if $95

6"

THE ARDEN SHAKESPEARE

GENERAL EDITORS:
RICHARD PROUDFOOT, ANN THOMPSON
and DAVID SCOTT KASTAN

THE FIRST PART OF
KING HENRY IV

THE ARDEN SHAKESPEARE

All's Well That Ends Well: edited by G. K. Hunter
Antony and Cleopatra: edited by M. R. Ridley
As You Like It: edited by Agnes Latham
The Comedy of Errors: edited by R. A. Foakes
Coriolanus: edited by Philip Brockbank
Cymbeline: edited by J. M. Nosworthy
Hamlet: edited by Harold Jenkins
Julius Caesar: edited by T. S. Dorsch
King Henry IV, Parts 1 & 2: edited by A. R. Humphreys
King Henry V: edited by John H. Walter
King Henry VI, Parts 1, 2 & 3: edited by A. S. Cairncross
King Henry VIII: edited by R. A. Foakes
King John: edited by E. A. J. Honigmann
King Lear: edited by Kenneth Muir
King Richard II: edited by Peter Ure
King Richard III: edited by Antony Hammond
Love's Labour's Lost: edited by Richard David
Macbeth: edited by Kenneth Muir
Measure for Measure: edited by J. W. Lever
The Merchant of Venice: edited by John Russell Brown
The Merry Wives of Windsor: edited by H. J. Oliver
A Midsummer Night's Dream: edited by Harold F. Brooks
Much Ado About Nothing: edited by A. R. Humphreys
Othello: edited by M. R. Ridley
Pericles: edited by F. D. Hoeniger
The Poems: edited by F. T. Prince
Romeo and Juliet: edited by Brian Gibbons
The Taming of the Shrew: edited by Brian Morris
The Tempest: edited by Frank Kermode
Timon of Athens: edited by H. J. Oliver
Titus Andronicus: edited by J. C. Maxwell
Twelfth Night: edited by J. M. Lothian and T. W. Craik
Troilus and Cressida: edited by Kenneth Palmer
The Two Gentlemen of Verona: edited by Clifford Leech
The Winter's Tale: edited by J. H. P. Pafford

THE ARDEN EDITION OF THE WORKS OF WILLIAM SHAKESPEARE

THE FIRST PART OF
KING HENRY IV

Edited by
A. R. HUMPHREYS

LONDON and NEW YORK

The general editors of the Arden Shakespeare have been

First Series
W. J. Craig (1899–1906) and R. H. Case (1909–44)

Second Series
Una Ellis-Fermor (1946–58), Harold F. Brooks (1952–82),
Harold Jenkins (1958–82) and Brian Morris (1975–82)

Third Series
Richard Proudfoot, Ann Thompson and David Scott Kastan

This edition of *King Henry IV, Part I*, by A. R. Humphreys,
first published in 1960 by
Methuen & Co. Ltd
Reprinted with minor corrections 1961, 1965 and 1967
Reprinted 1974

First published as a University Paperback in 1966
Reprinted ten times
Reprinted 1985

Reprinted 1988, 1989 (twice), 1992, 1994
by Routledge
11 New Fetter Lane, London EC4P 4EE
29 West 35th Street, New York, NY 10001

Editorial matter © 1960 Methuen & Co. Ltd

ISBN (hardbound) 0 416 47420 9
ISBN (paperback) 0 415 02750 0

Printed in England by Clays Ltd, St Ives plc

For Thomas Rice Henn,
in gratitude

"The judgment of Shakespeare in the selection of his materials, and in the manner in which he has made them, heterogeneous as they often are, constitute a unity of their own, and contribute all to one great end, is not less admirable than his imagination, his invention, and his intuitive knowledge of human nature."

Wordsworth, *Essay Supplementary to the Preface, 1815.*

CONTENTS

PAGE

PREFACE ix

INTRODUCTION xi
  1. Date xi
  2. The Question of Revision xv
    1. Changes of Name xv
    2. Further Revision? xviii
  3. Sources xxi
    1. Holinshed: *Chronicles of England* xxiii
    2. Daniel xxviii
    3. The "Wild Prince Hal" Stories xxix
    4. Stow xxxi
    5. *The Famous Victories of Henry the Fifth* . xxxii
    6. Other Prince Hal Plays? xxxiv
    7. *Woodstock* xxxvi
    8. *A Myrroure for Magistrates* xxxvii
    9. Ballads of Percy and Douglas xxxviii
    10. *Soliman and Perseda* xxxviii
    11. Other Possible Sources xxxix
  4. Falstaff xxxix
  5. The Unity of the Play xlv
  6. The Historical Outlook l
  7. The Spirit of the Play liii
  8. The Imaginative Impact lvii
  9. Establishment of the Copy-Text lxvi
  10. Editorial Methods lxxv
  11. Abbreviations lxxviii

THE FIRST PART OF KING HENRY THE FOURTH 1

APPENDICES
  1. The Title in Qq2–5, F1 165

II. The Date of *The Merry Wives of Windsor*   166

III. Source Material
    1. Holinshed   167
    2. Daniel   179
    3. *The Famous Victories of Henry the Fifth*   186

IV. Doubtful Sources
    1. Hall   195
    2. Holinshed: *The Historie of Scotland*   197
    3. Hayward   197
    4. Another Hotspur Play?   198

V. II. iv. 382—"King Cambyses' vein"   199

VI. III. ii. 39 ff.—"Had I so lavish of my presence been . . ."   200

VII. IV. i. 98–9—"All plum'd like estridges . . ."   201

VIII. The Mortimers   202

PREFACE

THIS edition has drawn freely on the illustrative material so abundantly provided by R. P. Cowl and A. E. Morgan in their previous Arden edition but is not otherwise based on their work, being an independent exploration of the introductory material and of textual problems. It owes much to the editions of John Dover Wilson (Cambridge, 1946), G. L. Kittredge (in *Sixteen Plays of Shakespeare*, Boston, 1946), and in particular S. B. Hemingway (the great New Variorum, Philadelphia, 1936), with the *Supplement* to this latter by G. Blakemore Evans in *The Shakespeare Quarterly*, vol. vii (New York, 1956). Its numerous debts to these and many other scholars are, I hope, adequately recognized in the introduction and commentary; they are boundless. The passages on pages lvi–lvii, from Cleanth Brooks's and Robert B. Heilman's book *Understanding Drama*, are quoted with the kind permission of the authors and of Henry Holt and Co., Inc., the publishers.

The work was finished under the dark shadow cast by the death of Una Ellis-Fermor, General Editor of the series, than whom no counsellor could have been more helpful, tolerant, and sympathetic; to have her encouragement eased many an hour of a long journey. Help was willingly afforded me by Dr T. W. Craik, Dr G. E. Dawson of the Folger Shakespeare Library, Dr Mary Isabel Fry of the Henry E. Huntington Library, Dr Charlton Hinman, Professor Harold Jenkins, Mr C. A. Luttrell, Dr G. H. Martin, Mr J. C. Maxwell (who furnished many items of value, including Appendix V), Miss Joyce Moody, Mr M. R. Ridley, and Miss Jean Robertson. I gladly acknowledge also the fresh insights and enthusiasm given by an adult-class research group of Vaughan College, an extra-mural department of the University of Leicester, which worked with me for some months on the play's problems. Above all, Dr Harold Brooks has given generously of his scanty time and abundant scholarship. What I owe to him cannot be sufficiently expressed, but my gratitude goes deep.

A. R. HUMPHREYS.

The University, Leicester.
December, 1959.

INTRODUCTION

This text is based on the earliest Quartos (Qo and Q1), modernized and punctuated as explained in "Editorial Methods" (pp. lxxv ff.). The introduction deals with the main questions which the play provokes, and the footnotes preserve much of the original Arden material for its relevance to Elizabethan language and life, though taking account too of the later harvest of scholarship.

I. DATE

The play is somewhat later than *King John* and *Richard II*, which are usually assigned to 1595–6.[1] Richer, riper, and far better built though it is than *King John*, John's troubled mind, Faulconbridge's irreverent vitality (so like Hotspur's), and the earlier play's poetic force find counterparts in it. Greatly though it differs from *Richard II*'s lyrical tragedy, the events of that play directly forecast it, as Carlisle prophesies "woefullest division" (*R2*, IV. i. 146), Richard foresees Northumberland's defection (*R2*, v. i. 55), and Bolingbroke laments his "unthrifty son" (*R2*, v. iii. 1); the two plays cannot be long separated, marvellously deeper and broader though Shakespeare's vision now is. In *Henry VI* he had struggled to present the whole national life; in *Richard III*, *King John*, and *Richard II* his scope had narrowed to baronial faction. Now he suddenly sees how to combine in a complex drama everyone from monarch to tapster, and all humours that have showed themselves humours since the old days of goodman Adam.

About 1598 the first part of *Henry IV* was much in the news.

(*i*) It was entered in the *Stationers' Register* to Andrew Wyse, on 25 February, though not called Part 1; this may or may not mean that Part 2 was unwritten or incomplete.

1597 [1598, new style] xxv° die ffebruarij. Andrew Wyse. Entred for his Copie vnder the[e] handes of Master Dix: and master Warden Man a booke intituled The historye of HENRY the IIIJth with his battaile of Shrewsburye against HENRY

1. As E. A. J. Honigmann observes, scholars have located *King John* in every year from 1591 to 1598. He himself argues for 1590 (*King John*, Arden edn, 1954, xliii–lviii).

HOTTSPURRE of the Northe with the conceipted mirthe of Sir JOHN FFALSTOFF.

(*ii*) There were two 1598 quarto editions. The earlier (Q0) survives only in a fragment (cf. "Establishment of the Copy-Text", p. lxvi). The later (Q1) was set up from it in the same printing-house, Peter Short's, and its title-page reads

THE | HISTORY OF | HENRIE THE | FOVRTH: | With the battell at Shrewsburie, | *betweene the King and Lord* | Henry Percy, surnamed | Henrie Hotspur of | the North. | *With the humorous conceits of Sir* | Iohn Falstalffe. | [Ornament] | AT LONDON, | Printed by *P. S.* for *Andrew Wise,* dwelling | in Paules Church-yard, at the signe of | the Angell. 1598.

Subsequent editions are recorded in Appendix I.

(*iii*) Francis Meres's *Palladis Tamia* (1598: entered *SR*, 7 September) cites "*Henry the* 4" (no part specified) as proving Shakespeare "most excellent . . . for Tragedy", and makes one of the three earliest-known Falstaff jokes (*Palladis Tamia*, xiv) by commending Michael Drayton's "vertuous disposition" in times "when there is nothing but rogery in villanous man".[1]

(*iv*) Between 25 and 28 February 1598, Essex wrote to Sir Robert Cecil asking him to tell their friend Sir Alex Ratcliff that "his sister is maryed to S^r Jo. Falstaff".[2] Gossip was linking Ratcliff's sister Margaret with Sir Henry Brooke, Lord Cobham. It is well known that Falstaff's original name was Oldcastle and that this was changed because Sir Henry, or his father Sir William Brooke, or both, being descendants of the historical Oldcastle, objected to their ancestor's mishandling. Shakespeare promptly rechristened his creation, and Sir Henry's enemies, it seems, promptly re-christened him likewise.

The Cobhams probably made their protest early in 1597. *The Merry Wives of Windsor* (written, according to John Dennis, in fourteen days at the Queen's command[3]) seems to have been hurriedly thrown together for the conferment of knighthoods of the Garter in April–May 1597 (cf. Appendix II). The name Falstaff had already memorably occurred in connection with Shakespeare's only previous prominent reference to the Order of the Garter, in which the heroic Talbot denounces an unworthy knight:

> When first this order was ordain'd, my lords,
> Knights of the Garter were of noble birth,

1. Cf. II. iv. 121–2: for other jokes see (*iv*), above, and v. i. 129–30, note.
2. L. Hotson, *Sh.'s Sonnets Dated*, 1949, 148.
3. Dedication to *The Comical Gallant*, 1702.

> Valiant and virtuous, full of haughty courage,
> Such as were grown to credit by the wars,
> Not fearing death, nor shrinking for distress,
> But always resolute in most extremes.
> He then that is not furnish'd in this sort
> Doth but usurp the sacred name of knight,
> Profaning this most honourable order,
> And should—if I were worthy to be judge—
> Be quite degraded.   (*1 Henry VI*, iv. i. 33–43)

The dastardly cause of this outburst was "Sir John Falstaffe" who deserted Talbot at the battle of Patay.[1] Busy with Garter preparations, and needing to rename his new antithesis of military honour, Shakespeare's mind leapt to his previous Garter-coward and with considerable violence to history pressed him, transformed, into immortal service.

Not only the first but both parts of *Henry IV* may have been performed before *The Merry Wives*; this latter play assumes that the spectators already know Justice Shallow, and they could do so only through *2 Henry IV*. Similarly, Pistol is elaborately introduced into *2 Henry IV* whereas in *The Merry Wives* Slender mentions him, with Nym and Bardolph, as a matter of course (i. i. 130). Both parts, moreover, seem to have reached the stage before the Brookes objected. The conclusion of Part 2's epilogue in the Folio text[2] comes in the Quarto at the end of the first paragraph; this presumably was where the epilogue originally concluded. The latter portion in both Q and F texts of the epilogue contains an apology dissociating Oldcastle from Falstaff. This looks like an afterthought, an apology added after the performance of the play had provoked the Brookes' protest. Traces of the original names indeed survive uncorrected in the Part 2 Q (1600): *Old.* appears as a speech-prefix at i. ii. 138, and "Sir Iohn Russel" in the ii. ii entry-direction. Why the Brooke family did not ensure a change of name until both parts were finished is uncertain; perhaps it swallowed Part 1 as it had done the previous Oldcastle appearance in *The Famous Victories of Henry the Fifth* but could not stomach the still further, and grosser, travesty in Part 2.

The precise dating of Part 1 is speculative, but the timetable may be as follows: *Richard II* being finished late in 1595, Shakespeare

1. The historical Fastolf (1378–1459) was one of Henry V's leaders and fought well at Agincourt and elsewhere. But at Patay (1429) his manœuvres went wrong, his men fled, and Talbot was captured. 16th-c. chroniclers followed Monstrelet's story that he was deprived of the Garter for cowardice, though in fact he was exonerated after an investigation into the defeat.

2. "and so [I] kneele downe before you: But (indeed) to pray for the Queene".

works on *1 Henry IV* in 1596 and it is played in the winter season of
1596–7. He carries on with Part 2, which reaches the stage also.[1]
Sir William Brooke, Lord Cobham, who is the Lord Chamberlain
(following Sir Henry Carey, first Lord Hunsdon and the players'
patron, who died on 22 July 1596), observes that these plays
increasingly misrepresent his ancestor, a Wycliffite hero for whom
he himself, being Puritanically inclined, probably feels particular
respect. Through his authority the plays are withdrawn. But on
5 March 1597 he himself dies; Sir George Carey, the second Lord
Hunsdon, succeeds him as Lord Chamberlain on 17 March, is (like
his father) the players' patron (they have been "Lord Hunsdon's
Men" and are now "The Lord Chamberlain's Men"), and
furthermore is to be elected Knight of the Garter on 23 April and
installed at Windsor in May. Moreover, the Queen wants to see
another play on the fat knight, tactfully renamed. Shakespeare
rushes *The Merry Wives* through in March/April (and presumably
as an actor is busy with the May production at Windsor too). Rely-
ing on the combination of Hunsdon's protection, the Queen's
favour, and the privilege of the occasion, he risks some anti-Brooke
jokes. Falstaff being sought after, the Host rather oddly says
"There's his Chamber, his House, his Castle" (*Merry Wives*, F text,
IV. v. 6; Q reads "Sir *John*, there's his Castle, his standing bed"
[l. 1305]), which may be an Oldcastle echo, and the jealous Ford
assumes the *nom de guerre* of "Brook" (II. i. 223).[2] Shakespeare might
during the summer of 1597 revise the offending names in both
parts of *Henry IV*, with some oversights.[3] From late July to early
October the Privy Council bans all stage performances, in retali-
ation for the production of Jonson and Nashe's "seditious" play
The Isle of Dogs. When the theatres re-open, the revised *Henry IV*
returns to the repertoire, and Part 1 is printed early in 1598 to publicize the change of names. Sir Henry Brooke, the new Lord Cobham, still feels aggrieved, however: *The Merry Wives* has mocked
him, and his enemies have nicknamed him Falstaff (cf. p. xii,
above). To pacify him, Part 2's epilogue is amplified to rehabilitate
his ancestor, *The Merry Wives*' "Brook" becomes "Broome", and

1. The question of the structural relationship between Parts 1 and 2 will be
discussed in the introduction to Part 2.
2. F changes this to "*Broome*", ruining Falstaff's joke about "such Brooks [F
Broomes]... that o'erflow such liquor" (*Wiv.*, II. ii. 159). The time-table suggested
above owes much to J. Dover Wilson, 'The Origins and Development of Sh.'s
H4' (*The Library*, 4th ser., xxvi, June 1945), and W. Bracy, *The Merry Wives of
Windsor: The History and Transmission of Sh.'s Text* (Univ. of Missouri Stud.,
xxv. 1, 1952).
3. As Dr Harold Brooks points out to me, Massinger overlooked some details
in recopying *Believe as you list* with altered names and setting.

after three years' perturbation of the Cobhams and diversion of everyone else the Drayton–Munday–Wilson–Hathaway play of *The true and honorable historie, of the life of Sir John Old-castle* (acted 1599, printed 1600) sets the long-suffering Wycliffite in the right light.

The dates suggested above for both parts are rather earlier than those often given, especially for Part 2, and raise the question why, if Part 2 already existed, the *SR* entry and the Q title-page of Part 1 have no reference to separate parts. Possibly Shakespeare wrote on his first page merely "The historye of Henry the IIIJth", and no-one amended it; Elizabethan registration- and publication-procedure is haphazard about details. Indeed, even after Part 2 was published, none of the Qq of Part 1 bore any indication that the play was divided. If both parts were written by the spring of 1597, the interval before their successor *Henry V* (1599) is long, but Shakespeare had other plays on hand. Some scholars have held that, as *2 Henry IV*'s epilogue promises, *Henry V* originally appeared "with Sir Iohn in it".[1] Such drastic revision as would be needed to excise Sir John from it needs, one may suggest, stronger arguments than have been adduced, and his absence may be due rather to the lapse of two years and the fact that Shakespeare, having already put him into three plays (besides the incidental appearance in *1 Henry VI*), may not have felt able to resuscitate him for a fourth.

2. THE QUESTION OF REVISION

That Shakespeare altered the *Henry IV* plays has always been recognized, but estimates of the degree of alteration range from the minimum assumption that he changed three names (Oldcastle, Harvey, and Russell giving place to Falstaff, Bardolph, and Peto) to the maximum that he pruned the history, rewrote and expanded the comedy, and reduced the status of Falstaff's cronies. Few scholars believe in radical changes but those few include Professors A. E. Morgan and Dover Wilson.

1. Changes of Name

Falstaff was certainly once Oldcastle. That is his name in *The Famous Victories*, and Shakespeare's text reflects it. "My old lad of the castle" (*1H4*, I. ii. 41), though also a cant term for a roisterer, is surely a pun. "Away, good Ned, Falstaff sweats to death" (ibid., II. ii. 103) would be decasyllabic like its context were the name

1. For a statement of this view, cf. *Henry V*, Arden edn, 1954, xlii–xlv.

"Oldcastle".[1] The surviving prefix *Old.* in the Q of Part 2 has been
mentioned, and the epilogue makes its apology. *The Merry Wives*,
as has been seen, may have its echo, though "Oldcastle" was not
necessarily the original name there too, as is sometimes suggested.
And finally, the *Sir John Oldcastle* play admits that its hero had been
travestied.

When, as Fuller puts it, Oldcastle was "relieved", other names
were changed too, doubtless because bearers of them at Court
might be offended. The Qq and F texts of Part 1 refer to "Falstalffe,
Haruey, Rossil, and Gadshill" (I. ii. 158), where editors beginning
with Theobald change the two middle names to Bardolph and
Peto. At II. iv. 172, 174, 178, the Qq have the prefix *Ross.*, which F
and editors change to *Gads.*[2] In Part 2, F substitutes "*Bardolfe*" in
the Q's entry-direction "*Sir Iohn Russel*" (II. ii). Russell was the
name of the Earls of Bedford, and Harvey that of Lord Southamp-
ton's mother's third husband. Shakespeare would be wise to avoid
offence.

Yet "Oldcastle" survived long in theatrical memory. On 6 March
1600 Rowland Whyte wrote to Sir Robert Sidney about a feast at
which "Sir John Old Castell" was performed by the Lord Chamberlain's Men, and since the play actually called *Sir John Oldcastle*
belonged not to the Lord Chamberlain's Men but the Lord
Admiral's, this is probably (though not certainly) a part of
Henry IV, which was sometimes called *Sir John Falstaff* (Hemingway, New Var., 477) and might informally retain the old name.
As late as 1639 the King's Men did "ould Castel" at court on 29
May, "the princes berthnyght" (Chambers, *W. Sh.*, ii. 353), and
this would hardly, one supposes, be the uninteresting Drayton–
Munday–Wilson–Hathaway play. In the anonymous *Meeting of
Gallants at an Ordinarie* (1604), the "fatte and pursie" Host is "a
madde round knaue, and a merrie one too: and if you chaunce to
talke of fatte *Sir Iohn Old-castle*, he wil tell you, he was his great
Grand-father, and not much vnlike him in Paunch" (sig. B4).
About 1610–11 Nathan Field's *Amends for Ladies*[3] asks:

> Did you neuer see
> The Play, where the fat Knight hight *Old-castle*,
> Did tell you truly what this honor was?

And the glutton in the anonymous *Wandering-Jew, Telling Fortunes*

1. The "Falstaff" at II. iv. 521 would also fit its decasyllabic context better as
"Oldcastle".
2. Save for Collier, who preferred *Bard.* Of course, *Gads.* for *Ross.* is not a re-
naming of the latter but a redistribution of his speeches.
3. Nathan Field, *Plays*, ed. W. Peery, 1950; *Amends for Ladies*, IV. iii. 23-5.

to Englishmen (c. 1628, printed 1640) claims that "*Sir Iohn Old-castle* was my greatgrandfathers fathers Uncle" (*SAB*, i. 446).

Seventeenth-century historians discussed the matter further. Dr Richard James, Sir Robert Cotton's librarian, wrote about 1625 to Sir Henry Bourchier relating that "a young Gentle Lady" inquired how Falstaff, banished for cowardice under Henry VI, could have died under Henry V. "I made answer", he says (*SAB*, i. 330):

> That Sʳ John Falstaffe was in those times a noble valiant souldier. . . . That in Shakespeares first shew of Harrie the fift [sic], the person with which he undertook to playe a buffone was not Falstaffe, but Sir Jhon Oldcastle, and that offence beinge worthily taken by Personages descended from his title . . . the poet was putt to make an ignorant shifte of abusing Sir Jhon Falstophe.

In *Trinarchodia, The Raigne of Henrie the Fifth* (1647), George Daniel the poet recognizes that Falstaff's name was used "lest scandall might / Creep backward, & blott Martyr" (i.e. libel Oldcastle). Best-known are Thomas Fuller's allusions. In his *Church History* (1655) he says:

> *Stage-Poets* have themselves been very *bold* with, and others very *merry* at, the Memory of Sʳ *John Oldcastle*, whom they have fancied a *boon Companion*, a *jovial Royster*, and yet a *Coward* to boot, contrary to the credit of all Chronicles, owning him a *Martial man* of merit. The best is, Sʳ *John Falstaffe*, hath relieved the Memory of Sʳ *John Oldcastle*, and of late is substituted *Buffoone* in his place, but it matters as little what *petulant Poets*, as what *malicious Papists* have written against him. (Book IV, xv cent., 168)

The phrase "of late is substituted Buffoone" is odd, fifty-seven years after *1 Henry IV* was published, but the Falstaff story is festooned with loose ends. In *The Worthies of England* (1662) Fuller is concerned to "relieve" Fastolf's memory as well as Oldcastle's (ii. 253):

> JOHN FASTOLFE Knight, was a native of this County [Norfolk] . . . To avouch him by many arguments valiant, is to maintain that the sun is bright, though since the *Stage* hath been over bold with his memory, making him a *Thrasonical Puff*, and emblem of *Mock-valour*. True it is, Sir *John Oldcastle* did first bear the brunt of the one, being made the *make-sport* in all plays for a *coward*. It is easily known out of what *purse* this black *peny* came. The *Papists* railing on him for a *Heretick*, and therefore he must also be a *coward*, though indeed he was a *man* of *arms, every inch of him,* and as valiant as any in his age.

Now as I am glad that Sir *John Oldcastle* is *put out*, so I am sorry that Sir *John Fastolfe* is *put in*, to relieve his memory in this base service, to be the *anvil* for every *dull wit* to strike upon. Nor is our Comedian excusable, by some alteration of his name, writing him Sir *John Falstafe* . . . seeing the *vicinity* of sounds intrench on the memory of *that worthy Knight,* and few do heed the *inconsiderable difference* in spelling of their name.

The thrasonical puff, however named, was never one to be ignored.

2. Further Revision?

In *Some Problems of Shakespeare's "Henry the Fourth"* (1924) Professor A. E. Morgan suggested more drastic revision, and Professor Dover Wilson supported him, with amendments, in *The Library,* xxvi (1945). The "Oldcastle" comedy, it is argued, was mainly in verse, and when the Cobhams' protests compelled revision Shakespeare both recast the vestigial "knights" Harvey and Russell as the lower-comedy Bardolph and Peto, and also rewrote the comic scenes in prose. Wilson says:

> I myself would date *1 Henry IV* in the autumn or winter of 1597, but I think that twelve months or more earlier Lord Hunsdon's Men were playing another *Henry IV* in which Oldcastle spoke comic blank verse like Juliet's Nurse and Robert Faulconbridge.

Morgan suggests that Shakespeare's first version (c. 1596) was in two parts, with more history and less comedy than at present, and that in revision the history was cut and the comedy expanded; Wilson holds that the first version was a single play which in revision grew into two parts. But these alternatives are less important than the common claim of a prior Shakespearean version with the comic scenes in verse. And this claim, brilliantly though it is argued, seems untenable.

Firstly, as Milton Crane points out in *Shakespeare's Prose* (1951), while poets have sometimes made prose drafts as a basis for versification, the contrary process is rare and occurs only for special reasons, as one would expect of a *modus operandi* which starts from the harder method of composition. Secondly, Shakespeare's company were busy actors who would hardly wish to forget a verse-version they knew in favour of learning a new prose one. Thirdly, Wilson has suggested similar prosifying in several other plays (e.g. *As You Like It, Two Gentlemen of Verona, Measure for Measure, The Tempest*)—but the more plays that are proffered the less likely does it become that a hard-working actor-dramatist would thus rewrite them. Fourthly, the "evidence" for the theory dissolves on close inspection.

(*a*) The historical verse scenes, it is argued, have been cut, have incomplete lines, and are retouched. Morgan sees curtailment in the jerky metre or curt action of I. i. 55–6, I. i. 62 ff., III. ii. 92–3, IV. i. 75, V. i. 22–9, v. i. 101–3. Dover Wilson finds reworking at III. ii. 173–6 (cf. note). Yet the historical scenes are quite as coherent and complete as one can properly expect in Elizabethan drama. Broken or rough lines and some confusion in the action are the ordinary accidents of the dramatist's workshop. They are not enough to prove curtailment.

(b) The comic prose scenes are said to contain "fossil" verses, relics of an earlier metrical version, surviving as decasyllabic rhythms in the prose "rewriting". These "fossils" are allegedly numerous in two areas—in the Gad's Hill preparations and robbery (the original "wild Prince" material), and in scene-endings where Shakespeare might preserve his original linkages with following scenes. The pure wit-comedy, however, not belonging to the Gad's Hill escapade, is held to be later and maturer addition.

There are fallacies in this, however. For instance, I. ii. 1–119 is wit-comedy without any "fossil" verses, and on Morgan's theory is later addition. Yet it contains three of the most evident echoes of the old *Famous Victories* story, in the "old lad of the castle" pun (I. ii. 41), the "most sweet wench" (cf. I. ii. 39–40, note), and Hal's promise to promote Falstaff hangman (cf. I. ii. 61–5, note). Scenes lacking fossil verses are evidently not necessarily later additions Shakespeare made while prosifying an "original" version.

The whole "fossils" argument is unreliable. It was not as clear to Shakespeare as to Monsieur Jourdain that everything that is not prose is verse, and everything that is not verse is prose. As McKerrow observes in the *Prolegomena for the Oxford Shakespeare* (1939):

> There are many passages in which it is difficult to be certain whether prose or verse was intended. . . The truth is, no doubt, that at least in dramatic writing there was no clear and consistent distinction between prose and verse, and that in many cases a more or less rhythmical prose took the place of formal verse.

Shakespeare often hovered betwixt and between, being a prolific verse-dramatist with decasyllables in his blood-stream.

But what if the "fossils" come not accidentally, at random, but clustered at scene-ends, as though surviving as links with the next verse-scene? "We should," says Morgan, "look for a preponderance of verse-fragments at the end of such scenes. That again is precisely what we find." We sometimes do find it, but not for Morgan's reason. Serious and comic are often thematically linked (cf. pp. xlvi–l), yet the linkage is not so specific that, were Shakespeare revising, comic scene-ends would resist change more than other parts. The verse or near-verse at comic scene-ends occurs rather for another reason, the reason that made Shakespeare write all of I. ii in prose save for Hal's final soliloquy. In other words, the scapegrace fun is in prose, but when Hal faces the outer world his different status calls for verse. In II. iv. 499–518 Hal and the sheriff speak in verse-rhythms (and Q mostly sets them up so) and these rhythms, whether intended as prose or verse, continue for a few lines after the sheriff leaves (519–22). Finally, Hal and Peto revert to prose (523–43). Similarly with III. iii: the fooling is in prose, but lines 194–203 are verse (albeit rough) because Hal (like his father at the end of III. ii) is giving orders for the campaign. These verses are not "fossils" but signs of Hal's function and status.

One scene-end (II. ii. 99–105), however, is so metrical that though QqF give it as prose nearly all editors follow Pope and arrange it as verse. Shakespeare may have intended verse but failed to make the lines clear. Of this there are other instances—for example, Q prints as prose (and that in a verse-scene) the clearly metrical speeches at II. iii. 71–3, 78–89, and III. i. 103–7, and the probably metrical speeches at III. i. 3–10. He may not have cared much how it appeared—"a lack of system, often even of decision, on Shakespeare's part", Wilson has called it—like the slipping in-and-out of metre at III. i. 227–30, 241–56, or v. iii. 40–55. But in this particular scene-end he has narrative to transmit. Here, as in the Gad's Hill onset, and the buckram-men episode too (II. iv), decasyllables abound. Is not the real reason that some spirited narrations are in prose because they are comedy, yet sound like verse (not that Shakespeare argued thus to himself) because they are comic heroics? The buckram-men scene, Morgan argues, shows "three strata of dramatic evolution": these are (a) a pre-Shakespearean verse-version with "a rudimentary deferential Oldcastle" (because once and once only, at II. iv. 173, Falstaff calls Hal "my lord"); (b) a Shakespearean verse-version revealed by "fossils" in the surviving text; (c) a Shakespearean prosified version "in which Falstaff rises to the topmost pitch of comedy". This might have weight were the "fossil" verse and mature prose uneasily yoked together. But when the very substance and phrase of the supposed "fossils" are the rich expression of mature comedy the argument must be dismissed. Verse-rhythm, coming to Shakespeare's pen in the full flow of the mature comedy, is there because the comic narrative stimulates him to metre while the wit-play stays in prose. Somebody else's verse-version may possibly have been intermediate between the original *Famous Victories* play(s) and the extant

Shakespearean text (cf. pp. xxxiv ff.), but there is no real evidence that Shakespeare himself first wrote these plays in a form different from their present one.

Wilson has raised one related point; some of Hotspur's speeches, he thinks, have been "deliberately prosified" to "break or roughen the smooth contours of the verse in which they were first written" and "to add bluntness and rudeness" to his character.[1] But if so, why did Shakespeare start prosifying only at III. i? Do these characteristics of Hotspur not emerge quite as well from the verse of, say, I. iii. 28 ff., as they could from any prose? To inquire thus is not to belittle Wilson's acuteness about the hesitancy the play often shows between prose- and verse-form; it is merely to assert that Hotspur's roughnesses, like Falstaff's rhythms, show the absence rather than the presence of revision. Other Elizabethan plays likewise hesitate as to medium; *Woodstock*, for instance, mixes verse- and prose-rhythms.[2] The practice will not support the theory propounded for the *Henry IV* plays.

3. SOURCES

Literary sources are, rightly speaking, the whole relevant contents of the writer's mind as he composes, and no account of them can be complete. To specify the *Henry IV* plays' "sources" is to run the risk of seeming too narrow, of circumscribing works that so generously embrace Elizabethan life and thought as to be an individual's expression of a whole nationhood. Definable origins there certainly are, some direct, on which Shakespeare demonstrably drew, and others indirect, which lie behind the direct sources or create the accepted popular traditions. There are plays —*Richard II*, *The Famous Victories* (or its presumed original—cf. pp. xxxiv ff.), *Woodstock, Soliman and Perseda*—directly drawn upon, as also are histories like Holinshed's *Chronicles*, Daniel's *Ciuile Wars*, the *Myrroure for Magistrates*, and probably Stow's *Annales*. Behind these, contributing to the historical tradition, though not directly to Shakespeare, are ranged other histories—Hall's and Fabyan's chronicles and their fifteenth-century antecedents, with the important MS translation (1513) of Tito Livio's *Vita Henrici Quinti*. There are numerous echoes of the Bible, and probably of the church *Homilies*, familiar from pulpit repetition. There are ballads, songs, and snatches of proverb-lore. Yet these are only identifiable portions of a rich complex which includes much else—

1. E.g. III. i. 3–5, 9–10, 15–17; these are prose in Qq.
2. E.g. Rossiter's edn, I. ii. 72–91, III. ii. 132–51, 174–239.

familiar legends, morality plays about the contests of Virtue and Vice, Renaissance conceptions of history as inculcating national unity and proper rule, and a popular spirit compounded of self-confidence and self-searching. Add a thousand strands of town and country life; of tavern cries and catches, revelry and play-acting; of army life with its practice of arms and malpractice of recruitment; of country life with its gentry and labourers, sowing and harvesting, buying and selling; of all the working, sporting, eating, drinking, travelling, praying, and preying, which always make a nation's life but which in Elizabethan idiom achieve an unrivalled vivacity. Fertilize all this with the fermenting linguistic, poetic, and dramatic experiment which attains its highest pitch in the mind of Shakespeare. Then some dim notion of what went into the plays becomes possible. The true "sources" are a whole national life, thought, and language as felt by a great poet; they far outrange any mere interleaving (as some critics have thought) of perfunctory history with vivid comedy or (as others have thought) of purposeful history with irrelevant (though welcome) comedy. Both history and comedy combine in surpassingly rich interrelationship, whose "source" is Shakespeare's myriad-mindedness. To Shakespeare's mind, as these plays reveal it, Coleridge's aphorism is splendidly apt:

No man was ever yet a great poet without being at the same time a profound philosopher. For poetry is the blossom and the fragrancy of all human knowledge, human thoughts, human passions, emotions, language.   (*Biographia Literaria*, xv)

To list a few documents is therefore to give no adequate account of the materials. Yet Shakespeare's indebtednesses are in fact great, and the more his identifiable sources are studied the more evident does it become that his structural power in uniting diverse material is as extraordinary as his psychological, moral, or poetic power. He modelled the interesting but inchoate substance of Holinshed by means of the spirit and shaping of Daniel; he enriched it with the graceless comedy of *The Famous Victories* (or its original) suitably modified by the humaner interpretations of Holinshed and Daniel and by the moral responsibility of the morality-play tradition. He maintained the popular heroism of the Percy story (which had already gone into the border ballads), the popular comedy of the current Oldcastle mythology, and the romanticism of Welsh history as his Welsh acquaintance breathed it. Like sherris-sack in Falstaff, this rich amalgam produced in his mind a stimulus "apprehensive, quick, forgetive, full of nimble, fiery, and delectable shapes".

1. Raphael Holinshed: "Chronicles of England" (2nd edition, 1587)

The history comes mainly from Holinshed,[1] though with most important adjustments from Daniel (cf. p. xxviii). Churton Collins thought that Holinshed contributed merely "the meagre outline of the purely historical portions" (*Studies in Sh.*, 1904, 259). Meagre it is not; it includes most of the major historical events and very many of the details. Holinshed tells his story well, though not so well as Shakespeare. Since Collins could not find in him "the pathetic character of the king" or "his position under Nemesis for the crime", and since others have credited to Hall rather than Holinshed a sense of the drama of history, it is proper to point out that pathos, Nemesis, and drama are movingly present. The "pathetic character" is evident when Henry's life is threatened (Hall omits the incident)[2]; and Henry's last hours are equally moving when, "sore troubled" with disease, he weeps to be reconciled with the Prince and regrets "with a great sigh" his criminal attaining of the crown. The marginal gloss reads: "A guiltie conscience in extremitie of sicknesse pincheth sore" (iii. 57). The Nemesis-theme is no less evident: it occurs immediately upon Richard II's murder when Bolingbroke is condemned for lack of "moderation and loialtie . . . for the whiche both he himselfe and his lineall race were scourged afterwards, as a due punishment vnto rebellious subiects" (ii. 869); it recurs when the Percys' revolt gathers way (iii. 24): and after Henry's death the theme of divine retribution sounds again, in significantly religious terms, over the severe rule Henry's subjects suffered under him:

And yet doubtlesse, woorthie were his subiects to tast of that bitter cup, sithens they were so readie to ioine and clappe hands with him, for the deposing of their rightfull and naturall prince king Richard.   (iii. 58)

Stressing the repeated troubles of Henry's reign, Holinshed sums it up as one of "great perplexitie and little pleasure" (iii. 57). Shakespeare may, as Dr Tillyard argues, have found a natural drama in Hall's chapter-headings (from "The Vnquiete Tyme of Kyng Henry the Fourthe" to "The Triumphant Reigne of Kyng Henry the VIII"). But Holinshed and Daniel could unaided inspire the retributive theme in the *Henry IV*s.

Shakespeare's discipleship is that of a playwright, not a research scholar: he follows errors as well as facts. Like Holinshed (and

1. The edition of 1587 has the word "pickthanks" (1587 edn, iii. 539) which Shakespeare picks up (III. ii. 25); the edition of 1577 does not. Except where otherwise stated, references are to the 6 vol. reprint of 1807-8.
2. See App. III, pp. 167-8.

Daniel too, *C.W.*, iii. 90) he confuses the Edmund Mortimer captured by Glendower with his nephew Edmund who was heir to the
crown (cf. I. iii. 144, note). He makes the Archbishop of York
"brother" instead of cousin to the Scrope executed at Bristol (cf.
I. iii. 264–5, note). Excusably he misreads Holinshed in making
Mordake the son of Douglas (cf. I. i. 71–2, note: this could not have
happened had his source been Hall), in applying to Glendower's
birth the occurrence (though not the kind) of portents really belonging to Mortimer's (cf. III. i. 11, note), and more carelessly in
taking the Scottish Earl of March to be one of the Mortimers, as
were the English Earls of March (cf. III. ii. 164, note). Hal's unhistorical killing of Hotspur is doubtless also a misreading of Holinshed (cf. v. iv. 38–40, note) made either direct or via Daniel, who
implies (*C.W.*, iii. 97) that the two met in single combat (cf.
Appendix III).

Appendix III indicates how Shakespeare resembles Holinshed.
But it is rather his alterations that suggest his shaping spirit of
imagination. These alterations consist of omissions, expansions,
and readjustments.

(*a*) *Omissions*. To specify all of these would be tedious. It must
suffice to say that the historical contents of both parts of *Henry IV*
use about one-fifth of Holinshed's material. From a shapeless
compilation of annual odds and ends, local anecdotes, religious
matters, and haphazard forays against the Scots, Welsh, and
French, Shakespeare takes those items which coherently relate the
Percys' defection and its consequences. In this, Daniel is his guide;
both poets achieve what is barely seen in Holinshed, a shape and
theme. One particular omission is noteworthy. While Shakespeare,
guided by the original *Famous Victories*, makes much more than
Holinshed of Hal's revelry, and indeed includes the highway
escapades which Holinshed does not mention, he omits Holinshed's curious story (quite grotesque in the *Famous Victories* version)
of how Hal submitted himself to his father dressed up in

> a gowne of blew satten, full of small oilet holes, at euerie hole the
> needle hanging by a silke thred with which it was sewed. About
> his arme he ware an hounds collar set full of SS of gold, and the
> tirets likewise being of the same metall.   (iii. 53)

Well known though this episode was, through the English translation of Tito Livio's *Vita* (cf. p. xxi), through Stow, Holinshed,
and the *Famous Victories*, its oddity (never convincingly elucidated)
would not accord with the maturity Shakespeare bestows upon
Hal. He omits it, as he tones down other moments of extravagance.

(*b*) *Expansions*. An exhaustive account of Shakespeare's germi-

nating power would be lengthy. But the growth of "meagre out-
lines" (the phrase is not unjustified here) into living personages is
worth observing, however inadequately. In some cases Shakespeare mainly realizes, magnificently, characterizations already
clear. In Holinshed, for instance, the bases of the King's character
are well laid in the demonstration of his acumen and "policy" over
Mortimer and the Percys, his vigorous initiatives against opposition, his military energy which surprises his enemies, his leadership
in battle, and his care-shadowed reign.[1] The gist of Worcester, too,
is well given; he is "the procurer and setter forth of all this mischeefe", he demands that Mortimer be ransomed, he confronts
Henry before Shrewsbury, and he conceals from Hotspur the
King's offered terms. Westmoreland, Northumberland, and
Douglas, too, Shakespeare brings vividly alive without originating
much. In Holinshed Westmoreland is a leading King's man
(though appearing only after Shrewsbury), Northumberland is
jealous of the King and absent from Shrewsbury, and Douglas is "a
right stout and hardie capteine". But something more original
happens with Mortimer; from Holinshed's brief reference to his
capture and his marriage to Glendower's daughter Shakespeare
makes the sensible negotiator, the devoted son-in-law and husband
(III. i). Blunt and Vernon, too, are brought forward. Holinshed
mentions Blunt merely as the King's standard-bearer at Shrewsbury; Shakespeare makes him the King's adviser and emissary
throughout (I. i, I. iii, III. ii, IV. iii, V. iii). Vernon, whom Holinshed
barely names, is given the splendid speeches about the redeemed
Hal in IV. i and V. ii, and a brief but vigorous part in IV. iii. As for
Lady Mortimer and Lady Percy, something delightful is made here
from almost nothing. To the former, Holinshed's mere "daughter
of the said Owen", Shakespeare gives her Welsh songs—a poignant
interlude in the theme of war, contrasting effectively with the
teasing passages between Lady Percy and Hotspur; to the latter,
whom Holinshed mentions simply as "Elianor [actually, Eliza-
beth], whom the lord Henrie Persie had married", Shakespeare
gives a truly human role.

The most striking developments, however, are those of Glendower, Hotspur, and Hal. In Holinshed, as in *A Myrroure for Magistrates*, Glendower is a predatory savage. He is, it is true, described
as trained in law, an esquire to either Richard II or Bolingbroke
(cf. III. i. 117), and famed for "art magike" (iii. 20). But otherwise
he is the outlaw issuing from inaccessible "lurking places" to commit outrages of which the Welshwomen's barbarities are examples

1. These points are stressed again in Daniel: cf. p. xxviii.

(cf. 1. i. 40–6). Shakespeare's visionary poet-scholar, framing many an English ditty to the harp, the "worthy gentleman . . . wondrous affable, and as bounteous / As mines of India" (III. i. 159–63), is so undiscoverable in the chronicles that the dramatist, it has been suggested, must have received this version of him from Welsh acquaintances in London between writing I. i and III. i.[1]

For Hotspur, Holinshed provides the basic elements but little more. As the impetuous leader his name suggests, "a capteine of high courage", Hotspur defies Henry and exhorts his soldiers to "aduancement & honor" or a liberating death. Daniel's *Ciuile Wars* merely lays a little more stress on his "peruers", "rash", and "furious" nature. Both authorities, though recognizing Hotspur's valour, tend to write of "the Persies" collectively rather than individually. These scanty traits Shakespeare develops into the dominating rebel, capable of such vehement brilliance as the popinjay-lord speech, the account of Mortimer's fight with Glendower, the quarrel over Glendower's magical and poetic gifts and the River Trent's meanders, and the heroics about honour and battle. For the fantastic comedy of the popinjay lord and his mission, Holinshed's only lead is a terse statement, of quite different tone, that the King "did diuers and sundrie times require deliuerance of the prisoners, and that with great threatenings". At Bangor, a colourless sentence in Holinshed (Daniel too) about the tripartite indenture burgeons into Shakespeare's conflict, so prophetic of the rebels' incohesion at Shrewsbury, between Hotspur and Glendower, with all the former's self-assertion and the latter's credulousness, soon to detain him from the battlefield "o'er-rul'd by prophecies". Hotspur's impatient humour is new: so is his rough comedy with Lady Percy. His unhistorical youthfulness is not new, however; it derives from Daniel.

As for Hal, all that Holinshed relates is that at Shrewsbury he "holpe his father like a lustie yoong gentleman", not retiring though wounded, and (nine years later) that he was reconciled to his father after misunderstandings provoked by "pickthanks". Both Holinshed and Daniel, however, as has been seen, may be misread as saying that Hal killed Hotspur, and both stress his valour. It is from Daniel that Shakespeare takes the King to be middle-aged, and Hotspur to be Hal's age (cf. pp. 182–5). The most striking amplification of Holinshed, and of Daniel too, is of course in the interleaving of the history with the Eastcheap life; it is obvious how much Shakespeare adds by incorporating the "wild Prince" stories, seeing them as a punishment for the King

1. Arthur E. Hughes, *Sh. and his Welsh Characters*, 1918, 23.

and an education in government for Hal, and making the theme of
Hal's redemption a leading dramatic interest. What does arouse
perpetual astonishment is the free creativity of Shakespeare's invention while he still remains faithful to the gist, and often the
detail, of his sources.

(c) *Readjustments.* The best-known readjustments of serious history are in the ages of Henry, Hal, and Hotspur, derived from
Daniel's account. Among others may be noted (i) the transference
of the intended Crusade from the last to the first years of the reign;
(ii) the arrival of the Percys at Windsor on the King's summons
rather than their own initiative; (iii) the postdating of Northumberland's sickness; (iv) the bringing forward by several years of
Prince John's soldiership and Hal's reconciliation with his father.

(i) This change makes the intended Crusade an expiation; it is so
in Daniel too, but only as Henry lies dying. What in Holinshed is a
late design for uniting Europe against the infidel (iii. 57) becomes
in Shakespeare the immediate prompting of remorse for Richard's
death (cf. *R2*, v. vi. 49), though the outbreak of domestic strife pre-
vents Henry from thus salving his conscience.

(ii) This change asserts Henry's dominance at the first stirrings
of rebellion; whatever his guilt, his supremacy is valid provided his
rule is effective.

(iii) This change makes more evident the rebels' rashness in committing their cause to unsafe ground. In Holinshed, Northumberland's sickness is known early (iii. 23) and there is no surprise about
it, whereas in Shakespeare it is announced on the eve of Shrewsbury
as an unforeseen aggravation of the hazard.

(iv) John's valour at Shrewsbury is an innovation; he was only
thirteen at the time, and Holinshed first mentions him two years
later when, with Westmoreland, he opposes the Archbishop's
revolt. Shakespeare probably wished to show the utmost consoli-
dation of the Lancastrian house in peril, and perhaps, too, to provide a staid foil for Hal (Cowl & Morgan, xiv). But also, since some
readers doubt whether Shakespeare intended a Part 2, it is interesting to find him looking at post-Shrewsbury material; John's
valour at Shrewsbury (which is not in any source) is presumably
prompted by his later military leadership and might well not be
introduced (like the Archbishop's scene with Sir Michael, iv. iv)
were not Part 2 already in mind. As for the predating of Henry's
and Hal's reconciliation, that is fundamental to the dramatic conduct of Part 1. To some extent Shakespeare queered his pitch with
it, for why in Part 2 should Henry seemingly have forgotten all
about it and still be dismayed at Hal's folly? The answer is that

while the historical events are in chronological sequence, the moral events (Hal's redemption in chivalry and justice) are in parallel, so that the reformation of Part 2 can proceed unaffected by that of Part 1. Certainly the effect in Part 1 is a great enrichment of Holinshed and Daniel. Daniel says nothing at all about discord between Henry and Hal; Holinshed says nothing until Henry's penultimate year about his suspicion of the Prince (iii. 53), and nothing until Hal's first year as King about "misrulie mates of dissolute order and life" (iii. 61). Shakespeare develops from Stow, via the original *Famous Victories*, the moral disorder which reinforces the political, and the private vindication of Hal which foreshadows the public.

2. Samuel Daniel: "*The First Fowre Bookes of the Ciuile Wars Between the Two Houses of Lancaster and Yorke*" (*1595*)

Daniel's poem helped Shakespeare markedly; in less than thirty stanzas (86–114) of the third Book it provided a lucid narrative stripped of Holinshed's irrelevances, clear stressing of the Nemesis theme through the repeated rebellions (98), plain statements of the Percys' turbulence and Mortimer's rights (87–90: he confuses the two Mortimers, cf. i. iii. 144, note), the tripartite division (91), the charges against Henry (92–3), Henry's celerity in advance (96, 99), and, in flat contradiction of Holinshed, the absence of the Welsh from Shrewsbury (99). Holinshed says that the Welsh "came to the aid of the Persies, and refreshed the wearied people with new succours" (iii. 25); Shakespeare keeps them away, though not for Daniel's reason (the King's rapid manœuvre) but through Glendower's superstition (IV. iv. 16–18). Above all, Daniel readjusts the relative positions of Henry, Hotspur, and Hal. Hotspur (b. 1364?) was in fact Henry's senior (b. 1367), a generation older than Hal (b. 1387). At Shrewsbury Henry was only thirty-six, and Hal all but sixteen. But Daniel without giving Henry's age distinguishes him from "young *Hotespur*" (97), who is coeval with Hal. So in Shakespeare the King is elderly (v. i. 13); Hotspur, whom Northumberland had introduced to Bolingbroke as "my son, young Harry Percy" (*R2*, II. iii. 21), is, as in Daniel, of an age with Hal (*1H4*, III. ii. 103), so that Henry wishes "some night-tripping fairy" had interchanged them (I. i. 86). Daniel accentuates from shadowy hints in Holinshed the heroic opposition of Hotspur and Hal at Shrewsbury; the former is not middle-aged but "young", "vndaunted", "With forward speed his forces marshalling", "wrong counsaild" and "peruers", yet a "great spirit" and "courage bold" fallen in a wrongful cause; the latter is "forward", "fierce", "Wonder of Armes, the terror of the field". He presents Hal in the role (which a loose reading of Holinshed could suggest) of the King's rescuer from Douglas and, by implication at least, of Hotspur's vanquisher.

Holinshed, then, provides adequate facts, a sketch of character-ization, and the theme of evil engendered by evil. Daniel unifies the material, reinterprets the leading relationships, accentuates the drama of personalities, and gives a high momentum.

3. The "Wild Prince Hal" Stories

Stories of Henry V's madcap youth date from his own times. In 1418 Thomas Walsingham records that on his accession he sud-denly reformed.[1] The virtually "official" *Vita Henrici Quinti* (c. 1437) by Tito Livio admits that his youthful pursuits were war, love, "and other things which licence allows to soldiers" ("et alia quae militaribus licentia praebere solet"). The Lambeth MS 84 (c. 1479) of the popular *Brut* chronicle tells how, as Prince of Wales, "he fylle & yntendyd gretly to ryot, and drew to wylde company; & dyuers Ientylmen and Ientylwommen folwyd his wylle", and how only three honest counsellors opposed his inclinations, whom "he louyd aftyrward best, for þere good counsayle".[2] Fabyan's *Chronicle* (1516; written before 1513) attributes to him "all vyce and insolency" with "ryottours and wylde disposed persones" (577), until on accession "suddenly he became a newe man" and banished the scapegraces ten miles from his person upon pain of death (the first recorded mention of this threat: cf. *2H4*, v. v. 68). In 1513 an English MS translation of Tito Livio's *Vita* made additions of first-rate interest. It added extra material from Enguerrand de Mons-trelet's *Chroniques* (including the crown-on-the-pillow incident; *2H4*, IV. v)[3] and, more importantly, from the recollections of the fourth Earl of Ormonde (1392–1452), whom Henry V knighted at Agincourt and whose information the translator derived probably from an amanuensis's report. Thence—that is, directly from one who knew Henry well—comes the story that the Prince would lie in ambush with his mates to rob his own receivers, that the King mis-liked "the acts of youth which he exercised more than meanly" and "the great recourse of people to him", that to make amends the Prince approached his father in the fantastic garb already cited from Holinshed (cf. p. xxiv), that when dying the King made

1. "Mox ut initiatus est regni insulis repente mutatus est in virum alterum" (*Historia Anglicana*, ed. H. T. Riley, 1863, ii. 290).
2. Ed. F. W. D. Brie, EETS, Orig. ser., 136, ii. 594–5.
3. *Chronicles of Enguerrand de Monstrelet*, trans. Thomas Johnes, 1809, i. 317, ch. ci.

him a speech of good counsel repenting of the usurpation, to which the Prince proudly replied that he would maintain the succession, and that while loose in morals before his accession he thereupon became strictly continent.[1]

Though this translation was not printed until 1911, its MS form was influential since its stories appeared in Stow's *Chronicles* (1580) and *Annales* (1592), and some of them (though not the receiver-robbing) in Holinshed. Together with the famous anecdote that the Prince struck the Lord Chief Justice and was sent to prison[2] they comprise the legend of the wild Prince, the origins of which thus date from the fifteenth century and seem reasonably authentic.

Professor Dover Wilson distinguishes a sevenfold tradition of these stories: (*i*) the general riot–repentance theme; (*ii–iii–iv*) three legends of wild exploits—highway robbery, Eastcheap unruliness, and the striking of the Lord Chief Justice; and (*v–vi–vii*) three legends of relations with the King—the submissive interview, the crown-taking, and the King's dying counsel. Of those that relate to *1 Henry IV*, the general wildness theme has been sketched already. That of highway ambush originates (as has been seen) with the Earl of Ormonde and is transmitted to Stow and *The Famous Victories* (though not Holinshed) by Tito Livio's English translator. That of Eastcheap unruliness is, it seems, derived from stories of princely riot extant in London histories.[3] Stow's *Chronicles* (1580) probably prompted *The Famous Victories* to make Hal the ringleader, for they say (573) that the riots occurred between "the kings sonne", "his men", and "men of the court". Stow's *Annales* (1592), however, like Gregory's *Chronicle* (cf. fn. 3, below) blame the trouble on "*Thomas* and *Iohn*, the kings sonnes being in Eastcheap at London, at supper, after midnight" (540).

While preserving the midnight revelry in Eastcheap, so prominent in *The Famous Victories*, Shakespeare ignores the "hurlynge" save for a possible oblique reference in *Richard II* (*R2*, v. iii. 5–9). The Lord Chief Justice story and Hal's dismissal from the Privy Council are mentioned briefly in *1 Henry IV* (*1H4*, III. ii. 32–3) and in *2 Henry IV* (*2H4*, I. ii. 61–3, 221–3, v. ii. 6–8, 63–101). After Elyot's *Governour* they appear in Redmayne's *Vita Henrici Quinti* (c. 1540), Hall (1548–50), Stow, Holinshed, and *The Famous Victories*. The Tudor historians attribute the dismissal to Hal's wild-

---

1. C. L. Kingsford, *The First Engl. Life of Henry V*, 1911, xxv–xxx.
2. This cannot be traced beyond Elyot's *Boke named the Governour*, 1531, but may descend from popular tradition or a non-extant London civic chronicle.
3. E.g. William Gregory's *Chronicle*, ed. James Gairdner, Camden Soc., 1876, 106—"the hurlynge in Estechepe by the lorde Thomas and the lorde John, the kyngys sone [*sic*]".

ness, yet they hint at the true reason, that he was suspected of intending treachery.[1] This suspicion is reflected in *1 Henry IV* at v. iv.
50–1 and perhaps at III. ii. 122–8, and Shakespeare appropriately
presents it as a retribution the usurping King feels to be impending.
Finally, the submissive interview (III. ii)—the only one of Wilson's
last three items relevant to this play—is Shakespeare's radical
improvement on and predating of the Ormonde–"Translator"–
Stow–Holinshed–*Famous Victories* visit in strange apparel.

The "wild Prince" materials, then, converge from many directions, mostly assembled in Stow and transmitted (though not the
highway robberies) to Holinshed. The original of *The Famous Victories* used Stow and was used by Shakespeare; Hal's companions
in *1 Henry IV* are not Stow's "yoong lords and gentlemen" but *The
Famous Victories'* rapscallions, and they rob not Hal's "owne
receivers" (as in Stow) but the King's (as in *The Famous Victories*).
At points in *1 Henry IV*, however, Shakespeare may have drawn
directly on Stow (cf. section 4, below). Lest the variety of chronicles
mentioned above suggests that Shakespeare ranged widely for his
comic material it should be emphasized that he seems virtually to
have been content with Stow, Holinshed, and the original *Famous
Victories*. As with his serious history he showed his genius in trans-
forming the handiest sources.

4. *John Stow: "The Chronicles of England"* (*1580*); *"The Annales of England"*(*1592*)

Though Shakespeare could find almost all the "wild Prince"
material in Holinshed or the original *Famous Victories* or both, at one
point (where Holinshed says nothing) he differs from *The Famous
Victories* and coincides with Stow. Stow relates (*Chronicles*, 583;
Annales, 547) that Hal practised highway robbery and that

> when his receiuers made to him their complaints how they were
> robbed in their comming vnto him, he would giue them dis-
> charge of so much mony as they had lost, and besides that, they
> shold not depart from him without great rewards for their
> trouble and vexation.

This restitution, which derives from the "Translator"[2] and is,
needless to say, quite foreign to the spirit of *The Famous Victories*,
may well have suggested the phrase "The money shall be paid back
again with advantage" (*1H4*, II. iv. 540–1). If Shakespeare looked
at Stow, his mind may have caught thence the word "starting-

1. In fact he was dismissed because of a scheme, urged in 1411–12 by the
Beauforts, to have the ailing King abdicate in his favour: cf. III. ii. 126, note.
2. Cf. C. L. Kingsford, *The First Engl. Life of Henry V*, 17.

hole" (cf. *1H4*, II. iv. 259, note). More significantly, he could have found in Stow's account of "Halydowne" (i.e. Holmedon), though not in Holinshed's English chronicle, that "Mordake" was the eldest son of the Duke of Albany (cf. I. i. 71–2, note). In *2 Henry IV*, he may have been impressed by Stow's very earnest account of the king's death-bed advice; in urgency and gravity Stow far outgoes Holinshed and Daniel. These details make indebtedness to Stow decidedly probable.

5. "*The Famous Victories of Henry the Fifth*" (*1594?–1598*)

Reading that chaotic anonymous production *The Famous Victories* is like going through the *Henry IV–Henry V* sequence in a bad dream, so close to Shakespeare is it in fragments, so worlds removed in skill. Entered on *SR* by Thomas Creede on 14 May 1594, it is not known in any edition before 1598, when the stimulus of *Henry IV* no doubt led to its publication or republication.

It consists of 1,563 lines, mostly ostensible verse but save for a possible 250 quite unmetrical. Although not printed in two parts it divides into a first half given almost entirely to the pranks of the Prince (called "Henry V" even in his father's lifetime) up to his accession and his comrades' banishment, and a second half corresponding closely to the course of *Henry V* from the Archbishop's recommendation of war to the winning of victory and "Katheren"'s hand. This half contains also, as the French wars are beginning, Henry's praise of the Lord Chief Justice, which Shakespeare more effectively places immediately after the accession. Some low-comedy characters from the first half (though not, curiously, the first half's Oldcastle, Ned, or Tom) provide the comedy of the French campaign.

The text is virtually unplayable, though the second half is less bad than the first. It seems to be a memorially-reconstructed abridgement of a longer *Henry V* play—perhaps two plays—probably done on a provincial tour when plague closed the London theatres in 1592–4. It is not a play of Henry IV's reign save inasmuch as Henry V is shown as the madcap Prince; there is nothing of Henry IV's "unquiet time", of the Percys and Glendower, and Shrewsbury and Hal's heroism. Shakespeare found in it (or its original) an outline of the youthful escapades but nothing on the penalties of usurpation or on education for kingship.

The play's resemblances to *1 Henry IV* are as follows: the Prince has three fellow-madcaps called (though not behaving as) "knights"—a status perhaps reflected in the Q entry-direction for "Sir Iohn Russel" at *2 Henry IV*, II. ii. They are Sir John Oldcastle,

Tom, and Ned, this last apparently the Prince's favourite (as is Ned Poins). They enter having taken £1,000 from the King's receivers (cf. *1H4*, II. iv. 157); Shakespeare's "money of the King's coming down the hill" (II. ii. 52) is nearer to this than to Stow, where the Prince robs "his owne receivers". They employ a "vilaine that was wont to spie out our booties" (cf. *1H4*, II. ii. 49—"our setter"), known variously as "the Theefe", "Cutbert Cutter", and "Gads Hill". He steals "a great rase of Ginger" from "a poore Carrier vpon Gads hill" (cf. *1H4*, II. i—the carriers suspicious of Gadshill, one of whom has "two razes of ginger" to deliver), and is pursued by a "hue and cry" from Deptford (cf. *1H4*, II. iv. 500). The Prince's crew visit "the olde Tauerne in East chepe" (cf. *1H4*, I. ii. 126) where "there is good wine: besides, there is a pretie wench / That can talke well" (cf. *1H4*, I. ii. 40). They expect the King's death as a time for joyful anarchy, and Ned is promised the office of Lord Chief Justice (the change by which the chief reprobate Falstaff, instead of the relatively uncorrupt Poins, is promised the office not of Lord Chief Justice but of hangman suggests Shakespeare's more responsible attitude). The Prince's riots, it is prophesied, imperil his succession (cf. *1H4*, III. ii. 36 ff.). He strikes the Lord Chief Justice and is gaoled (once referred to at *1H4*, III. ii. 32, but thrice in Part 2, at I. ii. 61–3, 221–2, v. ii. 70). There is a burlesque play (cf. *1H4*, II. iv. 371 ff.). The King laments the curse of a son who will destroy him with grief (cf. *1H4*, III. ii. 4–11).

Yet the differences reveal a totally different conception of similar material. Shakespeare's Prince is immeasurably more self-possessed and presentable than the hooligan who gets "belamd about the shoulders" by the receivers (as in Stow), wishes his father dead so that "we would all be kings", gets drunk and flings his drinking-pot against the wall, fights "a bloodie fray" in Eastcheap, is gaoled and escapes more than once, smites the Lord Chief Justice on the ear, promises to institute a reign of misrule, makes for Court at the first news of the King's illness "to clap the Crowne on my head", dresses fantastically, batters at the palace door with "a verie disordered companie", and after approaching the King with a drawn dagger suddenly and fulsomely repents. Oldcastle himself is neither old, thirsty, witty, jovial, untruthful, fat, nor voluble—he speaks in all about 250 words. It is hard to imagine an embryo less likely to grow, even with the fostering of genius, into Falstaff. As for the other rapscallions, there is no characterization, nothing of Poins's, Peto's, and Bardolph's admirable gradations of low comedy, nothing but names and knockabout. And the Hostess never appears at all.

Shakespeare's discretion shows high artistic tact. Some discreditable episodes he glances at but either without showing them or without making them more than venial ebullitions. In *Richard II* the Prince is said, but never seen, to beat the watch (*R2*, v. iii; cf. "the hurlynge in Estechepe"), to rob pedestrians, and to frequent the stews. In *1 Henry IV*, though apparently familiar with pursetaking (i. ii. 30 ff.), he bridles when the Gad's Hill affair is mooted, joins it only to jest at Falstaff (this seems entirely Shakespeare's innovation), and repays the money "with advantage" (ii. iv. 540–1). In ii. iv he may be merry with drink but he is not gross, and the place in Council, "rudely lost" through the Lord-Chief-Justice assault, is mentioned only quite obliquely (iii. ii. 32). In material Shakespeare owes his comic original much; in spirit he is nearer the sober Holinshed (cf. Appendix III, pp. 186 ff.). A primary purpose of Hal's much-discussed soliloquy (i. ii. 190 ff.) is to establish clearly that this is not the Prince of any such play as *The Famous Victories*, no reckless ribald but a good king in the making, taking a shrewd course and living by his own discipline.

6. Other Prince Hal Plays?

If the history of *The Famous Victories* could be established, a flood of light might be thrown on Shakespeare's use of this material. To investigate the relationship between the older play and Shakespeare's sequence one is almost bound to assume certain non-extant plays, though Sir Edmund Chambers conjectured that he may have used a vanished 1594 edition of *The Famous Victories* itself. That he used some form of *The Famous Victories* the resemblances show: that it was not the existing patchwork is suggested by, first, *The Famous Victories*' almost imbecile nature (in which not even Shakespeare, surely, could find inspiration), and, second, the fact that Oldcastle must have been more familiar to Elizabethan audiences when Shakespeare took him up than he could possibly be from *The Famous Victories*. Contrary to his general practice with newly-introduced characters, Shakespeare does not divulge Oldcastle–Falstaff's name in i. ii until Poins is broaching the jest to Hal (l. 158, after Falstaff's exit). Earlier he is nicknamed (Monsieur Remorse, Sir John Sack-and-Sugar), and this nick-naming before ever his true name is mentioned is striking. The audience is apparently assumed to recognize him at once as the debauched, sanctimonious misleader of youth. Admittedly Shakespeare does not always name his characters immediately; Richard III, Portia in *The Merchant of Venice*, and Mercutio are examples. Yet Richard makes clear that he is the crookback Yorkist; Portia has been discussed before her first entry; Mercutio, named only after the Queen Mab speech (*Rom.*, I. iv. 96), is plainly one of Romeo's friends. The same might be said of Falstaff; his naming may be unnecessary or its omission an accident. Yet surely, as one begins *I Henry IV*, I. ii, one feels that Shakespeare was putting before his audience a reborn but still a familiar "old acquaintance".[1]

There were certainly pre-Shakespearean Henry V plays; *I Henry VI* is already a sequel to some account of Henry V's victories. *Tarlton's Jests* contains the following passage:

At the [Red] Bull at Bishops-gate, was a play of Henry the fift, where in the judge was to take a box on the eare; and because he was absent that should take the blow, Tarlton himselfe, ever forward to please, tooke upon him to play the same judge, besides his owne part of the clowne.[2]

If this were the original *Famous Victories* it is not clear how Tarlton could do the clown's part and step into the Lord Chief Justice's also, but Elizabethan clowns, as we know from Hamlet's warning, were capable of anything. Tarlton died in 1588; there was, therefore, apparently a Henry V play before then. Dr Tillyard[3] and E. B. Everitt[4] have suggested that this was a very early Shakespeare play later corrupted into *The Famous Victories*, but this is quite unproved speculation.

A reference in Nashe's *Pierce Penilesse* (1592) calls up a scene like the end of *The Famous Victories* though not identical with it.

What a glorious thing it is to have Henrie the fifth represented on the stage leading the French king prisoner and forcing both him and the Dolphin to swear fealty.   (McKerrow, i. 213)

Then, on 14 May 1594, *SR* enters to Thomas Creede "a booke intituled *The famous victories of Henrye the Ffyft*". And finally, *Henslowe's Diary* (ed. W. W. Greg, i. 27) records as "ne[w]" *harey the v*, acted by the Lord Admiral's men at the Rose on 28 November 1595 and twelve times more by 15 July 1596.[5] If this last were derived from the original *Famous Victories* it must have been so

1. In the pre-Falstaff version, the "old lad of the castle" joke (I. ii. 41) would help to identify him; but even this requires the audience to recognize who he is.
2. *Sh. Jest-Books*, 1864, ed. W. C. Hazlitt, ii. 218.
3. *Sh.'s History Plays*, 1944, 149.   4. *The Young Sh.*, 1954, 171–2.
5. *Henslowe's Diary* (i. 17 ff.) seems to show the Lord Admiral's men at this time as appearing jointly with the Lord Chamberlain's at Newington; but for their separate tenure of the Rose see ibid., ii. 84, and E. K. Chambers, *El. St.*, ii. 141.

far redone as to appear a new play; and whatever its origin, Shakespeare was not likely to have based himself upon it (as has been suggested) since it belonged to a rival company and was still holding the stage as he was beginning on *1 Henry IV*.

The title-page of *The Famous Victories* proclaims that it was "plaide by the Queenes Maiesties Players" (the leading company of the 1580s, though declining in the 1590s). But if it was, there must have been a more coherent original form of it. In this, Oldcastle may have been prominent. If so, why is his part so exiguous in *The Famous Victories*? This is not an area in which one can see clearly at all. But as pure hypothesis one may put forward the following scheme, which owes much to previous scholars: that the original *Famous Victories* was in two parts, boiled down into one for provincial performance by needy players and memorially corrupted in the process; that its first part was a fuller version than survives in *The Famous Victories* of Hal's pranks (referred to in *Tarlton's Jests*), including more on the robbery, and its second part dealt with Henry V's French wars (referred to by Nashe); that the second was perhaps redone as *harey the v* and later drawn upon by Shakespeare (since *The Famous Victories* and *Henry V* are evidently related); and that the first was perhaps redone in a nonextant version which so familiarized the Elizabethan audiences with Oldcastle that Shakespeare took their familiarity for granted. Had the original *Famous Victories* contained an Oldcastle sufficiently prominent to be theatrically popular, the extant text, however corrupt, would surely make more of so valuable an asset. So a redone version may have existed which made more of him. Professors Morgan and Dover Wilson have of course suggested that the redoing was by Shakespeare himself, and followed the presumed form of the earlier text by being in verse; but this is unproven and indeed unlikely.

7. "*Woodstock*" (*c. 1591–4*)

The anonymous play *Woodstock* almost certainly influenced *Richard II*,[1] and seems to have affected *1 Henry IV*.[2] Its villain is "the old turkey-cocke Trissillian" (Mal. Soc. edn, l. 1877), a corrupt law-clerk appointed Lord Chief Justice during Richard II's anarchy, who boasts "me thinkes already / I am sweld more plump, then erst I was" (ibid., ll. 281–2).[3] He has a band of pillaging rascals under one Nimble, seeks out prosperous victims who bribe

1. Cf. *Woodstock*, ed. A. P. Rossiter, 1946, 47 ff.
2. Cf. J. J. Elson, 'The non-Shn *R2* and Sh.'s *1H4*', in *SP*, 32, 1935, 177–88.
3. 'The fall of Robert Tresilian chiefe Iustice of England' was familiar to the Elizabethans as the first story in *A Myrroure for Magistrates*.

him to avert spoliation, ambushes rich men coming from market, is contemptuous to his victims, flinches from danger, and is reputed for adroitness and for his "tricks" (ll. 1265, 1790, 1830; cf. *1H4*, II. iv. 259, 262). There are verbal similarities; as the farmers are fleeced there occur the phrases "ritch chuffes" (l. 1527), "ritch horesones" (l. 1542), "bacon fead pudding eaters" (l. 1615), and "catterpillers" (l. 1637), with "*Jesu* receaue my soule" (l. 1609) and "we can be but undone" (l. 1622) from the victims. The cluster of apparent echoes in *1 Henry IV* (II. ii. 79–85) is striking.[1] Finally, *Woodstock* integrates its Court drama and its mordant low comedy in presenting the tragic pillage of England; as in the *Henry IV*s, the two planes are organically interrelated.

8. "*A Myrroure For Magistrates*" (*1559*)

The first five stories of this sombre but long-popular collection—those of Tresilian, the Roger Mortimers, Thomas Duke of Gloucester, Lord Mowbray, and Richard the Second—are in the background of *Richard II*: the sixth, by Thomas Phaer, "Howe Owen Glendour seduced by false prophesies tooke vpon him to be prince of Wales", seems to have contributed to *1 Henry IV*. Phaer takes his material from Fabyan and Hall; he makes Owen relate how, "Entiste therto by many of Merlines tales", he aspired to be prince of Wales and how his alliance with Percy and Mortimer grew:

> And for to set vs hereon more agog
> A prophet came (a vengeaunce take them all)
> Affirming Henry to be Gogmagog
> Whom Merlyn doth a Mouldwarp euer call,
> Accurst of god, that must be brought in thrall
> By a wulf, a Dragon, and a Lyon strong,
> Which should deuide his kingdome them among.

> This crafty dreamer made vs thre such beastes
> To thinke we were these foresayd beastes in deede ...

In the corresponding passages Hall and Shakespeare both name Merlin (cf. III. i. 144—"the dreamer Merlin") but Holinshed does not, and it has been argued that this shows Shakespeare to be following Hall (Wilson, N.C.S., 160-1). But without opening Hall he could get Merlin from Phaer, and "dreamer" is like Phaer's "crafty dreamer" and Holinshed's "dreames of the Welsh prophesiers" but unlike Hall, who does not use the word. Shakespeare differs from the *Myrroure*, however, in a much more sympathetic presentation of Glendower (cf. p. xxvi; see also p. lxxxii).

1. Another possible echo in *1H4* is recorded in the note to II. ii. 43-4.

9. Ballads of Percy and Douglas

In confessing that "I never heard the olde song of Percy and Duglas that I found not my heart mooved more then with a trumpet" Sir Philip Sidney was surely not speaking for himself alone. The Percy story must have taken on a particular colour for Shakespeare, as for so many others, from the great ballads of Northumbrian battle like *The Hunting of the Cheviot* and *The Battle of Otterburn*. The Douglas–Percy theme of heroic combat, with Hotspur as the English hero, cannot be tied down to any single source, but the spirit of Shakespeare's treatment may owe something to the spirit of the ballads, and possible direct ballad influences may occur in the forms "the Percy" and "the Douglas" (cf. p. 197) and the detail by which Sir Harry Percy's Scottish enemies in *The Battle of Otterburn* number "forty thowsande . . . and fowre" (cf. IV. i. 130, note).

10. "Soliman and Perseda" (c. 1592)

E. E. Stoll[1] pointed out that Falstaff's soliloquy on honour (*1H4*, v. i. 127 ff.) is like Basilisco's after Erastus' murder (*Soliman and Perseda*, v. iii. 63 ff.). Shakespeare had already made fun of Basilisco in *King John*, I. i. 244. The parallel does not amount to an equation between *Soliman*'s braggart and Shakespeare's philosopher but it must have provided Elizabethan audiences with an entertaining overtone of the unheroic.

> *Basilisco:*   I will ruminate: Death, which the poets
>   Faine to be pale and meager,
>   Hath depriued *Erastus* trunke from breathing vitalitie,
>   A braue Cauelere, but my aprooued foeman.
>   Let me see: where is that *Alcides*, surnamed *Hercules*,
>   The onely Club man of his time? dead.
>   Where is the eldest sonne of *Pryam*,
>   That abraham-coloured Troian? dead.
>   Where is the leader of the Mirmidons,
>   That well knit Accill[es]? dead.
>   Where is that furious *Aiax*, the sonne of *Telamon*,
>   Or that fraudfull squire of *Ithaca*, iclipt *Vlisses*? dead.
>   Where is tipsie *Alexander*, that great cup conquerour,
>   Or *Pompey* that braue warriour? dead.
>   I am my selfe strong, but I confesse death to be stronger:
>   I am valiant, but mortall;
>   I am adorned with natures gifts,
>   A giddie goddesse that now giueth and anon taketh:
>   I am wise, but quiddits will not answer death:
>   To conclude in a word: to be captious, vertuous, ingenious,
>   Are nothing when it pleaseth death to be enuious.

1. *Shn Studies*, 1927, 459.

11. Other Possible Sources

Hall's *Chronicle*, Holinshed's *Historie of Scotland*, Sir John Hayward's *Life and Raigne of King Henry IV*, and a possible lost Hotspur play have also been proposed as sources. Their claims, which are not here accepted, are considered in Appendix IV.

4. FALSTAFF

Falstaff's transcendent prestige is reflected in a vast literature, and in such abundant reference as to occasion, in the *Shakspere Allusion-Book* index, the telling entry "For the purpose of this Index Falstaff is treated as a work". This eminence is not predictable from the life-story of his remote original Sir John Oldcastle (c. 1378–1417), High Sheriff of Herefordshire, who became Lord Cobham by marriage in 1409. Oldcastle steps into Holinshed in a role as remote as can be imagined from the reverend vice and vanity in years; he does not appear, moreover, until after the new-crowned Henry has banished his youthful mates. "A valiant capteine and a hardie gentleman" in the French wars, he has been "highly in the king's favour" (Hol., iii. 62), but is charged with Wycliffite heresy and condemned. Escaping from the Tower he hides in Wales, while his supporters are cruelly suppressed, but eventually he is captured and on Christmas Day 1417 is hanged and burnt.

The valiant Lollard could hardly have expected reincarnation as Oldcastle–Falstaff. Falstaff's Biblical quotations might just possibly reflect such antecedents; moreover, Oldcastle was cast off by the King after early favour (some traditions date the rejection before, some after, the accession); and during his trial he confessed

> that in my frayle youthe I offended thee (Lorde) moste greeuously, in Pride, Wrathe, and Glottony, in Couetousnes and in Lechery.[1]

But the resemblance is not strong. Oldcastle's posthumous story ran in two contrasting channels.[2] One, hostile to him, is that of anti-Wycliffite orthodoxy, and is found in the poet Hoccleve,[3] in popular political verses, and in chroniclers from Walsingham to Polydore Vergil. Fuller, it will be recalled, blamed "the *Papists* railing on him for a *Heretick*" as the fabricators of his disrepute as a

1. John Foxe, *Actes and Monuments*, 1563, 266.

2. Thoroughly plotted by Wilhelm Baeske, *Oldcastle-Falstaff in der engl. Literatur bis zu Sh.*, 1905.

3. Hoccleve, *Works. I. The Minor Poems* (EETS, Extra ser., lxi, 1892, 8–24, 'Address to Sir John Oldcastle').

coward. His flight to Wales and consequent absence from Henry's later wars were misconstrued as pusillanimity; his Lollardism was taken for presumption, blasphemy, and even diabolical instigation; his friendship with the King was restricted to Henry's unregenerate youth; and from his name he was wrongly assumed to be old. The contrasting, favourable, tradition emerged with Tudor Protestantism and is traceable to John Bale's *Brefe Chronycle Concernynge . . . Syr Iohn Oldecastell* (1544). This influenced Hall and was reprinted almost verbatim in Foxe's *Actes and Monuments*, later editions of which contained a long "Defence of the Lord Cobham" and furnished the historical materials for the Munday–Drayton–Wilson–Hathaway play. By this tradition "this most constaunt seruant of the lorde and worthy knight Sir John Oldecastell, the Lorde Cobham",[1] was a Protestant hero and martyr, "a principall fauourer, receiuer, and maintainer of . . . Lollards",[2] a scholar of philosophy and theology, a popular and virtuous leader, wild when young but a religious convert—"his youth was full of wanton wildness before he knew the scriptures", says Bale—and not rejected by Henry until some time after the coronation. Bale, however, mistakenly endorsed the error about his age. These, then, are the conflicting stories, germs of Oldcastle the vicious reprobate and Oldcastle the virtuous martyr, the former incorporated in *The Famous Victories* and Shakespeare, the latter in *Sir John Oldcastle*'s hero—

> It is no pamperd glutton we present,
> Nor aged Councellor to youthfull sinne,
> But one, whose vertue shone aboue the rest,
> A valiant Martyr and a vertuous peere.

How Oldcastle came to be involved in stories of youthful riot is a matter of speculation. The syllogism may have been that the companions of the young Henry were scapegraces; that Oldcastle was a companion of the young Henry; and that therefore Oldcastle was a scapegrace. Professor Dover Wilson suggests that his rejection by Henry welded itself in the popular mind with that of the scapegraces, the more readily since according to the hostile tradition both occurred approximately at Henry's accession ("Before the Kings coronacion [Oldcastle] was forsaken of the Kinge," says Tito Livio's translator[3]) and the "confession" reported by Foxe might be an effective link.

Since the historical Oldcastle was certainly neither old nor unmilitary and (being a warrior) probably not fat, these attributes of

1. John Foxe, *Actes and Monuments*, 1563, 263.   2. Ibid., 1596 edn, i. 513.
3. Cf. C. L. Kingsford, *The First English Life of Henry V*, 1911, 22.

Falstaff must arise otherwise than from history. In fact, several elements from the hostile tradition coalesced with features of the popular morality Vice. Oldcastle's age (thirty-nine at death) was exaggerated by the interpretation of his name on which Shakespeare puns in the "old lad of the castle"; but the Vice, too, was often the aged counsellor to youthful sin. The shortage of valour is derived from the hostile tradition, but it too was easily corroborated by the pusillanimity of Vices, parasites, and boasters. The "goodly portly" figure is in neither history nor *The Famous Victories*, and attempts have been made to explain it. It may be Shakespeare's dramatic contrast, Dover Wilson suggests, to that of the "starveling" Prince (II. iv. 240), whose lithe agility the chroniclers celebrate. Or something may come from *Woodstock*'s plump "old turkey-cocke". But here again the Vice has something to contribute, as will be seen.

Falstaff is indeed a rich amalgam, a world of comic ingredients. Source-seekers have proffered his components in great profusion. Of these the most important is the morality Vice, the ensnarer of youth. Since Quiller-Couch proposed this in *Shakespeare's Workmanship* (1918) the idea has been amply elaborated, and John W. Shirley has excellently explored the relevant characteristics of Gluttony, the Gula of the Seven Deadly Sins and a favourite morality-play tempter.[1] Vices often bragged, like Sensual Appetyte, or Ambidexter in *Cambises* (1569), or Lust, Sturdiness, and Inclination in *The Trial of Treasure*. They might sanctimoniously champion virtue; "Uertue is mocked of euery man", laments Incontinence in *The Longer Thou Livest*. Collectively they share their features with the farce-clowns like Huanebango the braggart of Peele's *Old Wives' Tale*, or the greedy cowardly Dericke of *The Famous Victories*, whom Falstaff copies in making his nose bleed with spear-grass (*1H4*, II. iv. 305). An Elizabethan audience would

---

1. 'Fal. an Elizabethan Glutton' (*PQ*, xvii, 1938). In *The Castell of Perseverance* (c. 1425), the World, Devil, and Flesh lead Mankind "with synnys al a-bowt"; Flesh is corpulent and accompanied by Gluttony, Lechery, and Sloth. In Medwall's *Nature* (c. 1486), aged Sensuality has Gluttony as an accomplice. In *The Nature of the Foure Elements* (1519), Sensual Appetyte under the guise of Friendship tempts Humanyte to the tavern, and in *Lusty Juventus* (c. 1540) the age-old Hypocrisy incites Juventus to lechery and self-indulgence. In William Wager's *The Longer Thou Livest the More Fool Thou Art* (c. 1586), Incontinence is as old as Idleness, "parent of all vice", and tempts Man with food, wine, and girls: in Lupton's *All for Money* (1578), Pleasure is glutton and lecher, and Gluttony prompts to "fine fare and gluttonie". Ryot, in *Youth* (c. 1550), is thief and tempter to wine and women; *The Trial of Treasure* (1567) has one Gredy-Gutte —"the cowe-bellied knaue", "the great-bellied loute". In *The Faerie Queene* (I. iv. 21–3) Spenser's Gluttony is, like Falstaff, "Not meet to be of counsell to a king", "Full of diseases", his belly "up-blowne with luxury".

recognize in Falstaff the familiar Vice-qualities of gluttony, idle-ness, and lechery, and in Hal the youth in danger. Throughout Falstaff is referred to in morality-idiom—iniquity, ruffian, vanity in years, beating Hal out of his kingdom with a dagger of lath, the abominable misleader of youth, the old white-bearded Satan; and in Part 2 he is rejected finally (as prospectively in Part 1, by Hal's soliloquy and many a hint) as the tutor and feeder of Hal's "riots" (a recognized morality-term), the old profane surfeit-swelled gor-mandizer. Hal's soliloquy (*1H4*, 1. ii. 190 ff.) tells the audience both that Hal is not the hooligan of *The Famous Victories* (which, inci-dentally, is not at all morality-influenced) and that he participates undeceived in the unyoked humours of idleness.

"Morality tradition" is a broad category. The various kinds of Vice-farce, with such conceits as clownage keeps in pay, furnish a wide panorama of aged, obese, gluttonous, wenching braggarts, comically outrageous in huffing, puffing, lying, thieving, and gor-mandizing. Somewhere in the picture are the *miles gloriosus*, with his bogus valour, and the witty parasite (both frequent in Plautine comedy), the fool, and the Elizabethan army officer often casti-gated for recruiting and other swindles. Enthusiasts have even sought Falstaff in historical persons—Tarlton the clown, Chettle the dramatist, and Captain Nicholas Dawtrey. Neglecting these agreeable whimsies we may admit something, though with reserve, in the other identifications. The *miles gloriosus* boasted of courage but avoided combat, like Bobadill in *Every Man in his Humour* or Parolles in *All's Well*, and scholars have worked out his contribu-tion to Falstaff. Yet since he was fatuous, humourless, and finally unmasked to derision we may agree with Maurice Morgann that elements of the *miles gloriosus* in Falstaff are so modified by wit and self-possession as to become something different, a mere trace of flavour in a succulent gallimaufry, like the *soupçon* of Basilisco in the soliloquy on honour (cf. p. xxxviii).

As for the parasite tradition, this contributed something; Iago has been called the culmination of the fatal parasite, Falstaff of the comic.[1] Butt, wit, sponger, trickster, and mocker, this classical type was familiar to the Elizabethan stage in such figures as Mathew Merygreke in *Ralph Roister Doister* or Cariosophus in *Damon and Pithias*. But again the relationship to Falstaff is only tangential; Falstaff is a parasite but a benefactor too, and much else besides.

His quality as Fool, however, is more noteworthy, for he shares not only some of the Fool's superficial features—comic bragga-docio, inventiveness of idea, dexterity with words, mock moraliz-

1. E. P. Vandiver, 'The Elizabethan Dramatic Parasite', *SP*, 1935, xxxii. 411.

ing, deliberate mistakings, absurd actions—but also the Fool's deeper significance, as liberator from convention. In Miss Enid Welsford's words:

> under the dissolvent influence of [the Fool's] personality the iron network of physical, social, and moral law, which enmeshes us from the cradle to the grave, seems—for the moment—negligible as a web of gossamer. The Fool does not lead a revolt against the law; he lures us into a region of the spirit where, as Lamb would put it, the writ does not run. (*The Fool*, 1935, 317)

We cannot always live in that region, as the play makes clear, nor is its freedom, as some Falstaff sentimentalists suggest, more precious than the network of law. But Miss Welsford does in fact admirably describe the effect Falstaff has upon our spirits.[1]

Falstaff as a whole is far greater than the sum of his parts; this Vice–Parasite–Fool–*Miles-Gloriosus*–Corrupt-Soldier is inspired by such humorous virtuosity as immeasurably to transcend such components. His whole nature is unified of paradoxical opposites, so that a man no more knows where to have him than he himself knew where to have the Hostess (III. iii. 126–7). Parasitical, he yet gives to life as much as he takes, and indeed provides amidst all his vices a vast salutary criticism of the world of war and policy. He is vicious, yet his vices are a tonic for human nature; he exploits his dependants, yet they remain indissolubly attached to him; he lies, yet would be dismayed if his lies were to be believed. He laments his age, corpulence, and lost agility, yet he behaves with the gaiety of youth, has intellectual legerity to offset his bulk, and is agile whenever it suits him. A reprobate, he yet quotes scripture for his purpose. Finally, is he or is he not a coward? No, say Morgann and Bradley: he is sought for in war, leads his men into danger, and philosophizes coolly on the battlefield. Yes, say Stoll and others: as Poins foretells, he runs at Gad's Hill and boasts afterwards; he hacks his sword, slubbers his garments, and is touchy when taunted; his Shrewsbury nonchalance is clown-foolery only; his ignominious stabbing of Hotspur is "one of the accepted *lazzi* of the coward on the stage"; and his capture of Colevile in Part 2 is buffoonery, like Pistol's of Monsieur le Fer in *Henry V*.

This tiresome question need not have arisen had not Morgann rightly desired to vindicate Falstaff from the ignominious clowning he received on the eighteenth-century stage. It would have been

1. Cf. C. L. Barber, 'From Ritual to Comedy', 24, in *English Stage Comedy*, ed. W. K. Wimsatt, 1955: "In the theatrical institution of clowning, the clown or vice, when Shakespeare started to write, was a recognized anarchist who made aberration obvious by carrying release to absurd extremes".

quickly settled had not Falstaff's vitality confused critics as to the difference between dramatic and real persons. This multifarious material is not to be reduced to a single realistic formula. That Falstaff's panic at Gad's Hill is not put on there is no doubt. It is a foretold outcome of the trick played on him; the point of "By the Lord, I knew ye as well as he that made ye" (II. iv. 263) is to show his resourcefulness in improbable excuse; and the surprised relief in "But by the Lord, lads, I am glad you have the money" (II. iv. 271–2) is proof that he had thought the booty to be lost. The multi-plication of buckram men does not mean either on the one hand that he expects to be believed or on the other that he has recognized his assailants and is pulling their legs: he is putting on the expected enjoyable show. And who, in fact, is "he"? "He", really, is the comic personality given a chance by the dramatist to revel in a comic role. The exaggerations are not to be explained realistically by the argument that so acute a wit cannot expect so absurd a yarn to be believed and is merely countermining the Prince and Poins for the trick he has detected: he has not detected it, but, like the brilliant stage-comic he is, he has an invention full of nimble and delectable shapes which he exercises on all possible occasions with the effect (eagerly expected by Prince, Poins, and audience alike) of landing himself in foreseeable quandaries and then unforeseeably extricating himself from them.[1] To schematize Falstaff's shotsilk variety into stable colour is absurd: his dramatic sphere of popular comedy allows a rapid shifting of attitudes. A real man who ran at Gad's Hill would not receive a charge of foot from his stampeder, nor would a dozen captains seek him out, nor even with Hal's con-nivance would anyone believe he had killed Hotspur. But the stage comic frees us from the restricting congruities of real life. Professor Empson has put it (it is Dover Wilson's plea too) that "the whole of the great joke is that you *can't* see through him, any more than the Prince could"—"the dramatic effect simply *is* the doubt, and very satisfying too".[2] Is Falstaff then inconsistent? Yes, if judged realis-tically. No, when taken, rightly, for what Empson calls his "Dra-matic Ambiguity", for the figure of dramatic comedy that he is, butt and wit together, equally amusing by his elephantine panic, exuberant fabrications, and comic aplomb in the midst of war. His philosophy of courage is, no doubt, to show as much or as little of it as circumstances require; he might observe, like the practical but not cowardly Bluntschli in Shaw's *Arms and the Man*, "It is our duty to live as long as we can", and like Bluntschli he keeps in his holster

1. A. J. A. Waldock comments well to this effect in 'The Men in Buckram'; *RES*, 1947, xxiii. 16–23.
2. W. Empson, 'Fal. and Mr Dover Wilson', *Kenyon Review*, 1953, xv. 223.

something better than pistols. Yet Bluntschli would hardly "roar" in flight, as Falstaff does (II. ii. 106), and the attempt to fit Falstaff into a formula of psychological realism must finally fail. Brilliant at timely evasions, he escapes this straitjacket as he escapes any other.

In other words, Falstaff, though immensely "living", is not like any single real man. But he is symbolically like life itself; the large comedy of humanity is embodied in him. He expresses the indispensable spirit of fun. When he runs away, the fun is at him; when he does not run away, the fun is through him. The consistency lies not in the congruence of one action with another, but in the whole function of providing mirth and a liberating irreverence. Falstaff differs in amplitude but not in kind from the stage funny man who, without incongruity, is both knocked about and knocker-about. In the words Whitman wrote on himself, he is large, he contains multitudes.

5. THE UNITY OF THE PLAY

Since Sir Edmund Chambers published *Shakespeare, A Survey* (1925), several critics have taken issue with his treatment of the *Henry IV*s. To query this treatment once again is not to undervalue his immense contribution to Shakespeare scholarship but it is to try to set in the right light plays on which a good many readers (fewer playgoers, perhaps) probably share Sir Edmund's views, expounded thus:

> In *Henry IV*, chronicle-history becomes little more than a tapestried hanging, dimly wrought with horsemen and footmen, in their alarums and excursions, which serves as a background to groups of living personages conceived in quite another spirit and belonging to a very different order of reality. . . All this . . . becomes the setting of a single great comic figure, and thereby the plays attain the unity which their intermediate position in the cycle . . . makes it difficult for them to accomplish in any other way. Instead of the dynamic unity of an emotional issue set and resolved in the course of the action, they have the static unity of a pervading humorous personality.

This, however, is precisely the opposite of what one should say. Far from the history's being merely a "dimly wrought" background to "groups of living personages" of superior reality, the historical themes are urged upon us with Shakespeare's utmost vigour. As Hazlitt observed, "the heroic and serious part of these two plays . . . is not inferior to the comic and farcical". And far from the unity's being "static", confined to the dominance of Falstaff, it is dynamic, complex, and organized from a wonderful interrelationship of material, so that one agrees with Elizabeth Montagu—"I cannot help thinking that there is more of contrivance and care in the execution of this play than in almost any he has written" (*Essay on the Writings and Genius of Shakespear*, 1769, 100). The co-existence of comic and serious plots is not confined to their efficient alternation, though their alternations are superbly efficient. The more they are scrutinized, the more connected they appear, the connection being sometimes of parallelism and reinforcement, sometimes of antithesis and contrast, sometimes a reversal by which serious or comic is judged by the other's values. There are, too, stylistic relationships by which, for instance, major types of imagery are common to both parts, or by which the texture and pace of prose scenes offset those of verse.

At first sight, one takes the two plots to be antithetical—court against tavern, nobility against commonalty, energy against sloth, time-saving against time-wasting, gravity against wit, verse against prose, and so on. To a hasty view the play seems to split into separate strata. These two different kinds of thing do indeed furnish different parts of the mind, stretch it, and make it feel extended over a wide dichotomy. Yet closer study shows a different state of things—branches belonging to a single trunk. The first speech expresses a hope for national unity; this hope is equally denied by both plots, by the Percys' rising and Hal's insubordination. Both these troubles reflect on Henry's own conduct—they have a causal, not casual, link with it, for the Percys, instruments of his usurpation, turn against him the very pretexts of national welfare on which his rise was based, and his own exclusion of the rightful heir (Mortimer) threatens to be repaid by a failure of the succession in Hal. Hal seems to Henry a replica of Richard II, for each man mingles his royalty with capering fools and enfeofs himself to popularity, and the benefits Richard flung recklessly upon Henry, Hal is recklessly flinging away again. Both serious and comic plots show the usurping Henry dogged by retribution: over both plots hangs the hand of constituted authority—defeat and death for rebels, the gallows or banishment for wastrels. Both plots sound the theme of ambition and rapacity—Hotspur will "cavil on the ninth part of a hair" and is as eager to monopolize honour as Falstaff to discard it. There is as little principle among barons as among thieves; Hotspur can no more depend on his fellow-conspirators, from the "lack-brain" (II. iii. 16) to Northumberland and Glendower, than Falstaff on Hal and Poins or they on him. There are all sorts of ways in which the two plots operate similarly; as the rebels'

self-seeking is masked by Hotspur's rhapsodies about honour, so the
rascals' exploits are romanticized (in their own eyes) by reference
to a world of legend, literature, and heroic service; Falstaff ideal-
izes highwaymen as vividly as sherris-sack—they are Diana's
foresters, minions of the moon, governed like the sea by celestial
power (I. ii). When Hotspur rants about the Mortimer–Glendower
fight (I. iii), and Falstaff about the buckram men (II. iv), we think
the former heroic and the latter outrageous, yet to fail to see a relationship is to miss part of the fabric of linkage. Another parody-
relationship is that between the Falstaff–Hal burlesque (II. iv) and
the King's genuine reproof (III. ii). Similar motifs appear seriously
and comically; the Gad's Hill bustle is the comic counterpart of
Hotspur's insurrection; Falstaff's sanctimoniousness has its serious
echo in Henry's yearnings for a Crusade; the predatory campaign-
ing is both heroic and preposterous at once; and motifs of bodily
states and actions, and particularly of disease, run thematically
through both plots.

The interrelationships form an intricate web among the main
characters. The connections between King, Prince, Hotspur, and
Falstaff compel us to assess them this way and that, from which
arises the play's moral value. The King and Hotspur, for instance,
are similar (rivals in the same game), but also antithetical (authority versus rebellion): the King and Falstaff, again, are alike
(fellows in subversion: elderly examples for Hal), but also opposite
(rule against misrule). Hotspur and Falstaff are both examples for
Hal of rebellious anarchy, contrasting however by their differing
codes of conduct and honour. Falstaff and Hal are simultaneously
allies (boon companions, fellow-scoffers), and opponents (Vicious
Age, Virtuous Youth). Hotspur and Hal, apparently at opposite
extremes of promise, meet on the ground of youth and valour.
Finally, the King and Hal, apparently opposed, are of the same
family, and have in common their "policy". As Professor Empson
has said, much of the play's value lies in this dramatic "ambiguity"
which leaves one deliberating this way and that, for and against all
the main characters.[1]

The moral structure of the play is, as Quiller-Couch affirmed, a
morality-structure, the "Contention Between Vice and Virtue for
the Soul of a Prince", though it is much more also. It is worth noting
how the possibilities are organized around Hal. In a simple sense,
Hotspur and Falstaff represent virtue and vice—the former the
hero, blunt, honest, too active to be sensual, enchanted by
honour; the latter his diametrical opposite. Yet merely opposite

1. 'Fal. and Mr Dover Wilson', *Kenyon Review*, 1953, xv. 221.

they are not; Hal cannot rule well by rejecting one model and following the other. Most importantly, he must inhabit the real world
while they both live their fantasies. Both men are dangerously
attractive, and their value to Hal is in showing what to seek (Hotspur's valour, Falstaff's ripeness), but equally what to avoid
(Hotspur's recklessness, Falstaff's indulgence). Both subvert the
decent conventions—Falstaff has no aim other than sensuality,
Hotspur none other than battle. Both, Brooks and Heilman put it in
Understanding Drama, "are *below* the serious concerns that fill the
play"—they "do not stand quite on the level of the adult world
where there are jobs to be done". To say that neither is serious
enough sounds pedantic: who wants a serious Hotspur, a serious
Falstaff? Why not love their brilliant displays of life? Yet it is
fundamental in both men that neither can see things in proportion:
Hotspur's imagination starts away from good judgement as fast as
Falstaff's. His greed for honour is for monopoly; he aims only at
war; he is as much a liability as an asset to his allies.[1]

As for Hal, mid-point between, he reflects on these plots and
codes of life. Non-committally poised, he provokes the maximum
dramatic expectation. It is to protract this expectation that though
the King and he are reconciled in Part 1 the process has to be
repeated in Part 2 as though Part 1 had not occurred—the Prince
still a companion to the common streets, the King mindless of his
virtues. Part 2 provides the matching half of a diptych, Hal's com-
mittal to gravity (the Lord Chief Justice) after frivolity. His prior
"loose behaviour" is a nodus of both serious and comic plots; Hotspur and the King, on their level, and Falstaff, on his, are all
punished for misreading him.

As Hotspur and Falstaff stand opposed to Hal as excess and defect of Honour, so the King and Falstaff stand as opposed versions of Age and Authority, responsible and irresponsible, but both
blemished by Anarchy. Brooks and Heilman observe that in taking
the King off in the tavern play Falstaff parodies not only Euphuism
but "the kind of seriousness with which authority has to express,
and take, itself; the carefully balanced antitheses, the allusions to
natural history, the appeal to learned authorities, the laboured
truism"; and it is this mocked authority which Hal (his father's representative as well as his mocker) ominously retorts upon Falstaff.

Yet these versions of authority, however opposed, are not simple
antitheses. Hal reaches kingly success by combining and tran-
scending them. To his father's masterfulness he adds Falstaff's
broad humanity, so that when king he commands not only "culled

1. See v. iv. 119, note, for a comment on rash valour.

and choice-drawn cavaliers" but "all the good lads in Eastcheap".
The King and Falstaff are complementary.

Moreover, both have a double function for Hal. On the face of
it, the King stands for rule, Falstaff for misrule, and Falstaff, like
the rebel lords, is to be suppressed. Yet Henry stands for rule only
because he has himself rebelled—the laws of England have been at
his command as Falstaff expects them to be at his, and woe to the
due succession. So Hal sees in Henry both regal firmness and regal
weariness: kingship is a glory but a burden.

Falstaff's function is more subtly dual. Anarchic though he is,
he gives Hal much of value, not only negatively (showing how not
to act) but positively. Professor Empson has made this point well:

> The idea is not simply that Falstaff is debauched and tricky,
> though that in itself made him give Hal experience . . . but that
> he had the breadth of mind and social understanding which the
> Magnanimous Man needed to acquire. . . Indeed, if you com-
> pare Hal to his brother and father, whom the plays describe so
> unflinchingly, it is surely obvious that to love Falstaff was a
> liberal education.[1]

Falstaff indeed makes the point himself in relating how "excellent
endeavour of drinking good and good store of fertile sherris" has in
Hal warmed the cold Bolingbrokian blood. However much Falstaff owes to the morality Vice, his function in respect of kingship
is much more than that of mere tempter.

Serious and comic themes are entwined by many other echoes
and links. They unite in a vision of national life both broad and
deep, and are expressed in a style of extraordinary energy, whether
in serious verse or comic prose. This vision of national life has its
comprehensive geographical range and its long perspectives of
time; it looks into the future and it reaches into the past, for retro-
spection is as integral to reminiscences of a comic past[2] as to those
of tragic history. The great idea of England is woven from all these
themes.

The structural coherence is equally organic. The Qq's lack of
scene-division makes evident the play's perpetual counterpointing. There are such interactions as that between what are now I. i
and I. ii: the former, in pressing strenuous verse, treats of mental
and bodily strain, the country's dangers, the swift succession of
military events; its emotions are grave, troubled, angry, its pace
increasingly swift. I. ii in lavish comic prose is the entire antithesis;
time, speed, and the making of appointments are rejected for time-

1. 'Fal. and Mr Dover Wilson', *Kenyon Review*, 1953, xv. 246-56.
2. Cf. *1H4*, II. iv. 310-12, 325-8; *2H4*, III. ii, passim.

less leisure; strung nerves give place to unbuttoned slumber; combat and worry yield to capons and wenches. Yet both express disorder and a prince's misconduct; in both a campaign is prepared—defiance to the Percys, robbery at Gad's Hill; and Hal's soliloquy at the end of I. ii knots both together. II. ii and II. iii are also related: the comic violence of Gad's Hill leads on to Hotspur's military exuberance—indeed, each scene sets forth its hero soliloquizing in exasperation at perfidious associates. In IV. i and IV. ii, we first have Vernon's great speech about the Prince's panoply and then meet Falstaff equally bound for war but scandalously cynical about his tattered men. The counterpointing is obvious, and rich; it would not need mentioning were the unity of the play more generally recognized. And finally, in this structural aspect, one notices that serious and comic plots, at first in quite different spheres, are progressively brought together. As the rebellion moves to its climax, Hal emerges from comic folly into serious leadership, and the comic scenes show every cognizance of the serious. Both are borne along on the tide running to Shrewsbury, and on the battlefield both attitudes to life are put to the test. The battle, however awkward on the stage, is the thematic resolution: Hal dispels the fears about him, Hotspur is proved to have been overweening, kingship is confirmed, and Falstaff is suddenly shown in a shocking light as he stabs the dead Hotspur. Shrewsbury is the touchstone which tries men and causes by Part I's criterion of prowess.

6. THE HISTORICAL OUTLOOK

In a discussion of Shakespeare's increasingly secular historical outlook, by which the "absolute moral values" of the *Henry VI–Richard III* series change into the Erastian criteria of *Henry IV–Henry V*, Professor John Danby offers a brilliant interpretation of the *Henry IV*s.[1] Instead of a kingdom, however evil, under God—which he takes to be the "vision" of the earlier sequence—he finds here one governed by purely secular motives of expediency and "Commodity", a morally sordid state however vigorous its physical life. Earlier, the issues had been "Is the King right or wrong? Is the state just or unjust?" Now, he avers, "the questions are reduced and vulgarized: Is the King strong or weak? Is the state secure or insecure?"

The difference between the sequences can easily be exaggerated; nevertheless it exists. Shakespeare's political instincts seem to have swung like a pendulum. In the first sequence, however selfish

1. *Sh.'s Doctrine of Nature*, 1949, pp. 81–101.

the actions of most of the characters (and supremely of Richard III), the presiding assumption is of divine superintendence, punishing sin. In the second, though this assumption is conventionally recognized, and Henry V puts himself religiously in the right, it lacks force. In *Macbeth* and *King Lear*, however, it more than regains its strength; both plays are myths expressing the religious conflict of moral law and moral anarchy.

The *Henry IV*s inhabit the Tudor Erastian world. Religious references are mostly perfunctory. Henry's wish for a crusade, true though it seems in Part 1, appears questionable in Part 2 (*2H4*, IV. v. 208–11). The rebels make much of Bolingbroke's gospel-sworn and broken oath, yet they themselves are parties to the guilt. In Part 2 Westmoreland urges the traditional sanctities against the Archbishop's rising (*2H4*, IV. i), but is answered with political necessity. Prince John's "God, and not we, hath safely fought to-day" (*2H4*, IV. ii. 122) frankly assimilates God to the wiles of state. The most striking sign of secularism is the King's rebound from remorseful reminiscence—for which one expects a moralizing conclusion—to a purely practical resolution (*2H4*, III. i. 92–3):

> Are these things then necessities?
> Then let us meet them like necessities.

Despite themes of sin and expiation the plays develop in terms not of a supernatural metaphysic of history but of the practical ends of worldly action; they reflect a necessitarian view of political action, a sense of compelling reality. Some qualifications, admittedly, should be made to this. Religious sanctions are not entirely superseded; Carlisle's prophesied disasters come to pass (*R2*, IV. i. 114 ff.); Henry IV suffers remorse; Henry V makes expiation (*H5*, IV. i. 312–25). But the effect is casual, and Dover Wilson rightly warns us not to overlay the *Richard II–Henry V* sequence with too much moralizing.[1] In this respect the chronicles point the way; they mostly perform a straddle by which they show Richard II as a bad king though they also lament his misfortunes and downfall, so that they condemn his follies yet extract emotion from his sufferings.[2] Shakespeare follows Holinshed who, while moralizing on sin and remorse (e.g. "A guiltie conscience in extremitie of sicknesse pincheth sore"), commits himself no more to Richard II than to Henry and, whatever emotion he derives from Henry's unquiet time, keeps the story secular. Henry's conscience troubles him, but

1. *Sh.'s Histories at Stratford*, 1951, 18–19.

2. The fifth story in *A Myrroure for Magistrates* is headed 'Howe kyng Richarde the seconde was for his euyll gouernaunce deposed from his seat, and miserably murdred in prison'.

mainly with a worried sense that his course was inevitable ("That I and greatness were compell'd to kiss": *2H4*, III. i. 74). To the question of *why* Henry's was an unquiet time the answer is that his abettors were unruly rather than that God was outraged; and to the question *why* they were unruly the answer is that they were ambitious rather than that the moral order was flouted (though flouted it certainly was).

Dr Irving Ribner has questioned whether Shakespeare deeply meant to show divine punishment for Richard's deposition.[1] If such punishment were the lesson of *Richard II*, why did Essex's followers launch their rebellion by having the play performed? Why publicize sacrilege? It is true that in the long run, interpreted by the "Tudor myth", Bolingbroke's crime resulted in divinely-prompted wars until exorcised in the blessed union of Lancastrian Henry VII and his Yorkist queen. But the second tetralogy looks less towards the remote *terminus ad quem* of the Tudor accession, however sanctified, than to the climax of Henry V's victories, and though *Henry V* is not without religious feeling that feeling is hardly distinguished from patriotic rant. Even in the *Henry IV*s the shadow of retribution does not prevent Henry's being the centre of authority and the rightful suppressor of rebellion.

Henry IV's career, then, proclaims less that God punishes deposition than that the king must rule. This was a sixteenth-century theme. Much as the Elizabethans execrated Machiavelli, he fascinated them by his cool recommendations of "policy". But even without Machiavelli the importance of rule was evident in the collapse of feudalism. Ribner quotes Tyndale's *Obedience of a Christian Man* (1528; ed. Locett, 1885, 93–4):

> Yea, and it is better to have a tyrant unto thy king than a shadow: a passive king that doth nought himself but suffreth other to do with him what they will and to lead him whither they list. For a tyrant, though he do wrong unto the good, yet he punisheth the evil, and maketh all men obey, neither suffreth any man to poll but himself only. A king that is soft as silk and effeminate, that is to say turned unto the nature of a woman— what with his own lusts, which are the longing of a woman with child, so that he cannot resist them, and what with the wily tyranny of them that ever rule him—shall be much more grievous unto the realm than a right tyrant. Read the chronicles and thou shalt find it ever so.

That describes the difference between Richard II and Henry IV, and Shakespeare shows Henry's efficiency. In the Bagot-Aumerle

1. 'The Political Problem in Sh.'s Lancastrian Tetralogy', *SP*, 1952, 171–84.

quarrel (*R2*, IV. i. 1–106) Henry dominates a situation such as
Richard had bungled with Mowbray and Bolingbroke; over
Aumerle and his conspiracy (which, be it noted, favours the "legi-
timate" king; *R2*, v. ii–iii) he combines strength and mercy. In
2 Henry IV the rebels fail even though led by an Archbishop who
displays "the blood / Of fair King Richard, scrap'd from Pomfret
stones" (*2H4*, I. i. 204–5). Richard falls through his own folly and
injustice, climaxed in the murder of the patriotic Gloucester (cf.
R2, I. ii. 1–3), which is the subject of the *Myrroure for Magistrates'*
third story[1] and the crux of *Woodstock*. Bolingbroke rises rather on
the Wheel of Fortune than by wicked purpose. In *Richard II* the
"formal and ceremonial" quality of which Dr Tillyard writes,[2] the
ritualistic character which Pater distinguishes,[3] mask the secular
situation behind poetry and symbolism; but peeping from behind
the ritual and ceremony there is, even here, the problem of efficient
rule. And in the *Henry IV*s this secular interest reduces the religious sentiment to subordination, just as it heightens the realistic
interest of lifelike men competing in the world of action.

7. THE SPIRIT OF THE PLAY

Professor Danby's analysis, however, goes beyond a mere asser-
tion of secularism to a striking characterization of the *Henry IV*s
which holds that they present a nation "disintegrated into mutually
exclusive spheres"—Court, tavern, dissidents, country fusspots—
motivated by "frigid opportunism, riotous irresponsibility, fatuous
inconsequence, quarrelsome 'honour'—with no common term
except the disease of each". " 'England',", the argument continues,

> is sometimes said to be the heroic composite thing that is por-
> trayed. If this is so, it is an England seen in her most unflattering
> aspects—an England pervaded throughout court, tavern, and
> country retreat by pitiless fraud.

Falstaff's unscrupulousness is the code by which all live—"if anything unifies this congeries of monads it is 'Commodity' ". "Order"
represents not Right, not God's Will, but effective Power: "Disorder" is not Unrighteousness, but secular Greed. So, Professor
Danby concludes,

> Analysis leaves us, then, with symbols of Power and Appetite as
> the keys to the play's meaning: Power and Appetite the two

1. 'Howe syr Thomas Duke of Wudstocke Duke of Glocester, vncle to king
Richarde the seconde, was vnlawfully murdred.'
2. E. M. W. Tillyard, *Sh.'s History Plays*, 1944, 245.
3. 'Sh.'s English Kings', in *Appreciations*.

sides of Commodity... The England depicted in *Henry IV* ... is neither ideally ordered nor happy. It is an England, on the one side, of bawdy house and thieves' kitchen, of waylaid merchants, badgered and bewildered Justices, and a peasantry wretched, betrayed, and recruited for the wars: an England, on the other side, of the chivalrous wolf-pack ... and of state-sponsored treachery, in the person of Prince John—the whole presided over by a sick King, hag-ridden by conscience, dreaming of a Crusade to the Holy Land as Monsieur Remorse thinks of slimming and repentance. Those who see the world of *Henry IV* as some vital, joyous, Renaissance England must go behind the facts that Shakespeare presents. It is a world where to be normal is to be anti-social, and to be social is to be anti-human. Humanity is split in two. One half is banished to an underworld where dignity and decency must inevitably submerge in brutality and riot. The other half is restricted to an over-world where the same dignity and decency succumb to heartlessness and frigidity.

If this were so, the play's unity would be a unity of moral chaos, an Elizabethan *Waste Land*. Professor Danby offers this not as a total view of the play, whose inventive vitality he fully admits, but merely of its themes, and even then only insofar as they reflect Shakespeare's increasing secularism. Yet, if this is offered as the play's tenor, even with these qualifications, one must reply that Shakespeare was not Ben Jonson, that the *Henry IV*s (particularly Part 1) are not *Volpone*, and that, related to the moralities though they are, this is not their true theme. Interpretations of this kind, it has been observed, "make a shambles of the heroic moments in the play, make them impossible to act".[1] Secular and realistic the plays have been admitted to be, and most of the characters are self-seeking, but their whole tenor forbids any summing-up in terms of mere greed. In a *Scrutiny* essay in 1934 Professor L. C. Knights (preceded by Ulrici in 1839, and followed by Professor Kenneth Muir in 1951) observed that in *1 Henry IV* "the Falstaff attitude is in solution, as it were, throughout the play", but pointed out also that "a set of complementary impulses is also brought into play". In other words, though Falstaff is, to quote Professor Muir, "a living criticism of the world of 'policy' ", satirizing the gulf between precept and practice in the world of rank, he has anything but the last word on the values of life.

But how does this happen? Surely not, as it were, antiseptically, by our being so faced with the spectacle of corruption that our codes of virtue are reinforced. Falstaff may be what Ulrici called

1. C. L. Barber, 'From Ritual to Comedy', 30 (in *English Stage Comedy*, ed. W. K. Wimsatt, 1955).

him, "the personified parody on the corrupt state of the chivalry and vassalry of the day", just as the chivalry's and vassalry's self-seeking throws into relief his hedonism. But should we feel the plays in this puritan-critical way? Surely not. Serious and comic do not reduce each other to shams; serious history enlarges itself to compass broad comedy, and comedy contributes more than mockery to our sense of history. "The heroic drama", Mr Mark Van Doren has said of these plays,

> is modified by gigantic mockery, by the roared voice of truth; but the result is more rather than less reality, just as a cathedral, instead of being demolished by merriment among its aisles, stands more august.   (*Shakespeare*, 1939, 116)

The greatness of the *Henry IV*s lies in their not taking a disapproving view. To quote Mr C. L. Barber again, "the dynamic relation of comedy and serious action is saturnalian rather than satiric". By the complex of cross-relationships that link together (as well as set off) the worlds of comedy and history one is left fully aware of human failings and yet impressed with great positives. The responsibilities of kingship, the honour of courage, the validity of justice, the energies of life, the zest of wit—these the plays fully assert, even though Henry is a usurper, Hotspur a firebrand, Hal a calculator, Falstaff a rogue. Fallible the persons may be, but their weaknesses are not what Shakespeare leaves uppermost in our minds. The Eastcheap comedy cannot be written down as "bawdy-house and thieves' kitchen", that of Gad's Hill as "waylaid merchants", that of Gloucestershire as "badgered and bewildered Justices", even that of Falstaff's recruitment as "a peasantry wretched, betrayed, and recruited for the wars". Nor can the history be only the sum of chivalrous wolf-pack, state-sponsored treachery, and hag-ridden King, though it includes those elements. Shakespeare, one feels sure, would have been startled at the idea. Usurper, yes; but Henry is an effective King. Firebrand, yes; but Hotspur is a true hero. Hal calculates, but becomes a good King; Falstaff is a rogue, yet he warms the heart. The fundamental Shakespearean fact is that at Eastcheap there is communal happiness as well as trickery; at Gad's Hill, mirth as well as robbery (and is anyone a ha'p'orth the worse?); in Gloucestershire, rustic comedy as well as bewilderment; in the recruitment, Feeble's courage as well as Falstaff's corruption. Hotspur deserves the great tribute his wife pays (*2H4*, II. iii. 18 ff.): state policy saves the nation: the King exerts a proper authority. The old view which sliced the play into independent alternating spectacles of politics and comedy was too casual, but the later one which interprets it through "the most

serious ethical scrutiny" is too narrow. The play stands ethical
scrutiny—that is its moral greatness—but it promotes a response of
which moral sums are only a small part and moral didacticism
abstracted from the rich dramatic context no part at all.[1] Shakespeare is not Jonson: cakes and ale exist alongside virtue. Instead of
a morally-corrective partial vision there is a wise inclusive vision,
derived from a true understanding of what men are like; in this, a
judgement of what they should be like takes only a secondary
place. "*Henry IV* is Shakespeare's vision of the 'happy breed of
men' that was his England." Dover Wilson's view, expressed thus
in his edition of *1 Henry IV*, is too roseate (it is, however, adjusted in
The Fortunes of Falstaff), but it shows a proper sympathy with what
is going on. Shakespeare loves his creatures (most of them, anyway)
before he judges them; his story demands rebels and buffoons, but
he thinks only on men.

The best analysis of this unified vision—the vision of many,
various, interrelated modes and codes of life—is Cleanth Brooks's
and Robert B. Heilman's.

> For the reader for whom the play does achieve a significant unity
> it may well seem that here Shakespeare has given us one of the
> wisest and fullest commentaries on human action possible to the
> comic mode—a view which scants nothing, which covers up
> nothing, and which takes into account in making its affirma-
> tions the most searching criticism of that which is affirmed. For
> such a reader, Shakespeare has no easy moral to draw, no simple
> generalization to make. . . The world which Shakespeare por-
> trays here is a world of contradictions—of mixtures of good and
> evil. His vision of that world is ultimately a comic vision. . . For
> the comic writer does not attempt to transcend the world of com-
> promises, even though the more thoughtful writers of comedy, as
> here, may be fully aware of the seriousness of the issues. Comedy,
> after all, does not treat the lives of saints or heroes: it does not
> attempt to portray the absolute commitment to ultimate issues—
> the total commitment which transcends, tragically and heroic-
> ally, the everyday world that we know. Shakespeare does not
> represent Prince Hal (as he might conceivably do in a tragic
> treatment) as a callous man, the scion of the "vile politician
> Bolingbroke". Hal will make a good ruler, and Falstaff would
> undoubtedly make a very bad ruler. Nor, on the other hand, is
> Falstaff portrayed as a villain: Falstaff too has his case. Fal-
> staff's wit—most of it at least—is not merely amusing trifling. It
> constitutes a criticism of the world of serious affairs, a criticism

1. This is not meant to imply for a moment that Professor Danby would, if
giving a full critical account, wish to abstract "moral didacticism" from the
"rich dramatic context".

which, on certain levels, is thoroughly valid. The rulers of the
world had better not leave it totally out of account.[1]

Shakespeare has it both ways, all ways—for and against Henry,
Hal, Hotspur, Falstaff, court-life, tavern-life, the thirst for battle,
the thirst for sack. So does life.

Yet this needs some qualification. Shakespeare is not here writing a problem play, leaving it doubtful which modes of action are
to be preferred. Were it otherwise, the argument that the *Henry IVs*
are related to the morality tradition would fall to the ground.
There is history here, as well as comedy—history which requires
responsible action. There are heroes here too, not superhuman
heroes but men who, having chosen their courses, must stand boldly
by them. Nature can be amoral. Comedy can, if it wishes, be
infinitely tolerant. But Shakespeare here is neither, wide though
his humanity shows itself. By understanding all points of view he
enables choices to be made in the light of full knowledge. He sets
virtues and vices in valid relationship; "the web of our life is of a
mingled yarn, good and ill together", *All's Well* was to proclaim.
The maturity of choice comes not from seeing life in black and
white but from knowing its manifold shades and then choos-
ing well. Shakespeare, undoctrinaire though he may be, is not
Laodicean; he upholds good government, in the macrocosm of the
state, and the microcosm of man. His vision is of men living, however conflictingly, in a nation, a political-moral family, in a world
of moral choices (a testing-ground of conduct), in mutual relationships which make their existence interesting and valuable. Life
moves by mixed impulses but not, on the whole, corrupt ones; it
animates, it challenges spirit and body to activity. To Chaucer,
even the Pardoner's rascality was delightful in its wholehearted-
ness; to Keats, even a street-quarrel was beautiful, such energy did
it release. To Shakespeare, the usurper, the rebel, the intriguer,
the credulous wizard, the toper, and the rest are not parts of a
disintegrated vulpine world. They combine in a totality which
affirms the worth, the wealth, of living.

8. THE IMAGINATIVE IMPACT

The play is about adventure—the adventure of conflict, the
adventure of Bohemianism. It is consequently also about danger
—the danger of defeat, the danger of retribution. And it is consequently also about courage—the courage of self-assertion, the
courage of disreputability (Falstaff may be a physical coward but

1. *Understanding Drama*, 1946, 386-7.

he is not a moral one, else he could not swim so buoyantly in his chosen element). It is therefore a very active play, and its style conveys its activity.

When Bernard Shaw observes that it shows "neither subtlety nor (for Shakespeare) much poetry in the presentation of the characters"[1] one must ask what he thinks poetry is. There is admittedly little of the lyrical-romantic (though cf. III. i. 194–220), or of the tragic-profound (though cf. v. iv. 76–82); nor does the action stop for set-pieces.[2] But almost every line works freshly and vivaciously in a spirited idiom which, like Hotspur's resolution,

> lends a lustre and more great opinion,
> A larger dare to our great enterprise.

And this is its poetry, the poetry of men in action.

The play insists on physical expressions and actions as these reflect emotions and tempers. From the outset the serious scenes sound a running theme of physical stress and strenuousness; the King and nation are shaken and wan with care, and frighted peace pants out short-winded accents of new broils. Foes confront each other with hostile paces and opposed eyes, with danger and disobedience showing in the moody frontiers of their brows. The defiance between Henry and the Percys, particularly Hotspur's speech on the popinjay lord, is packed with these physical portrayals (I. iii); so is Henry's comparison of Richard and himself (III. ii). As for the comic scenes, it is almost sufficient to remark that the centre of them is Falstaff; no dramatic figure makes more of physical bulk, condition, and behaviour, as these express the nature of the man, eating, drinking, sleeping, reporting the "wards, blows, extremities" of mock-heroism, flattering himself on "a cheerful look, a pleasing eye, and a most noble carriage".

The point needs no labouring; the play abundantly annotates emotions and behaviour as expressed physically. As is habitual with Shakespeare, states of mind are presented concretely; peace is frighted and pants, the edge of war cuts his master, haste is hot in question, news is uneven or smooth, riot and dishonour stain the brow, the humour of idleness is unyoked, reformation glitters o'er a fault, and so on. Again as is habitual with Shakespeare, animal imagery gives an active and vivid precision; Hotspur prunes himself, bristles up the crest of youth, is wasp-stung, stung with pismires, more splenetic than a weasel; the lord is a popinjay, Henry

1. *Dramatic Opinions*, 1906, 426.
2. Such "pieces" as the "popinjay" speech (I. iii) or Henry's retrospect (III. ii) are off-stage portions of the action; and Hotspur's passage on Honour is a recognized extravagance, in character.

a fawning greyhound; Falstaff's recruits fear gunshot worse than a struck fowl or a hurt wild-duck. And, supremely, Hal and his fellow-knights are plumed like estridges, bate like newly-bathed eagles, are wanton as youthful goats and wild as young bulls. This is the normal Shakespearean vitality, but never does it more vividly create a real, physical, life.

This reality is enriched by a wealth of off-stage incident, and of imaginatively-evoked social detail. Images of daily life abound; the inn-yard is full of them (II. i); so are the tavern-scenes with their banter and "unsavoury similes"; Hotspur uses them to scoff at Glendower's poetry (III. i. 122–58) or to chaff Lady Percy (III. i. 241–54). Falstaff indeed is presented in a context of meat and drink; he is chops, fat-kidneyed, brawn, ribs, tallow, sweet beef, fat as butter, a roasted Manningtree ox with a pudding in his belly, and he lards the lean earth. The comic scenes have an ample off-stage context, of habitual hedonism in the company of under-skinkers, drawers, and all the good lads in Eastcheap, subject to the reproof of the virtuous. We never in Part I see Falstaff's recruited ragamuffins, discarded unjust servingmen and the like, but they are as vivid to our minds as if they trooped before us. We glimpse the comic past, too—the two-and-thirty years Falstaff has main-tained Bardolph's nose, the eighteen years' history of Bardolph's blushing, the time when, at Hal's age, Falstaff could have crept into any alderman's thumb-ring, the time when he had not for-gotten what the inside of a church looked like. This rich embedding in social life is helped by the abundance of current and proverbial tags (cf. the notes, passim), of traditional similes and ejaculations—fragments of highwaymen's shouts, of ballads, of popular mytho-logy, of romance-reading, of morality plays and religious devotion The serious action, too, is compassed about with a great cloud of witnesses and of supporting actions; there are military disasters and successes reported from Wales and Scotland, Hotspur's popinjay-lord quarrel, and his restless sleep as Lady Percy describes it, long and repeated historical retrospects (III. ii; IV. iii; V. i), and the setting of a seething nation (I. i; I. iii; II. iii; II. iv. 329–67; III. ii; IV. ii; V. i). Armies clash, or march united; messengers arrive and depart. The impression of public importance is overwhelming; after all, the main serious concerns are the fate of kingdoms and the quest for honour (the latter here equated with public admiration). Personal actions encounter public comment; Richard's deposers "a world of curses undergo" and they must return "Into the good thoughts of the world again". They themselves remind Henry of the whole history of his exile; he retorts that by complaints "Proclaim'd at market crosses, read in churches" they have aroused the "fickle changelings and poor discontents" of the whole land.

This swarming social and national life is set in place and time. Pilgrims going to Canterbury, traders riding to London, men of Herefordshire fighting in Wales, the Scots discomfited at Holmedon, combattants by sandy-bottomed and sedgy-banked Severn, armies converging on Shrewsbury from the North or through Gloucestershire and the Midlands—all these insist on topographical reality. Indeed, the central scene on the rebels' side, that which most reveals them, is the Bangor meeting, with the map for the tripartite division and the quarrel over the "monstrous cantle" and the course of the Trent. Time presses as hard as does place on the attention; history-plays, after all, much more than comedies or tragedies fix the mind on the sequence of past, present, and future, and on the hour which strikes for action. The time here is sometimes the past, of Henry's accession and reign, sometimes the future, of expected misrule, sometimes the present, of planned council-meetings or purse-takings or campaign-details. But it always keeps us in the world of urgent events.

All this is history coming to life. Part of it is the theme of horsemanship, so incident to rapid messages and highway robbery and war and chivalry. Messengers "come with speed", "Stain'd with the variation of each soil", spurring "with winged haste". Blunt enters "newlighted" from his mission; Falstaff calls for his horse at Gad's Hill as urgently as Hotspur for his at Warkworth; Hal and Peto, with thirty miles to ride ere dinner-time, take "To horse, to horse". This equestrian vitality culminates, like the animal imagery, in the "fiery Pegasus" lines (IV. i. 109–10), and Hotspur's reply (IV. i. 119–23). Horsemanship is a symbol of chivalric prowess, which is a main subject of the play. When Hal appears most splendid he is vaulting on his horse; it is "hot horse to horse" that Hotspur yearns to encounter him. Falstaff's "charge of foot" marks his significantly unchivalric status, as well as being Hal's joke at his expense.

The style, not yet as profound as it was to become in the tragedies, has yet a full, active charge of meaning. It is vigorous and flexible in syntax, and given to rapid evolution of metaphor. It is mimetic —it expresses and enacts its meanings; it is powerful and resonant in sound. These points need discussion.

The charge of meaning is evident in the many quibbles which juggle consciously with semantic ambiguities, but it is present too where the ambiguities are subconscious. In these cases, instead of the meanings making fun of each other (which is the point of the conscious quibble) they combine in a solid body of significance. "Trenching" (I. i. 7) is an instance; it means "cutting deep and wide"[1] but also "encroaching, invading".[2] "Current" (I. iii. 67) means "running in, intruding" but also "valid, accepted as authentic". "To fill the mouth of deep defiance up" (III. ii. 116) means "To swell defiance's voice" but also, presumably, "To feast in defiant alliance". "A wild trick of his ancestors" (v. ii. 11) combines the senses of "trait" and "trickiness". "Make a head / To push against a kingdom" (IV. i. 80–1) means "raise a force" and "make a hostile advance", but also any related ideas of raising heads undaunted, and of pushing with head and shoulders against an obstacle.[3]

A greater complexity of sense arises in:

> The very *bottom* and the *soul* of hope,
> The very *list*, the very utmost *bound*
> Of all our fortunes.   (IV. i. 50–2)

The words italicized may be interpreted in two series, one meaning "farthest reach" and the other "restricting limitation", as follows: (*i*) last resource—irreducible essence—final account—ultimate reach; (*ii*) dregs—lowest footing (the "soul/sole" quibble?)—outside edge (IV. i. 51, note)—restricting border. The two series do not fight with each other; they "march all one way" to express "our utmost resources". One hardly distinguishes them, indeed, so thoroughly do they interact. Then there are cases like the following:

> To set the exact wealth of all our states
> All at one cast; to set so rich a main
> On the nice hazard of one doubtful hour. (IV. i. 46–8)

If one misses the metaphor (as modern readers may well do) this means "To risk all the military resources our possessions afford at one attempt, to venture so precious an army on the even chances of an unpredictable encounter". If one perceives the metaphor it means "To wager all our riches on a throw of the dice, to lay so high

1. Cf. *Ven.* 1052—"The wide wound, that the boare had trencht / In his soft flanke".

2. Cf. *OED*, "Trench. *v.* 7d." and Jonson, *Staple of News*, v. vi. 46–7 (H. & S., VI. 381)—"Who did? I? / I trench the liberty of the subject?"

3. In 'Imagery in *R2* and in *H4*' (*MLR*, xxxvii, 1942, 113) Miss Madeleine Doran discusses some words in *1H4* which "together with a figurative retain their literal meaning, and greatly enrich the context by this ambiguity": cf. notes on "balk'd" (I. i. 69), "malevolent" (I. i. 96), "countenance" (I. ii. 29), "frontier" (I. iii. 18), "nettled" (I. iii. 237), "bombast" (II. iv. 323), "common-hackney'd" (III. ii. 40), and "stain'd" (v. iv. 12).

a stake on the chancy outcome of a gamble". This, of course, is not an "ambiguity"; it is a normally-operating metaphor. The point is that to anyone not recognizing the metaphor the meaning is quite adequate, while to anyone recognizing it the literal and figurative meanings combine to make a broad front, a strong impact of well-controlled significance.

It is a style which, like a river, bears along a whole volume of effect. Hotspur's popinjay-lord speech conveys his own impatience, the lord's folly (the latter's idiom parodied within the idiom of the former), the attitudes of both men to war and to each other, and Hotspur's ambivalent attitude to the King—self-excusing, but with a dauntless autonomy. There are, moreover, swirling currents of metaphorical evolution. Sir Ifor Evans has noted in the play's first speech "a mounting and complicated imagery, where one notion is abandoned before it is fully developed as another comes crowding into the poet's mind".[1] The progression of effect in this speech may be traced thus:

> *weariness* ("shaken", "wan")—*gasping* ("pant", "breathe")—*thirst* ("thirsty")—*liquid* ("daub", "lips")—*blood-staining* ("daub", "blood")—*wounding* ("trenching", "channel")—*blows* ("bruise")—*trampling* ("armed hoofs")—*conflict* ("hostile paces")—*glinting hostility* ("opposed eyes")—*fiery celestial disorder* ("meteors", "troubled heaven")—*earthly disorder* ("intestine shock", "civil butchery")—*restored order* ("mutual . . . ranks")—*refreshed energy* ("march all one way").

An equal evolutionary inventiveness is evident in i. iii. 162–7:

> *subjection* ("you a world of curses undergo")—*subordinate instruments* ("agents", "base second means")—*methods of ascent* ("cords"[2], "ladder")—*brutal executioner of elevated victims* ("hangman"[3])—*degraded status* ("descend so low")—*sphere of life* ("line"[4])—*category* ("predicament" in the sense of "rank, station" [*OED*])—*danger* ("predicament" in the sense of "hazardous situation")—*roam in dangerous subjection* ("range", in the double sense of "move about" and "be ranked").

A chain of association unites these agile shifts of idea, each stage drawing some potency from the way it springs from its precursor and contributing some vitality to its successor, and the whole sug-

---

1. B. I. Evans, *The Language of Sh.'s Plays*, 1952, 62.
2. Perhaps a subconscious connection of "base–second–means–cords" as being all musical terms.
3. "Cords–ladder–hangman" form an obvious sequence.
4. "Line" may be prompted by "cords": its sense of "sphere of life" is illustrated at iii. ii. 85.

gesting a spontaneously active imagination which does not excogi-
tate a set-piece as it had done, for instance, in Richard II's studied
conceits (*R2*, v. v. 1–60). Shakespeare's command of metaphor is
now such that he need not stop to elicit its relevance, or use it as
applied decoration; the style is vitally metaphorical and carries its
sense not by explicit analogies but by half-conscious suggestion.

The words suggest physical activity. "Uneven" news comes "all
athwart"; prisoners are "surpris'd"; Hotspur will "prune himself
and bristle up / The crest of youth"; rebels "tread upon" Henry's
patience; a quarrel is the striking-up of heat; honour is to be leapt
for, dived for, plucked from the moon; danger, sent from east to
west, and honour crossing it from north to south, are to "grapple";
Hotspur in anger is "whipp'd and scourg'd with rods", and his
blood "stirs / To rouse a lion"; Henry, when ousting Richard,
"stole" courtesy from heaven and "dress'd" himself in humility (as
Hal will "throw off" loose behaviour), "to pluck allegiance from
men's hearts". This activity animates the whole play; of this, too,
as of other qualities Vernon's eulogy (iv. i. 97–110) is the crowning
example.

It is a style intensely dramatic. On a simple level this is evident in
the functional differentiation of verse and prose, each medium
suiting its own dramatic purposes. As expression for speech it is
unsurpassable; the words both in prose and verse all but sound
themselves aloud. From Lyly, either directly or as part of a pre-
vailing fashion, Shakespeare derived a prose of wit and rhetorical
point,[1] but Lyly never rivalled him in using the wit and point to
express vital dramatic ideas. Even the briefest glance at the prose
of, for instance, i. ii will reveal how fine and lively, even how elegant, a pattern it has for speaking. Characters as subordinate as
Gadshill and the chamberlain speak wittily (ii. i. 52–93), and every
stress is audibly expressive. As for Falstaff, could anyone ever go
wrong over the tone, manner, phrasing, and pointing of his
speeches? The Hostess is no whit behind him in this; her words
render her voice infallibly. Everywhere the cueing is excellent;
each phrase prompts the next, yet without giving it away in
advance.[2]

The serious scenes have an equal sense of the living voice. The
expressive impact of "To ransom home revolted Mortimer", or
"To be so pester'd with a popinjay", or "To shed my dear blood
drop by drop in the dust", or "Nettled, and stung with pismires",
could not be bettered, but this power is not confined to single lines.

1. Cf. Lyly, *Works*, ed. R. W. Bond, 1902, i. 150–4.
2. This may be amply studied in the buckram-men episode (ii. iv. 111–279)
or the succeeding comedy (ii. iv. 322–475).

The whole of I. iii is an object-lesson: its rendering of speech-stress gives it a hallucinatory air of reality as speech by speech it grows in defiance.[1] Poetry was never more mimetic, more evidently what (in another connection) an American critic calls "a verbal sign which somehow shares the properties of, or resembles, the objects which it denotes".[2]

It is an effective expository style, detailing facts and commands, with an onward pressure of rhythm. But even in such passages the lines gain their spirit not from the facts but from what the speaker feels about the facts: they are exposition, but dramatic exposition.[3] *A fortiori*, speeches specifically expressing feelings are livelier still, charged with attitudes arising from the whole context of the speaker's nature, purpose, situation, and estimate of his hearers. Hal's soliloquy (I. ii. 190–212) is relatively tame because relatively poor in such attitudes[4]; indeed, throughout there is less to Hal, despite the importance of his moral evolution, than there is to Henry, Hotspur, or Falstaff because there is less temperament expressed through the pressure of style. His speeches are lively enough in comedy, where they need not proceed from any weight of personality; in the serious scenes he is after all the observer, the learner still finding his way.

The last point of style relates to its richness as well as its vitality. The language of men is here not prosaically but imaginatively put down, and the Shakespearean imagination achieves—to use Keats's phrase—an "intensity, capable of making all disagreeables evaporate, from their being in close relationship with Beauty and Truth".[5] One's judgement that the play is not satirical or denigratory (cf. pp. liii–lvii) is encouraged by its eloquence, its grandiloquence. That Shakespeare knows the snares of grandiloquence is evident when Falstaff parodies Euphuism (II. iv. 393–426) or provides his comment on Honour to contrast with Hotspur's (though this does not mean that he is simply right and Hotspur simply wrong). But there is also a valid grandiloquence which asserts the positive values of the life it expresses. The serious scenes are en-

1. Consider Henry's anger in I. iii. 76–91, 112–22 (e.g. "Why, yet he doth deny his prisoners", "Thou dost belie him, Percy, thou dost belie him", and "Art thou not asham'd? But sirrah, henceforth . . ."), and every word of Hotspur's in the same scene (the popinjay speech, the exhortation [156–84], and the outbursts in 192–252).

2. W. K. Wimsatt, *The Verbal Icon*, 1954, x.

3. Contrast them with, e.g., the Salic-law harangue in *H5*, I. ii. 33–114.

4. Contrast, e.g., Hotspur's vigour in expressing himself about Glendower, III. i. 142–58.

5. Letter to George and Thomas Keats, [21 Dec. 1817].

riched by a language of vivid distinction. Glendower may be the credulous romancer who exasperates Hotspur; or he may be the bounteous and scholarly gentleman Mortimer describes. But whichever interpretation is being offered presents him richly and, as it were, appreciatively; even Hotspur's account of his tediousness is delightful. Hal may dismay his father but his failings are lamented with a poetic passion—he is "almost an alien to the hearts / Of all the court" and "the soul of every man / Prophetically do forethink thy fall". Henry, when still Bolingbroke, was rare like a comet, kept himself like a "robe pontifical", like a feast valued for unusualness. Richard on the contrary skipped, ambled, and so mingled his royalty with capering fools, with gibing boys and beardless vain comparatives, that his subjects, surfeited as if with honey or with the cuckoo in June, were glutted, gorged, and full. The two portraits are in the highest degree graphic, animated, vivid. So too with the qualities of war. It is horrible—blood daubing earth's mouth, the beastly shameless transformation of disfigurement, stained nobility lying trodden on: but it is also glorious—armies clash "in the very heat / And pride" of contention, warriors are "the theme of honour's tongue", "gallant", "ever-valiant and approved". They mount on horseback, plumed; gallantly armed, Hal drops into the saddle like an angel from the sky. With equal vividness they march as the tattered straggling rabble Falstaff describes. In each case the style is validly hyperbolical, committed to as spirited a meaning as possible. Its appreciative quality is as evident on the comic side as on the serious—and this again helps to avert too Puritanical a view of Eastcheap. After all, that Falstaff should mock authority in a parody of Euphuism, that in quizzing honour he should do so in the witty form of a catechism—this is part of the truth about him, that he is at home in a world of wit and style. His Biblical unction is part of the same truth, that he looks on fine phrases as a lover. Even the obloquy of which he is the appreciative victim (II. iv. 441–53) is grandiloquent, as fully flavoured as a nut or an apple. Our whole introduction to him (I. ii. 1–155) is in terms of spirited patterns of speech, with elegant alliterations, lofty comic periphrases, celestial invocations, literary and classical allusions, multiple mock-heroic similes, and Biblical idioms. The characteristic qualities of his own utterance have been excellently defined as follows:

> Falstaff has a trick of voice that recalls the great prose writers of the seventeenth century, the doctors and divines. He shows the same curious combination of abandon and economy, the fine frenzy blended with and wrought into an inevitable rhythmic

movement, that is so characteristic of their work. His words have
the air of being spoken extempore, and yet being under the
strictest control.[1]

This style, it may be objected, is a brilliant rhetorical gloss on a
sordid reality, and Falstaff knows it to be so. But until late in
2 Henry IV this moralistic view hardly presses itself; what takes the
attention is the utter enjoyment of life he so racily expresses. Unlike
Bobadill he is, until the end of Part 2, master of his vision, as well as
creator of it. This is what his style conveys. And a similar brilliance
of life is what the style as a whole conveys.

9. ESTABLISHMENT OF THE COPY-TEXT

Two Qq of 1598 provide the earliest and, as will be argued later,
the only authoritative texts. Of the earlier, Q0, only four leaves
survive[2]; on 25 May 1867 Halliwell recorded that they were "found
some years ago" in the binding of a copy of Thomas's *Rules of the
Italian Grammar* (1567); they must be of 1598, since that is the year
of the *SR* entry. A complete text is provided by Q1: it was set up
from Q0 (cf. Hemingway, New Var., 344–5) and in the same
printing-house, Peter Short's. Each later Q was set up from the one
before—Q2 (1599), Q3 (1604), Q4 (1608), Q5 (1613); the Folio
(1623) was set up throughout from Q5. Subsequent Qq (1622,
1632, 1639) and Ff (1632, 1664, 1685) have no authority; neither,
indeed, have Qq2–5,F, but since some editors have thought otherwise the transmission needs examining all the way from the MS to
the Folio.

Shakespeare would hand the players his MS of the Oldcastle
version. This would be his "foul papers". From these, or possibly
from a transcript, the prompt-book would be prepared. The play
would be acted, the Oldcastle fuss provoked, and the play withdrawn. The revisions of the offending names could be made either
in the prompt-copy and transferred to any MS (foul papers or
transcript) going to the printer, or vice versa.

But what copy went to the printer? Foul papers? A fair copy?
Prompt-book (or a transcript of it)? Prompt-book can be ruled out;
the stage-directions show no prompt-book features; exits and
entrances are defective,[3] and there is at times an indeterminacy

1. R. W. David, *The Janus of Poets*, 1935, 40.

2. C1–C4, from I. iii. 199 to II. ii. 106.

3. No entries for Blunt (I. i), Bardolph (II. ii), Servant (II. iii. 66; no exit,
either, at l. 73), Gadshill, Bardolph, Peto, and Francis (II. iv. 109), Vernon
(v. i. 8), Douglas (v. iv. 23). No exits for Fal. (I. ii. 155), Francis and Vintner
(II. iv. 79, 83), Bardolph and the Hostess before they re-enter (II. iv. 475), Hal's

which a prompt-book would settle.[1] Such defects suggest foul papers, and most bibliographical opinion holds that foul papers were Qo's "copy". Yet Qqo,1 (Q1 deriving closely from Qo) show some signs of a fair copy rather than foul papers, or at least of a MS somewhat spruced up. Speech-prefixes are fairly uniform, and follow the forms in the stage-directions; some colloquialisms have been thought to have undergone refinement. In addition, Wilson (N.C.S.) points out that the spelling is "far more normal than that for example of *Hamlet* Q2 or *Love's Labour's Lost* Q1", though he attributes the normality to the printers rather than a copyist. Each of these plays, incidentally, was printed at a different house.

Compared with a text unmistakably derived from foul papers, like the Q of *2 Henry IV*, *1 Henry IV* is strikingly uniform in speech-prefixes.[2] It has one important variant (IV. i reads *Per.* ten times for *Hot.*), but other variants are trifles of spelling or abbreviation, like *Wor.* | *Worst.*, *Hot.* | *Hotsp.*, *Falst.* | *Fal.* | *Fa.*, and *Poin.* | *Poi.* | *Poy.* | *Poynes* | *Po.* Part 2 is more irregular, too, in relating speech-prefixes to stage-directions.[3] These and other loosenesses in it indicate foul papers; and Part 1, though its directions need amendment, is much freer from them. Its "copy", therefore, has been thought to be a transcript of foul papers rather than foul papers themselves.

There is, however, another possibility. In accounting for its speech-prefix uniformity it must be remembered that the original Oldcastle, Harvey, and Russell had to be changed. This could be done, with the minimum of trouble, on any existing copy without

companions (II. iv. 497), Hal (v. i. 126), Prince John and Westmoreland (v. iv. 15), Worcester and Vernon (v. v. 15). No directions at all between III. iii and IV. i. Westmoreland enters with the King's company (v. i) though he is "engag'd" in the rebel camp.

1. *Enter Prince, Poines, and Peto, &c.* (II. ii) leaves Bardolph's entry uncertain; II. i. 32 is prefixed *Car.* (not *1* or *2 Car.*); II. ii prefixes *Trauel.* and *Tra.* without distinction of persons.

2. In *2H4*, I. ii, Fal.'s prefixes are *Iohn, sir Iohn, Falst.*, and even (once) *Old.*, and the Lord Chief Justice's are *Iustice, Iust., Lord*, and *Lo.*; in II. i Gower is *Gower* and *Mess.[enger]*; in IV. iv Thomas Duke of Clarence is *Clar.* (or *Cla.*) and *Tho.*, while Humphrey Duke of Gloucester is *Glo.* and *Hum.*; in v. v, after the rejection, Fal. changes from *Falst.* to *Iohn*, though *Iohn* is used immediately after for Prince John. Most notably, in II. iv Mistress Quickly and Doll Tearsheet are *Quickly, Qui., host.*, and *Ho.*, and *Tere., Doll, Dorothy, Dol., Teresh.*, and *Doro.*

3. In *2H4*, I. ii, Q's agreeable *Enter sir Iohn alone, with his page* results in the varied prefixes in note 2 above, as well as *Page* and *Boy*; in II. i, *an Officer or two* is followed by prefixes *Phang, Snare*, and *Offic.*; in II. ii, *sir Iohn Russel* (surviving from the original names?) enters in what is clearly a private Prince–Poins scene, and receives no speeches; in II. iii *the wife to Harry Percie* of the entry-direction speaks as *Kate*; III. i directs *Enter the King in his night-gowne alone*—but he addresses someone and calls for Surrey and Warwick, who enter accompanied by a speechless *sir Iohn Blunt*.

the need of a transcript. Anyone changing the names would stick to
fairly uniform substitutions. The serious scenes, with their historical
names, might be fairly uniform from the start—though there is the
Per. variant in IV. i. Or if they were not, anyone revising the comic
names might carry on regularizing throughout, in a copy going
to press; he might, too, ensure reasonable, though incomplete,
correspondence between entry-directions and speech-prefixes. In
other words, the text of the play has undergone unusual treatment
(the name-revision), and this treatment will necessarily produce
features that look like a transcript. Since the transcript theory has
its own difficulties[1] and is not in fact necessary to account for these
features, it seems that the most likely "copy" for Q0 was revised
foul papers. That foul papers were often the printer's copy is evident from the testimony in F of Heminge and Condell ("To the
great Variety of Readers"), that "His mind and hand went together: And what he thought, he vttered with that easinesse, that
wee haue scarse receiued from him a blot in his papers". The
strongest fact weighing against the transcript theory is that the text
is, in minute details, better than one would expect a transcript to
be. The punctuation has dramatic points that look like Shakespeare's own (cf. 'Editorial Methods', para. *viii*) and would, in a
transcript, be evidence of remarkable accuracy. The treatment of
past verb-forms points in the same direction. Hereward T. Price has
shown[2] that Shakespeare, for metrical reasons, was careful about
eliding weak verb past forms. *1 Henry IV* strikingly conforms to this
care: of past forms in the verse portions (the only ones to which the
test applies) Qq0,1 rightly elide 168 and rightly leave unelided

1. It is a little difficult to see why a transcript should be made. If the idea of
extensive revision be rejected (cf. Intro., pp. xviii ff.), revision merely of the
names would not appreciably mess up the MS or make it unusable. If a clean
version were needed for the censor, it is odd that the risky "old lad of the castle"
jibe at I. ii. 41 should survive, and "Haruey" and "Rossill" at I. ii. 158. If a
transcript were made by Shakespeare, one would expect him to remove these
relics (and the *Ross.* prefixes at II. iv. 172 ff.), insert stage-directions between
III. iii and IV. i, change *Per.* to *Hot.* in IV. i, align the metrical prose as verse in
such passages as II. iii. 71–3, 78–89, and, not least, alter the "most sweet wench /
As the hony of *Hibla*" sketch of the Hostess (I. ii. 40–1) to accord with the
totally different portrait he had worked out as the play proceeded. If a transcript were made by someone else, one would expect him to remove the relics
(knowing them to be part of the trouble), and perhaps to rectify the lack of
break between III. iii and IV. i, and the sudden *Per.* prefixes of IV. i. These
blemishes would be more easily overlooked by someone glancing through a
MS to amend it than by a transcriber going through in detail. It must be admitted, however, that any revision, by anyone, may leave a trail of inconsistencies.

2. In 'The First Quarto of Titus Andronicus', *English Institute Essays 1947*,
1948.

33; they wrongly elide I (at III. ii. 115, corrected in Q2), and wrongly leave unelided 10 (16 other apparent examples are of verb-stems ending in -w, -y, or a vowel, which tend to be exceptions anyway). Such counts, tedious both to make and to read about, remind one of Johnson's remark, "These are very slender disquisitions, but such is the task of the commentator". But they suggest a fidelity to the author's script closer than one would expect if a transcriber as well as a compositor had been at work.

Somewhere between Shakespeare's MS and the print, however, some colloquial details may have been lost. Qq0,1 have several lines which later editions have been tempted to make more metrical by introducing colloquial elisions:[1]

(a) Send vs your prisoners, or you wil [F you'l] heare of it.
                                       (I. iii. 122)
(b) And shed my deere bloud, drop by drop in the [Q5 i'th] dust. (I. iii. 132)
(c) Before the game is [Q5 game's] afoote thou still letst slip.
                                       (I. iii. 272)
(d) And tis no maruaile he is [Capell, he's] so humorous, Birlady he is [F hee's] a good musition. (III. i. 225-6)
(e) Come brother let vs [Q4 let's] to the highest of the field,
                                       (v. iv. 159)

The unelided forms are, it has been argued,[2] signs of a pedantic compositor committing "sedate expansions" (Dr Alice Walker attributes them to a transcriber[3]) in the desire to refine the text. It is indeed possible that the compositors erred in using such forms; they doubtless did so in many other lines where elision would help the metre and which eighteenth-century editors liked to amend (e.g. v. i. 15—"What say you to it [Pope, to't]? will you againe vnknit"). But the argument for compositorial pedantry is not strong; if some elisions seem "expanded", scores of others were accepted (as with "letst" and "tis" in (c) and (d) above). If, at these points, Qq0,1 depart from what Shakespeare wrote (and it is not certain that they do), the explanation is probably inadvertence. Later Qq and F may restore an original colloquialism (and it is again not certain that they do), but they operate by guess-work and have no authority in doing so. The present text retains the readings of Qq0,1 in most instances.

The case is the same with similar occurrences in the prose. There are several instances like the following:

1. Cf. also, e.g., collation notes for I. iii. 134, II. ii. 100, III. i. 66, 150, 153, 155, 188, III. ii. 123, IV. iii. 104, v. ii. 2, 70. Many other lines could also be regularized.

2. Wilson (N.C.S.), 104.   3. *Textual Problems of the First Folio*, 1953, 111.

(a) An it [F an't] be not foure by the day   (II. i. I)

(b) thou knowest [Q4 knowst] hee is [F hee's] no starueling
(II. i. 67–8)

(c) a plague vpon it [F vpon't]   (II. ii. 27)

(d) a cup of sacke with lime in it [F in't (uncorrected copies,
omitting 'lime'; cf. collation)]   (II. iv. 123)

(e) All is [Q3 All's] one for that   (II. iv. 153)

(f) Wel, breath a while, and then to it [F to't] againe
(II. iv. 245)

(g) Why then, it is [Q3 tis] like if there come a hote Iune
(II. iv. 357)

(h) I haue led my rag of Muffins [Rowe, Rag-o-Muffians;
Capell, ragamuffins] where they are pepperd   (V. iii. 36)

This last example is presumably the compositor's slip over Shakespeare's o' or a' (a like expansion occurs in "two of clocke" [III.
iii. 199]—surely not pedantry but carelessness). The others may be
"expansions", or they may be what Shakespeare wrote, knowing
that his whole text was a script for speaking and that the actors
would make the appropriate contractions. The elisions introduced
later than Qqo,1 are doubtless what the actors should (and will)
say, but there is no authority in the texts which introduce them (cf.
pp. lxxi–lxxv) and there is no need to adopt them (they could be
numerous) into the text. Indeed, in F it is significant that they
occur almost entirely in the portions[1] which Dr Walker has shown
to be set up by Compositor B, the much less conservative of the
two who set 1 Henry IV. B has sixteen of them while his careful
team-mate A has hardly any. They do not, therefore, though
Dover Wilson argues the contrary, indicate that F has any authority behind it; they merely show that B could sometimes guess
plausibly, as often he guesses most implausibly. This must also be
the conclusion about his most agreeable guesses, viz:

(a) In Richards time, what do you [F de'ye] call the place?
A plague vpon it [F vpon't], it is in Glocestershire;
(I. iii. 239–40)

(b) The Archbishop.
Of Yorke, is it [F is't] not? (I. iii. 264)

(c) lend me thy lanterne (quoth he) [F (quoth-a)]   (II. i. 38–9)

These have an authentic ring, and would doubtless be so spoken on
the stage; but again one queries B's freehandedness—in the last
example he may indeed have spoilt a mimicry the Carrier may
have been intended to make of Gadshill's (slightly) superior status,
a status reflected in the "Sirrah carrier" address in the next line.

Have any later editions any authority? Q2's title-page calls it

1. I. i. i. 1–II. iv. 147; III. iii. 110–IV. i. 19; IV. iv. 27–the end.

"Newly corrected by *W. Shake-speare*", which would be less mis-leading if "corrected" were followed by a full stop. Q2's changes are mostly printing-house variations—several decidedly for the worse, like "waspe-tongue" instead of "waspe-stung" (I. iii. 233), "loe, Mortimer" instead of "Lo: Mortimer" (I. iii. 289), or "carp-ing" instead of "capring" (III. ii. 63). No correction is made of un-doubted errors like "Haruey, Rossill" (I. ii. 158), the omitted *Hot.* before I. iii. 199, "present" (II. iv. 33), "so youth" (II. iv. 396), or "I my mind" (IV. i. 20). Qq0,1's "Oneyres" becomes "Oneyers" (II. i. 75), which helps the determination of the right reading in a negative way, by suggesting that no further amendment was thought necessary. Apart from corrected misprints, and a good deal of normalized punctuation, the changes that might at first sight seem to carry the weight of some authority are:

 (*a*) lyes [Q1 liues] the iest (I. ii. 185)
 (*b*) the [Q1 that] Earle of March (I. iii. 83)
 (*c*) *Enter Hotspur, Worcester, and Douglas* [Q1 omits the whole S.D.] (IV. i. S.D.)
 (*d*) *Hot.* [Q1 *Per.*] (for Hotspur's first ten speeches in IV. i)
 (*e*) busky [Q1 bulky] (V. i. 2)
 (*f*) thought's the slaue [Q1 thoughts the slaues] of life (V. iv. 80)
 (*g*) *Prince and* [Q1 omits *and*] *Iohn of Lancaster* (V. iv. 128 S.D.)

(*a*) and (*b*) are insignificant; (*c*), (*d*), and (*g*) are deducible from the context; and none transcends a compositor's sense. I judge (*f*), attractive though it is, to be a shade less relevant to Hotspur's situation (cf. V. iv. 80, note). One and all, despite the "Newly correct-ed", these changes stand or fall on their own probability rather than any sign of authority. On (*e*), see the annotation at V. i. 2.

 Q3's "improvements" are, apart from removal of evident errors:

 (*a*) Go hang [Qq0–2 Hang] (II. ii. 42)
 (*b*) yet [Qq1,2 so] youth (II. iv. 396)
 (*c*) rebel of that [Qq1,2 the] name (V. iv. 61)

There are also the colloquial contractions mentioned above (cf. p. lxx). Of the above three, (*b*) is self-evident; (*a*) and (*c*) are plausible but neither is so evidently right as to suggest anything more than chance alteration.

 Q4 introduces a colloquial contraction (cf. p. lxix) and also makes the commonsense substitution of the prefix *Poines* for *Prin.* at II. iv. 36.

 Q5 introduces two colloquial contractions (cf. p. lxix), inserts the prefix *Hot.* (hitherto omitted) at I. iii. 199, and corrects Qq1–4's "all vnder one" to "all vndone" (V. ii. 3); neither needs more than a compositor's common sense.

lxxii　　THE FIRST PART OF

The situation with regard to F is more complicated. Malone showed that it was printed from Q5, in that it repeats many errors and alterations first made in that edition: it was set up from a copy of Q5 made up of corrected sheets throughout (Hemingway, New Var., 352[1]). Q5 was its sole printed source as is indicated by its botching of errors which reference to earlier Qq would have cleared up, the most famous instance being at v. iii. 11:

> I was not borne a yeelder thou proud Scot,　(Qq1–4, subst.)
> I was not borne to yeeld, thou proud Scot,　(Q5, subst.)
> I was not borne to yeeld, thou haughty Scot,　(F)

See also the collations at i. i. 28; i. iii. 25, 70; ii. i. 13; iii. i. 29; iv. i. 85, 122, 123; v. iv. 83. But F's "copy" was a considerably edited Q5, and the alterations (some of which may originate, how-ever, with the compositors rather than an editor) are as follows:

(a) Act and scene divisions are introduced, though with no break between the present v. ii and v. iii.

(b) "Bardol(l)" becomes "Bardolph" (save for "Bardolfe" at F ii. ii. 50, "Bardol" at F ii. iv. 295). "Poins" is occasionally "Pointz".

(c) Oaths are mostly purged, in accordance with the Act of 1606.

(d) The stage-directions are somewhat altered.

(e) Such numerals as Qq give in figures F mostly gives in words.

(f) There is some re-lineation in both prose and verse passages.

(g) Along with many deteriorations, F has some plausible and some convincing new readings.

It has been argued that some of the changes show a copy of Q5 to have been amended by collation with the Globe prompt-book.[2] But none of the changes needs more than an editor's or compositor's wits can supply. Of those above, (a) is not beyond an editor's ability—the play's divisions indicate themselves. (b) could origi-nate in some acquaintance with the play—Bardolf(e) occurs throughout the Q of Part 2 (1600), though Bardol(l) persists through the successive Qq of Part 1. On (c) it has been cogently argued that expurgation need not originate in the prompt-book[3]; that "the dividing line between plays from which profanity was not expurgated and those from which it was, lies between the Comedies and the Histories"[4]; that this dividing line corresponds

1. At iv. iii. 80 the corrected Q5, followed by F, alters "lie" to "lay", probably in error; cf. collation.

2. Wilson (N.C.S.), 106–7.

3. W. W. Greg, *The Sh. First Folio*, 1955, 149–50.

4. Alice Walker, *RES*, 1951, ii. 225, and *Text. Problems of the First Folio*, 1953, 31.

to a break in F's printing from October 1621 to November 1622;
that in that break the easy-going Sir George Buc resigned as Master
of the Revels and a harsher policy was expected from his successor;
and that, therefore, the expurgation was not a prompt-book but a
literary operation, undertaken about 1621-2.[1]

The expurgation is only partial. Offending phrases are excised
(some of them very mild, like "by my troth" at I. ii. 20) or replaced by more-or-less inept substitutes. But the operation is oddly
performed. A good many profanities go but many others remain,[2]
while trivial changes occur like "confidence" for "saluation"
(II. iv. 9). "In faith" is sometimes cut, but it remains undisturbed in
a number of places; at II. iv. 437 it is thought a proper substitute
for "Zbloud". "Faith" remains at II. iv. 298 but is cut at II. iv.
299. At IV. iii. 32 "would to God" remains but at IV. iii. 38 "God
defend" yields to "Heauen defend", while at V. i. 120 "God
befriend vs" remains but at V. i. 126 "God" again yields to
"heauen". The cuts remove a Biblical irreverence like "wisedome
cries out in the streets" (I. ii. 86) or a harmless reference to weavers
singing "psalms" (II. iv. 130); yet other Biblical quips happily survive. The argument that expurgation was editorial in origin, and
not from the prompt-book, is confirmed by the excision at I. ii. 86
which makes nonsense of Hal's remark and Falstaff's reply, and
would hardly satisfy the actors.

(d) also weighs against prompt-book collation, for F's stage-
directions, despite some tinkering, are no more adequate than
Q5's. They fail to bring Blunt on in I. i, erroneously introduce
"Pointz" at the beginning of I. ii (ignoring his entry at 102), and
provide no exit for Falstaff in the same scene or entry for Bardolph
in II. ii. Throughout, though supplying some exits omitted in Qq
(generally evident from the context, e.g. at II. iv. 497, IV. iii. 113,
and V. v. 15), they do little to remedy deficiencies. Most strikingly,
they still retain Westmoreland in V. i, though no prompt-book
could do so.

(e) is simple editorial or compositorial amendment.[3]

(f) offers some puzzles. Some of F's re-lineations are real or
plausible improvements.[4] Others are merely turnovers made at

1. Alice Walker, *loc. cit.*

2. E.g. I. iii. 55, 147, 172, 251, 276; II. ii. 79; II. iii. 95; II. iv. 49, 59, 71, 129, 360,
385 (i'faith), 388; III. i. 235, 243; III. iii. 189; IV. i. 44; IV. iii. 29, 32, 60; V. i. 120;
V. ii. 35; V. iv. 35, 144.

3. This dealt, e.g., with I. i. 26; II. iv. 513; III. iii. 69, 72, 188; IV. ii. 13-14;
but not with V. iii. 37.

4. E.g. I. iii. 210-11; III. i. 3-9, 218; IV. i. 54-5; IV. iii. 13-14; V. ii. 26-7;
V. iv. 6-7.

about the medial pause rather than towards the line-end.[1] Not all these turnovers were, in fact, necessary and at III. i. 161–3 a quite unnecessary one has been made after "concealments" and has thrown the next two lines out—a sign of carelessness. Sometimes Q5's prose is semi-metrical and tempted F's compositors into inept versification.[2] Sometimes Q5's prose is quite unmetrical and yet was set up in F as irregular lines.[3] Sometimes, still more oddly, Q5's regular verse is irregularly redivided.[4] At I. iii. 209, after Q's "Good coosen giue me audience for a while", F adds the feeble tautology "And list to me", perhaps thinking that Hotspur's half-line "I crie you mercie" needed padding, which it did not. The collation at I. iii. 271 again shows wrong division and specious padding.

F makes guesswork attempts to smooth lines which all the Qq left rough or which Qq2–5's errors disarranged, but this implies no authority. The patent botches at I. iii. 70 (Q1 "What ere Lord *Harry Percie* . . ."; Qq2–5 "What e're *Harry Percie* . . ."; F "What euer *Harry Percie* . . ."), and at v. iii. 15, create no confidence that other regularizations, likely though some may be, are more than guesswork.[5]

(g) Do F's acceptable readings indicate prompt-book collation? They correct some evident misprints, and some other errors not beyond a compositor's wits, such as supplying the missing prefix (indicated by the context) at II. iv. 533, and changing "scantle" to "cantle" (III. i. 96), Qq's "monstrous scantle" being a virtual contradiction in terms. They alter the *Gad.*, *Ross.*, *Ross.*, *Ross.* prefixes of II. iv. 171, 172, 174, 178. They change "present", at II. iv. 33 to "President" (precedent), and "intemperance", at III. ii. 156, to "intemperature". The former change is clearly right, the latter argued to be right by Dover Wilson. Finally, they introduce the colloquialisms listed above (cf. pp. lxix–lxx). But does any of this confirm Dover Wilson's "firm link between the F *1 Henry IV* and the Globe prompt-book"?

Surely not. Though he missed the "Haruey, Rossill" at I. ii. 158, the editor could change the prefixes unaided (as the Dering MS copyist did)—he knows the play has no *Ross*. "Intemperature", though slightly preferable to "intemperance" (cf. III. ii. 156, note), may well arise from the "distemp'rature" which the same com-

1. E.g. I. iii. 271; III. i. 22, 64, 66, 136, 152, 184, 207; III. ii. 1–2, 29; III. iii. 204; IV. i. 15–16, 94, 111; IV. iii. 41, 52, 107.
2. E.g. III. i. 103–7, 241–4.
3. E.g. II. i. 90–1; III. i. 192–3; III. iii. 170–4, 176–7.
4. E.g. IV. i. 45–6, 84–5; IV. iii. 32–3; IV. iv. 4–5, 25–6.
5. E.g. I. iii. 252, 254, 264; v. i. 25.

positor (A) had set the scene before (III. i. 31). "President" is not
beyond an editor or compositor. The colloquialisms have been
dealt with already, but it may be noted that though B colloquial-
izes Q5's "An it be not foure by the day" (II. i. 1) and "quoth he"
(II. i. 39), he decolloquializes some of Q5's rusticity.[1] In short,
his erratic habits produce a few agreeable and many disagreeable
variants. Both kinds, it seems likely, are his work. Otherwise one
must postulate a collator who failed to remove major errors but
here and there inserted an authoritative apostrophe. Such collation
is inconceivable.

The conclusion, then, must be a conservative one, that Qq0,1
are the only substantive sources, that the prompt-book played no
discernible part, and that the variants in later Qq and F have
authority no greater than that of later editors, the authority merely
of the light of nature.

The Dering Manuscript. An early seventeenth-century MS survives in which both parts of *Henry IV* are abridged into a single
play. The abridgement, made perhaps for Court performance, is
further revised by the hand of Sir Edward Dering (1598–1644), of
Surrenden in Kent, possibly for private theatricals. The abridgement is based on Q5 (1613) of Part 1 and on Q (1600) of Part 2, and
though it coincides in some emendations with F it shows no real
signs of F influence. Sir Edward's revisions date from 1623 or 1624;
they include the marking of acts and scenes, not identical with those
of F. There are a few expurgations but most of Qq's profanities
remain. About three-quarters of the text is from Part 1 all of whose
scenes are represented save for II. i and IV. iv. The text has no
authority but, along with some deliberate and a great many heed-
less alterations, it has to its credit the emendation of QqF's "trustfull" to "tristfull" (II. iv. 388). It was edited in 1845 for the Shakespeare Society by J. O. Halliwell. The manuscript, now in the
Folger Shakespeare Library in Washington, is described with some,
though not full, collation by Hemingway (New Var., 495–501).

10. EDITORIAL METHODS

(*i*) Qq0,1 are judged to be the sole authoritative texts, for the
reasons given above.

(*ii*) Q1 (the Capell copy, at Trinity College, Cambridge) and F
(the Kökeritz-Prouty facsimile) have been collated throughout,
as has the unique copy of Q0, in the Folger Library. For other
QqFf I consulted in the first place the original Cambridge, the

1. Cf. II. i. 6, 10, 16.

THE FIRST PART OF

original Arden, and the New Variorum collations, but then checked every reading against original copies of QqFf. Qq after Q5 and Ff after F1 are cited only for adopted or significant alternative readings. Qq means Qq1–5 (or 0–5 where Q0 exists), unless otherwise indicated; F means F1.

(*iii*) The collation records (*a*) all significant departures from Qq0,1, including punctuation-changes which affect the sense; (*b*) the main links of transmission from Qq0,1 to F; (*c*) some interesting editorial emendations, whether acceptable or not. Unless the sense or transmission is affected the collation mostly ignores (*a*) accidentals, minor literals, and spelling- or italicization-details, and variant forms of proper names, to trace which direct consultation of the original texts is essential; (*b*) variant forms of stage-directions later than F, and of locations; (*c*) alternative Elizabethan spellings provided they are unambiguous—these are silently modernized (e.g. to/too, lose/loose, then/than). The lemmas are given in modernized form, even though the citations following are in the original. A modernized text can hardly avoid this discrepancy, but whenever the modernization is misleading, the original is given also in brackets. The first edition to give an accepted reading is recorded first, any earlier conjecture following. A collation such as that at I. i. 26, e.g. "fourteen hundred] *Qq* (1400.), *F*", means that Qq originate the reading, though in the form 1400., whereas F has it as in the text. "Subst." (=substantially) means that editions agree except for variations immaterial to the point under consideration.

(*iv*) Colloquial or metrical elisions in texts after Q1 are rarely adopted. They may be what Shakespeare intended, but the criteria for their adoption would be (*a*) that colloquial speech should be written in colloquial forms and (*b*) that verse lines should not be irregular. These criteria methodically practised would involve not only the adoption of the later QqF elisions and those of later regularizers like Pope and Capell but the making of other changes too. The former would affect phrases like "Now *Hal*, what time of day is it lad?" (I. ii. 1), or "There is nothing but rogery to be found in villanous man" (II. iv. 121–2)—both of which have been thought too precise to be natural; the latter would affect lines like "I would haue him poisoned with a pot of ale" (I. iii. 230), or "What say you to it? will you againe vnknit" (V. i. 15). *Metri gratia* one might also stretch out lines like "I thinke theres no man speakes better Welsh" (III. i. 47); but is it safe to assume (as Pope did) that Shakespeare wrote "there is no man"? Might he not have written the more pungent "there's no man here", or something similar? In short, a more adventurous editor would have amended the copy-text more often and in doing so would have introduced some corrections and some errors—but which would be which it is hard to say. Shakespeare perhaps wrote "horriblie" at II. iv. 362 (cf. collation for II. iv. 368). But how can one tell? Emendations, therefore, are admitted only when evident errors can be evidently rectified.

(*v*) Modernization raises problems. Some words no modernization will quite deal with; Hotspur's "parmacity" (I. iii. 57; "Parmacitie" in Q1) should not be pedanticized into "spermaceti" or bastardized into "parmaceti". Others, when Shakespeare perhaps chose between alternative forms, are left unmodernized provided that the reader will not be jolted with unfamiliarity; "vildly" (for "vilely"), though retained in some new Arden volumes, is not adopted, but milder archaisms are retained, like "stronds" (I. i. 4), "loaden" (I. i. 37), "Wild of Kent" (II. i. 54), and "bands" (III. ii. 157). "And" (="if") is not changed to "an".

(*vi*) Modernization of proper names is not easy. Trifling archaisms like Westmerland, Canturburie, or Sherley can be dealt with readily. But if Murrey becomes Murray, does Mordake become Murdoch? Sutton cophill can, phonetically, be Sutton Co'fil', and Bullenbrooke or Bullingbrooke is not much misrepresented by Bolingbroke, since this is pronounced Bollinbrook; but Shakespeare's Gawsey (Gausell in Holinshed) can hardly become the modern Goushill. The best course is to modernize names which would otherwise cause trouble, and leave the rest: Mighell and S. Albones would worry the reader, but Mordake and Holmedon will not. The trickiest problem is with Bardolph. In *1 Henry IV* Qq he is always Bardol(l), doubtless pronounced Bardle, in *2 Henry IV* Q Bardolf(e), in *1 Henry IV* F Bardolph (Bardolfe once, Bardol once), and in *2 Henry IV* F Bardolf(e) or Bardolph. One relinquishes Bardol(l) regretfully; *2 Henry IV* Q's Bardolf(e) perhaps represents Shakespeare's final choice, odd though it is to have two Bardolfes in that play. Yet since Bardolph is universally accepted, and the sound is identical, I here surrender to the Folio.

(*vii*) In the verse in this edition, -ed indicates the syllabic past verb-ending, 'd the non-syllabic. In the prose, the -ed is silent or syllabic according to modern usage; consequently the copy-text's contracted past forms indicating the non-syllabic ending (e.g. snatcht, lugd, talkt) need no collation when rendered in the prose into the uncontracted modern forms phonetically corresponding (e.g. snatched, lugged, talked). Other contracted forms in the copy-text which affect pronunciation (e.g. camst) are reproduced in the nearest modern equivalent (e.g. cam'st).

(*viii*) The punctuation is kept as close to Qq0,1 as is practicable

without distracting the reader. The original stopping is fairly light
—indeed, the comma sometimes seems to have been the compositors' (or Shakespeare's?) favourite resource. Sometimes the stopping suggests a dramatic point[1]; often it allows syntax to be
flexible. To reproduce Qq0,1's punctuation throughout is impossible, for much of it is haphazard. The main thing is not to clog the
lines by too many heavy stops.

(*ix*) Additions to and alterations of the directions of QqF are
indicated by square brackets.

II. ABBREVIATIONS

The abbreviated titles of Shakespeare's works are those of C. T. Onions,
A Shakespeare Glossary (2nd edn, 1919). Line numbers and texts of passages cited
or quoted are from the *Complete Works*, ed. W. J. Craig (Oxford, 1904). Quotations from the Bible, unless otherwise attributed, are from the Bishops' Bible,
1568. Qq indicates quartos 1–5 (or 0–5 where Q0 exists), unless otherwise
defined. F indicates the First Folio. F1 is used only when the First has to be distinguished from the later Folios, F2, F3, and F4. In the collation, numerals are
added after editors' names only when a particular edition is indicated. Other
references are to the first editions.

Abbott	E. A. Abbott, *A Shakespearian Grammar*, 3rd edn, London, 1870.
Bailey	Nathaniel Bailey, *Dictionary of Cant Words*, added to *The New Universal English Dictionary*, 4th edn, London, 1759.
Beau. & Fl.	Beaumont and Fletcher, *Works*, ed. Arnold Glover and A. R. Waller, 10 vols., Cambridge, 1905–12.
Bond	See Lyly.
Brome (Shepherd)	Richard Brome, *Dramatic Works*, [ed. R. H. Shepherd,] 3 vols., London, 1873.
Brooks & Heilman	Cleanth Brooks and Robert B. Heilman, *Understanding Drama*, New York, 1945.
Bullen (*Old Plays*)	*A Collection of Old English Plays*, ed. A. H. Bullen, 4 vols., London, 1882–5.
Cambr.	*The Works of William Shakespeare*, ed. W. G. Clark, J. Glover, and W. A. Wright, 9 vols., Cambridge, 1863–6.
Capell	*Mr. William Shakespeare His Comedies, Histories, and Trage-dies*, ed. Edward Capell, 10 vols., London, [1767–8].
Chambers (*W. Sh.*)	E. K. Chambers, *William Shakespeare, a Study of Facts and Problems*, 2 vols., Oxford, 1930.
Chambers (*El. St.*)	E. K. Chambers, *The Elizabethan Stage*, 4 vols., Oxford, 1923.
Chandler	*Henry IV, Part 1*, ed. F. W. Chandler, New York, 1911.

1. At I. ii. 4, 10, Q1 climaxes the successive phrases with semi-colons after
"noone" and "taffata". At I. iii. 229 a colon after "mischance" suggests Hotspur
savouring his outburst. In I. iii. 48–63 a volley of pattering commas, including an
explosive one after "saltpetre", conveys Hotspur's impatience. In III. iii. 170–4
Falstaff tosses off his instructions with a comma after every phrase.

Collier 2, 3	*The Works of Shakespeare*, ed. J. P. Collier, 1st edn, 8 vols., London, 1842–4; 2nd edn, 6 vols., London, 1858; 3rd edn, 8 vols., London, 1878.
Collier's MS	Manuscript annotations (allegedly of the seventeenth century, but actually forgeries) in J. P. Collier's copy of the Second Folio.
Cooper	Thomas Cooper, *Thesaurus Linguae*, London, 1565.
Cotgrave	Randle Cotgrave, *A Dictionarie of the French and English Tongues*, London, 1611.
Cowl & Morgan	*The First Part of King Henry the Fourth*, ed. R. P. Cowl and A. E. Morgan (The Arden Shakespeare), 4th edn, London, 1930.
Cowl (*Sources*)	R. P. Cowl, *Sources of the Text of King Henry IV* (various places of publication), 1929–48.
C.W.	Samuel Daniel, *The First Fowre Bookes of the Ciuile Wars*, London, 1595.
Dekker (Bowers)	Thomas Dekker, *Dramatic Works*, ed. Fredson Bowers, vols. I–III–(in progress), Cambridge, 1953–.
Dekker (Grosart)	Thomas Dekker, *Non-Dramatic Works*, ed. A. B. Grosart, 5 vols., London, 1884–6.
Dekker (Shepherd)	Thomas Dekker, *Dramatic Works*, [ed. R. H. Shepherd,] 4 vols., London, 1873.
Dyce 1, 2	*The Works of William Shakespeare*, ed. A. Dyce, 1st edn, 6 vols., London, 1857; 2nd edn, 9 vols., London, 1864–7.
EETS	The Early English Text Society.
Elton	*King Henry IV, Part I*, ed. O. Elton, London, 1889.
Evans (*Suppl.*)	G. Blakemore Evans, *Supplement* to the New Variorum edition of *Henry IV, Part I* (*Sh. Q.*, vii. 3), New York, 1956.
Fabyan	Robert Fabyan, *The New Chronicles of England and France*, ed. Sir Henry Ellis, London, 1811.
F.V.	*The Famous Victories of Henry the fifth*, ed. P. A. Daniel, Shakspere-Quarto Facsimiles 39, London, 1887.
Grant White	*The Works of William Shakespeare*, ed. R. Grant White, 12 vols., Boston, 1875.
Greene (Collins)	Robert Greene, *Plays and Poems*, ed. J. C. Collins, 2 vols., Oxford, 1905.
Greene (Grosart)	Robert Greene, *Life and Complete Works*, ed. A. B. Grosart, 15 vols., London, 1881–6.
Hall	Edward Hall, *The Vnion of the Two Noble and Illustre Famelies of Lancastre and Yorke*, London, 1809 edn.
Halliwell	*The Works of William Shakespeare*, ed. J. O. Halliwell, 16 vols., London, 1853–65.
Hanmer 1, 2	*The Works of Shakespear*, ed. Sir Thomas Hanmer, 1st edn, 6 vols., Oxford, 1744; 2nd edn, 6 vols., Oxford, 1771.
Hardinge	Notes on *1 Henry IV* by Nicholas Hardinge, in Lewis Theobald's edn of Shakespeare, 1733.
Hardyng	*The Chronicle of Iohn Hardynge . . . together with the Continuation by Richard Grafton*, ed. Sir Henry Ellis, London, 1812 edn.
Harvey	Gabriel Harvey, *Complete Works*, ed. A. B. Grosart, 3 vols., London, 1884–5.

Hazlitt's *Dodsley*	*A Select Collection of Old English Plays, originally published by Robert Dodsley . . . revised by W. Carew Hazlitt*, 15 vols., London, 1874–6.
Heath	Benjamin Heath, *A Revisal of Shakespear's Text*, London, 1765.
Hemingway (New Var.)	A New Variorum edition of Shakespeare: *Henry the Fourth Part I*, ed. S. B. Hemingway, Philadelphia, 1936.
Hemingway (Yale)	*The First Part of King Henry the Fourth* (The Yale Shakespeare), ed. S. B. Hemingway, New Haven, 1917.
Heywood, John	John Heywood, *Works*, ed. Burton A. Millington, Urbana, 1956.
Heywood, Thomas (Shepherd)	Thomas Heywood, *Dramatic Works*, [ed. R. H. Shepherd,] 6 vols., London, 1874.
Holinshed (or Hol.)	Raphael Holinshed, *Chronicles of England, Scotland and Ireland*, 6 vols., London, 1807–8 edn.
Hudson	*The Harvard Shakespeare*, ed. H. N. Hudson, 20 vols., Boston, 1880–1.
Hunt. L. Q.	*The Huntington Library Quarterly.*
JEGP	*The Journal of English and Germanic Philology.*
Johnson	*The Plays of William Shakespeare*, ed. Samuel Johnson, 8 vols., London, 1765.
Johnson, T. 1, 2	*The Works of Mr. William Shakespear*, pub. T. Johnson; 1st edn, 1710; 2nd edn, 1721.
Jonson (H. & S.)	Ben Jonson, *Works*, ed. C. H. Herford and Percy and Evelyn Simpson, 11 vols., Oxford, 1925–52.
Jorgensen	P. A. Jorgensen, 'Military Rank in Shakespeare', *Hunt. L.Q.*, 14, 1950–1.
Kittredge	*Sixteen Plays of Shakespeare*, ed. G. L. Kittredge, Boston, 1946.
Linthicum	M. C. Linthicum, *Costume in the Drama of Shakespeare and his Contemporaries*, Oxford, 1936.
Lyly (Bond)	John Lyly, *Complete Works*, ed. R. W. Bond, 3 vols., Oxford, 1902.
Madden	D. H. Madden, *The Diary of Master William Silence*, 2nd edn, London, 1907.
Malone	*The Plays and Poems of William Shakspeare*, ed. Edmond Malone, 10 vols., London, 1790.
Mal. Soc.	The Malone Society.
Marlowe	Christopher Marlowe, *Works*, gen. ed. R. H. Case, 6 vols., London, 1930–3.
Mason	John Monck Mason, *Comments on the last Edition of Shakespeare's Plays*, London, 1785.
Minsheu	John Minsheu, *Ductor in Linguas, The Guide into the Tongues*, London, 1617.
MLN	*Modern Language Notes.*
MLR	*The Modern Language Review.*
Moorman	*King Henry IV, Part I*, ed. F. W. Moorman, London, 1893.
Morgann	Maurice Morgann, *Essay on the Dramatic Character of Sir John Falstaff*, London, 1777.
Nashe (Grosart)	Thomas Nashe, *Complete Works*, ed. A. B. Grosart, 6 vols., London, 1881–5.
Nashe (McKerrow)	Thomas Nashe, *Works*, ed. R. B. McKerrow, 5 vols., London, 1904–10.

Noble	Richmond Noble, *Shakespeare's Biblical Knowledge*, London, 1935.
NQ	*Notes and Queries.*
OED	*A New English Dictionary*, Oxford, 1884–1928.
Onions	C. T. Onions, *A Shakespeare Glossary*, 2nd edn, revised, Oxford, 1919.
PMLA	*Publications of the Modern Language Association of America.*
Pope 1, 2	*The Works of Shakespear*, ed. Alexander Pope, 1st edn, 6 vols., London, 1725; 2nd edn, 10 vols., London, 1728.
PQ	*The Philological Quarterly.*
RES	*The Review of English Studies.*
Rowe 1, 3	*The Works of Mr William Shakespear*, ed. Nicholas Rowe, 1st edn, 7 vols., London, 1709; 3rd edn, 8 vols., London, 1714.
SAB	*The Shakspere Allusion-Book*, rev. J. Munro, re-issued with a preface by Sir Edmund Chambers, 2 vols., Oxford, 1932.
Schmidt	A. Schmidt, *Shakespeare-Lexicon*, rev., 2 vols., Berlin and Leipzig, 1923.
Sh. Q.	*The Shakespeare Quarterly.*
Sh.'s Engl.	*Shakespeare's England; an Account of the Life and Manners of his Age*, 2 vols., Oxford, 1916–17.
Singer	*The Dramatic Works of William Shakespeare*, ed. S. W. Singer, 10 vols., Chiswick, 1826.
Sisson	C. R. Sisson, *New Readings in Shakespeare*, 2 vols., Cambridge, 1956.
SN	*Studia Neophilologica.*
SP	*Studies in Philology.*
Spurgeon	Caroline Spurgeon, *Shakespeare's Imagery and what it tells us*, Cambridge, 1935.
SR	*A Transcript of the Registers of the Company of Stationers of London, 1554–1640 A.D.*, ed. Edward Arber, 5 vols., London, 1875.
Staunton	*The Plays of Shakespeare*, ed. Howard Staunton, 3 vols., London, 1858–60.
Steevens	*The Plays of William Shakespeare*, notes by Samuel Johnson and George Steevens, ed. Isaac Reed, 15 vols., London, 1793.
Stow	John Stow, *Chronicles of England*, London, 1580; *Annales of England*, London, 1592.
Sugden	Edward H. Sugden, *A Topographical Dictionary to the Works of Shakespeare and his Fellow Dramatists*, Manchester, 1925.
Theobald 1, 2	*The Works of Shakespeare*, ed. Lewis Theobald, 1st edn, 7 vols., London, 1733; 2nd edn, 8 vols., London, 1740.
Tilley	M. P. Tilley, *A Dictionary of the Proverbs in England in the Sixteenth and Seventeenth Centuries*, Ann Arbor, 1950.
TLS	*The Times Literary Supplement.*
Var. 1773	*The Plays of William Shakespeare*, ed. Samuel Johnson and George Steevens, 10 vols., London, 1773.
Var. 1778	*The Plays of William Shakspeare*, ed. Samuel Johnson and George Steevens, 10 vols., London, 1778.
Var. 1821	*The Plays and Poems of William Shakespeare*, ed. James Boswell, 21 vols., London, 1821.

Vauhgan   Henry H. Vaughan, *New Readings and New Renderings of Shakespeare's Tragedies*, 1878–86.

Walker   Wm S. Walker, *A Critical Examination of Shakespeare's Text*, 3 vols., London, 1860.

Warburton   *The Works of Shakespear*, ed. Wm Warburton, 8 vols., London, 1747.

Webster   John Webster, *Complete Works*, ed. F. L. Lucas, 4 vols., London, 1927.

Wilson (*Fortunes*)   John Dover Wilson, *The Fortunes of Falstaff*, Cambridge, 1943.

Wilson (N.C.S.)   *The First Part of the History of Henry IV*, ed. John Dover Wilson (The New Cambridge Shakespeare), Cambridge, 1946.

Wright   *King Henry IV, Part I*, ed. W. A. Wright, London, 1897.

ADDITIONAL NOTE TO THE INTRODUCTION

p. xxxvii: Another influence from the *Myrroure for Magistrates* probably occurs when Henry appoints Hal to accompany him against the Welsh (v. v. 39–40). Holinshed hints, but vaguely, about an intended campaign. The *Myrroure* follows Hall in relating that after Shrewsbury the Prince marched against Glendower, who consequently died in misery: Glendower declares ('Owen Glendower', ll. 197–200) that

> Whan Henry King this victory had wunne,
> Destroyed the Percies, put their power to flyght,
> He did appoynt prince Henry his eldest sunne
> With all his power to meete me if he might.

THE FIRST PART OF
KING HENRY THE FOURTH

CHARACTERS[1]

KING HENRY *the Fourth.*
HENRY, *Prince of Wales,*
LORD JOHN *of Lancaster,* } *sons to the King.*
EARL OF WESTMORELAND.
SIR WALTER BLUNT.
THOMAS PERCY, *Earl of Worcester.*
HENRY PERCY, *Earl of Northumberland.*
HENRY PERCY, *surnamed* HOTSPUR, *his son.*
EDMUND MORTIMER, *Earl of March.*
ARCHIBALD, *Earl of Douglas.*
OWEN GLENDOWER.
SIR RICHARD VERNON.
RICHARD SCROOP, *Archbishop of York.*
SIR MICHAEL, *a friend to the Archbishop of York.*
SIR JOHN FALSTAFF.
POINS.
PETO.
BARDOLPH.
GADSHILL.
LADY PERCY, *wife to Hotspur, and sister to Mortimer.*
LADY MORTIMER, *daughter to Glendower, and wife to Mortimer.*
MISTRESS QUICKLY, *hostess of the Boar's Head in Eastcheap.*

Lords, Officers, Sheriff, Vintner, Chamberlain, Drawers,
two Carriers, Ostler, Messengers, Travellers, and Attendants.

SCENE: *England and Wales.*

---

1. No list of characters appears earlier than Rowe.

THE FIRST PART OF THE HISTORY OF [KING] HENRY THE FOURTH

ACT I

SCENE I.—[*London. The Palace.*]

Enter the KING, LORD JOHN OF LANCASTER, EARL OF WESTMORELAND, [SIR WALTER BLUNT,] *with others.*

King. So shaken as we are, so wan with care,
    Find we a time for frighted peace to pant,
    And breathe short-winded accents of new broils
    To be commenc'd in stronds afar remote:
    No more the thirsty entrance of this soil   5

THE FIRST . . . FOURTH] THE HISTORIE OF / Henry the fourth. *Qq;* The First Part of Henry the Fourth, / with the Life and Death of HENRY / Sirnamed HOT-SPVRRE *F.* King] *Hanmer; not in QqF.*

ACT I

Scene 1

ACT I SCENE I.] *F (Actus Primus. Scœna Prima.); not in Qq. Location.*] *Capell (subst.).* S.D. *Lord John of Lancaster,*] *QqF; omitted Capell, some edd. Sir Walter Blunt,*] *Dering MS, Capell* (Blunt,) *Var. 1778; not in QqF.* 5. entrance] *QqF;* bosom *Dering MS;* Entrails *F4;* entrants *conj. Var. 1773;* Erinnys *Steevens, conj. Mason.*

Heading] Additions to and alterations of QqF's directions are indicated
by square brackets. All locations are
editorial; they are inserted merely in
deference to convention, and no undue
attention need be paid to them.

   1. *So . . . care*] The latter part of *R2*
shows Henry afflicted by his wild son,
by hostile conspirators, and by remorse, to dispel which he vows a crusade. Hol. records also a pestilence, an
ominous meteor, diabolic visitations,
an attempted assassination, and wars
threatened by the French and launch-

ed by the Scots and Welsh. The tone
here is caught from Hol.; cf. App. III,
pp. 167–8. This is the first of the abundant references to bodily states and
actions.

   4. *stronds*] A phonetic variant of
"strands".

   5–18. *No more . . . master*] The irony
of Henry's deluded hopes is present in
Daniel—"And yet new *Hydraes* lo,
new heades appeare / T'afflict that
peace reputed then so sure" (*C.W.,* iii.
86).

   5–6. *thirsty entrance . . . daub*] Malone

3

Shall daub her lips with her own children's blood,
No more shall trenching war channel her fields,
Nor bruise her flow'rets with the armed hoofs
Of hostile paces: those opposed eyes,
Which, like the meteors of a troubled heaven,   10
All of one nature, of one substance bred,
Did lately meet in the intestine shock
And furious close of civil butchery,
Shall now, in mutual well-beseeming ranks,
March all one way, and be no more oppos'd   15
Against acquaintance, kindred, and allies.
The edge of war, like an ill-sheathed knife,
No more shall cut his master. Therefore, friends,
As far as to the sepulchre of Christ—
Whose soldier now, under whose blessed cross   20
We are impressed and engag'd to fight—
Forthwith a power of English shall we levy,
Whose arms were moulded in their mothers' womb
To chase these pagans in those holy fields
Over whose acres walk'd those blessed feet   25

16. allies] *Qq1–3,5,F* (*subst.*); all eyes *Q4*.   22. Forthwith] *Qq1,2,4,5,F*;
Forth with *Q3*.   23. mothers'] *QqF* (mothers), *Theobald*; Mother's *F4*.

refers to *Gen.* iv. 11: "And nowe art
thou cursed from the earth, which
hath opened her mouth to receaue thy
brothers blood from thy hande".
Cain's fratricide of Abel perhaps
suggested to Shakespeare this violent image for the earth's crevices
splashed by civil slaughter. *R3*, v. iv.
36 ff., expresses a similar horror of
past civil war and hope for restored
peace.

9–10. *those opposed . . . heaven*] In the
meteor image the idea of enemy eyes
flashing fire coalesces with that of "a
troubled heaven" attending dynastic
disturbances. Cf. *R2*, II. iv. 7, 9—
" 'Tis thought the king is dead . . . /
And meteors fright the fixed stars of
heaven".

11. *All . . . bred*] "Meteor" was used
for various atmospheric phenomena,
"consisting of vapours drawn up into
the Middle Region of the Air"(Florio,

New World of Words). In Shelley it can
still mean any kind of fiery pheno-
menon (*Shelley's Prose*, ed. D. L. Clark,
1954, 61).

14. *mutual well-beseeming*] inter-
dependent, well-ordered.

19–22. *As far . . . levy*] Gosson's
Schoole of Abuse, 1579 (ed. Arber, 50),
has a similar usage: "*Scipio . . .* leuied
his force too the walles of *Car[t]hage*".
The proposed crusade, which the
chronicles put at the end of Henry's
reign, Shakespeare brings forward as
an expiation for Richard's murder
(*R2*, v. vi. 49–50), perhaps prompted
by an appeal the Emperor of Con-
stantinople made to Henry in 1400 for
aid against the Turks (Hol., iii. 17).

21. *impressed and engag'd*] conscripted
and pledged by our vow.

25–7. *blessed . . . cross*] "The king's
mood in this scene is heavy with religious emotion" (Noble, 169).

Which fourteen hundred years ago were nail'd
For our advantage on the bitter cross.
But this our purpose now is twelve month old,
And bootless 'tis to tell you we will go;
Therefor we meet not now. Then let me hear   30
Of you, my gentle cousin Westmoreland,
What yesternight our Council did decree
In forwarding this dear expedience.

West. My liege, this haste was hot in question,
And many limits of the charge set down   35
But yesternight, when all athwart there came
A post from Wales, loaden with heavy news,
Whose worst was that the noble Mortimer,
Leading the men of Herefordshire to fight
Against the irregular and wild Glendower,   40
Was by the rude hands of that Welshman taken,
A thousand of his people butchered,
Upon whose dead corpse there was such misuse,

---

26. fourteen hundred] *Qq* (1400.), *F*.   28. now is twelve month] *Qq1–3;* is
twelue month *Qq4,5;* is a tweluemonth *F*.   30. Therefor] *QqF* (Therefore),
this edn.   39. Herefordshire] *Q6,F;* Herdforshire *Qq1–3;* Herdfordshire
Qq4,5.   42. A thousand] *Qq;* And a thousand *F*.   43. corpse] *Q1,F* (corpes),
Var. 1821; corps *Qq2–5.*

28. *now . . . old*] Historically, two
years elapsed between Richard's murder (1400) and the battle of Holmedon
(1402).

30. *Therefor . . . now*] It is not for that
that we meet now.

31. *gentle cousin*] noble kinsman.
"Cousin" was used for various degrees
of kinship: Westmoreland's wife was
Henry's half-sister.

33. *dear expedience*] cherished and
urgent enterprise. The primary sense
of "expedience" is "speed" (cf. *H5,* IV.
iii. 69–70—"the French . . . will with
all expedience charge on us"): this
sense is taken up in Westmoreland's
first line.

34. *hot in question*] being eagerly debated.

35. *limits of the charge*] "To limit" can
mean "to assign"; cf. *R3,* v. iii. 25—
"Limit each leader to his several

charge". Since "charge" can mean
"business" and "duties" as well as
"expenditure", the phrase compre-
hensively signifies "assignments of resources and of commanders' duties in
the campaign".

37. *post*] messenger.

38–46. *the noble Mortimer . . . spoken
of*] See App. III, p. 168. On Mortimer's
identity see I. iii. 79, 144, notes.

40. *irregular and wild*] This accords
with the chronicles: "irregular"="engaged in 'guerilla' warfare" (Kittredge). For the courtly, scholarly
(though touchy) Glendower of III.
see Intro., p. xxvi.

43. *corpse*]=corpses; "corps" and
"corpes" were plural as well as singular. Similarly in F *2H4,* I. i. 192–3—
"My Lord (your Sonne) had onely but
the Corpes, / But shadowes, and the
shewes of men to fight".

Such beastly shameless transformation,
By those Welshwomen done, as may not be   45
Without much shame retold or spoken of.
King. It seems then that the tidings of this broil
  Brake off our business for the Holy Land.
West. This match'd with other did, my gracious lord,
  For more uneven and unwelcome news   50
  Came from the north, and thus it did import:
  On Holy-rood day, the gallant Hotspur there,
  Young Harry Percy, and brave Archibald,
  That ever valiant and approved Scot,
  At Holmedon met, where they did spend   55
  A sad and bloody hour;
  As by discharge of their artillery,
  And shape of likelihood, the news was told;
  For he that brought them, in the very heat
  And pride of their contention did take horse,   60
  Uncertain of the issue any way.
King. Here is a dear, a true industrious friend,
  Sir Walter Blunt, new lighted from his horse,
  Stain'd with the variation of each soil

---

49. did] *Qq1,2;* like *Qq3–5,F.*   lord,] *Qq1–5* (L.), *Q6,F* (Lord,).   50. For]
Qq1–4; Far *Q5,F* (*subst.*).   51. import] *Qq1–4;* report *Q5,F.*   55–6.] *As
QqF;* At . . . met, / Where . . . hour, / *Capell, most edd.*   62. a dear] *Qq4 corr.,
5,F;* deere *Qq1–3,4 uncorr.*   a true] *Qq1–4;* and true *Q5,F.*   64. Stain'd] *Qq;*
Strain'd *F, Dering MS.*

49–55. *This . . . met*] Nearly three
months separated the defeats of Mortimer (22 June 1402) and Douglas
(14 Sept.). Hol. dates the latter ("on
the Rood daie in haruest"—i.e. 14
Sept.) but not the former, and Shakespeare heightens the dramatic impact
by making them contemporaneous.

54. *approved*] of proved worth.

55–6. *At . . . hour*] The rhythmical
velocity seems better conveyed by this
lineation (of QqF) than by the usual
readjustment (cf. collation).

55. *Holmedon*] Humbleton near
Wooler in Northumberland.

57. *artillery*] Formerly used for any
missiles in war, not confined to gun-
fire.

58. *shape of likelihood*] the way
probability shaped itself.

58–9. *the news was . . . them*] "News"
could be plural as well as singular.
R2, III. iv, has "this news" in l. 74 and
"these news" in ll. 82, 100.

60. *pride*] highest pitch, supreme
position; cf. *Mac.,* II. iv. 12—"A falcon
towering in her pride of place".

60, 63. *horse*] References to urgent
horsemanship are numerous in both
parts of the play; cf. II. iii. 68 ff., IV.i.
104–10, 119–23, and Harry Levin,
'Falstaff Uncolted', *MLN,* 1946, 305–
10. The effect is to create a world
of vigorous movement and military
activity.

62. *true industrious*] loyally zealous.

Betwixt that Holmedon and this seat of ours; 65
And he hath brought us smooth and welcome news.
The Earl of Douglas is discomfited;
Ten thousand bold Scots, two and twenty knights,
Balk'd in their own blood, did Sir Walter see
On Holmedon's plains; of prisoners Hotspur took 70
Mordake, Earl of Fife and eldest son
To beaten Douglas, and the Earl of Athol,
Of Murray, Angus, and Menteith:
And is not this an honourable spoil?
A gallant prize? ha, cousin, is it not?
West.   In faith, 75

66. welcome] *Qq;* welcomes *F.*   69. blood, did] *Q5,F* (blood did); bloud.
Did *Qq1–4.*   71. Earl] *QqF;* the Earl *Pope.*   75–6. not? . . . conquest]
As Steevens; not?   In faith it is. / *West.* A conquest *Qq1,2;* not? In faith it is. /
West. A conquest *Qq3–5,F.*

66. *And he . . . news*] The King,
apparently dependent on Westmoreland for news of the Welsh and Scottish outbreaks, now proves the better-
informed. Some commentators take
this for duplicity, or as showing that a
passage has been cut. Neither assumption is necessary: the fact that Henry,
while knowing less of the Welsh rising
than his Council, knows more of the
Scottish one both emphasizes his leading position and reflects the confused
situation. The messenger was actually
one Nicholas Merbury, but Hol. gives
no name and Shakespeare can thus
enhance Blunt's role.
68. *two and twenty*] "three and twentie" in Hol., iii. 21.
69. *Balk'd . . . blood*] Lying defeated
in blood-stained ridges. A balk is a
ridge between furrows; "balk'd" here
carries too its other meaning "thwart-
ed". (M. Doran, 'Imagery in *R2* and
in *H4*', *MLR,* xxxvii, 1942.)
71. *Mordake, Earl*] Hol. has "Mordacke earle of Fife" (iii. 21) and Pope's
change (cf. collation) is unnecessary.
"R, 'the dog's letter', was so fiercely
spoken by the Elizabethans that it
might, in verse, be made to produce an
additional syllable where such was
wanted" (A. C. Sprague, *Poems of*

Samuel Daniel, 1930, p. xxxii, fn., citing
Delia, 1592, xxxv. 5—"And I, though
borne in a colder clime").
71–2. *eldest son . . . Douglas*] Murdoch
Stewart was the son of Robert, Duke
of Albany, Regent of Scotland; Hol.
calls him "the duke of Albanies
sonne" (iii. 22). Shakespeare here and
at I. iii. 257, however, follows a printer's error (Hol., iii. 21), where a
comma was omitted after "gouernor"
—"of prisoners among other were
these, Mordacke earle of Fife, son to
the gouernor Archembald earle Dowglas". That Murdoch was *eldest* son
Shakespeare could have found in
Hol., *Hist. Scot.,* v. 405–6—"Mur-
docke (eldest sonne to duke Robert)
earle of Fife"—or, more probably, in
Stow's account of Holmedon—"Mur-
dake the eldest sonne of the duke of
Albanie, that was heyre apparant to
the realme of Scotland" (*Annales,* 521).
73. *Menteith*] One of "Mordake" 's
titles. In making Menteith a separate
person Shakespeare follows Hol.—
"Mordacke earle of Fife . . . Robert
earle of Angus, and (as some writers
haue) the earles of Atholl & Menteith"
(iii. 21).
74, 80. *honourable spoil . . . honour's
tongue*] The "honour" theme, so asso-

It is a conquest for a prince to boast of.
King. Yea, there thou mak'st me sad, and mak'st me sin
     In envy that my Lord Northumberland
     Should be the father to so blest a son;
     A son who is the theme of honour's tongue,   80
     Amongst a grove the very straightest plant,
     Who is sweet Fortune's minion and her pride;
     Whilst I by looking on the praise of him
     See riot and dishonour stain the brow
     Of my young Harry. O that it could be prov'd   85
     That some night-tripping fairy had exchang'd
     In cradle-clothes our children where they lay,
     And call'd mine Percy, his Plantagenet!
     Then would I have his Harry, and he mine:
     But let him from my thoughts. What think you, coz, 90
     Of this young Percy's pride? The prisoners
     Which he in this adventure hath surpris'd
     To his own use he keeps, and sends me word
     I shall have none but Mordake, Earl of Fife.
West. This is his uncle's teaching, this is Worcester,   95
     Malevolent to you in all aspects,
     Which makes him prune himself, and bristle up

79. to] *Qq1–4;* of *Q5,F.*   87. lay] *Qq1,3–5,F;* say *Q2.*

ciated with Hotspur, is sounded at
once.

82. *minion*] darling.

86–7. *That some . . . lay*] Fairies, it
was thought, would substitute an ugly
changeling for a beautiful child. Like
Daniel, Shakespeare makes Hotspur
and Hal coeval, though Hotspur was
twenty-one years the elder.

91–4. *The prisoners . . . Fife*] Cf. App.
III, p. 170. By the law of arms (though
Hol. does not mention this) Hotspur
could retain the prisoners except for
the Earl of Fife who, as a prince of the
blood royal, must be surrendered to
the King. Cf. Sir J. Turner, *Pallas
Armata,* pr. 1683, 341: "The Ransome
of a Prisoner belongs to him who took
him, unless he be a person of very
eminent quality, and then the Prince,
the State, or their General seizeth on

him, giving some gratuity to those who
took him".

95–6. *Worcester . . . aspects*] Following
Walsingham, who calls Worcester "in-
ventor (ut dicitur) totius mali", Hol.
says that "his studie was euer (as some
write) to procure malice". Shakespeare likens him to a planet exerting
an evil influence in his "aspects" to the
earth. "Malevolent" and "aspects"
have an underplay of astrological significance; cf. "malevolent star" in
Massinger, *Duke of Milan,* I. iii. 313.

97. *prune*] A falconry term for the
hawk trimming her feathers for action:
typical, like the dog image in the next
lines, of the play's physical vitality.
Shakespeare shows a lively knowledge
of birds and "the special aspect of their
life which attracts him is their *movement*" (Spurgeon, 48).

       The crest of youth against your dignity.

King. But I have sent for him to answer this;
       And for this cause awhile we must neglect   100
       Our holy purpose to Jerusalem.
       Cousin, on Wednesday next our Council we
       Will hold at Windsor, so inform the lords:
       But come yourself with speed to us again,
       For more is to be said and to be done   105
       Than out of anger can be uttered.

West. I will, my liege.   *Exeunt.*

SCENE II.—[*London. An Apartment of the Prince's.*]

Enter PRINCE OF WALES *and* SIR JOHN FALSTAFF.

Fal. Now, Hal, what time of day is it, lad?
Prince. Thou art so fat-witted with drinking of old sack,

102–3. we / Will hold at] *T. Johnson 2, Pope;* we will hold / At *QqF.*   103. so]
Qq; and so *F.*   inform] *Qq1–4,F* (*informe*); informer *Q5.*

Scene II

SCENE II.] *F* (*Scæna Secunda.*); *not in Qq.*   Location.] *Theobald* (*subst.*).   S.D.]
Qq; Enter Henry Prince of Wales, Sir Iohn Falstaffe, and Pointz. | *F.*

97–8. *bristle . . . crest*] Cf. *John,* IV. iii.
148–9—"Now . . . / Doth dogged war
bristle his angry crest".

99. *I have . . . this*] To assert the
King's leadership Shakespeare varies
from Hol., who says that the Percys
themselves "came to the king vnto
Windsore (vpon a purpose to prooue
him)" (iii. 22).

105–6.] "The substance of the king's
speech is: 'Dismiss the lords until Wednesday next, but you yourself return to
me at once, for more is to be said and
done than I can say or do *in public,* in
my present angry condition' " (Hemingway, Yale). "Utter" has its Elizabethan sense of "make public". Quasi-
proverbial; see Tilley, N307—"Nothing is well said or done in a passion
(in anger)".

Scene II

Entry.] "The point of this [that Fal.
is supposedly 'discovered' asleep on
the inner stage] has eluded the
critics" (Wilson, N.C.S.). But can one
imagine the Prince entering un-
announced and doing the comic dis-
covery "business" as a mute solo?

1–12. *what time . . . the day*] "It is
indeed an absurdity for Fal. to ask the
time of day, for Fal. has properly nothing to do with the world of time. . .
For Fal., each day is a new day lived
for itself. The future does not cast a
cloud over the present" (Brooks and
Heilman, 382).

2. *fat-witted*] thick-witted. Cf. *LLL.*,
v. ii. 269—"Well-liking wits they
have; gross, gross; fat, fat".

sack] *OED,* "Sack, *sb.*³ Often

and unbuttoning thee after supper, and sleeping
upon benches after noon, that thou hast forgotten to
demand that truly which thou wouldst truly know.   5
What a devil hast thou to do with the time of the
day? Unless hours were cups of sack, and minutes
capons, and clocks the tongues of bawds, and dials
the signs of leaping-houses, and the blessed sun himself a fair hot wench in flame-coloured taffeta, I see   10
no reason why thou shouldst be so superfluous to
demand the time of the day.

Fal. Indeed, you come near me now, Hal, for we that
take purses go by the moon and the seven stars, and
not "by Phœbus, he, that wand'ring knight so fair":   15

---

4. after noon] *Qq;* in the afternoone *F.*   11. be so] *Q1,F;* be *Qq2–5.*
14. the seven] *Qq1–4;* seuen *Q5,F.*   15. "by . . . fair"] *This edn;* by . . .
faire *QqF.*

---

described as a sweet wine, though
Shakespeare's mention of sack and
sugar [cf. l. 110] shows that it was not
always such in the 16th c. A general
name for a class of white wines . . . from
Spain and the Canaries".

4–7. *that thou . . . the day*] The point is
hardly that, as Johnson supposed, Fal.
had asked in the *night* for the time of
day (the scene is not laid at night) but
that he is so bemused as to be asking
not after sack, capons, etc., but after
something quite irrelevant to him.
With typical quickness he seizes (ll.
13–15) on a sense of "day" (the opposite of night) different from Hal's.

6–12. *What a devil . . . the day*] Nashe
furnishes an apparent parallel—
"What haue we to doe with scales and
hower-glasses, except we were Bakers
or Clock-keepers? I cannot tell how
other men are addicted, but it is
against my profession to . . . keepe any
howers but dinner or Supper. It is a
pedanticall thing to respect times and
seasons" (*Summers Last Will*, McKerrow, iii. 247).

9. *leaping-houses*] brothels.

10. *flame-coloured taffeta*] Prostitutes
wore taffeta petticoats; cf. Dekker,
1 Honest Whore, II. i. 94–5—"The

knight, Sir *Oliuer Lollio*, swore he wold
bestow a taffata petticoate on thee, but
to breake his fast with thee" (Bowers,
ii. 46). *All's W.* refers to "your taffeta
punk" (II. ii. 24); in Barry's *Ram Alley*,
IV. i, a bawd sues a courtesan for "five
weeks' loan for a red taffata gown"
(Hazlitt's *Dodsley*, x. 344).

11. *superfluous*] A quibble: (*a*) need-
lessly inquisitive; (*b*) self-indulgent;
cf. *Lr.*, IV. i. 68—"superfluous and lust-
dieted man".

13. *you . . . near me*] you are near the
mark.

14. *go by*] A quibble: (*a*) are abroad
in; (*b*) tell the time by.

the seven stars] i.e. "the seauen
Starres, called the Pleiades" (Dekker,
King's Entertainment; Bowers, ii. 301).

15. "*by Phœbus . . . fair*"] Warburton
suggested, as is likely, that this is from
a lost ballad; Mr J. C. Maxwell points
out to me *OED*'s comment on the
"tag" use of "he"—"3*a* . . . Common
in ballad style . . . [citing *Chevy Chase*]"
—and examples in *Clyomon & Cla-
mydes* (Mal. Soc., 1913, 778, 827). As a
possible source for the allusion
Steevens refers to *The Mirrour of princely deedes and knighthood* by M[argaret]
T[yler], from Diego Ortuñez de Cala-

and I prithee sweet wag, when thou art king, as God
save thy Grace—Majesty I should say, for grace thou
wilt have none—

Prince. What, none?

Fal. No, by my troth, not so much as will serve to be pro-   20
logue to an egg and butter.

Prince. Well, how then? Come, roundly, roundly.

Fal. Marry then sweet wag, when thou art king let not us
that are squires of the night's body be called thieves
of the day's beauty: let us be Diana's foresters,   25
gentlemen of the shade, minions of the moon; and
let men say we be men of good government, being
governed as the sea is, by our noble and chaste mis-

---

16. king] *Qq2–5,F; a king Q1.*   20. by my troth] *Qq; not in F.*

horra's romance *Espejo de Principes y
Caballeros*; in this the Knight of the
Sun (El Donzel del Febo) appears, and
a jocose reference in Butler's *Hudibras*
(I. i. 15–16) shows that it was popular.
Douce suggests *The Voyage of the
Wandering Knight*, trans. 1581 by
William Goodyear from the French
of Jean de Cartigny (*Illust. of Sh.*, 1807,
i. 415).

16–17. *as . . . save*] *OED* gives "As.
†29. Formerly used to introduce an
imperative sentence. *Obs.*", and
quotes Chaucer's "as go we seene"
(let us go and see) and "As lene it
me" (Do lend it me), but no later
examples.

17. *grace*] A triple quibble: (*a*) Highness; (*b*) spiritual grace; (*c*) grace before meat.

21. *egg and butter*] Friday or Lenten
fare, presumably unworthy of more
than the minimum of grace; J. Eliot,
Ortho-epia Gallica, 1593, 117, has "It is
fasting day to day. . . There are egges
in the shell, butterd, poched, and
fride".

22. *roundly*] to the point (with a
glance at Fal.'s figure?).

24–5. *squires . . . beauty*] "Squires of
the body" were a nobleman's attendants. The following word-play seems
intended; "night–knight" (Bradley,

Sh's Engl., ii. 541, rejects this, arguing
that the "k" was sounded, but Wilson
(N.C.S.) points to the "nave–knave"
pun of *2H4*, II. iv. 278, and the "knight-
errant" [="night-sinner"] of ibid., v.
iv. 25); "body–bawdy" (cf. Middleton, *Family of Love*, v. i. 125—"the
liberality of your bawdies, not your
minds" (*Works*, ed. Bullen, iii. 98);
"body–beauty–booty". It is wrong to
tie these witticisms down to one prosaic meaning but approximately they
mean "Since we serve the night's ex-
citements, do not complain that we are
inactive by day". The German *Tages-
dieb*, thief of day (a euphemism for a
loafer), may provide a parallel.

25. *Diana's foresters*] Followers of
Diana as moon-goddess, they will
range abroad serving her also as
huntress. Cf. *Cym.*, II. iii. 74—"Diana's
rangers".

26. *gentlemen . . . shade*] "Cf. Gentlemen of the Chamber, etc., members of
the Royal Household" (Wilson,
N.C.S.).

minions . . . moon] So also Wilkins,
Miseries of Enforced Marriage, 1607, sig.
F3ᵛ—"the Moone, patronesse of all
purse-takers".

27. *of good government*] A quibble:
(*a*) well-behaved; (*b*) serving a good
ruler.

tress the moon, under whose countenance we steal.

Prince. Thou sayest well, and it holds well too, for the for-   30
tune of us that are the moon's men doth ebb and
flow like the sea, being governed as the sea is, by the
moon—as for proof now, a purse of gold most reso-
lutely snatched on Monday night, and most disso-
lutely spent on Tuesday morning, got with swearing   35
"Lay by!", and spent with crying "Bring in!", now
in as low an ebb as the foot of the ladder, and by and
by in as high a flow as the ridge of the gallows.

Fal. By the Lord thou say'st true, lad; and is not my hostess of the tavern a most sweet wench?   40

Prince. As the honey of Hybla, my old lad of the castle;
and is not a buff jerkin a most sweet robe of durance?

---

30. too] *Q1* (to), *Qq2–5,F.*   33. proof now,] *Wilson (N.C.S.);* proofe. Now
QqF.   39. By the Lord] *Qq; not in F.*   41. As the honey of Hybla] *Qq;*
As is the hony *F.*

---

29. *countenance*] Another quibble:
(a) face; (b) patronage.

steal] Another quibble: (a) go by
stealth; (b) thieve.

30. *it holds well*] the simile is apt.

36. *"Lay by!"*] Either "Stand and
deliver!" or perhaps "Drop your
weapons!"; cf. Brome (Shepherd, vol.
ii), *Covent-Garden Weeded* (p. 90)—
"Lay by your Armes, my Masters. I
bring none but friends".

"Bring in!"] "food and drink"
understood.

36–8. *now . . . gallows*] Cf. John Heywood, *Three Hundred Epigrammes*, 56:
"Thou art at an ebbe in Newgate,
thou hast wrong, / But thou shalt be
aflote at Tyburne ere long". Proverbial; Tilley, E56. "The foot of the
ladder" prompts the "gallows" association, since it was up a ladder that
the condemned man had to climb,
wearing the noose, to the crossbar
from which he was to drop.

39–40. *my hostess . . . wench*] An echo
of *F.V.*'s "pretie wench that can talke
well" at "the olde Tauerne in Eastcheape" (i. 89–91). The oblique-
ness of this innuendo, and Hal's rejec-

tion of it (l. 46), reflect Shakespeare's
care to keep Hal reputable.

41. *Hybla*] In Sicily, source of the
famous Hyblaean honey.

old lad . . . castle] A pun on "Oldcastle"; also a cant term for roisterer.
Gabriel Harvey's *Fovre Letters*, 1592
(Grosart, i. 225), refers to "old Lads of
the Castell", and his *Pierce's Supereroga-
tion*, 1593 (Grosart, ii. 44), to "a lusty
ladd of the Castell, that will bind
Beares, and ride golden Asses to
death". "Old Dick of the Castle"
occurs in Nashe's *Haue with You* (Mc-
Kerrow, iii. 5). In mediaeval homi-
letic literature the tavern was often the
devil's castle (Owst, *Lit. and Pulpit*,
438), which may help to explain the
term. Shakespeare's audience would
know, too, that one of Southwark's
principal brothels was called The
Castle (Stow, *Survay*, 'Bridge Ward
Without').

42. *buff . . . durance*] Hal seems to
mean "Mind you don't land in gaol".
A buff (leather) jerkin was the constable's jacket. "Durance" quibbles on
its hard-wearing qualities and the gaol
it suggested; cf. *Err.*, IV. iii. 24—"he

Fal. How now, how now, mad wag? What, in thy quips
and thy quiddities? What a plague have I to do with
a buff jerkin?

Prince. Why, what a pox have I to do with my hostess of
the tavern?

Fal. Well, thou hast called her to a reckoning many a
time and oft.

Prince. Did I ever call for thee to pay thy part?   50

Fal. No, I'll give thee thy due, thou hast paid all there.

Prince. Yea, and elsewhere, so far as my coin would
stretch, and where it would not I have used my
credit.

Fal. Yea, and so used it that were it not here apparent   55
that thou art heir apparent—But I prithee sweet
wag, shall there be gallows standing in England
when thou art king? and resolution thus fubbed as it
is with the rusty curb of old father Antic the law? Do
not thou when thou art king hang a thief.   60

Prince. No, thou shalt.

Fal. Shall I? O rare! By the Lord, I'll be a brave judge!

Prince. Thou judgest false already, I mean thou shalt
have the hanging of the thieves, and so become a rare
hangman.   65

Fal. Well, Hal, well; and in some sort it jumps with my
humour, as well as waiting in the court, I can tell
you.

55. it not] *Qq;* it *F.*   58. fubbed] *Qq* (fubd)*;* fobb'd *F.*   60. king] *Qq1–3;*
a King *Qq4,5,F.*   62. By the Lord] *Qq; not in F.*

[the sergeant] ... takes pity on decayed
men and gives them suits of durance".

44. *quiddities*] quibbles, subtleties.

48. *called ... reckoning*] (*a*) called her
to give an account of herself; (*b*) asked
her for the bill.

55–6. *here ... heir*] These (and "hair"
too) made a passable pun in Shakespeare's day. Were Hal not Prince of
Wales, Fal. suggests, he would get no
more credit.

58. *resolution . . . fubbed*] courage
robbed of its due reward.

59. *Antic*] "Speaking of the law as a
venerable buffoon is a right Falstaffian

stroke of humour" (Hudson)—and,
one may add, of irresponsibility.

60–1. *hang . . . shalt*] A strong innuendo: cf. Tilley, T119—"The great
thieves hang the little ones".

61–5.] Reminiscent of *F.V.* when
the Prince promises to make Ned
the Lord Chief Justice and Ned replies "By gogs wounds, ile be the
brauest Lord chiefe Iustice / That
euer was in England" (vi. 19–24). But
in Shakespeare Hal is revealingly
sardonic.

62. *brave*] fine.

67–9. *waiting ... court ... suits*] (*a*)

Prince. For obtaining of suits?

Fal. Yea, for obtaining of suits, whereof the hangman   70
hath no lean wardrobe. 'Sblood, I am as melancholy
as a gib cat, or a lugged bear.

Prince. Or an old lion, or a lover's lute.

Fal. Yea, or the drone of a Lincolnshire bagpipe.

Prince. What sayest thou to a hare, or the melancholy of   75
Moor-ditch?

71. 'Sblood] *Qq; not in F.*

being a suitor in the royal court for preferment; (*b*) waiting about the law-court for the felon's robes, which were the hangman's perquisite: cf. Brome (Shepherd, vol. i), *Mad Couple well Match'd* (p. 5)—"I will do some notorious death-deserving thing (though these cloaths goe to th' Hangman for't), what care I?" The "waiting-suits" jest was traditional; cf. John Heywood's *Epigrammes* (5th Hundred, 156), and Tilley, S962—"Suits hang half a year in Westminster Hall; at Tyburn half an hour's hanging ends all".

72. *gib cat*] *OED*, "Gib 2. A male cat ... in later dialectal use, one that has been castrated". The cat's melancholy was proverbial, perhaps because of its mournful outcries; cf. Tilley, C129. Mr J. C. Maxwell sends me a note: "A pleasant appearance of the melancholy cat is in [Dekker,] *1 Honest Whore* (Bowers), II. i. 131–2—'now you looke like an old he cat, going to the gallows' ". He wonders if there were a proverbial connection between cats and gallows. I can trace none, but Dr Harold Brooks reminds me that dogs were certainly hanged for misbehaviour—"Let gallows gape for dog, let man go free" (*H5*, III. vi. 44).

lugged] baited.

73. *old lion*] The forlorn expression of ageing lions might strike visitors to the royal menagerie at the Tower of London: in 1598 Hentzner saw one named Edward VI, born in that king's reign.

74. *drone*] Steevens and others show

that "Lincolnshire bagpipe" was applied to frogs and bitterns. But frogs croak and bitterns boom, so they are ruled out by "drone" ("At once the bass-pipe and its single note"—Wilson, N.C.S.). In Shakespeare's day the English bagpipe seems to have been associated with Lancs. and Lincs.; Robert Armin describes Christmas festivities where "a noyse of minstrells and a Lincolnshire bagpipe was prepared" (*Nest of Ninnies*, 1608, Sh. Soc. ed., 9). Drayton has "And *Bells and Bag-pipes* next belong to *Lincolne-shire*" (*Poly-Olb.*, xxiii. 266).

75. *hare*] "One of the moste melan-cholike beastes that is" (Turbervile, *Booke of Hunting*, 1575, 160). Kittredge cites Alanus de Insulis, *De Planctu Naturae*, in the 12th c. to the same effect (*Anglo-Lat. Satir. Poets*, ed. T. Wright, 1872, ii. 442). Tilley, H151, gives proverbial references.

76. *Moor-ditch*] Between Bishopsgate and Cripplegate, "a very narrow, and the same a filthy channel" (Stow, *Survay*, 'The Town Ditch'). It was associated with melancholy; Malone quotes John Taylor's *Pennyles Pilgrimage*, 1618, 129—"moody, muddy, Moore-ditch melancholy"; Kittredge refers to *The Penniless Parliament of Threadbare Poets*, 1608 (ed. C. Hindley, *Old Book Collector's Miscellany*, 1872, ii. 3)—"all such as buys this book, and laughs not at it, before he has read it over, shall be condemned of melancholy, and be adjudged to walk in Moorfields, twice a week".

Fal. Thou hast the most unsavoury similes, and art indeed the most comparative rascalliest sweet young
prince. But Hal, I prithee trouble me no more with
vanity. I would to God thou and I knew where a   80
commodity of good names were to be bought: an old
lord of the Council rated me the other day in the
street about you, sir, but I marked him not, and yet
he talked very wisely, but I regarded him not, and
yet he talked wisely, and in the street too.   85

Prince. Thou didst well, for wisdom cries out in the streets
and no man regards it.

Fal. O, thou hast damnable iteration, and art indeed able
to corrupt a saint: thou hast done much harm upon
me, Hal, God forgive thee for it: before I knew thee,   90
Hal, I knew nothing, and now am I, if a man should
speak truly, little better than one of the wicked. I
must give over this life, and I will give it over: by the
Lord, and I do not I am a villain, I'll be damned for
never a king's son in Christendom.   95

Prince. Where shall we take a purse tomorrow, Jack?

Fal. 'Zounds, where thou wilt, lad, I'll make one; an I do
not, call me villain and baffle me.

---

77. similes] *Q5;* smiles *Qq1–4,F.*   78. rascalliest] *Qq1–3;* rascallest *Qq4,5,F.*
80. to God] *Qq; not in F.*   86–7. wisdom . . . and] *Qq; not in F.*   89. upon] *Q1;*
vnto *Qq2–5,F.*   91. am I] *Qq;* I am *F.*   93–4. by the Lord] *Qq; not in F.*
97. 'Zounds] *Qq; not in F.*

78. *comparative*] fertile in (insulting)
comparisons; cf. III. ii. 67, and *LLL.*,
v. ii. 852—"Full of comparisons and
wounding flouts".

79–85. *But Hal . . . too*] "Fal. adopts
the Scriptural style of the sanctimonious Puritan" (Hemingway, New
Var.).

81. *commodity*] supply. *The Dis-
couerie of the Knights of the Poste*, 1597,
has "it were well, if they knew where a
good commodetie of names were to be
sould" (sig. C1).

86–7. *wisdom . . . it*] *Prov.*, i. 20, 24
— "Wisedome cryeth without, and
putteth foorth her voyce in the
streetes"; "Because I haue called,
and ye refused, I haue stretched out

my hande, and no man regarded".

88. *damnable iteration*] "a wicked
trick of repeating and applying holy
texts" (Johnson).

92. *the wicked*] Fal. mimics Puritan
idiom: cf. Overbury's *Characters, A
Button-Maker of Amsterdame*—"most of
the wicked (as hee calles them) be
there . . ."; and Butler's *Hudibras*, II. ii.
251–2—"She's of the Wicked, as I
guess / B'her looks, her language, and
her dress".

98. *baffle*] To baffle was to degrade a
perjured knight by hanging him, or
his effigy, or his shield, upside down;
cf. Spenser, *F.Q.*, VI. vii. 27—"He by
the heeles him hung vpon a tree, /And
baffuld so that all which passed by, /

Prince. I see a good amendment of life in thee, from
    praying to purse-taking.   100
Fal. Why, Hal, 'tis my vocation, Hal, 'tis no sin for a
    man to labour in his vocation.

                         Enter POINS.

Poins!—Now shall we know if Gadshill have set a
match. O, if men were to be saved by merit, what
hole in hell were hot enough for him? This is the   105
most omnipotent villain that ever cried "Stand!"
to a true man.
Prince. Good morrow, Ned.
Poins. Good morrow, sweet Hal. What says Monsieur
    Remorse? What says Sir John Sack—and Sugar?   110
    Jack! how agrees the devil and thee about thy soul,

---

102. S.D.] *Qq; not in F.*   103. Poins!—] *Q1* (Poynes), *Q2* (Poynes,), *Q3*
(*Poines,*); *Poines.* | *Qq4,5* (*as speech prefix*); *Pointz.* | *F* (*as speech prefix*).   104.
match] *Qq;* Watch *F.*   110–11. Sack—and Sugar? Jack!] *Cowl & Morgan;*
Sacke, and Sugar Iacke? *Qq1–4; Sacke* and *Sugar,* Iacke? *Q5;* Sacke and
Sugar: Iacke? *F;* Sack-and-Sugar? Jack! *Rowe.*

The picture of his punishment might
see".

  99. *amendment of life*] More Biblical
idiom, from the Geneva version
(*Matt.*, iii. 8, *Luke*, xv. 7, *Acts*, xxvi. 20)
and the Communion Service, Lit-
any, and *Homily on Repentance* (Noble,
61).

  102. *to labour . . . vocation*] *I Cor.*, vii.
20 (Geneva)—"let euerie man abide
in the same vocation wherein he was
called", a text often echoed by Protestant divines. Noble (70) cites the
Homily against Idleness—"so every one
. . . ought . . . to exercise himself,
according to the vocation, whereunto
God hath called him". Nashe, like
Fal., equates robbery with an honest
living—"He held it as lawful for hym
(since al labouring in a man's vocation
is but getting) to gette wealth as wel
with his sword by the High-way side,
as the Laborer with his Spade or
Mattocke" (*Christes Teares*, 1593; Mc-
Kerrow, ii. 64).

  103. *Gadshill*] This is the thief Cut-

bert Cutter's nickname in *F.V.* (ii.
67), from the scene of his exploits.
Shakespeare accepts it as a proper
name.

  103–4. *set a match*] Thieves' cant: =
"plan a robbery".

  104. *by merit*] "i.e. by works, not
faith" (Wilson, N.C.S.). *OED*, "Merit
sb. 3*b.*—spec. in *theology*, the quality, in
actions or persons, of being entitled to
reward from God".

  106. *omnipotent*] Used humorously =
"unparalleled". Nashe has "more
boystrous and cumbersome than a
payre of *Swissers* omnipotent galeaze
breeches" (*Haue with you*, McKerrow
iii. 35).

  107. *true*] honest; cf. *F.V.*—"*Theefe*:
It is not too late for true men to walke.
Law[*rence*]: We know thee not to be a
true man" (ii. 77–8).

  110–11. *Sack—and Sugar? Jack*] Qq1–
4's "*Sacke,* and Sugar *Iacke?*" is all but
impossible (though M. Mahood, *Sh.'s
Wordplay,* 1957, 15, thinks it means
"Sack-and-sugar Tankard" — *OED*

that thou soldest him on Good Friday last, for a cup
of Madeira and a cold capon's leg?

Prince. Sir John stands to his word, the devil shall have
his bargain, for he was never yet a breaker of pro-   115
verbs: he will give the devil his due.

Poins. Then art thou damned for keeping thy word with
the devil.

Prince. Else he had been damned for cozening the devil.

Poins. But my lads, my lads, tomorrow morning, by   120
four o'clock early at Gad's Hill, there are pilgrims
going to Canterbury with rich offerings, and
traders riding to London with fat purses. I have
vizards for you all; you have horses for yourselves.
Gadshill lies tonight in Rochester, I have bespoke   125
supper tomorrow night in Eastcheap: we may do
it as secure as sleep. If you will go, I will stuff your
purses full of crowns: if you will not, tarry at home
and be hanged.

Fal. Hear ye, Yedward, if I tarry at home and go not,   130
I'll hang you for going.

Poins. You will, chops?

119. had been] *Qq;* had *F.*   126. tomorrow night] *Qq;* to morrow *F.*

has "Jack . . . 20. A quarter of a pint").
Yet the comma suggests an inflection
which allows "sack" to quibble on (*a*)
sack-cloth (following Remorse); (*b*)
sherry; (*c*) the "stuffed cloak-bag of
guts". As for sack-and-sugar, Simon
Eyre equates it with old age—"lets be
merry whiles we are yong, olde age,
sacke and sugar will steale vpon vs ere
we be aware" (*Shoemaker's Holiday,* III.
iii. 22–3; Bowers, i. 55). Lyly, *Mother
Bombie,* II. v. 52, writes "Without wine
and sugar his veins wold waxe colde",
and sack is "that which doth an old
man good" (ibid., II. v. 14; Bond, iii.
193–4).

112. *Good Friday*] The strictest of
fasts, to elude which Fal. would go to
any lengths. Wilson (N.C.S.) quotes
John, I. i. 234–5—"Sir Robert might
have eat his part in me / Upon Good-
Friday and ne'er broke his fast".

115–16. *he was . . . due*] "Give every-

one his due" was proverbial (Tilley,
D634).

119. *cozening*] cheating.

121. *Gad's Hill*] I follow Wilson's
spelling (N.C.S.) to distinguish the
place from the man. On the London
road two miles N.W. of Rochester, it
was notorious for robberies. *F.V.*'s
thief is "a taking fellow / Vpon Gads
hill in Kent" (ii. 69–70); cf. Dekker
& Webster, *West-ward Hoe,* II. ii.
226 (Bowers, ii. 343)—"the way lies
ouer Gads-hill, very dangerous".

124. *vizards*] "High-Pads . . . have a
Vizor-Mask, and two or three Perukes
of different Colours and Make, the
better to conceal themselves" (Bailey).

126. *Eastcheap*] Cf. ll. 39–40, note.

130. *Yedward*] Dialectal for Edward.

132. *chops*] "Fafelu . . . *Puffed vp;
fat cheeked; a chops*" (Cotgrave). "You
whoreson chops" is Doll's characteristic endearment at *2H4,* II. iv. 234.

Fal. Hal, wilt thou make one?

Prince. Who, I rob? I a thief? Not I, by my faith.

Fal. There's neither honesty, manhood, nor good fel-   135
lowship in thee, nor thou cam'st not of the blood
royal, if thou darest not stand for ten shillings.

Prince. Well then, once in my days I'll be a madcap.

Fal. Why, that's well said.

Prince. Well, come what will, I'll tarry at home.   140

Fal. By the Lord, I'll be a traitor then, when thou art
king.

Prince. I care not.

Poins. Sir John, I prithee leave the Prince and me alone:
I will lay him down such reasons for this adventure   145
that he shall go.

Fal. Well, God give thee the spirit of persuasion, and
him the ears of profiting, that what thou speakest
may move, and what he hears may be believed,
that the true prince may (for recreation sake) prove   150
a false thief, for the poor abuses of the time want
countenance. Farewell, you shall find me in Eastcheap.

Prince. Farewell, the latter spring! Farewell, All-hallown summer!   [*Exit Falstaff.*]   155

134. by my faith] *Qq; not in F.*   141. By the Lord] *Qq; not in F.*   147–
8. God give thee . . . him] *Qq;* maist thou haue . . . he *F.*   155. S.D.] *F2;
not in Qq,F1.*

134. *I rob?*] Virtuous indignation
rather belied by l. 96.

137. *royal . . . ten shillings*] A royal
was worth 10s. "Stand for" = (*a*) be
worth; (*b*) make a fight for.

147–9. *God . . . move*] More Puritan
parody; Nashe, *Anat. of Absurditie* (Mc-
Kerrow, i. 22), has "they will make
men beleeue, they doe nothing where-
to the Spirit dooth not perswade
them", and Jonson, *Alch.*, III. i. 48–9
(H. & S., v. 342), "*Ananias:* The
motion's good, / And of the spirit".

150. *recreation sake*] A frequent usage;
see Abbott, 31, and "sport sake",
"credit sake" (II. i. 69, 71), "safety
sake" (v. i. 65).

154. *the latter spring*] Pope and other

edd. change to "thou", but the vocative definite article is found in the 16th
c.; cf. *3H6*, v. v. 38—"Take that, the
likeness of this railer here" (King Edward, stabbing Prince Edward), and
Lr., I. i. 271–2—"The jewels of our
father . . . / Cordelia leaves you". The
phrase means the youth or Indian
summer of old age; Mr J. C. Maxwell
refers me to Middleton, *Honourable
Entertainments* (Mal. Soc., 1953, *Entertainment viii*, 175–6)—"That in this
latter Spring of your graue yeares, /
You may be greene in Vertues"
(addressed to the Lord Mayor and
Aldermen).

154–5. *All-hallown summer*] *OED*,
"A season of fine weather in the late

Poins. Now, my good sweet honey lord, ride with us to-morrow. I have a jest to execute that I cannot manage alone. Falstaff, Bardolph, Peto, and Gads-hill shall rob those men that we have already way-laid—yourself and I will not be there: and when   160
they have the booty, if you and I do not rob them, cut this head off from my shoulders.

Prince. How shall we part with them in setting forth?

Poins. Why, we will set forth before or after them, and appoint them a place of meeting, wherein it is at   165
our pleasure to fail; and then will they adventure upon the exploit themselves, which they shall have no sooner achieved but we'll set upon them.

Prince. Yea, but 'tis like that they will know us by our horses, by our habits, and by every other appoint-   170
ment to be ourselves.

Poins. Tut, our horses they shall not see, I'll tie them in the wood; our vizards we will change after we leave them; and sirrah, I have cases of buckram for the nonce, to immask our noted outward garments.   175

Prince. Yea, but I doubt they will be too hard for us.

Poins. Well, for two of them, I know them to be as true-bred cowards as ever turned back; and for the third, if he fight longer than he sees reason, I'll for-swear arms. The virtue of this jest will be the in-   180
comprehensible lies that this same fat rogue will

---

158. Bardolph, Peto] *Theobald;* Haruey, Rossill *QqF.*   162. head off] *Qq1,2;* head *Qq3-5,F.*   163. How] *Qq;* But how *F.*   169. Yea] *Qq;* I *F.*   176. Yea, but] *Qq;* But *F.*   181. this same] *Qq1-4;* this *Q5,F.*

---

autumn [about 1 Nov., All Saints' Day]; also *fig.* brightness or beauty lingering or reappearing in old age". In similar reference to Fal.'s autumnal mellowness Poins in *2H4,* II. ii. 112, calls him "martlemas" (St Martin's day, 11 Nov.).

158. *Bardolph, Peto*] QqF's "Haruey, Rossill", Qq's speech-prefix "*Ross.*" (II. iv. 172, 174, 178), and Q *2H4*'s entry-direction "Sir Iohn Russel" (II. ii) are probably original names (though not found in *F.V.*), elsewhere changed when Oldcastle became Fal.

159–60. *waylaid*] set an ambush for.

170–1. *appointment*] accoutrement.

174. *sirrah*] "A form of *sir* used in familiar address. Poins is treating the Prince as a comrade" (Kittredge).

174–5. *cases . . . nonce*] rough cloth suits for the occasion.

176. *doubt*] fear.

180–1. *incomprehensible*] beyond "comprehension", or bounds. *OED* quotes *Book of Common Prayer,* 1548—"The father incomprehensible, the sonne incomprehensible: and the holy gost incomprehensible". Nashe writes

    tell us when we meet at supper, how thirty at least
    he fought with, what wards, what blows, what
    extremities he endured; and in the reproof of this
    lives the jest.   185

Prince. Well, I'll go with thee; provide us all things
    necessary, and meet me tomorrow night in East-
    cheap; there I'll sup. Farewell.

Poins. Farewell, my lord.   *Exit.*

Prince. I know you all, and will awhile uphold   190
    The unyok'd humour of your idleness.
    Yet herein will I imitate the sun,
    Who doth permit the base contagious clouds
    To smother up his beauty from the world,
    That, when he please again to be himself,   195
    Being wanted he may be more wonder'd at
    By breaking through the foul and ugly mists
    Of vapours that did seem to strangle him.
    If all the year were playing holidays,
    To sport would be as tedious as to work;   200
    But when they seldom come, they wish'd-for come,

---

185. lives] *Q1;* lyes *Qq2–5,F.*   189. S.D.] *QqF (Exit Poines. or Exit Pointz.),*
Dyce.

---

of "the incomprehensible corpulencie"
of a book (*Haue with You,* McKerrow,
iii. 35).

    183. *wards*] postures of defence.

    184. *reproof*] disproof.

    187. *tomorrow night*] They are to
meet at Gad's Hill in the morning, but
Shakespeare's mind is so intent on
Fal.'s fabrications that it jumps ahead
to tomorrow's supper, not tonight's.

    190–212. *I know ... I will*] Johnson's
excellent comment points out that this
speech combines a functional, expository purpose with an apparently
"natural picture" of Hal's mind.
"This speech is very artfully introduced to keep the prince from appearing vile in the opinion of the audience:
it prepares them for his future reformation, and, what is yet more valuable, exhibits a natural picture of
a great mind offering excuses to itself, and palliating those follies which

it can neither justify nor forsake".

    191. *unyok'd humour*] unbridled
inclination.

    192. *the sun*] Traditional symbol of
royalty.

    193. *contagious clouds*] "Pestilence
was thought to be generated in fog,
mist, and clouds" (Kittredge): cf.
MND., II. i. 90—"contagious fogs";
and "armies of pestilence" in the
clouds (*R2,* III. iii. 87). T. W. Baldwin
points out echoes of sonnet xxxiii—
"Anon permit the basest clouds to
ride / With ugly rack on his celestial
face, / And from the forlorn world his
visage hide", and of sonnet xxxiv—
"To let base clouds o'ertake me in my
way, / Hiding thy bravery in their
rotten smoke" (*On the Lit. Genetics of
Sh.'s Sonnets,* 1950, 235).

    198. *strangle*] stifle, eclipse; cf. *Mac.,*
II. iv. 7—"And yet dark night strangles
the travelling lamp".

And nothing pleaseth but rare accidents:
So when this loose behaviour I throw off,
And pay the debt I never promised,
By how much better than my word I am,   205
By so much shall I falsify men's hopes;
And like bright metal on a sullen ground,
My reformation, glitt'ring o'er my fault,
Shall show more goodly, and attract more eyes
Than that which hath no foil to set it off.   210
I'll so offend, to make offence a skill,
Redeeming time when men think least I will.   *Exit.*

SCENE III.—[*Windsor. The Council Chamber.*]

Enter the KING, NORTHUMBERLAND, WORCESTER, HOTSPUR,
SIR WALTER BLUNT, *with others.*

King. My blood hath been too cold and temperate,
    Unapt to stir at these indignities,
    And you have found me—for accordingly
    You tread upon my patience: but be sure
    I will from henceforth rather be myself,
    Mighty, and to be fear'd, than my condition,   5
    Which hath been smooth as oil, soft as young down,
    And therefore lost that title of respect

echoes Hol's language (handwritten marginal note)

210. foil] *Qq1–3* (foile); soile *Qq4,5;* soyle *F.*   212. S.D.] *Qq; not in F.*

Scene III

SCENE III.] *F (Scæna Tertia.); not in Qq.*   Location.] *Halliwell (Windsor. A Room in the Palace.), Wilson (N.C.S.).*   S.D. with] *Qq; and F.*

202. *rare accidents*] the exceptional and unexpected; cf. sonnet lii—"Therefore are feasts so solemn and so rare, / Since, seldom coming, in the long year set, / Like stones of worth they thinly placed are". For a further possible echo of this sonnet see III. ii. 58, note.

206. *hopes*] OED, "Hope. †3. Expectation (without implication of desire. *Obs.*)."

207. *sullen ground*] dull background

(with mental gloom also implied).

212. *Redeeming time*] Making amends for wasted time. Biblical; cf. *Ephes.,* v. 16—"Redeeming the tyme, because ye dayes are euyll".

Scene III

Location.] This meeting Shakespeare, following Hol., indicates to be at Windsor; cf. I. i. 103.

3. *found me*] found me so.
6. *condition*] natural disposition.

Which the proud soul ne'er pays but to the proud.

Wor. Our house, my sovereign liege, little deserves   10
    The scourge of greatness to be us'd on it,
    And that same greatness too which our own hands
    Have holp to make so portly.

North.   My lord,—

King. Worcester, get thee gone, for I do see
    Danger and disobedience in thine eye: 15
    O sir, your presence is too bold and peremptory,
    And majesty might never yet endure
    The moody frontier of a servant brow.
    You have good leave to leave us; when we need
    Your use and counsel we shall send for you.   20

                      Exit Worcester.

[*To North*.] You were about to speak.

North.   Yea, my good lord.
    Those prisoners in your Highness' name demanded,
    Which Harry Percy here at Holmedon took,
    Were, as he says, not with such strength deny'd
    As is deliver'd to your Majesty.   25
    Either envy therefore, or misprision,
    Is guilty of this fault, and not my son.

Hot. My liege, I did deny no prisoners,
    But I remember, when the fight was done,

---

20. S.D.] *Qq; not in F*.   21. S.D.] *Rowe; not in QqF*.   22. Highness' name] *Qq;*
Highnesse *F*.   24. deny'd] *Rowe;* denied *QqF*.   25. is] *Qq1–4;* he *Q5;* was *F*.
deliver'd] *Rowe;* deliuered *QqF*.   26. Either envy therefore] *Qq;* Who either
through enuy *F*.   27. Is] *Qq;* Was *F*.

12–13. *our . . . portly*] The Percys
were among Henry's first supporters
on his return from exile. Cf. I. iii. 158,
IV. iii. 54, V. i. 33, and *R2*, II. iii.
"Portly" is trisyllabic, cf. I. i. 71 note;
it = "stately", as in Spenser, *F.Q.*,
III. ii. 24—"Portly his person was and
much increast, / Through his Heroick
grace, and honorable gest".

18. *moody . . . brow*] angry defiance of
a subject's frown. "Frontier" = ram-
part, or border fortress, whence the
sense of something formidably defiant.
Like "front" (cf. III. i. 12) or "frontlet"
(*Lr.*, I. iv. 210) it can suggest the forehead and its expressions; *OED* gives

"Frontier. A.1†c. The forehead. *Obs.
rare:* Stubbes, *Anat. Abus.* I (1877), 67,
Their bolstred heir . . . standeth
crested round their frontiers".

26. *envy, misprision*] malice, mistake.

28 ff.] Of this speech, of Hotspur's
outbreaks about Glendower and Lady
Percy, and of Faulconbridge's idiom in
John, G. H. W. Rylands writes: "All
these passages have critical significance. . . These voices demanded a
new medium, verse which will allow
colloquial emphases and prose order.
. . . Dramatic effect must war with
poetic decoration" (*Sh. Criticism 1919–
35*, ed. Ridler, 383–4).

When I was dry with rage, and extreme toil,   30
Breathless and faint, leaning upon my sword,
Came there a certain lord, neat and trimly dress'd,
Fresh as a bridegroom, and his chin new reap'd
Show'd like a stubble-land at harvest-home.
He was perfumed like a milliner,   35
And 'twixt his finger and his thumb he held
A pouncet-box, which ever and anon
He gave his nose, and took't away again—
Who therewith angry, when it next came there,
Took it in snuff—and still he smil'd and talk'd: 40
And as the soldiers bore dead bodies by,
He call'd them untaught knaves, unmannerly,
To bring a slovenly unhandsome corse
Betwixt the wind and his nobility.
With many holiday and lady terms   45
He question'd me, amongst the rest demanded
My prisoners in your Majesty's behalf.
I then, all smarting with my wounds being cold,
To be so pester'd with a popinjay,

---

41. bore] *Qq;* bare *F.*   45. terms] *Qq* (termes *Qq1,4,* tearmes *Qq2,3,5*) ; tearme
F.   46. question'd] *F;* questioned *Qq.*   amongst] *Qq1,2;* among *Qq3–5,F.*
49. pester'd] *Qq1–4* (pestred) ; pestered *Q5,F.*

---

33. *reap'd*] close-clipped. Men of
fashion, at the date of the play, wore
close-clipped beards.

35. *perfumed . . . milliner*] A milliner
dealt in haberdashery, perfumed to
attract attention and originally imported from Milan. W. Rowley,
Search for Money, 1609 (Percy Soc. ed.,
17), says "the milliners threw out per-
fumes to catch him by the nose and
. . . sweete gloves to fit his hand".

37. *pouncet-box*] small box, with per-
forated lid, for aromatic powder.

40. *took . . . in snuff*] (*a*) was incensed;
(*b*) snuffed it up. The use of powdered
tobacco as snuff is traceable to the
early 1600s (cf. Hemingway, New
Var.), but "snuffs made of herbs,
aromatic and others, were us'd medi-
cally long enough before Henry the
fourth" (Capell, *Notes,* 1779, 153).

45. *holiday*] choice, not workaday.

Cf. Lodge & Greene, *Looking-Glass for
London* (Greene, *Plays & Poems,* i. 163,
ll. 591–4)—"she will call me Rascall,
Rogue, Runnagate, Varlet, Vaga-
bond, Slaue, Knaue, Why, alasse sir,
and these be but holi-day tearmes, but
if you heard her working-day words,
in faith, sir, they be ratlers like thunder, sir".

46. *question'd me*] Both "interrogated
me" and "talked away to me".

49. *To be . . . popinjay*] The slight syn-
tactical detachment of this line, which
F puts in parentheses, reflects Hotspur's impatience. "Popinjay" = parrot, prattler; cf. *Jack Juggler* (Mal.
Soc., 1933, ll. 237–8)—"She chaffeth
like a Pye all daye / And speaketh like
a paratt Poppagaye". Eliot's *Ortho-
epia Gallica,* 44, has "gay as a Papingay,
perke as a Sperhawke", which suggests the dandification of Hotspur's

Out of my grief and my impatience   50
Answer'd neglectingly, I know not what,
He should, or he should not, for he made me mad
To see him shine so brisk, and smell so sweet,
And talk so like a waiting-gentlewoman
Of guns, and drums, and wounds, God save the mark!
And telling me the sovereignest thing on earth   56
Was parmacity for an inward bruise,
And that it was great pity, so it was,
This villainous saltpetre should be digg'd
Out of the bowels of the harmless earth,   60
Which many a good tall fellow had destroy'd
So cowardly, and but for these vile guns
He would himself have been a soldier.
This bald unjointed chat of his, my lord,
I answer'd indirectly, as I said,   65
And I beseech you, let not his report
Come current for an accusation
Betwixt my love and your high Majesty.
Blunt. The circumstance consider'd, good my lord,

51. Answer'd] *Q1* (Answerd), *F;* Answered *Qq2–5.*   52. or he] *Qq;* or *F.*
56. sovereignest] *Qq1,2,5* (soueraignest); soueraignst *Qq3,4,F* (soueraign'st *F*).
59. This] *Qq;* That *F.*   61. destroy'd] *Qq4,5,F* (*subst.*); destroyed *Qq1–3.*
63. himself have been] *Qq1–3,F;* haue been himselfe *Qq4,5.*   65. I answer'd]
Qq (I answered), *Pope;* Made me to answer *F.*   66. his] *Q1;* this *Qq2–5,F.*
69. consider'd] *Rowe;* considered *QqF.*

visitor. *OED* gives "popinjay 4. *fig. b*—
a type of vanity or empty conceit, in
allusion to the bird's gaudy plumage,
or to its mechanical repetition of words
and phrases".

50. *grief*] pain; cf. v. i. 132.

54. *talk . . . waiting-gentlewoman*] "To
laugh like a wayting Gentlewoman" is
one of the "accoutrements" of a gallant, in Dekker's *Patient Grissil*, II. i. 67
(Bowers, i. 227).

55. *God . . . mark*] A phrase generally
deprecatory or apologetic, but here
indignant; cf. *Oth.*, I. i. 33—"I—God
bless the mark!—his Moorship's ancient". Originally perhaps a formula
invoking a blessing on the mark of the
cross made to avert evil.

57. *parmacity*] The spelling "parmacitie" or "parmacity" for "spermaceti" was apparently due to a fanciful
etymology from "Parma city". Thus
Minsheu gives "Parmacetie, *confectio
optima à Ciuitate Parmae ita dicta*". It was
credited with a penetrative medicinal
quality which resolved coagulated
blood and hence cured inward
bruises. Kittredge quotes Barnabe
Riche's *Farewell to the Military Profession*,
1581 (Sh. Soc. ed., 154): "The Doctor
tooke sparmaceti, and suche like
thynges that bee good for a bruse, and
recovered hymself in a shorte space".

61. *tall*] doughty, valiant.

65. *indirectly*] inattentively.

67. *Come current*] "be accepted at its
face value" (Kittredge); also, "in-
trude".

Whate'er Lord Harry Percy then had said   70
To such a person, and in such a place,
At such a time, with all the rest retold,
May reasonably die, and never rise
To do him wrong, or any way impeach
What then he said, so he unsay it now.   75
King. Why, yet he doth deny his prisoners,
But with proviso and exception,
That we at our own charge shall ransom straight
His brother-in-law, the foolish Mortimer,
Who, on my soul, hath wilfully betray'd   80
The lives of those that he did lead to fight
Against that great magician, damn'd Glendower,
Whose daughter, as we hear, the Earl of March
Hath lately marry'd: shall our coffers then
Be empty'd to redeem a traitor home?   85
Shall we buy treason, and indent with fears
When they have lost and forfeited themselves?
No, on the barren mountains let him starve;
For I shall never hold that man my friend
Whose tongue shall ask me for one penny cost   90

---

70. Whate'er Lord] *Q1;* What e're *Qq2–5;* What euer *F.*   76. yet he] *Qq;*
yet *F.*   80. on] *Qq1–2;* in *Qq3–5,F.*   82. that] *Qq1,2;* the *Qq3–5,F.*   83.
the] *Qq2–5,F;* that *Q1.*   84. marry'd] *Rowe;* married *QqF.*   85. empty'd]
Rowe; emptied *QqF.*   88. mountains] *Q1* (mountaines); mountaine *Qq2–5,F*
(*subst.*).   starve] *Qq1–3;* sterue *Qq4,5,F.*

70–5. *Whate'er . . . said*] "Whatever
he said then, in the circumstances
described, should be forgotten and not
cited to his harm, as proof that his
words were disloyal." "Shakespeare
has tied himself up in a little knot, but
the sense is clear" (Wilson, N.C.S.).

79. *brother-in-law*] Hotspur married
Elizabeth (though Shakespeare calls
her Kate), sister of the Sir Edmund
Mortimer (1376–1409) who was
Glendower's captive and son-in-law
(cf. l. 83); see Appendix VIII.

82–3. *that great magician . . . the Earl*]
Qq have "that" and F has "the" in
both places. The redoubled "that"s
seem too emphatic: most edd. sacrifice
one, or both. The first is kept as being

Q1's reading and significantly em-
phasizing Glendower, and the second
replaced since it probably slipped in by
contagion with the other "that"s in the
passage.

83–4. *Earl of March . . . marry'd*] The
Edmund Mortimer who was captured
and married Glendower's daughter
was not in fact Earl of March, that
title belonging to his nephew, a
younger Edmund (1391–1425).

86. *indent*] make an agreement.

with fears] "Fears" has both an
abstract sense (parallel to "treason")
and a personal one (="cowards"):
"shall we come to terms with cowardice when the cowards have given
themselves up?"; see III. ii. 43, note.

To ransom home revolted Mortimer.
Hot. Revolted Mortimer!
He never did fall off, my sovereign liege,
But by the chance of war: to prove that true
Needs no more but one tongue for all those wounds,   95
Those mouthed wounds, which valiantly he took,
When on the gentle Severn's sedgy bank,
In single opposition hand to hand,
He did confound the best part of an hour
In changing hardiment with great Glendower.   100
Three times they breath'd, and three times did they
     drink
Upon agreement of swift Severn's flood,
Who then affrighted with their bloody looks
Ran fearfully among the trembling reeds,
And hid his crisp head in the hollow bank,   105
Bloodstained with these valiant combatants.
Never did bare and rotten policy
Colour her working with such deadly wounds,
Nor never could the noble Mortimer
Receive so many, and all willingly: 110
Then let not him be slander'd with revolt.
King. Thou dost belie him, Percy, thou dost belie him,
He never did encounter with Glendower:
I tell thee, he durst as well have met the devil
     alone

95. tongue for] *Hanmer;* tongue: for *Qq;* tongue. For *F.*   107. bare] *Qq;* base *F.*
111. not him] *Qq;* him not *F.*   slander'd] *F* (sland'red)*;* slandered *Qq.*
114. thee, he] *QqF;* thee, / He *Steevens, most later edd.*

94–106. *to prove . . . combatants*]
"These ornate lines", Wilson (N.C.S.)
comments, "come oddly from Hotspur, who speaks the contemptuous
words of poets and poetry." But Hotspur always gets worked up when
thinking of combat (as in ii. iii. 48 ff.),
and these lines are rightly taken by
H. T. Price ('Sh. as Critic', *PQ,* July
1941, 391)—"When he makes Hotspur say [ll. 101–6] he is telling us
something about Hotspur—that he is a
windy man who rants".

99. *confound*] consume.

100. *changing hardiment*] matching
valour.

105. *crisp head*] Wilson (N.C.S.)
points out the quibbles: "crisp" = (a)
curled; (b) rippled: "head" = (a) surface; (b) pressure of water against a
bank (*OED sb.* 17).

107. *bare*] wretched, beggarly (cf.
iii. ii. 13), or perhaps, as Sisson suggests, bare-faced.
policy] cunning.

114.] Q1's lineation in this stormy
scene includes "irregular" lines which
it seems not only unnecessary but

As Owen Glendower for an enemy.   115
Art thou not asham'd? But sirrah, henceforth
Let me not hear you speak of Mortimer:
Send me your prisoners with the speediest means,
Or you shall hear in such a kind from me
As will displease you. My Lord Northumberland: 120
We license your departure with your son.
Send us your prisoners, or you will hear of it.

                          Exit King[, with Blunt and train.]

Hot. And if the devil come and roar for them
I will not send them: I will after straight
And tell him so, for I will ease my heart,   125
Albeit I make a hazard of my head.

North. What, drunk with choler? Stay, and pause
     awhile,
Here comes your uncle.

                [Re-]enter WORCESTER.

Hot.   Speak of Mortimer?
'Zounds, I will speak of him, and let my soul
Want mercy if I do not join with him: 130
Yea, on his part I'll empty all these veins,
And shed my dear blood, drop by drop in the dust,
But I will lift the down-trod Mortimer
As high in the air as this unthankful King,

---

120. you] *Qq;* ye *F.*   122. you will] *Qq;* you'l *F.*   S.D. *with Blunt and train*] *Capell (subst.); not in QqF.*   126. Albeit I make a] *Qq;* Although it be with *F.*   128. S.D.] *Qq1–4,F (Enter Wor.   or   Enter Worcester), Capell; not in Q5.*   129. 'Zounds] *Qq;* Yes *F.*   131. Yea, on his part] *Qq;* In his behalfe *F.*   132. in the] *Qq1–4;* i'th *Q5,F.*   133. down-trod] *Qq;* downfall *F.*   134. in the] *Qq1–4;* in'th *Q5;* i'th *F.*

damaging to cure by setting the hyper-metrical portion on a separate line, as most edd. do. Similar metrical speed and passion, through elision or irregular stress or both, occur at ll. 16, 32, 112, 116, 216, 221, and 244 in this scene, and need no smoothing.

122. *you will*] Wilson (N.C.S.) prefers F's "you'l", as presumably the authentic abbreviation. But these phrases involving colloquial elision

seem to have been set up, and were perhaps written, haphazardly, and F, though undoubtedly representing what should be spoken, has no authority: cf. Intro., pp. lxix–lxx.

123. *the devil . . . them*] An echo of *1 Peter,* v. 8—"your aduersarie the deuyll, as a roaryng lion"; reminiscent too of the "roaring devil i' the old play" of popular drama (cf. *H5,* IV. iv. 76).

As this ingrate and canker'd Bolingbroke.   135
North. Brother, the King hath made your nephew mad.
Wor. Who struck this heat up after I was gone?
Hot. He will forsooth have all my prisoners,
    And when I urg'd the ransom once again
    Of my wife's brother, then his cheek look'd pale,   140
    And on my face he turn'd an eye of death,
    Trembling even at the name of Mortimer.
Wor. I cannot blame him: was not he proclaim'd,
    By Richard that dead is, the next of blood?
North. He was, I heard the proclamation: 145
    And then it was, when the unhappy King
    (Whose wrongs in us God pardon!) did set forth
    Upon his Irish expedition;
    From whence he, intercepted, did return
    To be depos'd, and shortly murdered.   150
Wor. And for whose death we in the world's wide mouth
    Live scandaliz'd and foully spoken of.
Hot. But soft, I pray you, did King Richard then
    Proclaim my brother Edmund Mortimer
    Heir to the crown?
North.   He did, myself did hear it.   155
Hot. Nay, then I cannot blame his cousin King,
    That wish'd him on the barren mountains starve.
    But shall it be that you that set the crown
    Upon the head of this forgetful man,

135. Bolingbroke] *QqF* (Bullingbrooke), *Pope.*   143. not he] *Qq;* he not *F.*
150. murdered] *Qq;* murthered *F.*   154. brother Edmund] *Q1;* brother *Qq2-*
5,F.   157. starve] *Qq;* staru'd *F.*

135. *canker'd Bolingbroke*] rotten at heart. Bolingbroke, spelt Bullen- or Bullingbrook(e) in Hol. and QqF, is pronounced Bollinbrook.

141. *an eye of death*] Either "an eye menacing death" (Johnson) or "an eye of mortal fear" (Kittredge). There are parallels to the former sense (e.g. *Cor.*, III. iii. 69—"Within thine eyes sat twenty thousand deaths"), but the latter seems right for the context; cf. the king's alleged pallor at III. i. 8.

144. *the next of blood*] The same con-

fusion as before (ll. 79, 83-4). The proclaimed heirs were (a) Roger Mortimer, Earl of March; (b) on Roger's death (1398) his son Edmund, Earl of March. Hotspur's "brother Edmund Mortimer" (l. 154) was, as aforesaid, this Edmund's uncle, not the heir; and the heir himself, at III. i. 190, refers to Hotspur's wife as "my aunt Percy"; see Appendix VIII.

147. *Whose . . . us*] the wrongs we inflicted on whom.

149. *intercepted*] interrupted.

154. *my brother*] Cf. l. 144, note.

And for his sake wear the detested blot   160
Of murderous subornation—shall it be
That you a world of curses undergo,
Being the agents, or base second means,
The cords, the ladder, or the hangman rather?
—O, pardon me, that I descend so low,   165
To show the line and the predicament
Wherein you range under this subtle King!
Shall it for shame be spoken in these days,
Or fill up chronicles in time to come,
That men of your nobility and power   170
Did gage them both in an unjust behalf
(As both of you, God pardon it, have done)
To put down Richard, that sweet lovely rose,
And plant this thorn, this canker Bolingbroke?
And shall it in more shame be further spoken,   175
That you are fool'd, discarded, and shook off
By him for whom these shames ye underwent?
No, yet time serves wherein you may redeem
Your banish'd honours, and restore yourselves
Into the good thoughts of the world again: 180
Revenge the jeering and disdain'd contempt
Of this proud King, who studies day and night

160. wear] *Qq;* wore *F.*   165. me] *Qq1-4;* if *Q5,F.*

161. *murderous subornation*] aiding
and abetting murder.
162-7. *That you . . . King*] Cf. Intro.,
p. lxii.
166-7. *line . . . predicament . . . range*]
The surface sense is "degree and category in which you are ranked". For
"line" as "degree" *OED* ("Line. *sb.*
†18. Degree, rank, station") cites
"Skiparis and seruandis of euery
line" from *Extracts Aberd. Reg., 1528.*
"Predicament" was originally a logi-
cians' term for a category of objects,
a "classification". But the passage
illustrates the richness of Shakespeare's
meanings: "line" carries from l. 164
implications of hangman's rope, and
"predicament" suggests its modern
sense of "dangerous situation"; cf.

Mer.V., iv. i. 358—"In which predicament [i.e. danger of death], I say, thou
stand'st".
171. *gage them both*] pledge their
nobility and power.
174. *canker*] *OED* gives "Canker †5.
An inferior kind of rose: the dog-rose".
Shades of meaning from "canker"
as "canker-worm" (which destroys
plants) and as "ulcer" are probably
present. The imagery in ll. 173-4 is
characteristically biased.
181. *disdain'd*] disdainful. This form
is here not participial but = "charac-
terized by"; cf. "the guiled shore / To
a most dangerous sea" (*Mer. V.,* iii. ii.
97-8), and "some distressed stroke"
(*Oth.,* Q, i. iii. 157, where F has "dis-
tressefulle").

  To answer all the debt he owes to you,
  Even with the bloody payment of your deaths:
  Therefore, I say—
Wor.   Peace, cousin, say no more. 185
  And now I will unclasp a secret book,
  And to your quick-conceiving discontents
  I'll read you matter deep and dangerous,
  As full of peril and adventurous spirit
  As to o'er-walk a current roaring loud 190
  On the unsteadfast footing of a spear.
Hot. If he fall in, good night, or sink, or swim!
  Send danger from the east unto the west,
  So honour cross it from the north to south,
  And let them grapple: O, the blood more stirs 195
  To rouse a lion than to start a hare!
North. Imagination of some great exploit
  Drives him beyond the bounds of patience.

183. to you] *Qq1–4;* you *Q5;* vnto you *F.* 188. you] *Qq1–4,F;* your *Q5.*
195. O, the] *Qq1–4;* the *Q5,F.*

183–4. *debt . . . deaths*] This word-play (cf. v. i. 126–7) occurs as early as the first Engl. trans. of *De Imit. Christi* (c. 1400, EETS, Extra ser., lxiii, 1893, 88)—"gode menne þat payed her dette of holy deþe".

189–91. *As full . . . spear*] This, like *2H4*, I. i. 170–1 ("You knew he walk'd o'er perils, on an edge, / More likely to fall in than to get o'er"), refers to the "perilous bridge" or "sword-bridge" of medieval romances. In *Mabinogion* ('Kilwch and Olwen', Everyman Lib., 103), "Osla Gyllellvawr . . . bore a short broad dagger" which, laid over a torrent, "would form a bridge sufficient for the armies of . . . Britain". Lancelot, Dr Harold Brooks points out to me, crosses a dangerous bridge in Chrétien de Troyes (*Erec and Enid*, Everyman Library, 308–9)—"The bridge across the cold gleaming stream consisted of a polished gleaming sword; but the sword was stout and stiff, and was as long as two lances. At each end there was a tree-trunk in which the sword was firmly fixed. . . [He] preferred to maim himself rather than fall from the bridge and be plunged in the water . . . [so] he passes over with great pain and agony, being wounded in the hands, knees and feet". See also H. R. Patch, *The Other World*, 1950, for sword-bridge refs. and illustration facing p. 306.

192. *If . . . swim*] "A man falling in such an adventure is doomed, whether he sink or swim: let us salute his passing."

196. *To rouse . . . hare*] "Rouse" and "start" were hunting terms, the latter for the hare, the former for bigger game. Turbervile, *Booke of Hunting*, 1575, writes "We . . . Vnherbor a Harte, we . . . rowse a Bucke . . . ; we . . . starte a Hare; we . . . bolt a Conie . . . ; we . . . vnkenell a Fox" (239); and Lyly, *Midas*, IV. iii. 47–8 (Bond, iii. 148), has "thou shouldest say, start a hare, rowse the deere, spring the partridge". Hotspur's idiom is typically energetic.

Hot. By heaven, methinks it were an easy leap
  To pluck bright honour from the pale-fac'd moon,   200
  Or dive into the bottom of the deep,
  Where fathom-line could never touch the ground,
  And pluck up drowned honour by the locks,
  So he that doth redeem her thence might wear
  Without corrival all her dignities: 205
  But out upon this half-fac'd fellowship!
Wor. He apprehends a world of figures here,
  But not the form of what he should attend:
  Good cousin, give me audience for a while.
Hot. I cry you mercy.
Wor.   Those same noble Scots   210
  That are your prisoners—
Hot.   I'll keep them all;
  By God he shall not have a Scot of them,
  No, if a Scot would save his soul he shall not.
  I'll keep them, by this hand!
Wor.   You start away,
  And lend no ear unto my purposes: 215

199. *Hot.* By] *Q5,F;* By *Qqo–4.*   209. a while] *Qq;* a-while, / And list to me *F.*
210–11. Those . . . Scots / That . . . prisoners—] *As F;* Those . . . Scots that . . .
prisoners *Qq.*   212. God] *Qq;* heauen *F.*

199–205. *By heaven . . . dignities*] Hotspur's extravagance is indicated by an oration in Ercles' vein, popularized by Shakespeare's early contemporaries. Cf. Marlowe, *1 Tamb.*, iv. iv. 17–19— "Ye Furies . . . / Dive to the bottom of Avernus' pool, / And in your hands bring hellish poison up"; Greene, *Frier Bacon*, ll. 1537–8 (*Plays & Poems*, ii. 61)—"thou knowest I haue diued into hell / And sought the darkest pallaces of fiendes"; *Tit.*, iv. iii. 43–4 —"I'll dive into the burning lake below, / And pull her out of Acheron by the heels".

205. *corrival*] partner, associate, as in iv. iv. 31.

206. *half-fac'd fellowship*] skimpy sharing of honours. Hotspur wants them all himself. *OED* defines "half-faced" at *2H4,* iii. ii. 286 ("this same half-faced fellow, Shadow"), as "Of a coin, having a profile stamped upon it; hence of persons, having a thin, pinched face", and, as used here, "imperfect, incomplete, half-and-half".

207. *apprehends*] snatches at.

figures] "*Figure* is here used equivocally. As it is applied to Hotspur's speech it is a rhetorical mode [i.e. it = figures of speech]; as opposed to *form* it means appearance or shape" (Johnson).

213. *if a Scot*] A quibble on "scot", a small payment: cf. v. iv. 113, note. On the phrase "We will not lose a *Scot*" Fuller comments "That is, *we will lose nothing, how inconsiderable soever.* . . . This *Proverb* began in the *English borders*, when . . . they had little *esteem* of, and less *affection* for, a *Scotch-man*" (*Worthies,* 1662, ii. 303).

Those prisoners you shall keep—

Hot.   Nay, I will: that's flat!
He said he would not ransom Mortimer,
Forbade my tongue to speak of Mortimer,
But I will find him when he lies asleep,
And in his ear I'll holla "Mortimer!"   220
Nay, I'll have a starling shall be taught to speak
Nothing but "Mortimer", and give it him
To keep his anger still in motion.

Wor. Hear you, cousin, a word.

Hot. All studies here I solemnly defy,   225
Save how to gall and pinch this Bolingbroke:
And that same sword-and-buckler Prince of Wales,
But that I think his father loves him not,
And would be glad he met with some mischance—
I would have him poison'd with a pot of ale!   230

Wor. Farewell, kinsman: I'll talk to you
When you are better temper'd to attend.

---

220. holla] *F;* hollow *Qqo–2;* hollo *Qq3–4;* hallow *Q5.*   221. Nay, I'll] *QqF;*
Nay, / I'll *Steevens, many later edd.*   230. him poison'd] *Qq* (him poisoned), *Pope;*
poyson'd him *F.*   232. temper'd] *Qqo,1,F;* tempered *Qq2–5.*

220. *And . . . "Mortimer!"*] An echo
of Marlowe, *Ed.2,* II. ii. 125–7—"*Mor.
jun.:* Cousin, and if he will not ransom
him, / I'll thunder such a peal into his
ears / As never subject did unto his
king".

221. *Nay, . . . speak*] Many edd. make
"Nay" a separate line, but this is just
like the colloquially slurred "Nay, I
will" of l. 216 or "Why, it cannot
choose" of l. 273, and suggests Hotspur's velocity; cf. note on l. 114.

starling] Elizabethan texts have
many talking starlings: e.g. Florio's
Montaigne, II. xii (Tudor Trans., ii.
159)—"We teach Blacke-birds, Star-
lins, . . . to chat"; and Drayton, *The
Owle* (l. 634)—"Like a *Starling,* that is
taught to prate".

225. *All . . . defy*] I . . . renounce all
concerns.

227. *sword-and-buckler*] swashbuck-
ling. Cf. *Tarlton's Jests* (W. C. Hazlitt,
Sh. Jest-Books, 1864, ii. 197)—"Not

long since lived a little swaggerer,
called Blacke Davie, who would at
sword and buckler fight with any
gentleman or other for twelve pence".
Hal's tastes, Hotspur implies, are plebeian: when Shakespeare was a boy,
gentlemen began to adopt the rapier
instead of the sword, which was retained by serving-men. Kittredge
cites *Quarrel between Hall and Mallerie,*
c. 1580 (*Miscellanea Antiqua Anglicana,*
1816, 13)—"Mallerie drew his rapier,
and bad his man take him to his sword
and buckler". Cf. also Porter, *Two
Angry Women of Abington,* 1599 (Mal.
Soc., 1912, ll. 729–30)—"Wher's your
blew coate, your sword and buckler,
sir? / Get you such like habite for a
seruingman". Cf. II. iv. 165–6, note.

230. *pot of ale*] i.e. Hal's drinking
habits too are plebeian.

231. *Farewell . . . you*] With a rolled
"r" and a glided "I'll" this is passably
metrical, and certainly expressive.

North. Why, what a wasp-stung and impatient fool
    Art thou to break into this woman's mood,
    Tying thine ear to no tongue but thine own!   235
Hot. Why, look you, I am whipp'd and scourg'd with rods,
    Nettled, and stung with pismires, when I hear
    Of this vile politician Bolingbroke.
    In Richard's time—what do you call the place?
    A plague upon it, it is in Gloucestershire—   240
    'Twas where the mad-cap Duke his uncle kept,
    His uncle York—where I first bow'd my knee
    Unto this king of smiles, this Bolingbroke,
    'Sblood, when you and he came back from Ravenspurgh.
North. At Berkeley castle.   245
Hot. You say true.
    Why, what a candy deal of courtesy
    This fawning greyhound then did proffer me!

---

233. wasp-stung] *Qqo,1;* waspe-tongue *Qq2–5;* Waspe-tongu'd *F.*   236.
whipp'd] *Qq1–5,F* (whipt); whip *Qo.*   239. do you] *Qq;* de'ye *F.*   240. upon
it] *Qq;* vpon't *F.*   242. bow'd] *F;* bowed *Qq.*   244. 'Sblood, when] *Qq;*
When *F;* 'Sblood! / When *Cambr.*   247. candy] *Qqo–2;* candie *Qq3–5;*
caudie *F.*

---

237. *Nettled*] Irritated as if stung with
nettles. Hotspur's criteria of impatience are as vivid as could be desired.
   pismires] ants.
   238. *politician*] A word almost always sinister in Elizabethan usage;
Chapman, *Revenge of Bussy* (*Works*,
1873, ii. 119), has "This was a sleight
well maskt. O what is man, / Vnless he
be a Politician".
   239–40. *do you call . . . upon it*] Cf. collation, note on l. 122, and Intro.,
p. lxx.
   241. *mad-cap Duke*] Edmund Langley, Duke of York, fifth son of Edward
III, is described in Hol. as "a man
rather coueting to liue in pleasure,
than to deale with much businesse"
(ii. 831), and similarly in Hardyng's
Chronicle (1812 ed., 340)—"Edmonde
hyght of Langley of good chere, / Glad
and mery . . . / When all [the] lordes to
councell and parlyament / [Went,] he
wolde to hunte and also to hawekyng,
/ All gentyll disporte [as to a lorde]

appent / He vsed aye". Neither *Woodstock* nor *R2*, however, shows him in the
least "mad-cap", unless Shakespeare
has in mind the sputtering testiness of
his loyalty to Richard (*R2*, II. ii–iii)
and later to Henry (ibid., v. ii–iii).
The trait may be traditional.
   kept] dwelt, lived.
   244. *'Sblood*] To make this a separate
line, as some edd. do, breaks Hotspur's
impetuosity, and I follow Qq's rough
velocity.
   Ravenspurgh] The Yorkshire har-
bour, near Spurn Head, since sub-
merged by the sea, where in 1399
Bolingbroke landed on returning from
exile.
   247. *candy deal*] sugary quantity.
   248. *fawning greyhound*] The association of sticky sweetmeats and fawning treacherous dogs is frequent in
Shakespeare, e.g. *Cæs.*, III. i. 42–3—
"With that which melteth fools; I
mean sweet words, / Low-crooked
curtsies, and base spaniel fawning";

"Look when his infant fortune came to age",
And "gentle Harry Percy", and "kind cousin":   250
O, the devil take such cozeners!—God forgive me!
Good uncle, tell your tale; I have done.

Wor.   Nay, if you have not, to it again,
    We will stay your leisure.

Hot.   I have done, i'faith.

Wor. Then once more to your Scottish prisoners;   255
    Deliver them up without their ransom straight,
    And make the Douglas' son your only mean
    For powers in Scotland, which, for divers reasons
    Which I shall send you written, be assur'd
    Will easily be granted.—[*To North.*] You, my lord,   260
    Your son in Scotland being thus employ'd,
    Shall secretly into the bosom creep
    Of that same noble prelate well-belov'd,
    The Archbishop.

Hot.   Of York, is it not?

---

249. his] *Qq0–2,5,F;* this *Qq3,4.*   252. I] *Qq;* for I *F.*   253. to it] *Qq;* too't *F.*
254. We will] *Qq;* Wee'l *F.*   i'faith] *Qq;* insooth *F.*   260. granted.—[*To
North.*] You, my lord,] *Theobald;* granted you my Lord. *Qqo,1,4;* granted you,
my Lord. *Qq2,3,5,F.*   261. employ'd] *F;* emploied *Qq.*   264. is it] *Qq;* is't *F.*

Ham., III. ii. 65–7—"let the candied
tongue lick absurd pomp / . . . Where
thrift may follow fawning"; and *Ant.,*
IV. x. 33–6—"The hearts / That spaniel'd me at heels . . . / . . . do discandy,
melt their sweets / On blossoming
Caesar". Spurgeon thinks that Shakespeare fastidiously disliked dogs beg-
ging for sweetmeats at table and lick-
ing hands (Spurgeon, 197). There are,
however, many non-Shakespearean
instances of canine fawning (Cooper's
Thesaurus defines "adulatio" as "Properly the fawninge of a dogge; Flat-
terie"), and of sugary or honeyed
obsequiousness. The image-cluster
may be Shakespearean, but its parts
are popular tags; cf. Tilley, "Dog"
(D459), "Spaniel" (S704), and
"Whore" (W327), and J. L. Jackson,
'Sh.'s Dog-and-Sugar Imagery' (*Sh.
Q.,* I. iv, 1950, 260–3).
    249. "*Look when* . . ."] Idioms like

"Look how", "Look what", "Look
when" are misinterpreted if commas
are inserted after "Look". They mean
"However", "Whatever", "Whenever"; e.g. *Ven.,* 289—"Look when a
painter would surpass the life"; and
R3, I. iii. 290—"Look when he fawns
he bites" (Mark Eccles, 'Sh.'s Use of
"Look how" and similar Idioms',
JEGP, 1943, 386 ff.).
    251. *cozeners*] cheats (with, of course,
the play on "cousin").
    257. *the Douglas' son*] The definite
article designates the head of distinguished Scottish families. For Shakespeare's error in Mordake's parentage
see I. i. 71–2, note.
    262. *into . . . creep*] wind yourself into
the confidence. Proverbial; Tilley,
B546—"He will creep into your
bosom". Worcester has a sly idiom.
    264.] A crowded line which sug-
gests the urgent exchanges. Cf. col-

Wor.   True, who bears hard
  His brother's death at Bristow, the Lord Scroop.   265
  I speak not this in estimation,
  As what I think might be, but what I know
  Is ruminated, plotted, and set down,
  And only stays but to behold the face
  Of that occasion that shall bring it on.   270
Hot. I smell it. Upon my life it will do well!
North. Before the game is afoot thou still let'st slip.
Hot. Why, it cannot choose but be a noble plot;
  And then the power of Scotland, and of York,
  To join with Mortimer, ha?
Wor.   And so they shall.   275
Hot. In faith it is exceedingly well aim'd.
Wor. And 'tis no little reason bids us speed,
  To save our heads by raising of a head;
  For, bear ourselves as even as we can,
  The King will always think him in our debt,   280
  And think we think ourselves unsatisfy'd,
  Till he hath found a time to pay us home:
  And see already how he doth begin
  To make us strangers to his looks of love.
Hot. He does, he does, we'll be reveng'd on him.   285
Wor. Cousin, farewell. No further go in this
  Than I by letters shall direct your course.
  When time is ripe, which will be suddenly,
  I'll steal to Glendower, and Lord Mortimer,
  Where you, and Douglas, and our powers at once,   290
  As I will fashion it, shall happily meet,

---

271. it. Upon] *Qq;* it: / V pon *F.* well] *Qq;* wond'rous well *F.* 272. game is]
Qqo–4; game's *Q5,F.* 281. unsatisfy'd] *Rowe;* vnsatisfied *QqF.* 287. course.]
Johnson; course *QqF.* 288. suddenly,] *Qqo,1;* suddenly: *Qq2–5,F (subst.).* 289.
Lord] *Qqo,1* (Lo:), *Rowe;* loe, *Qq2–5,F.* 290. powers] *Qqo,2–5;* powres *Q1,F.*

---

lation, note on l. 122, and Intro., p.
lxx.

 264–5. *who . . . Scroop*] Shakespeare
follows Hol. in making Scrope the
Archbishop's brother; he was in fact
his cousin. His execution in 1399 at
Bristol is recorded in *R2,* III. ii. 142.
"Bears hard" = "takes ill".

 266. *estimation*] conjecture.

 272. *game is*] Cf. collation, note on
l. 122, and Intro., p. lxix.

 thou . . . slip] you're always letting
the hounds loose.

 278. *a head*] a force of arms.

 282. *pay us home*] i.e. "pay us out"—
with the implication of "give us a
home thrust".

 288. *suddenly*] at once, immediately.

　　To bear our fortunes in our own strong arms,
　　Which now we hold at much uncertainty.
North. Farewell, good brother; we shall thrive, I trust.
Hot. Uncle, adieu: O, let the hours be short,　　　295
　　Till fields, and blows, and groans applaud our sport!

　　　　　　　　　　　　　　　　　　　　　Exeunt.

292. bear our] *Qq1–5,F;* bear out *Qo.*　　296. S.D.] *Qq; exit / F.*

ACT II

SCENE I.—[*Rochester. An Inn Yard.*]

Enter a Carrier with a lantern in his hand.

First Car. Heigh-ho! An it be not four by the day I'll be
hanged; Charles' wain is over the new chimney, and
yet our horse not packed. What, ostler!

Ost. [*Within*] Anon, anon.

First Car. I prithee, Tom, beat Cut's saddle, put a few   5
flocks in the point; poor jade is wrung in the withers
out of all cess.

Enter another Carrier.

Sec. Car. Peas and beans are as dank here as a dog, and
that is the next way to give poor jades the bots: this

ACT II

Scene 1

Act II Scene I.] *F* (*Actus Secundus. Scena Prima.*); *not in Qq.*   Location.] *Capell.*
1. An it] *Qq;* an't *F.*   4. S.D.] *Theobald; not in QqF.*   6. poor] *Qq;* the
poore *F.*   9. that] *Qq;* this *F.*

1. *by the day*] in the morning.

2. *Charles' wain*] the Plough, Great
Bear.

3. *horse*] horses. Often plural in
Elizabethan usage; cf. the unchanged
plural "hors" in O.E.

5. *beat Cut's saddle*] i.e. in order
to soften it. "Cut" = a labouring
horse (*OED*), either a curtal or
gelding. Minsheu defines it as "a
Curtall horse without a taile . . . court
de queue".

5–6. *put . . . point*] stuff some wool
into the pommel.

6. *poor jade is*] The terse idiom, as in
l. 11, implies rusticity.

6–7. *wrung . . . cess*] sadly galled
on the ridge between the shoulder-
blades; "out of cess" = excessively.

8. *dank as a dog*] This is as meaning-
less as most alliterative similes. Dogs
seem liable to these odious comparisons, so suggested emendations like
"bog", "dock", "fog" are unnecessary.
John Taylor, *A Dogge of Warre* (*Works
. . . from Folio Ed. of 1630*, Spenser Soc.,
pt. II, 1868, 232), asserts that "I haue
heard a Man say, I am as hot as a
Dogge, or, as colde as a Dogge, I
sweat like a Dogge, (when indeed a
Dog neuer sweates,) as drunke as a
Dogge, hee swore like a Dogge". One
could also be as dry, greedy, idle, low,
melancholy, sick, and weary as a dog;
Tilley, D433–41.

9. *next way*] nearest, quickest way.

bots] "little short wormes [in horses'
intestines] with great red heads, and

house is turned upside down since Robin Ostler died.　10

First Car. Poor fellow never joyed since the price of oats
　　rose, it was the death of him.

Sec. Car. I think this be the most villainous house in all
　　London road for fleas, I am stung like a tench.

First Car. Like a tench! By the mass, there is ne'er a king　15
　　christen could be better bit than I have been since
　　the first cock.

Sec. Car. Why, they will allow us ne'er a jordan, and then
　　we leak in your chimney, and your chamber-lye
　　breeds fleas like a loach.　　20

First Car. What, ostler! Come away, and be hanged,
　　come away!

Sec. Car. I have a gammon of bacon, and two razes of

10. Ostler] *Qq;* the Ostler *F.*　　13. be] *Qqo–4;* to be *Q5;* is *F.*　　15. By the
mass] *Qq; not in F.*　　16. christen] *Qq;* in Christendome, *F.*　　18. they]
Qqo–4; you *Q5,F.*

long small white Tailes . . . ingendred
by foule and naughty feeding" (Gervase Markham, *Maister-Peece of Farri-
ery,* 1615, ch. 74). They are in fact
hatched from eggs laid on leaves which
the horse swallows.

11–12. *never . . . rose*] Oats averaged
about 6s. a quarter in 1593, 11s. in
1594, 12s. in 1595, and 18s. in 1596,
dropping to about 14s. in 1597 and
10s. in 1598 (J. E. T. Rogers, *Hist. of
Agric. & Prices,* 1887, v. 268). The
Queen's *Proclamation for the Dearth of
Corne* (31 July 1596) forbids extortion-
ate prices (*Bibl. Lindesiana,* vol. v, *Cat.
of Tudor . . . Proclamations,* ed. R.
Steele, 1910, i, No. 884).

14. *stung like a tench*] The tench's
spotted markings may have suggested
vermin bites. Or cf. l. 20, note.

15. *By the mass*] Elyot, in *The
Governour,* 1531, III. vii, says that "the
masse . . . is made by custome so simple
an othe, that it is nowe used amonge
husbande men and artificers": Earle
in 1628 calls it "an olde out-of-date
innocent othe" (*Microcosmographie,*
'A Blunt Man'). Nevertheless F expur-
gates it.

15–16. *king christen*] "a Christian

king. The Carrier implies that kings
have the best of everything" (Kittredge).

17. *first cock*] "The times of cock-
crow were conventionally fixed as follows: first cock, midnight; second
cock, 3 a.m. . . .; third cock, an hour
before day" (Kittredge).

18–19. *jordan . . . chimney*] "jordan"
= chamberpot; "chimney" = fire-
place. Andrew Boorde condemns this
insanitary custom—"Be ware of emp-
tying of pysse-pottes, and pyssing in
chymnes, so that all euyll and con-
tagyous ayres may be expelled"
(*Dyetary of Helth,* 1542, EETS, Extra
ser., x, 1870, 236–7).

19. *chamber-lye*] urine.

20. *loach*] Cf. l. 14, note. Pliny
asserts that "some fishes there be,
which of themselves are given to breed
fleas and lice" (*Nat. Hist.,* trans. Holland, 1601, IX. xlvii).

21. *Come away*] Come here, come
along.

23–4. *razes of ginger*] An echo of the
robbed carrier's complaint in *F.V.*—
"hee hath . . . taken the great rase of
Ginger, that bouncing Besse . . . should
haue had" (iv. 28–31). "Raze" =

ginger, to be delivered as far as Charing Cross.

First Car. God's body! The turkeys in my pannier are   25
quite starved. What, ostler! A plague on thee, hast
thou never an eye in thy head? canst not hear? And
'twere not as good deed as drink to break the pate on
thee, I am a very villain. Come, and be hanged!
Hast no faith in thee?   30

Enter GADSHILL.

Gads. Good morrow, carriers, what's o'clock?
[*First*] *Car.* I think it be two o'clock.
Gads. I prithee lend me thy lantern, to see my gelding in
the stable.
First Car. Nay, by God, soft! I know a trick worth two of   35
that, i'faith.
Gads. I pray thee lend me thine.
Sec. Car. Ay, when? Canst tell? Lend me thy lantern,
quoth he! Marry I'll see thee hanged first.
Gads. Sirrah carrier, what time do you mean to come to   40
London?
Sec. Car. Time enough to go to bed with a candle, I war-
rant thee; come, neighbour Mugs, we'll call up the
gentlemen, they will along with company, for they
have great charge.   *Exeunt* [*Carriers*].   45

25. God's body] *Qq; not in F.*   28. deed] *Qqo–3;* a deed *Qq4,5,F.*   on]
Qqo–4; of *Q5,F.*   31, 32. o'] *QqF* (a), *Theobald.*   32. First Car.] *Hanmer*
(*1 Car.*); *Car. | QqF.*   35. by God, soft] *Qq;* soft I pray ye *F.*   36. i'faith]
Qq; not in F.   37. pray thee] *Qqo–2;* prethee *Qq3–5,F.*   38. Ay, when?]
Qqo,1 (I when), *Qq2–5,F* (I, when,) *Pope.*   39. quoth he] *Qq;* quoth-a *F.*
45. S.D. *Carriers*] *Rowe; not in QqF.*

"obs. form of *race*, i.e. root (of ginger);
OF. *rais, raiz,* Lat. *radicem*" (*OED,*
"Race. *sb.* 6"). Ginger, used medi-
cinally and as a spice in food or drink,
was imported in root form.

24. *as far as Charing Cross*] Then a
separate village, and on the far side of
London from Rochester.

28. *as good . . . drink*] A popular tag;
cf. II. ii. 22.

35–6. *I know . . . that*] "I'm not such a
fool": a popular tag (Tilley, T518).

38. *Ay . . . tell*] A retort to an incon-

venient request. Tilley, T88, cites
Marlowe, *Faustus,* III. iiiB. 27—
"*Vint.* Come, give it me again. *Robin.*
Ay, much; when? can you tell?"—
and other instances.

39. *quoth he*] F's "quoth-a" is more
colloquial; cf. I. iii. 122, note, and
Intro., p. lxx.

42. *Time . . . candle*] Evasive rustic
wit.

45. *great charge*] much to look after
(whether baggage, business, or valu-
ables).

Gads. What ho! Chamberlain!

Enter Chamberlain.

Cham. "At hand, quoth pick-purse."

Gads. That's even as fair as "At hand, quoth the cham-
    berlain": for thou variest no more from picking of
    purses than giving direction doth from labouring;   50
    thou layest the plot how.

Cham. Good morrow, master Gadshill. It holds current
    that I told you yesternight: there's a franklin in the
    Wild of Kent hath brought three hundred marks
    with him in gold, I heard him tell it to one of his   55
    company last night at supper, a kind of auditor,
    one that hath abundance of charge too, God knows
    what; they are up already, and call for eggs and
    butter—they will away presently.

46. S.D.] *Kittredge; QqF (after line 45).*

46. S.D.] Capell and some edd. put
this entry after l. 51 because of the
delayed answer (l. 52), and prefix
"[*Within*]" to l. 47. But an exactly
similar entry, satirical comment, and
delayed greeting occur at I. ii. 102-9.

47. *At hand, quoth pick-purse*] A
popular tag—"Ready, sir, as the pick-
purse said": cf. Cotgrave—"A la
main. *Nimbly, readily, actiuely, at hand
(quoth pick-purse)*"; and *Apius and Vir-
ginia* (Mal. Soc., 1911, l. 531)—"*Haphazard:* At hand (quoth picke purse)
here redy am I".

49-51. *thou . . . how*] Chamberlains,
like other inn-servants, had a poor
reputation. "Manie an honest man",
says Harrison's *Description of Engl.*
(Hol., *Chron.*, i. 414-15), "is spoiled of
his goods as he trauelleth to and fro
. . . for when he commeth into the inne
. . . the chamberlaine . . . giueth warning to such od ghests as hant the house
and are of his confederacie, to the
vtter vndoing of manie an honest yeoman as he iournieth by the waie."

50. *giving direction*] (*a*) overseeing;
(*b*) thieves' cant for planning a
"match": cf. Jonson, *E.M.O.O.H.H.*,

IV. vi. 31-4 (H. & S., iii. 547)—"sig-
nior Clog, that was hang'd for the robbery . . . gaue all the directions for the
action".

51. *layest the plot*] "Equivocal: plot=
(*a*) overseer's plan for workmen; (*b*)
highwayman's plot" (Wilson, N.C.S.).

53. *franklin*] freeholder. Franklins
were rich yeomen; John Russell's
Boke of Nurture, c. 1440 (EETS, Orig.
ser., xxxii, 1894, 73), ranks "Mar-
chaundes & Franklonz, worshipfulle
& honorable" as "peregalle to a
squyere of honoure", and to Serjeants
of Law, ex-Mayors of London, Masters of Chancery, and Apprentices of
Law.

54. *Wild*] Weald.

three hundred marks] £200. The mark
was the value of 13s. 4d., not a coin.

56. *auditor*] A royal officer who examined the accounts of receivers and
other "under Officers Accomptable"
(Minsheu, "Auditor"). This may be
in apposition to "franklin" or to "one
of his company"; probably the latter,
to give this confidant some reality.

58-9. *eggs and butter*] Cf. I. ii. 21, note.

59. *presently*] at once.

Gads. Sirrah, if they meet not with Saint Nicholas' clerks,   60
I'll give thee this neck.

Cham. No, I'll none of it, I pray thee keep that for the
hangman, for I know thou worshippest Saint Nicholas, as truly as a man of falsehood may.

Gads. What talkest thou to me of the hangman? If I hang,   65
I'll make a fat pair of gallows: for if I hang, old Sir
John hangs with me, and thou knowest he is no
starveling. Tut, there are other Troyans that thou
dream'st not of, the which for sport sake are content
to do the profession some grace, that would (if mat-   70
ters should be looked into) for their own credit sake
make all whole. I am joined with no foot-landrakers,
no long-staff sixpenny strikers, none of these mad

---

62. pray thee] *Qq;* prythee *F.*   67. knowest] *Qqo–3;* knowst *Q4,F;* knowes *Q5.*
he is] *Qq;* hee's *F.*   68. Troyans] *Qo;* Troians *Qq1–5,F.*   72. foot-landrakers]
Q4; footland rakers *Qqo–3 (subst.);* foot-land rakers *Q5;* Foot-land-Rakers *F.*

---

60. *Saint . . . clerks*] Like "Saint
Nicholas' clergymen" (*OED*, "clergymen", 2) a euphemism for highway
robbers. *Martin's Months Minde* (by
Nashe?; Grosart, i. 151) has "like the
Saint Nicholas Clarkes on Salsburie
plaine [he] stept out before vs in the
high waie, and bidde vs stand"; and
Belman of London (Dekker; Grosart,
iii. 151) says "The theefe that commits the *Robbery,* and is cheife clerke to
Saint *Nicholas,* is called the *High Law-
ver".* St Nicholas was patron-saint of
children, scholars, sailors, shepherds,
and travellers. "From wandering
scholars the saint's protection seems
rapidly to have been extended to
other vagabonds . . . and by the 16th c.
the same phrase has a less respectable
connotation for highwaymen" (O. E.
Albrecht, *Four Latin Plays of St Nicholas,*
1935, 34). The saint's attributes are
three balls or purses of gold, deriving
either from money he threw in a poor
man's window, or from treasure he
miraculously made robbers restore
(cf. *Ludus super Iconia S. Nicolai,* Pollard,
Engl. Miracle Plays). Perhaps, as Hemingway (New Var.) and Wilson

(N.C.S.) suggest, the balls or purses
made him look like the patron of
robbers. In the popular mind there
may have been a punning association
between Nicholas and necklace (=
noose: G. S. Haight, *TLS,* 16 Sept.
1944, 451).
    64. *truly . . . falsehood*] The "true/
false" antithesis in the sense "honest/
dishonest" is frequent: cf. ll. 91–2, and
II. ii. 23.
    67. *thou . . . he is*] Cf. I. iii. 122, note.
    68. *Troyans*] Troyans or Trojans,
like Corinthians and Ephesians, were
boon companions. Kemp, *Nine Daies
Wonder,* 1600 (Camden Soc., 1840, 13),
has "he was a kinde good fellow, a true
Troyan".
    69, 71. *sport sake, credit sake*] Cf. I. ii.
150, note.
    72. *foot-landrakers*] vagabond foot-
pads. To rake is to roam about.
    73. *long-staff . . . strikers*] Footpads,
says Bailey, are "a Crew of Villains
. . . using long Poles or Staves, with an
Iron Hook at the End, with which
they either pull Gentlemen from their
Horses, or knock them down". "Sixpenny" = paltry; cf. "euerie six

mustachio purple-hued maltworms, but with nobility and tranquillity, burgomasters and great onyers,   75
such as can hold in, such as will strike sooner than

74. mustachio purple-hued] *Qq* (*subst.*)*; Mustachio-purple-hu'd- F.*   75.
onyers] *Wilson* (*N.C.S.*), *conj. Malone; Oneyres Qqo,1; Oneyers Qq2–5,F;
Oneraires conj. Pope 1; One-eyers conj. Pope 2; Moneyers Theobald, conj. Hardinge;
owners Hanmer; mynheers Capell; one-yers Johnson; ones; —yes Collier MS,
Collier 2.*   76. in,] *F; in Qq.*

pennie slaue" (Nashe, *Anat. of Absurditie*; McKerrow, i. 7). "To strike" is
thieves' cant for purse-cutting or
pocket-picking; the act of "figging"
(pocket-picking), says Greene, is
known as "striking" (*Notable Discov. of
Coosnage*, 1591; Grosart, x. 38).

73–4. *mad . . . maltworms*] roaring be-
whiskered purple-faced soakers. Fierce
moustaches supposedly betokened
valour. "Maltworm" = toper; *A
Wonderfull . . . Prognostication* (by
Nashe?; McKerrow, iii. 383) foretells
"yᵉ dearth that by their deuout drinking is like to ensue of Barly, if violent
death take not away such co[n]suming
mault worms".

75. *tranquillity*] Many needless emendations have been proposed. The
word is in the vein of travesty which
gives us "I did impeticos thy gratillity"
(*Tw. N.*, II. iii. 28). It contrasts the
serene "nobility" with the landrakers
and strikers.

onyers] QqF's "Oneyres" or "One-
yers" has been much emended (cf. collation). Observing that the verb "to
ony" was still used in the Exchequer of
his day, from *o.ni.*, a fiscal techni-
cality, Malone suggested "onyers" as a
possibility, the sense being "sheriffs
accountable to the King for moneys
due". *OED* gives "O.Ni, oni. *Obs.* An
abbreviation of the Latin words
*oneratur, nisi habeat sufficientem exonera-
tionem*, 'he is charged, or legally responsible, unless he have a sufficient
discharge', with which the account of
a sheriff with the King was formerly
marked in the Exchequer: sometimes
used subst. as a name for this phrase or
the fact itself." *OED* also quotes Coke
On Littleton, iv. 16 (1628)—"The

course of the Eschequer is, that as soon
as a Sheriffe or Escheator enter into
his account for issues, amerciaments,
and mean profits, to mark upon his
head O.Ni. which is as much as to say
[Latin phrase as above], and presently he is become the King's deb-
tor"; and also "Oni, o'ni *v. trans.*
to mark with *O.Ni*". John Cowell, *The
Interpreter*, repeats Coke almost verbatim (1684 edn, Aaa2ʳ; the term does
not occur in the editions of 1607,
1637). The only doubt is whether
Shakespeare would at this plebeian
moment launch an Exchequer tech-
nicality at his audience, though law-
terms were certainly more familiar to
the litigious Elizabethans. Another
possibility is "oneyers"—"as he terms
them in merriment by a cant termina-
tion, great one-yers, as we say pri-
vateer, auctioneer, etc." (Johnson);
Lettsom cited Dickens in corrobora-
tion—"'Miss Sally's such a one-er for
that, she is.' 'Such a what?' said Dick.
'Such a one-er,' returned the Mar-
chioness' (*Old Cur. Shop*, ch. lviii). The
equally odd, and oddly similar, title
"An-heires" occurs in *Wiv.*, II. i. 227,
from an equally jocular speaker the
Host, who likes high-flown appella-
tions (e.g. "Cavaliero", "Bully-
Rook"). What is wanted in both
places is something facetiously grandiloquent, recognizable as a title yet
far-fetched; "Ameires" ("Amirs") has
been suggested for *Wiv.* and is possible
here.

76. *hold in*] A quibble: (*a*) keep
counsel; (*b*) stick together; (*c*) stick
to the quarry (a hunting term: cf.
Madden, 53).

76–8. *strike . . . pray*] assault sooner

speak, and speak sooner than drink, and drink
sooner than pray—and yet, 'zounds, I lie, for they
pray continually to their saint the commonwealth,
or rather not pray to her, but prey on her, for they   80
ride up and down on her, and make her their boots.

Cham. What, the commonwealth their boots? Will she
hold out water in foul way?

Gads. She will, she will, justice hath liquored her: we
steal as in a castle, cock-sure: we have the receipt of   85
fern-seed, we walk invisible.

Cham. Nay, by my faith, I think you are more beholding
to the night than to fern-seed for your walking invisible.

Gads. Give me thy hand, thou shalt have a share in our   90
purchase, as I am a true man.

Cham. Nay, rather let me have it, as you are a false thief.

Gads. Go to, *homo* is a common name to all men: bid the

---

78. 'zounds] *Qq; not in F.*   79. to] *Qq;* vnto *F.*   80. pray] *Qq;* to pray *F.*
prey] *Q5,F;* pray *Qqo–4.*   87. by my faith] *Qq; not in F.*   think] *Qq;* thinke
rather, *F.*   88. fern-seed] *Qq;* the Fernseed *F.*   90–1.] *As Qq;* Give ... hand./
Thou ... purpose, / As ... man *F (verse).*   91. purchase] *Qq;* purpose *F.*

---

than speak to a man (with a pun on
"strike" as meaning rob; cf. l. 73,
note); speak to him (e.g. swearing
"Lay by", as at I. ii. 36) even sooner
than drink; and certainly drink sooner
than pray. To speak to or with a victim was thieves' cant for holding him
up; cf. *OED,* "Speak, *v.* 13h, 16†d".
Bailey gives "To SPEAK *with,* to steal".
"Talk with" seems similarly used
in *F.V.* (ii. 13–16)—cf. App. III, p.
189.

81. *boots*] spoils.

83. *hold ... way*] Literally, "let us
go dryshod in muddy roads"; figu-
ratively, "protect you in difficulty".

84. *justice ... her*] Those who control
the laws have (*a*) "greased" her (with
ref. to "boots" and perhaps bribery),
and (*b*) made her drunk.

85. *in a castle*] Proverbial; "in complete security". Kittredge suggests an
"Oldcastle" echo.

85–6. *receipt of fern-seed*] = "the

fern-seed formula". Fern-seed was
thought to be visible only on St John's
(Midsummer) Eve (23 June) and, if
gathered then, to render the wearer
invisible. Cf. Jonson, *New Inn,* I. vi. 16–
18 (H. & S., vi. 418)—"*Fer*[*ret*]. I had /
No med'cine, Sir, to goe inuisible: /
No Ferne-seed in my pocket".

91. *purchase*] Euphemistic for "plun-
der". Cf. *H5,* III. ii. 45–6—"They will
steal any thing and call it purchase".

91–2. *true man ... false thief*] Cf. l. 64,
note.

93. homo ... men] A frequently-
cited tag from Lily and Colet's *Shorte
Introduction of Grammar* (1549)—"a
Noune Substantive either is Proper
... Or else is common, as, Homo is a
Name common to all men". Nashe repeats it, as Wilson (N.C.S.) points out,
in *Pierce Penilesse* (McKerrow, i. 187–
8). Gadshill has promised as a "true
man"; the chamberlain bids him promise as a "false thief"; to which he

ostler bring my gelding out of the stable. Farewell,
you muddy knave.   [*Exeunt.*]   95

SCENE II.—[*Gad's Hill. The Highway.*]

Enter PRINCE, POINS, *and* PETO.

Poins. Come, shelter, shelter! I have removed Falstaff's
horse, and he frets like a gummed velvet.
Prince. Stand close!   [*They retire.*]

Enter FALSTAFF.

Fal. Poins! Poins, and be hanged! Poins!
Prince. [*Coming forward*] Peace, ye fat-kidneyed rascal,   5
what a brawling dost thou keep!

94. my] *Qq;* the *F.*   95. you] *Qqo,1;* ye *Qq2–5,F.*   S.D.] *F; not in Qq.*

Scene II

SCENE II.] *F (Scæna Secunda.); not in Qq.*   Location.] Capell *(Gad's-Hill. The Road
down it.).*   S.D.] *F; Enter Prince, Poines, and Peto, &c. | Qq.*   3. S.D.] *Dyce;
not in QqF.*   5. S.D.] *Dyce; not in QqF.*

replies that he is a (true) man for *homo*
is common to all men, including
(false) thieves.

95. *muddy*] dull-witted.

Scene II

S.D.] Some edd. reserve this entry
merely for the Prince and Poins, and
bring Peto and Bardolph in with
Gadshill; in QqF it is Bardolph who at
l. 50 is applied to for news and at l. 51
gives it. Other edd. bring on all four
here and give Gadshill a solo entry at
l. 46 (as in QqF), making him the one
applied to for news, and furnishing it
(cf. collation, ll. 46, 49–50, 51). On the
face of it one would expect Gadshill to
be separate and to act as informant,
and the other four to keep together.
But Qo's entry does not specifically
bring Bardolph on here (the "&c"
may indicate Fal.), while Qo does
specifically name Peto here and make

Bardolph the informant later (though
not showing any indication of entry).
Sisson argues that were a speech-
prefix for Bardolph, not a vocative,
intended in l. 50, Shakespeare would
have written not Bardoll, but Bar., and
that "the Quarto text and punctuation
give no support to emendation". The
arrangement adopted here and at
ll. 47–51 involves the least amendment
of Qo.

2. *frets . . . velvet*] chafes; a quibble on
human irritation and the "fretting" or
fraying of velvet treated with gum to
give a showy gloss. Marston, *Malcon-
tent*, I. ii. 13–14 *(Plays,* ed. H. H. Wood,
1934, i. 145), has "Ile come among
you . . . as Gum into Taffata, to fret, to
fret". Tilley, T8, gives other examples.
In Eliot's *Ortho-epia Gallica*, ii. 69, a
customer for velvet asks "Is it not
gummed?" and the salesman replies
"No I assure you of my faith".

Fal. Where's Poins, Hal?

Prince. He is walked up to the top of the hill; I'll go seek
    him.   [*Retires.*]

Fal. I am accursed to rob in that thief's company; the   10
rascal hath removed my horse and tied him I know
not where. If I travel but four foot by the squier further afoot, I shall break my wind. Well, I doubt not
but to die a fair death for all this, if I scape hanging
for killing that rogue. I have forsworn his company   15
hourly any time this two and twenty years, and yet
I am bewitched with the rogue's company. If the
rascal have not given me medicines to make me love
him, I'll be hanged. It could not be else, I have
drunk medicines. Poins! Hal! A plague upon you   20
both! Bardolph! Peto! I'll starve ere I'll rob a foot
further—and 'twere not as good a deed as drink to
turn true man, and to leave these rogues, I am the
veriest varlet that ever chewed with a tooth: eight
yards of uneven ground is threescore and ten miles   25
afoot with me, and the stony-hearted villains know
it well enough. A plague upon it when thieves can-

---

7. Where's] *Qqo,1;* What *Qq2–5,F.*   9. S.D.] *Dyce; not in QqF.*   10. thief's]
Qq; Theefe *F.*   the] *Qq;* that *F.*   12. squier] *QqF* (squire), *Cambr.*   16. two
and twenty] *Qqo–4* (xxii.), *Q5* (22.), *F.*   years] *Qqo,1* (yeares); yeare *Qq2–5,F*
(*subst.*).   21. Bardolph] *F;* Bardol *Qo;* Bardoll *Qq1–5.*   I'll rob] *Qq;*
I rob *F.*   22. as drink] *Qq;* as to drinke *F.*   27. upon it] *Qq;* vpon't *F.*

10–11. *the rascal . . . horse*] A possible
echo of Nashe, 'The complaint of
Gluttonie' (*Pierce Penilesse*; McKerrow, i. 201)—"The *Romane* Censors, if
they lighted vpon a fat corpulent man,
they straight tooke away his horsse,
and constrained him to goe a foote:
positiuely concluding his carkasse was
so puft vp with gluttonie or idlenesse.
If we had such horse-takers amongst
vs, and that surfit-swolne Churles, who
now ride on their foot-cloathes, might
be constrained to carrie their flesh
budgets from place to place on foote,
the price of veluet and cloath would
fall with their belies . . . *Plenus venter nil
agit libenter*".

  12. *squier*] measure; an obs. form of
square, a measuring instrument. Cf.

Spenser, *F.Q.*, II. i. 58—"Temper-
ance . . . with golden squire / Betwixt them both can measure out a
meane".

  18. *medicines*] potions.

  21. *Bardolph*] On the spellings "Bar-
dol(l)"/ "Bardolfe" / "Bardolph" see
Intro., p. lxxvii.

  starve] die—the original meaning;
cf. O.E. "steorfan", to die.

  27–8. *thieves . . . another*] Besides
glancing paradoxically at "true" (=
honest; cf. II. i. 64, note), "he gives the
principle of honour among thieves a
comic application, as if honour were
more to be expected of thieves than
of honest men" (Kittredge). Tilley,
T121a, quotes "Thieves are never
rogues among themselves".

not be true one to another! (*They whistle.*) Whew! A
plague upon you all, give me my horse, you rogues,
give me my horse and be hanged!   30

Prince. [*Coming forward*] Peace, ye fat guts, lie down, lay
thine ear close to the ground, and list if thou canst
hear the tread of travellers.

Fal. Have you any levers to lift me up again, being down?
'Sblood, I'll not bear my own flesh so far afoot again 35
for all the coin in thy father's exchequer. What a
plague mean ye to colt me thus?

Prince. Thou liest, thou art not colted, thou art uncolted.

Fal. I prithee good Prince Hal, help me to my horse,
good king's son.   40

Prince. Out, ye rogue, shall I be your ostler?

Fal. Hang thyself in thine own heir-apparent garters!
If I be ta'en, I'll peach for this: and I have not ballads made on you all, and sung to filthy tunes, let a

---

29. upon] *Qq*; light vpon *F*.   give me] *Qq*; Giue *F*.   31. S.D.] *Dyce, not in*
QqF.   32. canst] *Qqo,1*; can *Qq2–5,F*.   35. 'Sblood] *Qq; not in F*.   my]
Qo; mine *Qq1–5,F*.   41. ye] *Qqo,1*; you *Qq2–5,F*.   42. Hang] *Qqo–2*; Go
hang *Qq3–5,F*.   44. on you] *Qqo–2*; on *Qq3–5,F*.

---

37. *colt*] trick.

42. *Hang . . . garters*] "Alluding to the
Order of the Garter, in which he was
enrolled as heir-apparent" (Johnson),
and also to the popular tag "He may
hang himself in his own garters"
(Tilley, G42). Q3 et seq. read "Go
hang", but the phrase existed without
"go" as well as with it; see *Tw. N.*, I.
iii. 12—"And [these boots] be not
[good enough to drink in], let them
hang themselves in their own straps",
and Tourneur, *Ath. Trag.*, II. v (Mer-
maid edn, 285), "I bid him hang himselfe in his owne garters".

43. *peach*] turn king's evidence, lay
information.

43–4. *ballads . . . tunes*] Wilson
(N.C.S.) points out a Nashe parallel
(*Christes Teares*, 1593; McKerrow, ii.
103)—"Ignominious Ballads made of
you, which euery Boy woulde chaunt
vnder your Nose". One could hire
ballad-writers to lampoon one's enemies; cf. *Woodstock*, ll. 1659–60—

"I'll have these verses sung to their
faces by one of my schoolboys, wherein
I'll tickle them all i' faith"; and Jonson, *Bart. Fair*, II. ii. 15–17 (H. & S.,
vi. 41)—"and thou wrong'st me, I'll
finde a friend shall right me, and make
a ballad of thee". Topical ballads were
sold in the streets by ballad-singers,
and stuck upon tavern walls: Fal. proposes to have his capture of Colevile
"in a particular ballad" (*2H4*, IV. iii.
52). "Ten-groat rhymers", Massinger
calls their writers (*Bondman*, v. iii. 216),
and Hal when King disparages
flowery speeches with "A rhyme is but
a ballad" (*H5*, v. ii. 166). Ballads had
their appropriate tunes; thus *Fortune
my Foe* was the Hanging Tune, for
ballads about executions; cf. Samuel
Rowley, *Noble Souldier*, III. ii (Bullen,
Old Plays, i. 293)—"I shall have
scurvy ballads made of me / Sung to
the Hanging Tune". See H. E. Rollins,
A Pepysian Garland (1922) and *The Pack
of Autolycus* (1927), and C. H. Firth,

cup of sack be my poison—when a jest is so forward, 45
and afoot too! I hate it.

Enter GADSHILL [*and* BARDOLPH].

Gads. Stand!

Fal. So I do, against my will.

Poins. O, 'tis our setter, I know his voice. [*Coming forward
with* PETO] Bardolph, what news? 50

Bard. Case ye, case ye, on with your vizards, there's
money of the King's coming down the hill, 'tis going
to the King's exchequer.

Fal. You lie, ye rogue, 'tis going to the King's tavern.

Gads. There's enough to make us all. 55

Fal. To be hanged.

Prince. Sirs, you four shall front them in the narrow lane:
Ned Poins and I will walk lower—if they scape from
your encounter, then they light on us.

Peto. How many be there of them? 60

Gads. Some eight or ten.

Fal. 'Zounds, will they not rob us?

Prince. What, a coward, Sir John Paunch?

Fal. Indeed, I am not John of Gaunt your grandfather,
but yet no coward, Hal. 65

Prince. Well, we leave that to the proof.

Poins. Sirrah Jack, thy horse stands behind the hedge;

---

45. when a] *Qqo,1,F;* when *Qq2–5.*   46. S.D. *and Bardolph] Rowe; not in QqF.*
49–50. voice. Bardolph, what] *Qo* (voice. Bardoll, what), *Q1* (voice, Bardoll,
what), *Q2* (voyce, Bardoll, what), *Qq3–5* (voyce: *Bardol* what [*subst.*]), *F* (voyce /
Bardolfe, what); voice. / *Bard.* What *Var. 1773, many edd.,* conj. *Johnson.*   S.D.]
Dyce (Coming forward with Bardolph and Peto)*; not in QqF.*   51. *Bard.*] *QqF; Gads.
Johnson, many edd.*   54. ye] *Qqo–2;* you *Qq3–5,F.*   57. Sirs, you] *Qqo–2;*
You *Qq3–5,F.*   58. Poins] *Qq; not in F.*   60. How many be there] *Qqo,1;*
How many be they *Q2;* But how many be they *Qq3–5;* But how many be *F.*
62. 'Zounds] *Qq; not in F.*   64. your] *Qqo–4,5 corr., F;* our *Q5 uncorr.*   66.
Well, we] *Qqo–2;* Well, weele *Qq3–5;* Wee'l *F.*

'Ballads and Broadsides' (*Sh.'s Engl.,*
ii. 511 ff.).

  49. *setter*] informant (thieves' cant).

50–1. *Bardolph . . . Bard.*] The collation shows how "Bardolph" (l. 50)
came in some edns to be the speaker of
"What news?". Arguing that Gadshill should be the news-bringer, some

edd. alter Bard. (l. 51) to Gads., but
the change is unnecessary.

  51. *Case ye*] Mask yourselves.

  64. *John of Gaunt*] "Fal.'s pun . . . did
not lack personal application, for
Prince Hal was tall and thin; cf. the
exchange . . . in II. iv. 240–4" (Kittredge).

when thou need'st him, there thou shalt find him.
Farewell, and stand fast.

Fal. Now cannot I strike him, if I should be hanged.   70
Prince. Ned, where are our disguises?
Poins. Here, hard by, stand close.   [*Exeunt Prince and Poins.*]
Fal. Now, my masters, happy man be his dole, say I—
every man to his business.

Enter the Travellers.

[*First*] *Trav.* Come, neighbour, the boy shall lead our   75
horses down the hill; we'll walk afoot awhile and
ease our legs.
Thieves. Stand!
[*Second*] *Trav.* Jesus bless us!
Fal. Strike, down with them, cut the villains' throats!   80
Ah, whoreson caterpillars, bacon-fed knaves, they
hate us youth! Down with them, fleece them!
[*First*] *Trav.* O, we are undone, both we and ours for ever!
Fal. Hang ye, gorbellied knaves, are ye undone? No, ye
fat chuffs, I would your store were here! On, bacons,   85

---

72. S.D.] *Malone* (*subst.*) ; *not in QqF.*   73. say I] *Qqo–4,F; say Q5.*   74. S.D.
the] *Qq; not in F.*   75. First Trav.] *Capell; Trauel. / QqF* (*subst.*).   78. Stand]
Qqo–4; Stay *Q5,F.*   79. *Sec. Trav.*] *Dyce 2; Trauel. / QqF* (*subst.*).   Jesus] *Qq;*
Iesu *F.*   81. Ah] *QqF* (a), *Rowe.*   83. *First Trav.*] *Capell; Tra. / QqF* (*subst.*).
84. are ye] *Qq;* are you *F.*

---

73. *happy . . . dole*] Proverbial: "May
each one's fortune be to be a happy
man".

74. *every . . . business*] Proverbial:
"Every man as his business lies"
(Tilley, M104).

81. *whoreson caterpillars*] Intro., p.
xxxvii, gives *Woodstock* parallels. As
with "gorbellied knaves" and "fat
chuffs" Fal. deflects his own failings on
to his opponents: the receivers, he implies, are battening on society. The
caterpillar metaphor is as frequent in
the 16th c. as "parasite" in the 20th c.;
e.g. *R2*, II. iii. 166—"The caterpillars
of the commonwealth".

bacon-fed knaves] = "great lumber-
ing bumpkins". *Woodstock*, l. 1615, has
"baconfead pudding-eaters". Boorde,

Dyetary of Helth, 1542 (EETS, Extra
ser., x, 1870, 273), says that "Bacon is
good for carters and plowmen, and
whiche be euer labourynge in the
earth or dunge".

84. *gorbellied*] "Pançu . . . *Gorbellied,
great-paunched*" (Cotgrave). Nashe has
"an vnconscionable vast gorbellied
Volume" (*Haue with you*; McKerrow,
iii. 35).

85. *chuffs*] Often applied to rich or
avaricious farmers or citizens. "Franc-
gontier. *A good rich Yeoman, substantiall
yonker, wealthie chuffe*" (Cotgrave);
"ritch chuffes" (*Woodstock*, l. 1527).
"A fat chuffe" and "rich Chuffes"
occur in Nashe (McKerrow, i. 163, ii.
107).

store] "all you possess" (Kittredge).

on! What, ye knaves! young men must live. You are
grandjurors, are ye? We'll jure ye, faith.

Here they rob them and bind them. Exeunt.

[*Re-*]*enter the* PRINCE *and* POINS[*, disguised*].

Prince. The thieves have bound the true men; now could
   thou and I rob the thieves, and go merrily to London, it would be argument for a week, laughter for a   90
   month, and a good jest for ever.
Poins. Stand close, I hear them coming.   [*They retire.*]

Enter the Thieves again.

Fal. Come, my masters, let us share, and then to horse
   before day; and the Prince and Poins be not two
   arrant cowards there's no equity stirring; there's no   95
   more valour in that Poins than in a wild duck.

As they are sharing the PRINCE *and* POINS *set upon them.*
Prince. Your money!
Poins. Villains!

*They all run away, and Falstaff after a blow or two
runs away too, leaving the booty behind them.*
Prince. Got with much ease. Now merrily to horse:
   The thieves are all scatter'd and possess'd with fear   100
   So strongly that they dare not meet each other;

87. ye, faith] *Qq0–2;* yee yfaith *Qq3–5;* ye ifaith *F.*   87. S.D. *Exeunt.*] *Qq0–3;*
not in *Qq4,5,F.*   Re-enter] *QqF (Enter), Malone.*   disguised] *Cambr.; not in QqF.*
92. S.D. *They retire*] *Dyce; not in QqF.*   Enter the] *Qq; Enter | F.*   96. more] *Qq;*
moe *F.*   96. S.D.–98. S.D.] *As Dyce; [On the left:—]Prin. . . . money. | Poin.*
Villaines. [*bracketed, on the right:—*] *As . . . Poins | set . . . and | Falstaffe . . . away |
too, . . . them. | Qq (subst.); [S.D.s undivided after line 98]F.*   98. S.D. and . . . too]
Qq; not in F.   99–105.] *As Pope; prose, QqF.*   100. are all] *Qq0,1;* are
Qq2–5,F.   scatter'd] *F* (scatt'red); scattered *Qq.*

87. *grandjurors*] Only men of some
wealth or standing could serve on a
grand jury. Nashe writes "Wealthy
saide I? nay I'le be sworne hee was a
grande iurie man in respect of me"
(*Lenten Stuffe;* McKerrow, iii. 155).

jure ye] A widely popular form of
comic retort.

90. *argument*] something to talk
about.

95. *no equity stirring*] "no such thing
as correct judgment in the world"
(Kittredge).

99–105.] QqF print this as prose,
but it is markedly decasyllabic and
Pope and most later edd. arrange it as
verse, assimilating it to those other
scene-ends when Hal asserts his status
by rising to metre (e.g. I. ii, III. iii, v.
iii, v. iv).

Each takes his fellow for an officer!
Away, good Ned—Falstaff sweats to death,
And lards the lean earth as he walks along.
Were't not for laughing I should pity him.   105
Poins. How the fat rogue roared.   *Exeunt.*

SCENE III.—[*Warkworth. The Castle.*]

Enter HOTSPUR *solus, reading a letter.*

[*Hot.*] "But, for mine own part, my lord, I could be well
contented to be there, in respect of the love I bear
your house." He could be contented: why is he not
then? In respect of the love he bears our house: he
shows in this, he loves his own barn better than he   5
loves our house. Let me see some more. "The purpose you undertake is dangerous"—Why, that's
certain; 'tis dangerous to take a cold, to sleep, to
drink; but I tell you, my lord fool, out of this nettle,
danger, we pluck this flower, safety. "The purpose   10
you undertake is dangerous, the friends you have
named uncertain, the time itself unsorted, and your
whole plot too light, for the counterpoise of so great
an opposition." Say you so, say you so? I say unto

---

103. sweats] *Qq0–2,F;* sweares *Qq3–5.*   106. the fat] *Qo;* the *Qq1–5,F.*

Scene III

SCENE III.] *F (Scæna Tertia.); not in Qq.   Location.] Capell (subst.).   1. Hot.]
Capell; not in QqF.   4. respect] Q6,F;* the respect *Qq1–5.*

102. *Each . . . officer*] An echo of the
proverb "The thief does fear each bush
an officer" (Tilley, T112). Wilson
(N.C.S.) cites it from Nashe (*Unfortunate Traveller;* McKerrow, ii. 319)—
"A theefe . . . mistakes euerie bush for
a true man".

104. *lards*] bastes.

Scene III

Location.] Warkworth, in Northumberland, was the principal seat of
the Percys. Capell first fixed the scene

here. Scholars have discussed the
identity of the letter-writer, which,
however, since Shakespeare has not
named him, is hardly more worth
determining than is the size of Lady
Macbeth's family. Nameless, he is all
the more representative of the fickle
"diuerse noblemen" mentioned by
Hol. (cf. App. III, p. 171).

9–10. *out . . . safety*] Echoing the proverb "Danger and delight grow both
upon one stalk [stock]" (Tilley, D28).

12. *unsorted*] ill-chosen.

you again, you are a shallow cowardly hind, and you   15
lie: what a lack-brain is this! By the Lord, our plot is
a good plot, as ever was laid, our friends true and constant: a good plot, good friends, and full of expectation: an excellent plot, very good friends; what a
frosty-spirited rogue is this! Why, my Lord of York   20
commends the plot, and the general course of the
action. 'Zounds, and I were now by this rascal I
could brain him with his lady's fan. Is there not my
father, my uncle, and myself? Lord Edmund Mortimer, my Lord of York, and Owen Glendower? Is   25
there not besides the Douglas? Have I not all their
letters to meet me in arms by the ninth of the next
month, and are they not some of them set forward
already? What a pagan rascal is this, an infidel! Ha!
You shall see now in very sincerity of fear and cold   30
heart will he to the King, and lay open all our proceedings! O, I could divide myself, and go to buffets,
for moving such a dish of skim milk with so honourable an action! Hang him, let him tell the King, we
are prepared: I will set forward tonight.   35

Enter LADY PERCY.

How now, Kate? I must leave you within these two
hours.

Lady. O my good lord, why are you thus alone?
For what offence have I this fortnight been

16. By the Lord] *Qq;* I protest *F.*   17. a good] *Qq;* as good a *F.*   friends]
Qq1–3; friende *Qq4,5,F* (*subst.*).   22. 'Zounds] *Qq;* By this hand *F.*   and]
Qq; if *F.*   29. this, an] *Q1;* this, and *Qq2–5;* this? An *F.*   33. skim]
Qq; skim'd *F.*   34. King, we] *Qq;* King we *F.*   35. forward] *Qq;* forwards
F.   35. S.D. *Lady Percy*] *Rowe; his Lady QqF.*

29. *pagan*] unbelieving.
32. *divide . . . buffets*] split myself in
two and set the halves to cuffing each
other.
36. *Kate*] Hol. calls her "Elianor";
her real name was Elizabeth. Shakespeare seems fond of "Kate": cf.
Henry's courtship in *H5;* and the
heroine of *Shr.;* and Kate who had "a
tongue with a tang" (*Tp.,* II. ii. 52).

38. *O my good lord*] Critics remark
that this scene resembles that between
Brutus and Portia (*Cæs.,* II. i. 233 ff.).
But more notable still is the differentiation Shakespeare could manage, as
always, in treating similar material;
there is all the difference in the world
between the vivid comic spirit of this
scene and the troubled sadness of the
other.

A banish'd woman from my Harry's bed?   40
Tell me, sweet lord, what is't that takes from thee
Thy stomach, pleasure, and thy golden sleep?
Why dost thou bend thine eyes upon the earth,
And start so often when thou sit'st alone?
Why hast thou lost the fresh blood in thy cheeks,   45
And given my treasures and my rights of thee
To thick-ey'd musing, and curst melancholy?
In thy faint slumbers I by thee have watch'd,
And heard thee murmur tales of iron wars,
Speak terms of manage to thy bounding steed,   50
Cry "Courage! To the field!" And thou hast talk'd
Of sallies, and retires, of trenches, tents,
Of palisadoes, frontiers, parapets,
Of basilisks, of cannon, culverin,
Of prisoners' ransom, and of soldiers slain,   55
And all the currents of a heady fight.
Thy spirit within thee hath been so at war,
And thus hath so bestirr'd thee in thy sleep,
That beads of sweat have stood upon thy brow
Like bubbles in a late-disturbed stream,   60
And in thy face strange motions have appear'd,
Such as we see when men restrain their breath
On some great sudden hest. O, what portents are
  these?

48. thy] *Qq1–3*; my *Qq4,5,F.*   thee have] *Qq1–3,F*; thee *Qq4,5.*   49. thee
murmur] *Qq2–5,F*; the murmur, *Q1.*   52. of trenches, tents] *Q1* (of trenches
tents), *Qq2–3*; trenches, tents *Qq4,5,F.*   55. ransom] *QqF* (ransome); ransom'd *Dyce 2, conj. Capell.*   56. currents] *Qq1–3*; current, *Qq4,5*; current *F.*
59. beads] *Q1*; beds *Qq2–5,F.*   have] *Qq1–3*; hath *Qq4,5,F.*   63. hest] *Q1*;
haste *Qq2,3*; hast *Qq4,5,F.*

47. *thick-ey'd . . . curst*] dull-sighted,
ill-tempered.

50. *manage*] manège, horsemanship.

53. *palisadoes*] a defence of iron-
pointed stakes in the ground.

frontiers] Cf. I. iii. 18, note.

54. *basilisks . . . culverin*] Of ord-
nance, the basilisk was the largest kind
(named from the fabulous reptile
which blasted by its breath or gaze,
hatched by a serpent from a cock's
egg), the cannon a comprehensive

category, and the culverin (Fr.
"couleuvrine", after "couleuvre", an
adder) the smallest.

55. *prisoners' ransom*] QqF "prisoners
ransome". Capell's conjectural "ran-
somd" (the common "e/d" misprint)
would make this a parallel to "soldiers slain".

63. *hest*] behest, command. Or perhaps "resolve"; *OED* quotes Stany-
hurst, *Æneis*, ii. 64—"In one heast hee
stieflye remayned".

Some heavy business hath my lord in hand,
And I must know it, else he loves me not.   65
Hot. What ho!

[*Enter a Servant.*]

Is Gilliams with the packet gone?
Serv. He is, my lord, an hour ago.
Hot. Hath Butler brought those horses from the sheriff?
Serv. One horse, my lord, he brought even now.
Hot. What horse? A roan, a crop-ear is it not?   70
Serv. It is, my lord.
Hot.   That roan shall be my throne.
Well, I will back him straight: O Esperance!
Bid Butler lead him forth into the park.   [*Exit Servant.*]
Lady. But hear you, my lord.
Hot. What say'st thou, my lady?
Lady. What is it carries you away?   75
Hot. Why, my horse, my love, my horse.
Lady. Out, you mad-headed ape!
A weasel hath not such a deal of spleen
As you are toss'd with. In faith,   80
I'll know your business, Harry, that I will;
I fear my brother Mortimer doth stir

---

66. S.D.] Capell; (*after line 65*) Dering MS; (*after line 66*) Rowe; not in QqF.   67.
ago] *Qq1,2;* agoe *Qq3–5;* agone *F.*   70. A roan] *Qq3–5,F;* Roane *Qq1,2.*   71–
3. That . . . park] *As Pope; prose, QqF.*   72. O] *Qq1–4; not in Q5,F.*   73. S.D.]
Dering MS, Hanmer; not in QqF.   78–84.] *As Capell (reading* Now, in sooth, in
sooth, *for* In faith,*); prose, QqF.*   80. In faith] *Qq;* In sooth *F.*

68. *horses*] Cf. I. i. 60, 63, note.
70. *A roan*] Madden (252) notes Shakespeare's fondness for roan horses. Blundevill (*Foure Chiefest Offices of Horsemanship,* 1580) says that the perfect horse which "doth participate of all the foure elements equallie and in due proportion" is often "a faire rone" (Madden, 251). Hal knows of Hotspur's preference in horses—cf. II. iv. 104–5.
72. *Esperance*] "Esperance" or "Esperance ma comforte" was the Percy motto; cf. v. ii. 96.
76. *carries you away*] (*a*) takes you

from home; (*b*) excites, "transports" you.
78–89.] Prose in QqF. Edd. from Pope on arrange as verse.
79. *weasel . . . spleen*] Cf. *Cym.,* III. iv. 162—"As quarrelous as the weasel"; and *Songs . . . of the Fifteenth Century* (ed. Thomas Wright, Percy Soc., xxiii, 5) —"Ther wer 3 angry, 3 angry ther wer: A wasp, a wesyll, and a woman". The spleen was thought to be the source of irritable emotions, and Hotspur is "govern'd" by his; cf. v. ii. 19.
82. *my brother Mortimer*] Cf. I. iii. 79, 144, notes; see Appendix VIII.

About his title, and hath sent for you
To line his enterprise. But if you go—

Hot. So far afoot I shall be weary, love.   85

Lady. Come, come, you paraquito, answer me
Directly unto this question that I ask;
In faith, I'll break thy little finger, Harry,
And if thou wilt not tell me all things true.

Hot. Away,   90
Away, you trifler! Love! I love thee not,
I care not for thee, Kate; this is no world
To play with mammets, and to tilt with lips;
We must have bloody noses, and crack'd crowns,
And pass them current too. God's me! my horse!   95
What say'st thou, Kate? What wouldst thou have
      with me?

Lady. Do you not love me? Do you not indeed?
Well, do not then, for since you love me not

86–9.] *As Pope; prose, QqF.*   87. ask] *Q1; shall aske Qq2–5,F.*   88. In faith]
Qq; Indeede F.   89. And if] *Qq; if F.*   me all things] *Qq; me F.*   90–1.
Away, / Away] *As Capell; Away, away QqF.*   97. you . . . you] *Qq; ye . . . ye F.*

84. *line*] strengthen (as lining
strengthens a garment); cf. *John*, IV.
iii. 24–5—"We will not line his
[John's] thin bestained cloak / With
our pure honours".

88. *break . . . finger*] To wring the
little finger was (is?) a lovers' endearment. W. Cornish (*XX So[n]ges*, 1530)
gives a lady's song with the refrain:
"Bewar my lytyl fynger syr I yow
desyre bewar my lytyl fynger. . . Ye
wryng my hand to sore"; and G. Fen-
ton (*Tragicall Discourses*, 1567, Tudor
Trans., ii. 102) has "No sortes of
kysses or follyes in love were forgotten,
. . . no pinchyng by the lytle finger";
cf. "paddling palms and pinching
fingers" (*Wint.*, I. ii. 116). Anders
(*Sh.'s Books*, 1904) and Wilson (N.C.S.)
refer to a sentence about Lady Percy
given in the New York *Nation* (11 Mar.
1875; repr. in *New Sh. Soc. Trans.*,
1875/6, 124) and there erroneously
attributed to Polydore Vergil, xxvi. 2,

which may indicate some unidentified
source for this detail: "Saeva in
familiares, petulans etiam erga mari-
tum, cujus secreta se exquaesituram
minitabat, vel *frangendo digitorum
ossicula*, si veritatem pandere constan-
tius recusaret".

91. *Love!*] In his abrupt way Hotspur suddenly reverts to Lady Percy's
words in l. 65.

93. *mammets*] dolls, from "mawmet", an idol of Mahomet whom
Saracens supposedly worshipped.
Stubbes, *Anat. of Abuses* (ed. Furnivall,
I. 75), writes "when they haue all these
goodly robes vppon them, women
seeme to be . . not Women of flesh &
blod, but rather puppits or maw-
mets of rags & clowtes compact together".

94–5. *crack'd crowns . . . current*] A
popular quibble, on the currency of
cracked coins.

95. *God's me*] "God save me" (*OED*).

I will not love myself. Do you not love me?
Nay, tell me if you speak in jest or no.   100
Hot. Come, wilt thou see me ride?
And when I am a-horseback I will swear
I love thee infinitely. But hark you, Kate,
I must not have you henceforth question me
Whither I go, nor reason whereabout: 105
Whither I must, I must; and, to conclude,
This evening must I leave you, gentle Kate.
I know you wise, but yet no farther wise
Than Harry Percy's wife; constant you are,
But yet a woman; and for secrecy   110
No lady closer, for I well believe
Thou wilt not utter what thou dost not know;
And so far will I trust thee, gentle Kate.
Lady. How? so far?
Hot. Not an inch further. But hark you, Kate,   115
Whither I go, thither shall you go too:
Today will I set forth, tomorrow you.
Will this content you, Kate?
Lady.   It must, of force.   *Exeunt.*

100. you speak] *Qq;* thou speak'st *F.*   105, 106. Whither] *Qq;* Whether *F.*
107. you] *Qq;* thee *F.*   108. farther] *Qq;* further *F.*   111. well] *Qq1–3;* wil
Q4; will *Q5,F.*   113. far will] *Qq1–4;* farewill *Q5;* farre wilt *F.*

112. *Thou … know*] A venerable jest, traceable as far as the elder Seneca (*Controv.*, II. xiii. 12)—"Nec tam magnum consilium . . . commisi muliebri garrulitati, quae id solum potest tacere quod nescit". Tilley, W649, gives several instances of the proverb "A woman conceals what she knows not", including a version of the Seneca (above) which Nashe wrongly attributes to Valerius's *Epistle to Rufinus* and translates "who will commit any thing to a womans tatling trust, who conceales nothing but that shee knowes not?" (*Anat. of Absurditie;* McKerrow, i. 14). Hotspur's very caution emphasizes his masculinity.

118. *of force*] of necessity.

SCENE IV.—[*Eastcheap. The Boar's Head Tavern.*]

Enter PRINCE *and* POINS.

Prince. Ned, prithee come out of that fat room, and lend
    me thy hand to laugh a little.

Poins. Where hast been, Hal?

Prince. With three or four loggerheads, amongst three or
    fourscore hogsheads. I have sounded the very base-   5
    string of humility. Sirrah, I am sworn brother to a
    leash of drawers, and can call them all by their
    christen names, as Tom, Dick, and Francis. They
    take it already upon their salvation, that though I be
    but Prince of Wales, yet I am the king of courtesy,   10
    and tell me flatly I am no proud Jack like Falstaff,

Scene IV

SCENE IV.] *F* (*Scena Quarta.*)*; not in Qq.*   *Location.*] *Pope* (*The Tavern in* Eastcheap.), *Theobald* (*subst.*).   4. amongst three] *Qq*; amongst 3. *F.*   7. them all]
Qq; them *F.*   8. christen names] *Qq* (*Q5* Christian names)*;* names *F.*
9. salvation] *Qq*; confidence *F.*   11. and tell] *Qq*; telling *F.*   no] *Qq1–3,F*;
not *Qq4,5.*

Location.] The place is not, of
course, specified in QqF S.D.s. In
F.V. the Prince's companions frequent
"the olde Tauerne in Eastcheape"
(i. 89). Though Shakespeare mentions Eastcheap from time to time, he
does not name the Boar's Head; but he
implies it at *2H4*, II. ii. 159, when Hal
asks, "Doth the old boar feed in the old
frank?" and Bardolph answers, "At
the old place, my lord, in Eastcheap".
Wilson (N.C.S.) suggests other hints in
references to Fal. as "brawn" or "boar
pig" (*1H4*, II. iv. 108; *2H4*, I. i. 19, II.
iv. 250). "This famous hostelry . . was
on the N. side of Gt. Eastcheap . . .
where the statue of Wm. IV now
stands" (Sugden). Sugden traces its
possible ancestry back to the tavern of
Glutton's debauch in *Piers Plowman*, B,
v. 306 ff., and refers to Lydgate too.
For its 17th-c. association with Fal.,
Chambers (*El. St.*, ii. 443) cites E.
Gayton, *Pleasant Notes upon Don Quixot*,
1654, 277—"Sir John of Famous
Memory; not he of the Boares-head in
Eastcheap".

1. *fat*] This could certainly = "vat"
(cf. *Ant.*, II. vii. 122—"In thy fats our
cares be drown'd"; Bunyan, *P. Prog.*—
"Every fat must stand on its own bottom" [World's Classics ed., 38]), but
it could also = "stuffy", and since it
is Hal himself who has been among
the hogsheads this sense better suits
Poins's whereabouts.

4–5. *With* . . . *hogsheads*] Drawers
would invite favoured guests to share
the sociable atmosphere of the cellar.
Gallants are counselled in Dekker's
Guls Horn-booke "to accept of the
courtesie of the Celler when tis
offered you by the drawers" (Grosart,
ii. 260).

7. *leash of drawers*] trio of tapsters.
Leash = set of three (espec. of hounds,
foxes, etc.).

8. *christen names*] Dekker, *Guls Horn-
booke* (Grosart, ii. 256), says "Your
first complement shall be to grow most
inwardly acquainted with the drawers, to learne their names, as *Iack*, and
Will, and *Tom*".

11. *Jack*] fellow.

but a Corinthian, a lad of mettle, a good boy (by the
Lord, so they call me!), and when I am King of England I shall command all the good lads in Eastcheap.
They call drinking deep "dyeing scarlet", and when   15
you breathe in your watering they cry "Hem!" and
bid you "Play it off!" To conclude, I am so good a
proficient in one quarter of an hour that I can drink
with any tinker in his own language during my life. I
tell thee, Ned, thou hast lost much honour that thou   20
wert not with me in this action; but, sweet Ned—to
sweeten which name of Ned I give thee this pennyworth of sugar, clapped even now into my hand by

12–13. (by . . . me!)] *Qq; not in F.*   16. they] *Qq;* then they *F.*

12. *Corinthian*] a boon companion;
cf. II. i. 68, note. Corinth was noted
for gay dissipation.

15. *dyeing scarlet*] The most evident reference is to topers' complex-
ions; cf. Eliot's prayer (on the inter-
ruption of the French wine-trade)
"that we may safelie fetch that deifi-
yng liquor, which dieth quickly our
flegmaticke faces into a pure sanguine
complexion" (*Ortho-epia Gallica*, sig.
A3). That urine was a reagent for
fixing dyes seems possibly relevant
also; Mr J. C. Maxwell refers me to
Middleton, *Widow*, IV. ii. 7–9, where
Occulto says, of an old mason troubled
with the stone, "He's swoln most
piteously: / Has urine in him now was
brewed last March", and Latrocinio
replies, " 'Twill be rich gear for
dyers". The same ingredient is said to
be used in the Hebrides (cf. Wilson,
N.C.S., 145). Rabelais tells of outrageous dogs which "made a stream
with their urine wherein a duck might
have very well swimmed, and it is the
same current that now runs at St
Victor, in which Gobelin dieth
scarlet" (Bk II, ch. xxii; Urquhart's
trans.).

16. *breathe . . . watering*] stop for
breath in your drinking—a sign of
imperfect prowess.

Hem] = "Clear your throat" (Wilson, N.C.S.); a drinking exhortation.

At *2H4*, III. ii. 234–5, Shallow recalls
his revels—"Our watchword was,
'Hem, boys!' " In Eliot's *Ortho-epia
Gallica*, pt. ii. 41, the drinkers cry
"Hem, ha-hem!" while quaffing.

17. *Play it off*] Get on with it;
cf. Rowlands, *Letting of Humours Blood*
(1600), cited Var. 1821—"A pox of
piecemeal drinking William says, /
Play it away, we'll have no stops and
stays".

18–19. *drink . . . language*] Tinkers
were noted tipplers and had their own
cant. "Gypsies . . . drink more like
Swine than human Creatures, entertaining one another all the Time with
Songs in the *Canting* Dialect" (Bailey).
In Overbury's *Characters* the Tinker
is found "where the best Ale is . . .
His tongue is very voluble, which,
with Canting, proves him a Linguist".

21. *action*] engagement.

22–3. *pennyworth of sugar*] Sugar to
sweeten sack was sold by the tapsters
in small packets. Cf. Dekker, *Guls
Horn-booke* (Grosart, ii. 258–9)—
"Enquire what Gallants sup in the
next roome, and, if they be any of your
acquaintance, do not you (after the
City fashion) send them in a pottle of
wine; and your name, sweetned in two
pittiful papers of Suger, with some
filthy Apology cramd into the mouth
of a drawer".

an underskinker, one that never spake other English
in his life than "Eight shillings and sixpence", and   25
"You are welcome", with this shrill addition, "Anon,
anon, sir! Score a pint of bastard in the Half-moon",
or so. But Ned, to drive away the time till Falstaff
come:—I prithee do thou stand in some by-room,
while I question my puny drawer to what end he   30
gave me the sugar, and do thou never leave calling
"Francis!", that his tale to me may be nothing but
"Anon". Step aside, and I'll show thee a precedent.

                                        [*Poins retires.*]

Poins. [*Within*] Francis!
Prince. Thou art perfect.   35
Poins. [*Within*] Francis!

                Enter [FRANCIS, *a*] *Drawer.*

Francis. Anon, anon, sir. Look down into the Pomgarnet,
       Ralph.
Prince. Come hither, Francis.
Francis. My lord?   40
Prince. How long hast thou to serve, Francis?
Francis. Forsooth, five years, and as much as to—
Poins. [*Within*] Francis!
Francis. Anon, anon, sir.
Prince. Five year! By'r lady, a long lease for the clinking   45

28. the time] *Qq1–3*; time *Qq4,5,F.*   31. do thou] *Qq1–3*; doe *Qq4,5,F.*   33.
precedent] *F* (President), *Pope;* present *Qq.*   33. S.D.] *Theobald; not in QqF.*
34, 36. S.D. *Within*] *Dyce; not in QqF.*   36. *Poins.*] *Qq4,5,F; Prin. | Qq1–3 (subst.).*
S.D. *Francis, a*] *Rowe (subst.); not in QqF.*   43, 51, 55, 62, 76. S.D.] *Capell; not
in QqF.*   45. year] *Qq1,2;* yeeres *Qq3–5,F (subst.).*

24. *underskinker*] under-tapster: to
skink is to draw wine.
26–7. *Anon, anon, sir*] Coming, sir.
Nashe provides a parallel—"his tapster ouerhearing him, cried, anone,
anone sir, by and by" (*Unfortunate
Traveller*; McKerrow, ii. 212).
27. *bastard*] A sweet Spanish wine.
OED cites Surflet & Markham, *Country
Farm,* 1616—"Bastards ... seeme to me
to be so called, because ... oftentimes
adulterated and falsified with honey".

Half-moon] Inn-rooms had, and
often still have, fancy names—cf.
Pomgarnet (l. 37).
30. *puny*] *OED*, "3. Raw, inexperi-
enced". "Puisne" or "puny" was a
term for Oxford freshmen and new
students at Inns of Court.
33. *show ... precedent*] give you a fore-
taste. On Qq's reading cf. Intro., p.
lxxiv.
42. *five years*] Apprenticeships lasted
seven years.

of pewter; but Francis, darest thou be so valiant as to
play the coward with thy indenture, and show it a
fair pair of heels, and run from it?

Francis. O Lord, sir, I'll be sworn upon all the books in
England, I could find in my heart—   50

Poins. [*Within*] Francis!

Francis. Anon, sir.

Prince. How old art thou, Francis?

Francis. Let me see, about Michaelmas next I shall be—

Poins. [*Within*] Francis!   55

Francis. Anon, sir—pray stay a little, my lord.

Prince. Nay but hark you, Francis, for the sugar thou
gavest me, 'twas a pennyworth, was't not?

Francis. O Lord, I would it had been two!

Prince. I will give thee for it a thousand pound—ask me   60
when thou wilt, and thou shalt have it.

Poins. [*Within*] Francis!

Francis. Anon, anon.

Prince. Anon, Francis? No, Francis, but tomorrow,
Francis; or, Francis, a-Thursday; or indeed, Francis, 65
when thou wilt. But Francis!

Francis. My lord?

Prince. Wilt thou rob this leathern-jerkin, crystal-button,
not-pated, agate-ring, puke-stocking, caddis-garter,
smooth-tongue Spanish pouch?   70

---

49. all the] *Qq1–3,F;* all *Qq4,5.*   52. Anon] *Qq;* Anon, anon *F.*   56. pray]
Q1; pray you *Qq2–5,F.*   59. Lord] *Qq;* Lord sir *F.*   65. a-] *Qq1,2* (a); on
Qq3–5,F.   70. Spanish pouch?] *Qq;* Spanish pouch. *F;* Spanish-pouch,—
Capell, most edd.

47–8. *show . . . heels*] Proverbial; "He
shows a fair pair of heels" (Tilley,
P31).

49. *books*] Bibles, or prayer-books.
Pulton, *Abstract of Penal Statutes*, 1577,
fol. 155, says "When a free manne
shall doe fealtie to his Lorde, hee shall
holde his right hande uppon a booke,
and shall saye thus . . ."

68. *rob*] i.e. by breaking your indenture.

leathern-jerkin, crystal-button] Greene's
pawn-broker wears "a black taffata
doublet and a spruice leather ierkin,

with Christall buttons" (*Quippe for an
Vpstart Courtier*; Grosart, xi. 242); cf.
Foure Letters Confuted (by Nashe?;
Grosart, ii. 221)—"a Broker, in a
spruse leather ierkin". About the
tenth year of Queen Elizabeth, says
Howes (Stow's *Annales*, 1631 ed.,
1039), "many young Citizens and
others, began to weare Christall buttons upon their doublets, coats and
Ierkins".

69. *not-pated*] crop-headed. Chaucer's Yeoman had "a not-heed" (*Prol.
Cant. T.*, 109). "The custom of wearing

Francis. O Lord, sir, who do you mean?

Prince. Why then your brown bastard is your only drink:
for look you, Francis, your white canvas doublet will
sully. In Barbary, sir, it cannot come to so much.

Francis. What, sir?   75

Poins. [*Within*] Francis!

Prince. Away, you rogue, dost thou not hear them call?

> *Here they both call him; the Drawer stands*
> *amazed, not knowing which way to go.*

Enter Vintner.

Vintner. What, stand'st thou still and hear'st such a calling? Look to the guests within. [*Exit Francis.*] My
lord, old Sir John with half-a-dozen more are at the   80
door—shall I let them in?

Prince. Let them alone awhile, and then open the door.
[*Exit Vintner.*] Poins!

74. In Barbary] *Qq1–3,4 corr., 5,F;* Barbary *Q4 uncorr.*   77. thou not] *Qq;*
thou *F.*   79. S.D.] *Johnson* (*Exit Drawer.*), *Hanmer 2; not in QqF.*   83. S.D.
Exit Vintner] *Theobald; not in QqF.*

the hair short was more common
among the lower and middle classes,
and the Puritans got the nickname
of roundheads because they for the
most part belonged to these ranks"
(Wright).

agate-ring] Carved agates were
mounted as seals; cf. *Rom.,* I. iv. 56–7—
"an agate-stone / On the fore-finger of
an alderman".

puke-stocking] wearing heavy dark
woollen stockings. "Puke" was a dark
grey or blue-black woollen cloth.

caddis-] worsted-tape.

70. *Spanish pouch*] A Spanish-leather
pouch was part of a vintner's outfit. Of
a country innkeeper Dekker says "A
leatherne pouch hung at his side"
(*Wonderfull Yeare*; Grosart, i. 138).
Spanish leather was considered
tougher than English. Qq's "Spanish
pouch?" seems better than Capell's
(and later edds.') "Spanish-pouch,
—" since doubtless Francis, however
agitated, does not interrupt the Prince.

72–4. *Why.... much*] "The Prince is
talking incoherent nonsense to mystify
Francis. One is tempted to make sense
of it, and perhaps Hal has some
thought or other in the back of his
mind: 'You'd better stick to your
trade and learn to serve wine. If you
rob your master you'll become a fugi-
tive. A white doublet like that you are
wearing will not keep clean long'"
(Kittredge). This is perhaps the best
one can do: the passage is, in fact (to
quote an 18th-c. commentator), "totally in the humbug style".

it=sugar, grown in Barbary; cf.
"your Barbary Sugars" (Thos. Heywood [Shepherd], i. 252).

78–9. *What. . . . within*] Wilson
(N.C.S.) cites a Nashe parallel (*Unfortunate Traveller*; McKerrow, ii. 214)
about an innkeeper who "ran hastely
to his Tapster, and all to belaboured
him about the eares, for letting
Gentlemen call so long and not looke
in to them".

[*Re-*]*enter* POINS.

Poins. Anon, anon, sir.

Prince. Sirrah, Falstaff and the rest of the thieves are at   85
the door; shall we be merry?

Poins. As merry as crickets, my lad; but hark ye, what
cunning match have you made with this jest of the
drawer: come, what's the issue?

Prince. I am now of all humours that have showed them-   90
selves humours since the old days of goodman Adam
to the pupil age of this present twelve o'clock at midnight.

[*Re-enter* FRANCIS.]

What's o'clock, Francis?

Francis. Anon, anon, sir.   [*Exit.*]   95

Prince. That ever this fellow should have fewer words
than a parrot, and yet the son of a woman! His industry is up-stairs and down-stairs, his eloquence the
parcel of a reckoning. I am not yet of Percy's mind,
the Hotspur of the north, he that kills me some six   100
or seven dozen of Scots at a breakfast, washes his

S.D. *Re-enter Poins*] F (*Enter Poines*), Capell; *Enter Poines* Qq (*after line 84*).   92, 94. o'] QqF (a), Theobald.   93. S.D.] Malone (*Re-enter Francis, with wine*); *Re-enter Drawer, with Bottles.* | Capell; not in QqF.   95. S.D.] Collier; not in QqF.

87–9. *what cunning . . . issue*] what's the game? what's the point of all this?

90. *I . . . humours*] "I am in the mood to indulge any fancy that any man has ever had since the creation" (Kittredge).

96. *fewer words*] Other dramatists also mock the meagre vocabulary of drawers; e.g. Thomas Heywood, *Faire Maid of the West*, III. iv—"You rogue, how many yeares of your prentiship have you spent in studying this set speech?"—to which the reply is "The first line of my part was, Anon anon, sir: and the first question I answerd to, was logger-head, or block-head" (Pearson, ii. 302). Also T. Nabbes, *Totenham-Court*, III. i (Bullen, *Old Plays*, New ser., i. 133)—"*Tap-*ster. Y'are welcome, Gentlemen. *James.* Now, my parrat of froth . . ."

97–8. *His industry . . . down-stairs*] Overbury perhaps echoes this: *Characters, A Chamber-Mayde*—"Her industrie is up-staires, and down-staires like a drawer".

99. *parcel . . . reckoning*] items of a bill.

99. *I am . . . mind*] This change of subject is surprising. The connection may lie, as Johnson suggested, in Hal's contrasting his "all humours" with Hotspur's homicidal monomania; or in Francis's busy-ness, or his limitation of ideas; or in all these. This is Hal's first reference to Hotspur and he instinctively recognizes the antithesis between his own sociable nature and his rival's combative militarism.

hands, and says to his wife, "Fie upon this quiet
life, I want work". "O my sweet Harry", says she,
"how many hast thou killed today?" "Give my roan
horse a drench", says he, and answers, "Some   105
fourteen", an hour after; "a trifle, a trifle". I prithee
call in Falstaff; I'll play Percy, and that damned
brawn shall play Dame Mortimer his wife. *Rivo!*
says the drunkard: call in Ribs, call in Tallow.

Enter FALSTAFF[, GADSHILL, BARDOLPH, *and* PETO;
followed by FRANCIS, *with wine*].

Poins. Welcome, Jack, where hast thou been?   110
Fal. A plague of all cowards, I say, and a vengeance too,
marry and amen! Give me a cup of sack, boy. Ere I
lead this life long, I'll sew nether-stocks, and mend
them and foot them too. A plague of all cowards!
Give me a cup of sack, rogue; is there no virtue   115
extant?   *He drinketh.*
Prince. Didst thou never see Titan kiss a dish of butter

109. S.D. *Gadshill, Bardolph, and Peto;*] *Theobald; not in QqF.*   *followed . . . wine*]
Dyce; not in QqF.   114. them and foot them] *Qq;* them *F.*   116. S.D.] *Qq1–4;
not in Q5,F.*   117–18. butter (pitiful-hearted] *Warburton;* butter, pittiful
harted *QqF (subst.).*

103. *work*] i.e. real fighting; cf. *Ant.*,
IV. vii. 2—"Caesar himself has work"
(= is fighting hard).
106. *an hour after*] Hal hits off Hotspur's preoccupied delayed response,
as at II. iii. 91.
107. *I'll play Percy*] Nothing comes of
this proposal, but the liking for play-
acting which it suggests becomes evident later (ll. 371 ff.).
108–9. *brawn . . . Ribs . . . Tallow*]
"The epithets and comparisons which
Hal and Poins apply to him, or he himself makes use of, . . . recall the chief
stock-in-trade of the victuallers and
butchers of Eastcheap, namely meat
of all kinds" (Wilson, *Fortunes,* 27).
Tallow = dripping.
108. *Rivo*] A bacchanalian cry of
uncertain origin, frequent in dramatists. "App. of Spanish origin; perh.
Sp. *arriba,* up, upwards" (*OED*); cf.

Marlowe, *Jew of M.,* IV. vi. 10—"Hey
Riuo Castiliano, a man's a man", where
it may mean the Castilian stream, or
liquor. Marston, *What You Will,* II. i,
has "weele quaffe or anything: *Rivo*"
(*Works,* ed. H. H. Wood, ii. 248), and
"Rivo, drinke deepe, give care the
mate" (ibid., ii. 252).
113. *nether-stocks*] stockings.
117. *Titan*] the sun; cf. *Cym.,* III. iv.
164–6—"Exposing it [your cheek] . . .
to the greedy touch / Of common-
kissing Titan".
117–19. *Didst . . . sun's*] A much-
discussed passage. The sense is: "Look
at that combination—that round rosy
visage and the vanishing liquor it peers
over, like Titan the sun with a dish of
butter melting before his amorous
addresses (this, though, is a very soft-
hearted Titan—he wouldn't hurt a fly,
would he?)". Theobald read "pitiful-

(pitiful-hearted Titan!), that melted at the sweet
tale of the sun's? If thou didst, then behold that
compound.   120

Fal. You rogue, here's lime in this sack too: there is nothing but roguery to be found in villainous man, yet
a coward is worse than a cup of sack with lime in it.
A villainous coward! Go thy ways, old Jack, die
when thou wilt—if manhood, good manhood, be   125
not forgot upon the face of the earth, then am I a
shotten herring: there lives not three good men un-
hanged in England, and one of them is fat, and
grows old, God help the while, a bad world I say.

118. Titan!)] *Warburton;* Titan *QqF;* Titan, *Pope;* Butter, *Theobald;* creature,
Cowl & Morgan.   119. sun's] *Cambr.;* sonnes *Qq1,2;* sunne *Qq3–5,*F.   123.
than] *Qq1–4,5 corr.,* F (then); the *Q5 uncorr.*   lime in it] *Qq;* in't F *uncorr.;*
lime *F corr.*

hearted Butter", to avoid the apparent
indication in QqF ("pittifull harted
Titan that melted") that Titan melted
at the sun's (i.e. Titan's own) tale.
Theobald's is a cogent reading, since
by it Titan kisses the butter which then
soft-heartedly melts at his blandish-
ments. The compositor (indeed, the
author) might have repeated "Titan"
when he should have repeated
"butter". Yet "pitiful-hearted" seems
a rather pointless epithet here with
"butter", whereas with "Titan" it is
surely Hal's sarcastic innuendo on
Fal.'s "heroism", as well as his sun-like
visage and vast girth. Cowl substituted
"creature" for "Titan" (l. 118), thinking "pitiful-hearted creatures" in
Marmion's *Antiquary*, III. i, to be an
echo. But Warburton's brackets and
exclamation mark (as above) provide
a sound meaning.

121. *lime*] Used for doctoring wine
to make it dry and sparkling. Eliot's
Ortho-epia Gallica, ii. 40, is forthright on
the subject—"Worse [i.e. than watering down the wine] do the vintners of
London, who put in lime, brimstone,
honie, allume, and other more
beastly things to be spoken, and nothing is more hurtfull to mens bodies,
whome men ought to chastise pub-

likely as theeues and murtherers: for
thence proceed infinit maladies, and
specially the goutes".

121–2. *nothing . . . man*] Quoted by
Meres, *Palladis Tamia,* 1598; cf.
Intro., p. xii.

126–7. *a shotten herring*] as lank as a
herring that has shot its roe; a frequent
simile. E.g. Greene, *Never Too Late*
(Grosart, viii. 187)—"thou hadst a-
late . . . a louely fat paire of cheekes,
and now thou lookest like a shotten
herring". "The objects Fal. chooses as
a contrast to his person, objects excessively thin, wizened, or meagre, are
. . . often taken from the food-shops.
There is, for instance, the shotten
herring, the soused gurnet, the bunch
of radish, the rabbit-sucker, or
poulter's hare, and, wittiest of all perhaps, the carbonado—the rasher of
bacon, we should say" (Wilson, *Fortunes,* 31).

127. *there . . . men*] Elizabethan usage
allows a singular verb before a plural
subject. The ambiguity in "good"—
(*a*) valiant; (*b*) virtuous—allows Fal.
to modulate characteristically from
infrequency of valour to infrequency
of virtue.

129. *God . . . while*] God help these
times.

I would I were a weaver; I could sing psalms, or   130
anything. A plague of all cowards, I say still.

Prince. How now, wool-sack, what mutter you?

Fal. A king's son! If I do not beat thee out of thy kingdom with a dagger of lath, and drive all thy subjects
afore thee like a flock of wild geese, I'll never wear   135
hair on my face more. You, Prince of Wales!

Prince. Why, you whoreson round man, what's the
matter?

Fal. Are not you a coward? Answer me to that—and
Poins there?   140

Poins. 'Zounds, ye fat paunch, and ye call me coward
by the Lord I'll stab thee.

Fal. I call thee coward? I'll see thee damned ere I call
thee coward, but I would give a thousand pound I

130-1. psalms, or anything] *Qq;* all manner of songs *F.*   139. not you] *Q1;*
you not *Qq2–5,F.*   141. *Poins.*] *Qq1–4; Prin. | Q5,F.*   'Zounds, ye fat] *Qq;*
Ye fatch *F.*   142. by the Lord] *Qq; not in F.*   144. thee coward] *Qq;* the
Coward *F.*

130. *I would . . . psalms*] Weavers
sang at their work and many were
Puritans given to psalmody; cf. the
clown's reference (*Wint.*, IV. ii. 48) to
the Puritan who "sings psalms to
hornpipes". Shakespeare alludes elsewhere to weavers' love of singing—"a
catch that will draw three souls out of
one weaver" (*Tw. N.*, II. iii. 62–3).
D'Avenant (*Wits*, 1636, I. i. 84–7) has
"She's more devout / Than a weaver
of Banbury, that hopes / T'entice
Heaven, by singing, to make him lord /
Of twenty looms".

133-4. *beat . . . lath*] "The old Vice
. . . / Who with dagger of lath, / In his
rage and his wrath, / Cries, 'Ah, ah!'
to the devil" and offers to "pare thy
nails, dad" (*Tw. N.*, IV. ii. 138–44)
was reputedly a favourite interlude-
figure. Harsnet remarks (*Declaration of
Popish Impostures*, 1603, 114–15) that
"It was a prety part in the old Church-
playes, when the nimble Vice would
skip vp nimbly like a Iacke an Apes
into the deuils necke, and ride the
deuil a course, and belabour him with
his woodden dagger, til he made him

roare". Fal. differs from the "nimble"
Vice, but the reference is part of the
morality-associations which indicate
to the audience how to take him.
In extant plays, however, the Vices do
not assault the Devil (L. W. Cushman,
The Devil & the Vice, 1900, 69, suggests Punch-and-Judy shows as an
exception). Dr T. W. Craik points out
to me that the chief comic character
(whether Vice or Fool—e.g. Moros in
William Wager's *The Longer Thou
Livest*) often bore a wooden dagger and
fought his low-comic associates; a possible Devil-beating may have occurred,
e.g., at the end of Fulwell's *Like Will to
Like* when the Vice "rideth away on
the Devil's back" (at his invitation)
and remarks "Now for a pair of spurs
I would give a good groat! / To try
whether this jade do amble or trot"
(Hazlitt's *Dodsley*, iii. 356). "This
roaring devil i' the old play, that every
one may pare his nails with a wooden
dagger" (*H5*, IV. iv. 76–8) suggests (as
does the *Tw. N.* verse, above) some
actual incident, apparently entirely
familiar to an Elizabethan audience.

could run as fast as thou canst. You are straight   145
enough in the shoulders, you care not who sees your
back: call you that backing of your friends? A
plague upon such backing, give me them that will
face me! Give me a cup of sack: I am a rogue if I
drunk today.   150

Prince. O villain! Thy lips are scarce wiped since thou
drunk'st last.

Fal. All is one for that. (*He drinketh.*) A plague of all
cowards, still say I.

Prince. What's the matter?   155

Fal. What's the matter? There be four of us here have
ta'en a thousand pound this day morning.

Prince. Where is it, Jack, where is it?

Fal. Where is it? Taken from us it is: a hundred upon
poor four of us.   160

Prince. What, a hundred, man?

Fal. I am a rogue if I were not at half-sword with a
dozen of them two hours together. I have scaped by
miracle. I am eight times thrust through the doublet, four through the hose, my buckler cut through   165
and through, my sword hacked like a handsaw—
ecce signum! I never dealt better since I was a man:
all would not do. A plague of all cowards! Let them

---

153. All is] *Qq1,2; All's Qq3–5,F.*   153. S.D.] *Qq1–4; He drinkes. | Q5,F.*
156. There . . . here] *Qq1,2; here be foure of vs Qq3–5,F.*   157. this day]
Qq1,2; this Qq3–5,F.

153. *All is*] Cf. collation; and see I.
iii. 122, note, and Intro., p. lxx.

157. *a thousand pound*] Since Fal. fled
before the sharing was complete, this
sum derives rather from *F.V.*—"We
haue a thousand pound about vs"
(i. 87). At II. i. 54 and II. iv. 513 the
booty is put at 300 marks (£200).

this day morning] this morning.

162. *half-sword*] very close quar-
ters.

165–6. *buckler . . . sword*] Fal.'s claim
to sturdy old-fashioned manhood (ll.
125–9) extends also to his choice of
weapons: on the outmoded nature of
these see I. iii. 227, note. The point

implied here is made in Henry Porter's
Two Angry Women of Abington, 1599
(Mal. Soc., 1912, ll. 1339–44)—"I see
by this dearth of good swords, and
dearth of swoord and buckler fight,
begins to grow out [sic], I am sorrie for
it, I shall neuer see good manhood
againe, if it be once gone, this poking
fight of rapier and dagger will come vp
then, then a man, a tall man and a
good sword and buckler man, will be
spitted like a cat or a conney".

167. *ecce signum*] behold the
sign: a popular tag in Elizabethan
literature, of uncertain origin; cf. Tilley, S443, and Cowl & Morgan.

speak—if they speak more or less than truth, they
are villains, and the sons of darkness.   170

Prince. Speak, sirs, how was it?

Gads. We four set upon some dozen—

Fal. Sixteen at least, my lord.

Gads. And bound them.

Peto. No, no, they were not bound.   175

Fal. You rogue, they were bound, every man of them,
or I am a Jew else: an Ebrew Jew.

Gads. As we were sharing, some six or seven fresh men
set upon us—

Fal. And unbound the rest, and then come in the other.   180

Prince. What, fought you with them all?

Fal. All? I know not what you call all, but if I fought not
with fifty of them I am a bunch of radish: if there
were not two or three and fifty upon poor old Jack,
then am I no two-legg'd creature.   185

171. *Prince.*] F, *Dering MS; Gad.* | *Qq.*
Bard. | *Dering MS, Collier MS, Collier.*
Gad.); Lord. | *Ross.* And   *Qq;*
and   *Dering MS.*   175. *Peto*] *QqF; Bard.* | *Dering MS.*
Qq2–4.   178. *Gads.*] *See l. 172, collation.*
181. you] *Q1;* ye *Qq2–5,F (subst.).*   182. you] *Q1;* ye *Qq2–5,F (subst.).*

172, 178. *Gads.*] F (*Gad.*) ; *Ross.* | *Qq;*
173–4. lord. | *Gads.* And] F (*reading*
lord. | *Bard.* And   *Collier MS, Collier;* lord,
177. an] *Qq1,5,F;* and
six or seven] *QqF (Qq3,4* 6. or 7.).

170. *sons of darkness*] More of Fal.'s
Biblical idiom; cf. *1 Thessalonians,* v. 5
—"Ye are all the chyldren of lyght . . . :
we are not of the nyght, neither of
darkenesse".

171. Prince.] The speech is given in
Qq to *Gad.,* and ll. 172, 174, and 178 to
Ross. (cf. I. ii. 158, note). F redistri-
butes as here and most edd. follow.
One expects the burning question to
come from Hal, who otherwise would
be taking a back seat, not from a minor
participant who knows the situation
already. Wilson (N.C.S.) suggests
plausibly that the MS read "*Prin.*",
"*Ross.*", "*Ross.*", "*Ross.*", and that to
replace the "*Ross.*"es a single "*Gad.*"
was written in, which the printer mis-
placed. On F's correction cf. Intro.,
p. lxxiv.

177. *an Ebrew Jew*] "Humorously
emphatic: 'A Jew of Jews'" (Heming-

way, New Var.). "Jew" as a term of
opprobrium was not limited to ava-
rice; cf. "If I do not take pity of her, I
am a villain; if I do not love her, I am
a Jew" (*Ado,* II. iii. 283–5).

180. *the other*] Often plural. It was
Hol.'s phrase "the other on his part"
(= the others on his side) which
Daniel and Shakespeare seem to have
taken as "the other one, for his part",
so making Hal out to be Hotspur's
vanquisher (cf. App. III, p. 176).

183. *a bunch of radish*] "A symbol of
leanness. Elyot, *Castle of Health,* 1539,
35, writes 'Radyshe rootes haue the
vertu to extenuate or make thin' "
(Wilson, N.C.S.).

184. *three and fifty*] This strikingly
verisimilar figure seems a reminiscence
of "fiftie three gainst one" in Gervase
Markham's *Most Honorable Tragedie of
Sir Richard Grinuile,* 1595, or at least of

Prince. Pray God you have not murdered some of them.

Fal. Nay, that's past praying for, I have peppered two of
    them. Two I am sure I have paid, two rogues in
    buckram suits. I tell thee what, Hal, if I tell thee a
    lie, spit in my face, call me horse. Thou knowest my   190
    old ward—here I lay, and thus I bore my point.
    Four rogues in buckram let drive at me—

Prince. What, four? Thou saidst but two even now.

Fal. Four, Hal, I told thee four.

Poins. Ay, ay, he said four.   195

Fal. These four came all afront, and mainly thrust at
    me; I made me no more ado, but took all their seven
    points in my target, thus!

Prince. Seven? Why, there were but four even now.

Fal. In buckram?   200

Poins. Ay, four, in buckram suits.

Fal. Seven, by these hilts, or I am a villain else.

---

186. *Prince.*] *Qq1–4 (subst.); Poines. | Q5,F (subst.).*   God] *Qq;* Heauen *F.*
murdered] *Q1* (murdred); murthered *Qq2–5,F.*   191. ward] *Qq1–4;* word
Q5,F.   bore] *Qq1,2,3 corr., 4,5,F;* boare *Q3 uncorr.*   193. What, four?]
Qq2–5,F; What foure? *Q1.*   197. made me] *Qq1,2;* made *Qq3–5,F.*

---

popular interest in Grenville's fight
(G. R. Stewart, *PQ*, 1935, xiv. 274–5).
Ralegh (*The Fight about the Iles of
Açores*, 1591; ed. Arber, 1871, 22),
gives the number, "fiftie and three
saile", and Markham (ed. Arber,
1871) harps on it—"fiftie three strong
ships" (64), "fiftie three great ships"
(81), "fiftie three saile" (41, 57),
"fiftie three Tygers" (66), and
especially "fiftie three gainst one"
(65). Fal.'s fight assumes the propor-
tions of a national epic.

188. *paid*] settled with, killed.

190. *horse*] This, like "cut" (a curtal
horse) or "ass", was contemptuous,
and "Call me horse [or cut]" was a
popular tag: "if thou hast her not i'the
end, call me cut," says Sir Toby Belch
(*Tw. N.*, II. iii. 205); and Heywood, *If
You Know Not Me* (Shepherd, i. 256),
has "And I do not show you the right
trick . . . Ile giue you leaue to call me
Cut".

191. *ward*] guard, posture of defence.

here . . . point] this is the guard I took,
and thus I pointed my sword.

196. *afront*] abreast.

mainly] with might and main.

198. *target*] Here identified with the
buckler (l. 165), though strictly the
target was broader than the buckler
and was held on the arm, whereas the
buckler was grasped in the centre
(Planché, *Costume of Sh.'s King Henry
the Fourth*, 27).

202. *hilts*] The hilt being divided in
three parts—pommel, handle, and
shell (Sir Wm Hope, *Compleat Fencing
Master*, 1691, 2–3)—could be spoken
of as plural; cf. *R3*, I. iv. 160–1—
"Take him over the costard with the
hilts of thy sword". To swear upon
one's sword (a kind of cross), as Hamlet swears his friends to secrecy "upon
my sword" (*Ham.*, I. v. 147), was an
old form of oath.

Prince. Prithee let him alone, we shall have more anon.

Fal. Dost thou hear me, Hal?

Prince. Ay, and mark thee too, Jack.   205

Fal. Do so, for it is worth the listening to. These nine in
    buckram that I told thee of—

Prince. So, two more already.

Fal. Their points being broken—

Poins. Down fell their hose.   210

Fal. Began to give me ground; but I followed me close,
    came in, foot and hand, and, with a thought, seven
    of the eleven I paid.

Prince. O monstrous! Eleven buckram men grown out of
    two!   215

Fal. But as the devil would have it, three misbegotten
    knaves in Kendal green came at my back and
    let drive at me, for it was so dark, Hal, that thou
    couldst not see thy hand.

Prince. These lies are like their father that begets them,   220
    gross as a mountain, open, palpable. Why, thou
    clay-brained guts, thou knotty-pated fool, thou
    whoreson obscene greasy tallow-catch,—

---

205. too, Jack] *Qq2–5,F (subst.)*; to iacke *Q1*.   210. their] *Q1*; his *Qq2–5,F,*
220. their] *Q1*; the *Qq2–5,F.*   223. catch,—] *QqF (catch.), Pope*; chest. *Dering
MS (orig. written* catch. *and altered)*; ketch,— *Hanmer*; keech,— *Var. 1778, conj.
Johnson*; cake,— *Cowl & Morgan.*

209–10. *points . . . hose*] "The double
meaning of points must be remembered, which signifies the sharp
end of a weapon and the lace [fasten-
ing hose to doublet] of a garment"
(Johnson).

212. *with a thought*] quick as thought.

217. *Kendal green*] coarsish cloth
worn by lower-class people, woodmen,
servants, country folk, and perhaps
rogues and vagabonds as a disguise:
cf. Robert Armin—"Truth, in plaine
attire, is the easier knowne: let fixion
[fiction] maske in Kendall greene"
(*Nest of Ninnies*, ed. Collier, xvi).
"Fal.'s imaginary 'knaves' had dressed
true to form, either as robber woodmen or as low-class thieves" (Linthicum, 79).

222. *knotty-pated*] block-headed.
OED cites Ascham's *Scholemaster*—"A
witte . . . that is not ouer dulle, knottie
and lumpishe".

223. *tallow-catch*] Most simply explained as a dripping pan under roast-
ing meat ("tallow" is animal fat). Of
emendations (cf. collation) the best is
"keech" (the lump of fat rolled up by
the butcher for candle-making). The
butcher's wife in *2H4*, II. i. 104, is
named "goodwife Keech", and the
butcher's son, Wolsey, in *H8*, I. i. 55–7,
is a "keech" whose "bulk" keeps the
sun's rays from the earth. The superb
appropriateness of this to Fal. tempts
one to take "tallow-catch", with Kittredge, as "apparently a variant form
of *tallow-keech*".

Fal. What, art thou mad? art thou mad? Is not the
truth the truth?   225

Prince. Why, how couldst thou know these men in Kendal green when it was so dark thou couldst not see
thy hand? Come, tell us your reason. What sayest
thou to this?

Poins. Come, your reason, Jack, your reason.   230

Fal. What, upon compulsion? 'Zounds, and I were at
the strappado, or all the racks in the world, I would
not tell you on compulsion. Give you a reason on
compulsion? If reasons were as plentiful as blackberries, I would give no man a reason upon com-   235
pulsion, I.

Prince. I'll be no longer guilty of this sin. This sanguine
coward, this bed-presser, this horse-back-breaker,
this huge hill of flesh,—

Fal. 'Sblood, you starveling, you eel-skin, you dried   240

231. 'Zounds, and I were] *Qq;* No: were I *F.*   234. plentiful] *Q1;* plentie
Qq2–5,F (subst.).   240. 'Sblood] *Qq;* Away *F.*   eel-skin] *Hanmer;* elsskin
Qq1–2 (elfskin); elfskin *Qq3–5;* Elfe-skin *F.*

232. *strappado*] Steevens quotes
Randle Holme's *Academy of Armory and
Blazon*, 1688, iii. 310: "The *Half Strappado*, is to have the Mans hands tyed
cross behind his Back, and so by them
to be drawn up to a considerable
height, and so let down again; this in
the least of it, cannot but pull either
the Shoulders or Elbows or both out of
Joynt.—The *Whole Strappado*, is when
the person is drawn up to his height,
and then suddenly to let him fall half
way with a jerk, which not only break-
eth his Arms to pieces, but also shaketh
all his Joynts out of Joint; which
Punishment is better to be hanged,
than for a Man to undergo". It was,
according to Minsheu, "Italis et His-
panis familiare".

234–5. *reasons . . . blackberries*] A frequent pun, "reason" and "raisin"
being often pronounced alike.

237–8. *sanguine coward*] An oxy-
moron, cowards being supposedly
pale and thin whereas the full-blooded
man was sanguine, ruddy, corpulent,

and given to valour. Oriel MS 76,
quoted by Skeat (Chaucer, *Prol. Cant.
T.*, 333) defines the sanguine man as
"Largus, amans, hilaris, ridens, rubei-
que coloris, Cantans, carnosus, satis
audax atque benignus". Fal.'s dis-
quisition on sherris (*2H4*, IV. iii. 92 ff.)
draws the distinction between "de-
mure boys" of over-cool blood, with a
male green-sickness, who are fools and
cowards, and the sack-enriched blood
which produces courage.

240. *eel-skin*] Hanmer's emendation.
The point in these base comparisons is
Hal's lankiness. The *Life of Henry V*
(c. 1513, ed. Kingsford, 1911, 16) says
"This Prince Henrie exceeded the
meane stature of men: he was beaw-
tious of visage, his necke was longe, his
bodie slender and leane, his boanes
smale", and Stow takes this over almost verbatim (*Chron.*, 1580, 582). Hol.
calls him "rather leane than grose,
somewhat long necked" (iii. 134). In
John, I. i. 141, the Bastard refers to
Robert Faulconbridge's skinny arms as

neat's-tongue, you bull's-pizzle, you stock-fish—O
for breath to utter what is like thee!—you tailor's-
yard, you sheath, you bow-case, you vile standing
tuck!

Prince. Well, breathe awhile, and then to it again, and   245
when thou hast tired thyself in base comparisons
hear me speak but this.

Poins. Mark, Jack.

Prince. We two saw you four set on four, and bound
them and were masters of their wealth—mark now   250
how a plain tale shall put you down. Then did we
two set on you four, and, with a word, out-faced you
from your prize, and have it, yea, and can show it
you here in the house: and Falstaff you carried your

241. you bull's-pizzle] *Qq1,2;* buls-pizzel *Qq3–5,*F *(subst.).*   242. utter what
. . . thee,] *Q1;* vtter, what . . . thee? *Qq2–5 (subst.);* vtter. What . . . thee? *F.*
245. to it] *Qq;* to't *F.*   246. tired] *Qq1–4,*F; tried *Q5.*   247. this] *Qq1–3;*
thus *Qq4,5,*F.   254. you here] *Qq;* you *F.*

"eel-skins stuff'd"; in *2H4,* III. ii. 353–
4, Fal. says of the "starved justice"
Shallow that "you might have thrust
him and all his apparel into an eel-
skin"; and Nathan Field, in *A Woman
is a Weathercock,* I. ii. 146–7 (*Works,* ed.
Peery, 81), in what seems an echo of
this passage, has "that little, old dri'de
Neats tongue, that Eele-skin". Did
these parallels not point so aptly to this
particular emendation there would be
a strong case for "elshin" or "elsin",
an awl (as suggested by Evans (*Supp.*),
the first commentator to observe the
reading of Qq1,2 (cf. collation), which
edd. had taken as "elfskin"). E. M.
Wright (*Rustic Speech and Folk-Lore,*
1913, 166) lists "to sup sowans [oat-
meal and water] with an elshin [a
shoemaker's awl]" as a country
phrase for trying the impossible.
OED's citations for "elsin" are, however, only from trade sources or northern dialect contexts; and though the
image would suit Hal's tall spindliness,
Fal.'s outburst down to "stock-fish"
concentrates rather on his skinniness.
Had the word occurred after "tuck",

the reading "elsin" would have been
almost irresistible.

241. *neat's*] ox's.

pizzle] The dried bull's pizzle was
used as a whip: the idea of elongated
shrivelled dryness is brought out in all
these metaphors.

stock-fish] dried cod.

243. *bow-case*] A long (usually
leather) holder for unstrung bows.
The lean Penurio in Beau. & Fl.'s
Women Pleased, III. ii (*Works,* vii. 268),
is a "starv'd rascal . . . precious bow-
case".

243–4. *standing tuck*] stiff, upended
rapier. "Standing" is a quibble; a
blade was said to "stand" when it lost
its resiliency.

249. *set . . . bound*] Such alteration in
mood is not uncommon; cf. IV. i. 106–7.
Wright cites North, *Plutarch, Julius
Caesar*—"He sawe a private souldier of
his thrust in among the Captaines, and
fought so valliantlie . . ."

252. *with a word*] Edd. explain as "in
a word, in short". But Hal seems rather
to mean that a brief shout was enough
to rout the highwaymen.

guts away as nimbly, with as quick dexterity, and   255
roared for mercy, and still run and roared, as ever I
heard bull-calf. What a slave art thou to hack thy
sword as thou hast done, and then say it was in
fight! What trick, what device, what starting-hole
canst thou now find out, to hide thee from this open   260
and apparent shame?

Poins. Come, let's hear, Jack, what trick hast thou now?

Fal. By the Lord, I knew ye as well as he that made ye.
Why, hear you, my masters, was it for me to kill the
heir-apparent? should I turn upon the true prince?   265
Why, thou knowest I am as valiant as Hercules: but
beware instinct—the lion will not touch the true
prince; instinct is a great matter. I was now a
coward on instinct: I shall think the better of myself, and thee, during my life—I for a valiant lion,   270
and thou for a true prince. But by the Lord, lads, I
am glad you have the money. Hostess, clap to the
doors! Watch tonight, pray tomorrow!—Gallants,

256. run] *Qq*; ranne *F*.   roared, as] *Q1* (roard, as); roare, as *Qq2–5*; roar'd, a ↓
F.   263. By the Lord] *Qq*; not in *F*.   264. you] *Qq*; ye *F*.   268. was now]
Q1; was *Qq2–5,F*.   271. by the Lord] *Qq*; not in *F*.

259. *starting-hole*] bolt-hole, hiding
place. Stow reports Hotspur as saying
before Shrewsbury "neither can we,
though we would, seeke any starting-
hole: stand to it manfully therefore"
(*Annales*, 1592, 523).

261. *apparent*] manifest.

267–8. *the lion . . . prince*] This belief
is traceable back to Pliny, and Koel-
bing gives many examples (*Engl. Stu-
dien*, xvi, 1892, 454 ff.). In the *Myrroure for Magistrates* (Lord Hastings,
ll. 282–3), "Lyons . . . feare the sacred
lawes / Of prynces bloud"; in Spenser
the lion recognizes Una (*F.Q.*, I. iii. 5–
6); in Munday's trans. (1588) of *Pal-
merin d'Oliva* (pt II, ch. v), "The Lyons
comming about him, smelling on his
clothes would not touch him; but (as
it were knowing the bloud royall) lay
downe at his feet and licked him"; and
Topsell's *Historie of Foure-footed beastes*
(1658 ed., 370) tells of a lion in Eng-

land "which by evident token was
able to distinguish betwixt the King,
Nobles, and vulgar sort of people". In
"true prince" some commentators
have seen a dig at Hal's dubious right
to succeed, but Fal. always accepts
him as undoubted heir.

269–70. *I shall think . . . life*] A popular idiom; cf. Middleton, *A Trick to
Catch the Old One*, IV. iii ad fin.—"I
shall think the better of myself as long
as I live".

273. *Watch . . . pray*] Fal. again quoting Scripture for his purpose; cf.
Matt., xxvi. 41, "Watche, and praye,
that ye enter not into temptation".
The Genevan version (1560) has
"Watch & pray" as a page-heading
above *Luke*, xxii. Fal. quibbles on
"watch" (= (*a*) keep vigil; (*b*) car-
ouse—cf. Jasper Heywood, *Thyestes*,
1560, III. i. 143, "nightes paste foorth
in watche and wine"), and makes the

lads, boys, hearts of gold, all the titles of good fellowship come to you! What, shall we be merry,   275
shall we have a play extempore?

Prince. Content, and the argument shall be thy running
away.

Fal. Ah, no more of that, Hal, and thou lovest me.

Enter Hostess.

Host. O Jesu, my lord the Prince!   280

Prince. How now, my lady the hostess, what say'st thou
to me?

Host. Marry, my lord, there is a nobleman of the court
at door would speak with you: he says he comes
from your father.   285

Prince. Give him as much as will make him a royal man,
and send him back again to my mother.

Fal. What manner of man is he?

Host. An old man.

Fal. What doth gravity out of his bed at midnight?   290
Shall I give him his answer?

Prince. Prithee do, Jack.

---

274. titles of good] *Qq;* good Titles of *F.*   280. O Jesu] *Qq; not in F.*   283.
lord] *Q1* (Lo.), *Qq2–5* (L.), *F.*   nobleman] *QqF* (noble man *Qq1,4,5,F;*
noble-man *Qq2,3*).

usual "pray-prey" joke. The sanctimonious words pun respectively on the
"Bring in" and "Lay by" (I. ii. 36) by
which purses are spent and got.

274. *hearts of gold*] A popular tag: in
H5, IV. i. 44, Pistol proclaims "The
king's a bawcock, and a heart of gold".

276. *a play extempore*] Extempore
plays were features of tavern life; cf.
ll. 107–8 and 371 ff. Thomas Heywood's *2Ed.4* (Shepherd, i. 93)
describes a tipsy impromptu: "Then
comes a slave, one of these drunken
sots, / In with a tavern-reckoning for
a supplication, / Disguised with a
cushion on his head, / A drawers apron
for a heralds coate, / And tells the
Count, the King of England craves /
One of his worthy honours dog-ken-

nels, / To be his lodging for a day or
two, / With some such other tavern-
foolery."

283, 286. *nobleman . . . royal man*]
A pun dear to Tudor hearts. A noble
was worth 6s. 8d., a royal 10s. Stubbes,
Anat. of Abuses (ed. Furnivall, pt II, 85),
classifies sermons, with reference to
the preachers' fees, as "roiall sermons,
angell sermons, and noble sermons"
(an angel, though once the same as a
noble [cf. *OED*, "Angel. 6."], coming
to be of variable value between the
other two).

290. *gravity*] Fal. invents a morality
character representing aged respect-
ability. In some moral interludes (e.g.
Youth, Hickscorner), the Vice scores in
the early stages off aged Virtue.

Fal. Faith, and I'll send him packing.   *Exit.*

Prince. Now, sirs: by'r lady, you fought fair, so did you,
Peto, so did you, Bardolph; you are lions too, you   295
ran away upon instinct, you will not touch the true
prince, no, fie!

Bard. Faith, I ran when I saw others run.

Prince. Faith, tell me now in earnest, how came Falstaff's sword so hacked?   300

Peto. Why, he hacked it with his dagger, and said he
would swear truth out of England but he would
make you believe it was done in fight, and per-
suaded us to do the like.

Bard. Yea, and to tickle our noses with spear-grass, to   305
make them bleed, and then to beslubber our gar-
ments with it, and swear it was the blood of true
men. I did that I did not this seven year before, I
blushed to hear his monstrous devices.

Prince. O villain, thou stolest a cup of sack eighteen years   310
ago, and wert taken with the manner, and ever
since thou hast blushed extempore. Thou hadst
fire and sword on thy side, and yet thou ran'st away
—what instinct hadst thou for it?

---

294. by'r lady] *Qq* (birlady), *Pope; not in F.*   295. Bardolph] *Rowe;* Bardol
QqF.   lions too,] *Q1 corr.* (lions to, *Devonshire-Huntington copy*), *Qq2–5,F;*
lions, to *Q1 uncorr.* (*Brit. Mus. and Trin. Coll. Cambr. copies*).   299. Faith] *Qq;*
not in F.   305. Bard.] *Q1* (Bar.), *F; Car. | Qq2–5.*   308. year] *Qq1–3;*
yeeres *Qq4,5,F.*

302. *swear . . . England*] Middleton's
Family of Love, I. iii (*Works,* ed. Dyce,
1840, ii. 121–2) refers to gallants who
so overdid their swearing by "their
gentility" that "they had almost
sworn away all the ancient gentry out
of the land". Fal. will put truth to rout
in any contest of asseveration.

305. *tickle . . . -grass*] An echo of
F.V. (xix. 17–19), where Dericke ex-
plains how he feigned wounds in the
French wars—"Euery day when I
went into the field, / I would take a
straw and thrust it into my nose. / And
make my nose bleed". The precise
identification of spear-grass is both un-

certain and unimportant; Ellacombe
(*Plant Lore of Sh.,* 295) says that in
eastern counties couch-grass is still
called spear-grass.

311. *taken with the manner*] Under
"Mainour, alias Manour . . . (or
Maner)" Minsheu has "taken with
the manner, that is, having the thing
stolne about him". "A term of Anglo-
French law, orig. 'mainoure' (= Fr.
manœuvre, lit. hand-work), which ac-
quired the concrete sense of 'thing
stolen' " (Onions). Costard, courting
Jaquenetta, is "taken with the manner" (*LLL.,* I. i. 203).

313. *fire*] i.e. Bardolph's ruddiness.

Bard. My lord, do you see these meteors? do you behold   315
    these exhalations?
Prince. I do.
Bard. What think you they portend?
Prince. Hot livers, and cold purses.
Bard. Choler, my lord, if rightly taken.   320
Prince. No, if rightly taken, halter.

[*Re-*]*enter* FALSTAFF.

Here comes lean Jack, here comes bare-bone. How
now, my sweet creature of bombast, how long is't
ago, Jack, since thou sawest thine own knee?
Fal. My own knee? When I was about thy years, Hal, I   325
    was not an eagle's talon in the waist, I could have
    crept into any alderman's thumb-ring: a plague of
    sighing and grief, it blows a man up like a bladder.
    There's villainous news abroad: here was Sir John
    Bracy from your father; you must to the court in   330
    the morning. That same mad fellow of the north,

321 S.D.] F (*Enter Falstaffe*), Theobald; Qq (*after line 320*).   326. talon] QqF
(talent), Q7 (tallon).   330. Bracy] Qq1,2; Braᴄy Q3; Braby Qq4,5,F.   to]
Qq1–4; go to Q5,F (*subst.*).   331. That] Qq1–4; The Q5,F.

316. *exhalations*] fiery meteors; cf.
I. i. 11, note.
319. *Hot . . . purses*] The antithetical
results of potations. Charmian in *Ant.*,
I. ii. 25, says "I had rather heat my
liver with drinking", and Wilson
(N.C.S.) points to "hot liuered dron-
kards" in Nashe's *Unfortunate Traveller*
(McKerrow, ii. 247).
320. *Choler . . . taken*] "A choleric
(bilious) temperament, if properly interpreted" (Kittredge). The choleric
man, whose excess of bile showed in
his red face, was supposedly irascible.
321. *No . . . halter*] "Prince Hal's
pun is a masterpiece. In a speech only
five words long he puns on three
words" (Kittredge)—i.e. "rightly"
(justly), "taken" (arrested), "halter"
(collar, noose).
323. *bombast*] cotton stuffing;
Stubbes, *Anat. of Abuses* (ed. Furnivall,
pt 1, 55), speaks of monstrous doub-

lets "stuffed with foure, fiue or six
pound of Bombast at the least". But
the metaphorical sense is present too;
cf. *Oth.*, I. i. 13–14—"bombast circumstance / Horribly stuff'd with epithets
of war"—and Greene's sarcasm that
Shakespeare "supposes he is as well
able to bombast out a blanke verse as
the best of you" (*Groatsworth of Wit*, ed.
G. B. Harrison, 45).
327. *alderman's thumb-ring*] Worn in
Shakespeare's time by aldermen and
substantial citizens; cf. Brome (Shepherd, vol. iii), *Northern Lasse*, II. i (p.
23)—"A good man i'th'City is . . . one
that . . . wears . . . a thumb-Ring with
his Grandsirs Sheep-mark, or Gran-
nams butter-print on't, to seal Baggs,
Acquittances and Counterpanes" (i.e.
"counterparts" of an indenture).
330. *Bracy*] Neither Bracy nor Braby
(cf. collation) has been traced in the
chronicles.

Percy, and he of Wales that gave Amamon the bastinado, and made Lucifer cuckold, and swore the
devil his true liegeman upon the cross of a Welsh
hook—what a plague call you him?   335

Poins. O, Glendower.

Fal. Owen, Owen, the same; and his son-in-law Mortimer, and old Northumberland, and that sprightly
Scot of Scots, Douglas, that runs a-horseback up a
hill perpendicular—   340

Prince. He that rides at high speed, and with his pistol
kills a sparrow flying.

Fal. You have hit it.

Prince. So did he never the sparrow.

Fal. Well, that rascal hath good mettle in him, he will   345
not run.

Prince. Why, what a rascal art thou then, to praise him
so for running!

Fal. A-horseback, ye cuckoo, but afoot he will not budge
a foot.   350

Prince. Yes, Jack, upon instinct.

Fal. I grant ye, upon instinct: well, he is there too,
and one Mordake, and a thousand blue-caps more.
Worcester is stolen away tonight; thy father's beard
is turned white with the news; you may buy land   355
now as cheap as stinking mackerel.

336. O,] *Qq2–5,F;* O *Q1;* Owen *Dering MS.*   338. that] *Qq1–2;* the *Qq3–5,F.*
sprightly] *Qq1,2,F;* sprightie *Q3;* sprighty *Q4;* sprighly *Q5.*   341. his] *Qq1,2;*
a *Qq3–5,F.*   349. afoot] *Qq2,3;* a foote *Qq1,4,5,F.*   354. tonight] *Qq1–4;*
by night *Q5,F.*

332. *Amamon*] A principal devil.
Reginald Scot's *Discov. of Witchcraft,*
1584, xv. iii, mentions "Amaymon,
king of the east", and again (xv. xxix)
"king Baell, or Amoimon, which are
spirits reigning in the furthest regions
of the east".

332–3. *bastinado*] cudgelling (strictly,
on the soles of the feet).

333. *cuckold*] i.e. made the horns
grow on his head.

334–5. *cross . . . Welsh hook*] A kind of
Irish bull: the devil swore allegiance,
says Fal., on the cross not of the sword,

as customary, but of the crossless
Welsh bill-hook.

345–6. *good mettle . . . run*] Q1
"mettall"; "mettle" and "metal"
are "differentiated spellings of the
same word" (Onions). Puns: good
"metal" does not easily "run", or melt.

347–8. *to praise . . . running*] i.e. if not
to run be praiseworthy, you are a
rascal to praise him (l. 339) for running.

349. *ye cuckoo*] you witless echoer.

353. *blue-caps*] Scots in their "blue
bonnets".

Prince. Why then, it is like if there come a hot June, and
this civil buffeting hold, we shall buy maidenheads
as they buy hob-nails, by the hundreds.

Fal. By the mass, lad, thou sayest true, it is like we shall   360
have good trading that way. But tell me, Hal, art not
thou horrible afeard? Thou being heir apparent,
could the world pick thee out three such enemies
again, as that fiend Douglas, that spirit Percy, and
that devil Glendower? Art thou not horribly   365
afraid? Doth not thy blood thrill at it?

Prince. Not a whit, i'faith, I lack some of thy instinct.

Fal. Well, thou wilt be horribly chid tomorrow when
thou comest to thy father; if thou love me practise
an answer.   370

Prince. Do thou stand for my father and examine me
upon the particulars of my life.

Fal. Shall I? Content! This chair shall be my state, this
dagger my sceptre, and this cushion my crown.

Prince. Thy state is taken for a joint-stool, thy golden   375
sceptre for a leaden dagger, and thy precious rich
crown for a pitiful bald crown.

Fal. Well, and the fire of grace be not quite out of thee,
now shalt thou be moved. Give me a cup of sack to
make my eyes look red, that it may be thought I   380

357. Why then] *Qq1,2;* Then *Qq3–5,F.*   it is] *Qq1,2;* tis *Qq3–5,F (subst.).*
June] *Qq1–3;* sun *Qq4,5, F (subst.).*   362. horrible] *Qq1,2,4,5,F;* horribly *Q3.*
365. thou not] *Qq1,2;* not thou *Qq3–5,F.*   horribly] *Qq1–3;* horrible *Qq4,5,F.*
367. i'faith] *Qq; not in F.*   368. horribly] *Qq1–3 (Q1* horriblie); horrible
Qq4,5,F.   369. love] *Qq1,2;* doe loue *Qq3–5,F.*   375. stool] *Qq1–4,F*
(stoole); Stole *Q5.*   380. my] *Qq1,2;* mine *Qq3–5,F.*

357–8. *hot ... buffeting*] The connection between these is, perhaps, "Given
the heat of summer, and the excite-
ments of civil war, the girls won't
resist us at all".

364. *spirit*] i.e. of mischief; "spirit. 3.
A supernatural being . . . frequently
conceived of as troublesome, terrify-
ing, or hostile to mankind" (*OED*).

366. *thrill*] shiver with cold; cf.
Meas., III. i. 121—"thrilling region of
thick-ribbed ice".

373. *state*] chair of state, a throne on

a dais beneath a canopy. On extempore plays see l. 276, note.

375. *taken for*] seen to be.

joint-stool] "A stool made by a joiner
of parts joined and fitted together, as
distinguished from one of more clumsy
workmanship" (*OED*).

376. *leaden dagger*] A theatrical pro-
perty, "type of ineffectual weapon"
(*OED*); cf. Beau. & Fl., *Little French
Lawyer,* II. ii (*Works,* iii. 396)—
"There's twelve pence, go buy you
two leaden Daggers".

have wept, for I must speak in passion, and I will do
it in King Cambyses' vein.

Prince. Well, here is my leg.

Fal. And here is my speech. Stand aside, nobility.

Host. O Jesu, this is excellent sport, i'faith.   385

Fal. Weep not, sweet Queen, for trickling tears are vain.

Host. O the Father, how he holds his countenance!

Fal. For God's sake, lords, convey my tristful Queen,
For tears do stop the floodgates of her eyes.

Host. O Jesu, he doth it as like one of these harlotry   390
players as ever I see!

Fal. Peace, good pint-pot, peace, good tickle-brain.—
Harry, I do not only marvel where thou spendest
thy time, but also how thou art accompanied. For

385. O Jesu] *Qq; not in F.*   388. tristful] *Dering MS, Rowe;* trustfull *QqF.*
390. Jesu] *Qq;* rare *F.*

381. *in passion*] with deep emotion.

382. *King Cambyses' vein*] i.e. that of
Thomas Preston's *Lamentable Tragedie,
mixed full of plesant mirth, containing the
Life of Cambises, King of Percia,* 1569.
Johnson surmised that Shakespeare
knew it only by hearsay, since he did
not imitate its tempting rhymed four-
teener measure (the "very tragical
mirth" of Pyramus and Thisbe seems,
however, to parody its title—*MND,*
v. i. 57); Wilson (N.C.S.) thinks that
such imitation existed in an earlier
version of *1H4,* but in revision was
discarded for up-to-date echoes of
Lyly or Greene. But the style parodied
in ll. 386, 388–9, is so much the staple
of the time that unmistakable identification is impossible. The idiom is as
much like Preston as anybody, and, as
for the metre, "King Cambyses' vein"
seems to imply the ludicrous
rant of such plays rather than any particular specimen, as it does in Bucking-
ham's *Rehearsal,* 1672, Prologue—
"There, strutting Heroes, with a grim-
fac'd train, / Shall brave the Gods, in
King Cambyses' vein". Even the evident Lyly parody (ll. 393 ff.) might be
included under such a generalized
"Cambyses" label. See App. V.

383. *leg*] bow.

386–9. *Weep . . . eyes*] Preston's
Cambises has a S.D. "At this tale told,
let the Queen weep", followed by
"*Queen.* These words to hear makes
stilling tears issue from crystal eyes. /
King. What doest thou mean, my
spouse, to weep for loss of any prize?"
(Hazlitt's *Dodsley,* IV. 236). Other
echoes suggested are from Greene's
Alphonsus, l. 1825—"Then, daintie
damsell, stint these trickling teares";
Myrroure for Magistrates (ed. Camp-
bell, 271, l. 96)—"Full manye a trick-
lyng teare theyr mouthes did drynke";
and *Soliman and Perseda,* IV. i. 94–
5—"[mine eyes] are stopt with flouds
of flowing teares".

387. *holds his countenance*] keeps a
straight (or solemn?) face.

390. *harlotry*] scurvy, knavish; sometimes, as here, used rather appreciatively.

392. *pint-pot . . . tickle-brain*] Names
suggesting the hostess's occupation.
"Tickle-brain" was slang for a kind of
strong liquor; Davenport, *New Tricke
to Cheat the Divell,* III. i (Bullen, *Old
Plays,* New ser., iii. 232), has "A Cup
of Nipsitate, briske and neate; / The
Drawers call it Tickle-braine".

though the camomile, the more it is trodden on the   395
faster it grows, yet youth, the more it is wasted the
sooner it wears. That thou art my son I have partly
thy mother's word, partly my own opinion, but
chiefly a villainous trick of thine eye, and a foolish
hanging of thy nether lip, that doth warrant me. If   400
then thou be son to me, here lies the point—why,
being son to me, art thou so pointed at? Shall the
blessed sun of heaven prove a micher, and eat

395. trodden on] *Qq1–3* (troden on); trodē on *Q4*; troden *Q5,F*.   396. yet]
Qq3–5,F; so *Qq1,2*.   397. That thou] *Qq1,2*; thou *Qq3–5,F*.   398. my
own] *Qq1,2*; my *Qq3–5,F*.   400. thy] *Qq1–3,5,F*; the *Q4*.   401. lies] *Qq1–2*;
lieth *Qq3–5,F* (*subst.*).   403. sun] *Q1* (sunne); sonne *Qq2–5,F*.

395-7. *camomile . . . wears*] Cf. Lyly,
Euphues, Anatomy of Wyt (Bond, i. 196)
—"Though the Camomill, the more
it is trodden and pressed downe, the
more it spreadeth yet the violet the
oftner it is handled and touched, the
sooner it withereth and decayeth".
Gerard's *Herball* (1633 ed., 754–5)
says "The common Cammomill hath
many weak and feeble branches trail-
ing vpon the ground, taking hold on
the top of the earth as it runneth,
whereby it greatly increaseth". Tilley,
C34, gives several examples of this
simile, including three before Lyly.
Among the euphuistic traits Fal. parodies are the use of similes from natural
history, the affectation of recondite
learning, trite quotations, rhetorical
questions, and verbal antitheses and
alliterations.

396. *yet youth*] Unauthoritative
though Q3 is, the sense, as well as the
Lyly parallel, requires this emendation.

399. *trick*] characteristic.

399-400. *foolish . . . lip*] "foolish"
probably in the sense of "wanton",
"roguish"; cf. Beau. & Fl., *Philaster*,
IV. i (*Works*, i. 117)—"a foolish twink-
ling with the eye". A hanging lower
lip was a mark of beauty and wantonness: cf. John Day, *Law-Tricks* (Mal.
Soc., 1949/1950, ll. 1005–6)—"*Em-*
[*ilia*]: Marke but the glance of his eye.
Iul[*io*]: The hanging of his neither

[sic] lip"; and Brome (Shepherd, iii.
476), *Queens Exchange*, II. i—"the hanging of the nether lip, / Which the best
Phisiognomists do tell us / Shews
women apt to lust, and strong incontinence". The features Fal. mentions
have no warrant in the chronicles.

402. *pointed at*] i.e. derisively. In
2H6, II. iv. 46–7, the Duchess of Gloucester is "a pointing-stock / To every
idle rascal follower".

402-9. *Shall . . . defile*] In *NQ*, vol.
199, 19, Arnold Davenport points out
that this passage parallels Lyly's
Campaspe (Bond, ii. 329–30), where
Hephestion, in rhetorical questions,
rebukes Alexander for forgetting his
royal station and falling in love with a
captive girl. He begins "What! is the
sonne of *Phillip*, king of Macedon, become the subiect of *Campaspe*, the cap-
tiue of *Thebes*?", and observes "Bewty
is like the blackberry, which seemeth
red, when it is not ripe". In reply,
Alexander compares his fallen condition with that of the sun in eclipse.
The rhetorical manner, the reproof
to fallen royalty, and the king's-
son–heaven's-sun–blackberry elements
suggest a probable connection.

403-4. *micher . . . blackberries*] To
mitch, mich, or mooch is "to play
truant, espec. . . . in order to gather
blackberries" (Wright, *Engl. Dial.
Dict.*). Miching and blackberrying
have long been and still are associated.

blackberries? A question not to be asked. Shall the
son of England prove a thief, and take purses? A   405
question to be asked. There is a thing, Harry, which
thou hast often heard of, and it is known to many
in our land by the name of pitch. This pitch (as
ancient writers do report) doth defile, so doth the
company thou keepest: for, Harry, now I do not   410
speak to thee in drink, but in tears; not in pleasure,
but in passion; not in words only, but in woes also.
And yet there is a virtuous man whom I have often
noted in thy company, but I know not his name.

Prince. What manner of man, and it like your Majesty?   415
Fal. A goodly portly man, i'faith, and a corpulent; of a
cheerful look, a pleasing eye, and a most noble carriage; and, as I think, his age some fifty, or by'r lady
inclining to threescore; and now I remember me,
his name is Falstaff. If that man should be lewdly   420
given, he deceiveth me; for, Harry, I see virtue in
his looks. If then the tree may be known by the fruit,
as the fruit by the tree, then peremptorily I speak it,
there is virtue in that Falstaff; him keep with, the
rest banish. And tell me now, thou naughty varlet,   425
tell me where hast thou been this month?

---

410. Harry, now] *Q1 corr. (Devonshire-Huntington copy), Qq2–5,F;* Harry now, *Q1
uncorr. (Brit. Mus. and Trin. Coll. Cambr. copies).*   421. deceiveth] *Qq1,2;*
deceiues *Qq3–5,F.*

J. E. Cross offers a modern French
parallel—"faire l'école buissonière"
('On the Meaning of "A-Blakebery-
ed"', *RES*, New ser., II, 1951, 373).

405. *son*] The sun/son quibble has
here a deeper resonance, a virtual
identification, from the traditional
association of kingship and the sun. In
these speeches Fal. develops a formal
rhetorical pattern, in which traditional symbols, Biblical echoes, and citation of authorities combine.

408–9. *pitch . . . defile*] *Ecclus.*, xiii. 1
—"Who so toucheth pytch, shalbe de-
fyled withall"; an appropriate part of
the Lyly parody since Lyly himself
quotes it in *Euphues to Philautus* (Bond,
i. 250), and *Letters Writ by Euphues*

(Bond, i. 320). Fal.'s echo is doubly apt.
412. *passion*] Cf. l. 381.
416. *portly*] of stately bearing; cf. I.
iii. 12–13, note.
corpulent] "full-bodied—not in the
modern sense of 'extremely stout' "
(Kittredge).
420. *lewdly*] "2. wickedly, evilly;
vilely, mischievously . . . 4. lascivi-
ously" (*OED*).
422–3. *If . . . tree*] A popular tag,
from *Matt.*, xii. 33—"The tree is
knowen by his fruite"; similarly *Luke,*
vi. 44. As in ll. 408–9, Fal. can cite
Scripture and Lyly concurrently;
Euphues (Bond, i. 207) has "No, no, yᵉ
tree is known by his fruits".
423. *peremptorily*] decisively.

Prince. Dost thou speak like a king? Do thou stand for
    me, and I'll play my father.

Fal. Depose me? If thou dost it half so gravely, so majes-
    tically, both in word and matter, hang me up by the   430
    heels for a rabbit-sucker, or a poulter's hare.

Prince. Well, here I am set.

Fal. And here I stand. Judge, my masters.

Prince. Now, Harry, whence come you?

Fal. My noble lord, from Eastcheap.   435

Prince. The complaints I hear of thee are grievous.

Fal. 'Sblood, my lord, they are false: nay, I'll tickle ye
    for a young prince, i'faith.

Prince. Swearest thou, ungracious boy? Henceforth ne'er
    look on me. Thou art violently carried away from   440
    grace, there is a devil haunts thee in the likeness of
    an old fat man, a tun of man is thy companion. Why
    dost thou converse with that trunk of humours,
    that bolting-hutch of beastliness, that swollen par-
    cel of dropsies, that huge bombard of sack, that   445
    stuffed cloak-bag of guts, that roasted Manningtree

---

437. 'Sblood] *Qq*; Yfaith *F*.   438. i'faith] *Qq; not in F*.   442. an old fat]
Qq1–4; a fat old *Q5,F*.

431. *rabbit-sucker . . . hare*] baby rabbit . . . hare hanging in a poulterer's
shop. "The jest is in comparing himself to something thin and little"
(Johnson).

432. *set*] seated.

437–8. *I'll . . . prince*] i.e. "Watch me
play a young prince; this will tickle
you"; cf. Thomas Heywood, *Mayden-
head well lost* (Shepherd, iv. 139)—
"*Clowne*: I did but doo't to make you
smile: Nay, Ile tickle you for a
Doctor".

439. *ungracious*] graceless, profane.

440–1. *violently . . . devil*] This, Wilson
(N.C.S.) points out, may echo Nashe,
Pierce Penilesse (McKerrow, i. 220)—
"the Diuell . . . violently carries him
away to vanitie, villanie, or monstrous hypocrisie".

443. *humours*] "morbid secretions
. . . ; practically equivalent to diseases" (Kittredge).

444. *bolting-hutch*] sifting-bin.

445. *bombard*] a big leather wine
vessel, whose portliness is indicated in
Tp., II. ii. 20–2—"Yond same black
cloud, yond huge one, looks like a foul
bombard that would shed his liquor".

446. *cloak-bag*] portmanteau. Similarly used in *Return from Parnassus*, pt 2
(ed. J. B. Leishman, IV. ii. 1656–7)
—"you that are a plagie stuffed
Cloake-bagge of all iniquitie".

446–7. *roasted . . . ox*] East Anglia
was famous for fat oxen, but why
Shakespeare picked on Manningtree
in Essex is uncertain. The morality-
references in Hal's mind ("grace",
"devil", "vice", "iniquity","ruffian",
"vanity") may have suggested Manningtree by association, for it was
known for morality-play performances. Malone quotes Dekker, *Seuen
Deadly Sinnes*, 1606 (Grosart, ii.
73)—"the old Morralls at *Maningtree*

ox with the pudding in his belly, that reverend vice,
that grey iniquity, that father ruffian, that vanity in
years? Wherein is he good, but to taste sack and
drink it? wherein neat and cleanly, but to carve a   450
capon and eat it? wherein cunning, but in craft?
wherein crafty, but in villainy? wherein villainous,
but in all things? wherein worthy, but in nothing?

Fal. I would your Grace would take me with you: whom
means your Grace?   455

Prince. That villainous abominable misleader of youth,
Falstaff, that old white-bearded Satan.

Fal. My lord, the man I know.

Prince. I know thou dost.

[acted] by Trades-men", and *Choise of Valentines* (by Nashe?; McKerrow, subscribers' ed., iii. 404)—"To ... see a playe of strange moralitie / Shewen by Bachelrie of Maningtree; / Where-to the Contrie franklins flock-meale swarm / And thou and Jone com marching arme in arme". The "strange moralitie" was apparently the reason why in 1611 certain inhabitants complained to the King's commissioners that "at whitsontyde some vayne and ill disposed stage players haue very muche abused the said place" (i.e. the premises of the town chapel), and were promised that there would be a prohibition of "any stage playes or suche lyke vayne or profane exercise" (C. Fell Smith, 'A Note on Manningtree in 1611', *Essex Review*, 1906, xv. 155). Manningham's *Diary*, 1602-3 (Camden Soc., 1868, 130), says "The towne of Manitre in Essex holdes [its fair rights?] by stage playes", and Heywood's *Apology for Actors*, 1612 (Sh. Soc. ed., 61), is to the same effect. This idea is probably erroneous, but it does associate the plays with the fair. Both fairs and performances might well have been accompanied by ox-roastings and be well reputed among hungry troupers.

447. *pudding*] stuffing. "An extension of the orig. meaning of the word = 'mixture of meat, herbs, &c. stuffed into an animal's stomach or intestine', which survives in 'black pudding' " (Onions). Wilson (N.C.S.) cites, from Nashe, "All the rest of his inuention is nothing but an oxe with a pudding in his bellie" (*Christes Teares*; McKerrow, ii. 180).

vice] Cf. ll. 133-4, note.

447-8. *vice ... iniquity ... ruffian ... vanity*] Morality-references. Jonson, *The Devil is an Ass*, i. i. 40-3 (H. & S., vi. 165), has "*SAT[AN]*: What *Vice?* ... *Pug.* Why any, *Fraud*; / Or *Couetousnesse*; or Lady *Vanity*; / Or old *Iniquity*". " 'Ruffian' was a cant word for the Devil, e.g. in the Chester miracle plays (cf. *OED*, 'ruffin')" (Wilson, N.C.S.). But also, "ruffian" meant the interlude hooligan. The point of "father ruffian" and "vanity in years", Dr T. W. Craik points out to me, is that the interlude "ruffian" and "vanity" were normally young. Hal taunts Fal., who should by now be aged "gravity", with arrested development at the young-scapegrace stage.

450. *cleanly*] deft, dextrous.

451. *cunning*] skilful.

454. *take ... you*] "Go no faster than I can follow you" (Johnson).

456. *misleader of youth*] The fundamental morality-role of the Devil and his agents.

Fal. But to say I know more harm in him than in myself 460
were to say more than I know. That he is old, the
more the pity, his white hairs do witness it, but that
he is, saving your reverence, a whoremaster, that I
utterly deny. If sack and sugar be a fault, God help
the wicked! If to be old and merry be a sin, then 465
many an old host that I know is damned: if to be fat
be to be hated, then Pharaoh's lean kine are to be
loved. No, my good lord; banish Peto, banish Bardolph, banish Poins—but for sweet Jack Falstaff,
kind Jack Falstaff, true Jack Falstaff, valiant Jack 470
Falstaff, and therefore more valiant, being as he is
old Jack Falstaff, banish not him thy Harry's company, banish not him thy Harry's company, banish
plump Jack, and banish all the world.

Prince. I do, I will.   [*A knocking heard. Exeunt* 475
        Hostess, Francis, and Bardolph.]

        [*Re-*]*enter* BARDOLPH, *running.*

Bard. O my lord, my lord, the sheriff with a most monstrous watch is at the door.

Fal. Out, ye rogue! Play out the play! I have much to
say in the behalf of that Falstaff.

        [*Re-*]*enter the Hostess.*

Host. O Jesu, my lord, my lord!   480

464. God] *Qq;* Heauen *F.* 467. lean] *Qq2–5,F;* lane *Q1.* 468–9. Bar-
dolph] *F;* Bardoll *Qq (subst.).* 475. S.D.] *Malone; Enter Bardoll running.* |
QqF (subst.). 476. most] *Qq;* most most *F.* 478. ye] *Q1;* you *Qq2–5,F.*
479. S.D. Re-enter] *QqF (Enter),* Theobald. 480. Jesu] *Qq;* not in *F.*

467. *Pharaoh's lean kine*] Gen., xli.
19–21.

469–72. *sweet . . . Jack Falstaff*] A
probable echo of Nashe, *Haue with you,*
1596 (McKerrow, iii. 5–6)—"curteous
Dicke, comicall Dicke, liuely Dicke,
louely Dicke, learned Dicke, olde
Dicke of Lichfield".

475. S.D. A knocking . . . Bardolph]
QqF S.D. here simply reads *Enter Bardoll running,* and at l. 479 *Enter the hostesse,* having marked no previous exits

for them. Sisson would have them
leave after l. 392. Wilson (N.C.S.)
thinks they must have slipped out at
some unspecified time, since if they
now leave and return "the stage [is]
silent for several moments, which is
absurd". But the stage-business of
tumult "off" is hardly "silence" and
abundantly covers their momentary
absence. Who has the heart to deprive
two such devoted Falstaffians of any
part of their master's performance?

Prince. Heigh, heigh, the devil rides upon a fiddle-stick,
    what's the matter?

Host. The sheriff and all the watch are at the door; they
    are come to search the house. Shall I let them in?

Fal. Dost thou hear, Hal? Never call a true piece of gold   485
    a counterfeit: thou art essentially made without
    seeming so.

Prince. And thou a natural coward without instinct.

Fal. I deny your major. If you will deny the sheriff, so; if
    not, let him enter. If I become not a cart as well as   490
    another man, a plague on my bringing up! I hope
    I shall as soon be strangled with a halter as another.

Prince. Go hide thee behind the arras, the rest walk up

---

481. *Prince.*] *Qq1-3; Fal. | Qq4,5,F (subst.); Poyn. | Dering MS.*   486. made]
QqFf1,2, mad *Ff3,4, many edd.*

481. *Heigh . . . fiddle-stick*] i.e. "The
Devil's leading this dance". Proverbial; Tilley D263. "The association
of the devil with dancing and dance
music is a venerable notion, not to be
ascribed (as has been thoughtlessly
suggested) to a Puritan origin"
(Kittredge).

485-7. *Never . . . so*] A much-discussed passage. Many edd. follow
Ff3,4, changing "made" to "mad",
but this hardly helps the sense, though
by balancing with "coward" (l. 488)
"mad" may seem to connect the two
speeches. The idea behind Fal.'s
"flying quibble" (Elton) is that of
"genuine worth mistaken for falsity";
both he himself and Hal might be thus
misjudged. He says, therefore, "Listen
to me, Hal: don't denounce me, a true
piece of gold, as a counterfeit (and so
peculiarly obnoxious to the law); you
yourself are the real thing, though you
may not look like it (and the same is
true of me)". The prince's reply then
is "You are getting into a panic as you
did before", whereupon Fal. rallies
with a quibble and a pun. Fal. may
possibly, however, mean that Hal is
the true piece of gold; "prove true in
your friendship, do not play me false,
for you are made of true gold, though

you do not look it". Massinger, *Parliament of Love*, III. ii. 150-1, has "I
proved true gold, / And current in my
friendship".

489. *your major*] QqF "your Maior";
i.e. "your major premiss" (a term in
syllogistic logic), quibbling on "major/
mayor", pronounced and often spelt
alike. Hardin Craig (*Sh. and Formal
Logic*, 1929, 385) reconstructs the supposed syllogism thus: "*Major premiss:*
Natural cowards are cowards without
instinct. *Minor premiss:* Fal. is a
natural coward. *Conclusion:* Fal. is a
coward without instinct". But, he
comments, what Fal. in fact denies in
the above is the *minor* premiss, though,
eager for his pun, he confuses the
two.

490. *If . . . cart*] If I am not a credit
to the cart taking me to the gallows.

491. *bringing up*] (*a*) breeding; (*b*)
summoning before a law court. In the
prodigal plays, Dr T. W. Craik suggests to me, the stress was on the prodigal's bad upbringing which led him
to the gallows. Fal.'s jest is that at the
gallows he will bear himself well because his upbringing was good.

493. *arras*] curtain before the inner
stage. In actual houses the arras stood
away from the walls on wooden frames

above. Now, my masters, for a true face, and good
        conscience.   495
Fal. Both which I have had, but their date is out, and
        therefore I'll hide me.   [*Exeunt all but the Prince and Peto.*]
Prince. Call in the sheriff.

                    Enter Sheriff and the Carrier.

        Now, master sheriff, what is your will with me?
Sher. First, pardon me, my lord. A hue and cry   500
        Hath follow'd certain men unto this house.
Prince. What men?
Sher. One of them is well known, my gracious lord,
        A gross fat man.
Car.   As fat as butter.
Prince. The man I do assure you is not here,   505
        For I myself at this time have employ'd him:
        And sheriff, I will engage my word to thee,
        That I will by tomorrow dinner-time
        Send him to answer thee, or any man,
        For anything he shall be charg'd withal;   510
        And so let me entreat you leave the house.

---

497. S.D.] *Collier; Exit. | F; not in Qq.*   499. Now] *Theobald; Prin.* Now *QqF*
(*subst.*).   499–504.] *As Pope; prose, QqF.*   501. follow'd] *Rowe; followed QqF.*

and could provide concealment; cf.
Beau. & Fl., *Woman-Hater*, III. iv
(*Works*, x. 109)—"Farewell, my fellow
Courtiers all, with whom, / I have of
yore made many a scrambling meal /
In corners, behind Arasses, on stairs".

497. S.D. Exeunt . . . Peto] Qq have
no S.D. for this, and F has merely *Exit.*
Who remains with Hal—Peto, or
Poins? QqF give Peto the speeches at
ll. 521, 526, 543 (there is no prefix at
l. 528) and make Hal use his name at
l. 542. But the Dering MS, though it
makes Poins go out here, gives him
Peto's speeches in the remainder of the
scene and reads "Poins" at l. 542.
Johnson preferred Poins as Hal's companion and the recipient of an "honourable" place (l. 538), and some edd.
follow. At III. iii. 196 the same uncertainty arises. Confusion might have
occurred if the MS speech-prefixes

were *Po.*, which occurs for *Poins* in
Q0. But it still remains true that
"Peto" occurs in l. 542, and anyone
substituting "Poins" there ignores the
fact that Hal's form of address is normally not "Poins" but "Ned" (e.g.
I. ii. 108; II. ii. 71, 103; II. iv. 1, 20–2,
28). He uses "Poins" once (II. iv. 83),
only in summoning him from off-
stage, and "Ned Poins" once (II. ii.
58), only to third parties. Poins himself is usually more familiar than
l. 543's "good my lord" (e.g. "Hal",
"sweet Hal", "my good sweet honey
Prince", "sirrah", "my lad"). So
Peto seems the likelier companion
here, and there is no need to amend
QqF.

500. *hue and cry*] In *F.V.*, "the
Towne of Detfort is risen / With hue
and crie after your man / Which . . .
robd a poore Carrier" (i. 19–22).

Sher. I will, my lord: there are two gentlemen
    Have in this robbery lost three hundred marks.
Prince. It may be so: if he have robb'd these men
    He shall be answerable; and so, farewell.   515
Sher. Good night, my noble lord.
Prince. I think it is good morrow, is it not?
Sher. Indeed, my lord, I think it be two o'clock.

                        Exit[, with Carrier.]

Prince. This oily rascal is known as well as Paul's: go call
    him forth.   520
Peto. Falstaff!—Fast asleep behind the arras, and snort-
    ing like a horse.
Prince. Hark how hard he fetches breath—search his
    pockets. (*He searcheth his pockets, and findeth certain
    papers.*) What hast thou found?   525
Peto. Nothing but papers, my lord.
Prince. Let's see what they be, read them.
Peto. [*Reads*] Item a capon   .   .   .   2s. 2d.
            Item sauce .   .   .   .   4d.
            Item sack two gallons .   .   5s. 8d.   530
            Item anchovies and sack after supper 2s. 6d.
            Item bread   .   .   .   ob.
Prince. O monstrous! but one halfpennyworth of bread
    to this intolerable deal of sack? What there is else
    keep close, we'll read it at more advantage. There   535
    let him sleep till day; I'll to the court in the morn-
    ing. We must all to the wars, and thy place shall be
    honourable. I'll procure this fat rogue a charge of

---

513. three hundred] *Qq* (300.), *F.*   518. S.D. *with Carrier*] *Hanmer* (*subst.*);
not in QqF.   521, 526, 543. *Peto*] *QqF*; *Poins | Dering MS, Var. 1773, conj. John-
son.*   524. S.D. *pockets*] *Qq4,5,F*; *pocket Qq1–3.*   525. *papers.*) *What*] *Hanmer*;
papers. | Pr. What QqF (*subst.*).   527. *see . . . be,*] *Q1*; see what they be: *Qq2,3*;
see what be they: *Qq4,5*; see, what be they? *F.*   528. *Peto.*] *F*; *not in Qq*; *Poins. |
Dering MS, Var. 1773, conj. Johnson.*   528. S.D.] *Capell*; *not in QqF.*   533.
Prince.] *F*; *not in Qq.*

---

531. *anchovies*] Eaten to provoke
thirst: "twelve penyworth of An-
choves, 18*d*" is a tavern-item for four
sea-captains in Thomas Heywood's
Faire Maid of the West, II. i (Shepherd,
ii. 280).

532. *ob.*] obolus, half-penny.

534. *intolerable*] "1.†c. extreme, exceedingly great" (*OED*).

538–9. *charge of foot*] Cf. III. iii. 185.
"A company of infantry commanded
by a captain and including subordi-
nates from the recruit to the lieutenant" (Jorgensen).

foot, and I know his death will be a march of twelve
score. The money shall be paid back again with   540
advantage. Be with me betimes in the morning;
and so, good morrow, Peto.

Peto. Good morrow, good my lord.   *Exeunt.*

539. march] *Qq1–3;* match *Qq4,5,F.*   542. Peto] *QqF;* Poins *Dering MS, Var.*
1773, conj. Johnson.

  539–40. *twelve score*] sc. "paces".   541. *advantage*] interest.

ACT III

SCENE I.—[*Bangor. The Archdeacon's House.*]

Enter HOTSPUR, WORCESTER, LORD MORTIMER,
OWEN GLENDOWER.

Mort. These promises are fair, the parties sure,
And our induction full of prosperous hope.
Hot. Lord Mortimer, and cousin Glendower, will you
sit down?
And uncle Worcester. A plague upon it!
I have forgot the map.
Glend.   No, here it is: 5
Sit, cousin Percy, sit, good cousin Hotspur;
For by that name as oft as Lancaster doth speak of you
His cheek looks pale, and with a rising sigh
He wisheth you in heaven.

ACT III

Scene 1

ACT III SCENE I.] *F* (*Actus Tertius. Scena Prima.*); *not in Qq.*   *Location.*] *Theobald*
(*The Archdeacon of Bangor's House in Wales*).   3–9. Lord . . . heaven] *As F* (*subst.*;
line 3 reading Lord . . . *Glendower,* / Will . . . downe?); *prose, Qq.*   8. cheek looks]
Qq; Cheekes looke *F.*   sigh] *Qq1,5,F*; sight *Qq2–4.*

Location.] Since QqF specify no
locality, none need really be provided;
but if the scene must have a local habi-
tation and a name this, which Theobald derived from Hol. (cf. App. III,
p. 170), is the best.

2. *induction*] opening scene, before
the main action of a play.

3–10.] Qq print as prose, and presumably the original "copy" looked
like prose. But the scene should be
conceived in verse from the beginning,
and Dr Harold Brooks suggests how
the error arose. Shakespeare seems at
times to have written 1½ lines as 1,
especially where hemistiches were involved: if he wrote line 3 thus, and
carried on in 1½ lines (ending *down?* /
map. / *Hotspur;* / *of you* / *heaven.* / *spoke
of.*), the compositor would see the passage as prose. The present ll. 3 and 7
are perhaps portions of this "free"
composition where Shakespeare himself lost track of his line-lengths. Since
they cannot be reduced to decasyllables without producing surplus
words which improperly halt the
rhythm they have been left in their
overgrown condition; the movement
is lithe enough.

Hot.   And you in hell,
    As oft as he hears Owen Glendower spoke of.   10
Glend. I cannot blame him; at my nativity
    The front of heaven was full of fiery shapes,
    Of burning cressets, and at my birth
    The frame and huge foundation of the earth
    Shak'd like a coward.
Hot.   Why, so it would have done   15
    At the same season if your mother's cat
    Had but kitten'd, though yourself had never been born.
Glend. I say the earth did shake when I was born.
Hot. And I say the earth was not of my mind,
    If you suppose as fearing you it shook.   20
Glend. The heavens were all on fire, the earth did tremble—
Hot. O, then the earth shook to see the heavens on fire,
    And not in fear of your nativity.
    Diseased nature oftentimes breaks forth
    In strange eruptions, oft the teeming earth   25
    Is with a kind of colic pinch'd and vex'd
    By the imprisoning of unruly wind

9–10. And . . . of.] *As Collier; prose, QqF.*   14. and huge] *Q1;* and *Qq2–5,F.*
15. Shak'd] *Q5,F;* Shaked *Qq1–4.*   15–17. Why . . . born] *As Pope; prose,*
QqF.   21. tremble—] *Qq1,2* (tremble,)*;* tremble. *Qq3–5,F.*   22. O . . .
fire] *Qq (reading* Oh)*;* Oh . . . shooke / To . . . fire *F.*   25. oft] *Qq1–3;* of *Q4;*
and *Q5,F.*

11. *my nativity*] For portents on Mortimer's birth (which might be confused with Glendower's), see App. III,
p. 169. Shakespeare's portents, however, are different, and may owe
something to the "blasing starre"
which in 1402 foretold Glendower's
defeat of Lord Grey (Hol., iii. 19).

13. *cressets*] stars like fire-baskets, or
beacons.

25. *eruptions*] outbreaks, "with notion of a 'breaking out' of latent disease
or of peccant humours" (*OED*).

25–30. *oft . . . towers*] This explanation goes back at least to classical antiquity, e.g. Aristotle, *Meteorologica*, II.
7–8, Pliny, *Nat. Hist.*, II. lxxxi, and
Plutarch, *Opinions of Philosophers*, Bk
III. xv (in *Morales of Plutarch*, trans.

Holland, 1603). Gabriel Harvey's
*Pleasant . . . Discourse of the Earthquake in
Aprill Last*, 1580 (Grosart, i. 52), says
"The Materiall Cause of Earthquakes
(as . . . is sufficiently prooued by Aristotle in ye second Booke of his *Meteors*)
is no doubt great aboundance of
wynde, or stoare of grosse and drye
vapors, and spirites fast shut vp, & as a
man would saye, emprysoned in the
Caues, and Dungeons of the Earth:
which winde or vapors, seeking to be
set at libertie . . . violently rush out . . .
which forcible Eruption, and strong
breath, causeth an Earthquake". As
late as the 18th c. Young writes "As
yawns an earthquake, when im-
prison'd air / Struggles for vent" (*Last
Day*, i. 286–7).

Within her womb, which for enlargement striving
Shakes the old beldam earth, and topples down
Steeples and moss-grown towers. At your birth   30
Our grandam earth, having this distemp'rature,
In passion shook.

Glend.   Cousin, of many men
I do not bear these crossings; give me leave
To tell you once again that at my birth
The front of heaven was full of fiery shapes,   35
The goats ran from the mountains, and the herds
Were strangely clamorous to the frighted fields.
These signs have mark'd me extraordinary,
And all the courses of my life do show
I am not in the roll of common men.   40
Where is he living, clipp'd in with the sea
That chides the banks of England, Scotland, Wales,
Which calls me pupil or hath read to me?
And bring him out that is but woman's son
Can trace me in the tedious ways of art,   45
And hold me pace in deep experiments.

Hot. I think there's no man speaks better Welsh:
I'll to dinner.

Mort. Peace, cousin Percy, you will make him mad.

---

29. topples] *Qq1–4*; toples *Q5*; tombles *F.*   33. crossings] *Qq1,2,5,F*; crossing
Qq3,4.   41. he] *Qq1–3*; the *Qq4,5,F.*   42. Wales] *Qq1–4*; and Wales *Q5,F.*
44. son] sonne, *Q1 corr. (Brit. Mus. copy), Qq2–5,F*; sonne? *Q1 uncorr. (Trin. Coll.
Cambr. and Devonshire-Huntington copies).*

29. *beldam*] grandmother, grandam
(l. 31).

31. *distemp'rature*] constitutional disorder, earthly or celestial; Nashe
satirizes the author of "an absurd
Astrologicall Discourse of the terrible
Coniunction of *Saturne* and *Iupiter,*
wherein (as if hee had lately cast the
Heauens water, or beene at the anato-
mizing of the Skies entrailes . . .) hee
prophecieth of such strange wonders
to ensue from stars destemperature"
(*Pierce Penilesse*; McKerrow, i. 196).

32. *passion*] spasm of suffering.

42. *chides*] A characteristically living
image for the chafing sea. "The more
we study . . . the clearer it becomes that

there is one quality . . . which over-
poweringly attracts [Shakespeare]
throughout, and that quality is *movement*: nature and natural objects in
motion" (Spurgeon, 50).

43. *read to*] lectured, tutored.

45. *trace me*] follow my tracks.

47. *speaks better Welsh*] (*a*) "talks his
own tongue better (and that's all he's
good at)"; (*b*) (as it were) "talks more
double Dutch"—Welsh being thought
almost unintelligible; cf. l. 115, and
Webster, *White Devil,* III. i. 42—"Why
this is welch to Lattin" (*Works,* i. 138);
(*c*) "brags better", the Welsh being
much satirized on the stage for boast-
ing.

Glend. I can call spirits from the vasty deep.   50
Hot. Why, so can I, or so can any man,
          But will they come when you do call for them?
Glend. Why, I can teach you, cousin, to command the devil.
Hot. And I can teach thee, coz, to shame the devil,
          By telling truth; tell truth, and shame the devil.   55
          If thou have power to raise him, bring him hither,
          And I'll be sworn I have power to shame him hence:
          O, while you live, tell truth, and shame the devil!
Mort. Come, come, no more of this unprofitable chat.
Glend. Three times hath Henry Bolingbroke made head   60
          Against my power, thrice from the banks of Wye
          And sandy-bottom'd Severn have I sent him
          Bootless home, and weather-beaten back.
Hot. Home without boots, and in foul weather too!
          How scapes he agues, in the devil's name?   65
Glend. Come, here is the map, shall we divide our right
          According to our threefold order ta'en?
Mort. The Archdeacon hath divided it

---

53. you] *Qq1-4;* thee *Q5,F.*   command the] *QqF;* command / The *Capell, many edd.*   54. coz] *Qq1-4* (coose)*;* coosen *Q5;* Cousin *F.*   59. come, no] *QqF;* come, / No *Pope, many edd.*   62. sent] *Qq1-3;* hent *Qq4,5,F.*   64. boots, and] *Qq;* Bootes, / And *F.*   66. here is] *Qq;* heere's *F.*   map, shall] *Qq;* Mappe: / Shall *F.*

---

50. *I can call spirits*] Scot, *Discov. of Witchcraft*, 1584, Bk xv, ch. 1, describes conjurors who "deale with no inferiour causes; these fetch divels out of Hell, and angels out of Heaven", and "take upon them also the raising of tempests, and earthquakes, and to doo as much as God himselfe can doe. These are no small fooles, they go not to worke with a baggage tode, or a cat, as witches doo, but with a kind of Majestie, and with authoritie they call up by name, and have at their commandement seventie and nine principall and princelie divels, who have under them, as their ministers, a great multitude of legions of pettie divils".

53. *Why . . . devil*] Most edd. divide this at "command", but given the kind of slur frequent in this scene

("cous'n", "t'command") it makes an acceptable line and a better rhythmic parallel to l. 54.

55. *tell . . . devil*] Proverbial; Tilley, T566.

60–3. *Three . . . back*] i.e. in 1400, 1402, and (antedated by Shakespeare) 1405 (Hol., iii. 17, 20, 39). Hardyng (358) says, "The kyng Henry thryce to Wales went, / . . . In euery tyme were mystes and tempestes sent, / Of wethers foule that he had neuer power / Glendour to noye". If Shakespeare saw this he perhaps assumed that all three preceded Shrewsbury. For Henry's defeat in 1402 by "art magike" see App. III, p. 168.

63. *Bootless*] Unsuccessful. Q1's "booteless" is perhaps trisyllabic.

66. *here is*] Cf. collation, I. iii. 122, note, and Intro., p. lxix.

Into three limits very equally:
England, from Trent and Severn hitherto,   70
By south and east is to my part assign'd:
All westward, Wales beyond the Severn shore,
And all the fertile land within that bound,
To Owen Glendower: and, dear coz, to you
The remnant northward lying off from Trent.   75
And our indentures tripartite are drawn,
Which being sealed interchangeably,
(A business that this night may execute)
Tomorrow, cousin Percy, you and I
And my good Lord of Worcester will set forth   80
To meet your father and the Scottish power,
As is appointed us, at Shrewsbury.
My father Glendower is not ready yet,
Nor shall we need his help these fourteen days.
[*To Glend.*] Within that space you may have drawn
    together   85
Your tenants, friends, and neighbouring gentlemen.
Glend. A shorter time shall send me to you, lords,
And in my conduct shall your ladies come,
From whom you now must steal and take no leave,
For there will be a world of water shed   90
Upon the parting of your wives and you.
Hot. Methinks my moiety, north from Burton here,
In quantity equals not one of yours:
See how this river comes me cranking in,
And cuts me from the best of all my land   95
A huge half-moon, a monstrous cantle out.

---

85. S.D.] *Capell; not in QqF.*   96. cantle] *F; scantle Qq.*

69. *limits*] "limit *sb.*†3. The tract or region defined by a boundary" (*OED*).

76–7. *indentures tripartite . . . interchangeably*] contracts reciprocally sealed between the three parties; each party sealed all three copies and kept one for himself.

83. *father*] father-in-law.

92. *moiety*] share (not necessarily half).

96. *cantle*] F; Qq's "scantle" per-haps caught the "s" from "monstrous". A "scantle" is a small portion; *OED*, "scantle. *sb.*2", quotes Vilvain, *Theorem. Theol.*, vii. 194 (1654)—"The future cannot be confined to so short a scantle". A "cantle" (segment) seems nearer the required meaning. Cf. *Ant.*, III. viii. 16—"The greater cantle of the world is lost"; and Dray-ton, *Poly-Olb.*, i. 81—"Rude Neptune cutting in, a cantle forth doth take".

I'll have the current in this place damm'd up,
And here the smug and silver Trent shall run
In a new channel fair and evenly;
It shall not wind with such a deep indent,   100
To rob me of so rich a bottom here.
Glend. Not wind? It shall, it must—you see it doth.
Mort. Yea,
But mark how he bears his course, and runs me up
With like advantage on the other side,   105
Gelding the opposed continent as much
As on the other side it takes from you.
Wor. Yea, but a little charge will trench him here,
And on this north side win this cape of land,
And then he runs straight and even.   110
Hot. I'll have it so, a little charge will do it.
Glend. I'll not have it alter'd.
Hot.   Will not you?
Glend. No, nor you shall not.
Hot.   Who shall say me nay?
Glend. Why, that will I.
Hot. Let me not understand you then, speak it in Welsh.   115
Glend. I can speak English, lord, as well as you,
For I was train'd up in the English court,
Where being but young I framed to the harp
Many an English ditty lovely well,
And gave the tongue a helpful ornament—   120

---

97. damm'd] *Qq3–5* (damd); damnd *Qq1,2,F* (*subst.*).   102. wind?] *Qq2–5,F*; wind *Q1*.   103–7.] *As Steevens* (*verse*); Yea, ... course, / And ... side, / Gelding ... much, / As ... you. *F* (*verse*); *prose, Qq.*

98. *smug*] smooth, unruffled. Eliot's *Ortho-epia Gallica*, ii. 171, translates "Elle a la face luysante & Angelique" by "she hath a smug and a glistering face".

101. *bottom*] river-valley.

103–7.] Prose in Qq, garbled verse in F. It is so clearly metre that all edd. print it so, generally making a separate line of "Yea" or "Yea, but".

106. *Gelding ... continent*] Cutting a vital piece from the opposite bank. "Continent" = that which contains.

In *MND*, ii. i. 92, the flooded rivers "have overborne their continents".

112. *I'll*] Pope and many edd. change QqF's "Ile" to "I will". But Glendower's Welsh tune can make "I'll" quite long enough; cf. "she'll" (l. 188), "we'll" (l. 259), and l. 205, note.

115. *Welsh*] Cf. l. 47, note (*b*).

117. *train'd ... court*] See App. III, p. 167.

120. *gave ... ornament*] graced the words with music.

         A virtue that was never seen in you.
Hot. Marry and I am glad of it with all my heart!
         I had rather be a kitten and cry "mew"
         Than one of these same metre ballad-mongers;
         I had rather hear a brazen canstick turn'd,   125
         Or a dry wheel grate on the axle-tree,
         And that would set my teeth nothing on edge,
         Nothing so much as mincing poetry—
         'Tis like the forc'd gait of a shuffling nag.
Glend. Come, you shall have Trent turn'd.   130
Hot. I do not care, I'll give thrice so much land
         To any well-deserving friend:
         But in the way of bargain, mark ye me,
         I'll cavil on the ninth part of a hair.
         Are the indentures drawn? Shall we be gone?   135
Glend. The moon shines fair, you may away by night:
         I'll haste the writer, and withal
         Break with your wives of your departure hence.
         I am afraid my daughter will run mad,
         So much she doteth on her Mortimer.   *Exit.*   140
Mort. Fie, cousin Percy, how you cross my father!
Hot. I cannot choose; sometime he angers me

---

122. Marry and] *QqF;* Marry, / And *Dyce.*   124. ballad-mongers] *Q1*
(ballet mongers), *Qq2–5* (ballet-mongers), *F.*   125. canstick] *Qq;* Candle-
stick *F.*   127. on] *Qq3–4;* an *Qq1,2,5,F.*   136. fair, you] *Qq;* faire, /
You *F.*

122. *Marry . . . heart*] One line, QqF.
Some edd. separate "Marry", but the
slur ("Marry'and I'm") is just like
Hotspur.
    124. *metre ballad-mongers*] "Metre"
often implied "doggerel verse"; cf.
Peele, *Ed. I* (Mal. Soc., 1911, ll. 556–7)
—"lets haue a few more of these
meeters, he hath great store in his
head"; and Campion, *Observations*
(*Elizn Crit. Essays*, ed. G. G. Smith,
1904, ii. 329)—"that vulgar and easie
kind of Poesie which . . . we abusively
call Rime and Meeter". A more reputable sense occurs in Stow (*Annales*,
1592, 547)—"He [Prince Henry] de-
lighted in songs, meters, and musicall

instruments". On the low repute of
street ballads cf. II. ii. 43–4, note.
    125. *brazen . . . turn'd*] A vivid image
of cacophony. "Canstick" = candle-
stick. The Lothbury founders, says
Stow, "cast candlesticks . . . and doe
afterwards turne them . . . to make
them smooth and bright with turning
and scrating . . . making a lothsome
noise to the by-passers" (*Survay*, "Cole-
man Street Ward").
    128. *mincing*] tripping on affected
poetic feet.
    142. *he angers me*] This anger is fully
vindicated when "prophecies" keep
Glendower away from Shrewsbury,
IV. iv. 18.

With telling me of the moldwarp and the ant,
Of the dreamer Merlin and his prophecies,
And of a dragon and a finless fish,   145
A clip-wing'd griffin and a moulten raven,
A couching lion and a ramping cat,
And such a deal of skimble-skamble stuff
As puts me from my faith. I tell you what—
He held me last night at least nine hours   150
In reckoning up the several devils' names
That were his lackeys: I cried "Hum", and "Well, go to!"
But mark'd him not a word. O, he is as tedious
As a tired horse, a railing wife,
Worse than a smoky house. I had rather live   155
With cheese and garlic in a windmill, far,

---

143. of] *Qq1–4,F; of of Q5*.   150. last] *QqF;* up last *T. Johnson;* the last *Pope;*
but last *Steevens*.   152. lackeys: I] *Qq;* Lacqueyes: / I F.   153. he is] *QqF;*
he's *Pope, many edd*.   155. I had] *QqF;* I'ad *Pope;* I'd *Theobald*.

143–7. *moldwarp . . . cat*] "moldwarp" = mole. For Hol.'s comment
on this credulity see App. III, p. 171.
For an echo of *A Myrroure for Magistrates* see p. xxxvii. *Archaeologia*, xx,
1824, 250–71, discussing Merlin prophecies from antiquity, cites some current under Richard II and Henry IV
in which Henry figures as the mole
cursed by the mouth of God (cf. *Lev.*,
xi. 29–30—"These also shall be un-
clean . . . the mole . . ."") and the others
as the dragon, lion, and wild boar.
The dragon, lion, and boar (really, the
white wolf) were the crests respectively of Glendower, Percy, and Mortimer (G. R. French, *Sh.'s Genealogy*,
1869, 64). There seem, however, no
references to the ant, fish, griffin,
raven, or cat; these may derive orally
from Shakespeare's Welsh acquaintances (cf. Intro., p. xxvi).
144. *dreamer Merlin*] Cf. Intro.,
p. xxxvii.
147. *couching . . . ramping*] Burlesque
of the heraldic "couchant" (lying) and
"rampant" (rearing).
148. *skimble-skamble*] Apparently
"coined by Shakespeare for Hotspur's
use. *OED* defines it as *nonsensical* and

records no prior use of it" (Hemingway, New Var.).
149. *puts . . . faith*] makes me a scep-
tic, even about Christianity.
150. *He . . . hours*] Scot's *Discov. of
Witchcraft*, 1584, Bk xv, ch. 2, fills
eight folio pages with a list of devils'
names. Reading it, as Steevens remarks, one sympathises with Hotspur.
151. *several*] various.
154–5. *a railing . . . house*] Traditional, from *Prov.*, xxvii. 15—"A
brawling woman and the roofe of the
house dropping in a raynie day, may
well be compared together". Tilley,
H781 and S574, gives many examples
of the "smoky house" variant, found
also in Chaucer, *Wyf of Bathe's Prol.*,
278–80—"smoke / And chiding wives
maken men to flee / Out of hir owen
hous". In *Piers Plowman*, B, xvii. 315–
26, "a wikked wyf", a leaky roof, and a
smoky house are said to make home
untenable.
156. *cheese . . . windmill*] The least
agreeable diet and residence. "Cheese
and onions" were proverbially poor
fare; Thomas Heywood, *Captives* (Mal.
Soc., 1953, ll. 2383–4), has "the poore
can still / with cheese and onions [fill

> Than feed on cates and have him talk to me
> In any summer house in Christendom.
> *Mort.* In faith, he is a worthy gentleman,
>   Exceedingly well read, and profited   160
>   In strange concealments, valiant as a lion,
>   And wondrous affable, and as bountiful
>   As mines of India. Shall I tell you, cousin?
>   He holds your temper in a high respect
>   And curbs himself even of his natural scope   165
>   When you come 'cross his humour, faith he does:
>   I warrant you that man is not alive
>   Might so have tempted him as you have done
>   Without the taste of danger and reproof:
>   But do not use it oft, let me entreat you.   170
> *Wor.* In faith, my lord, you are too wilful-blame,
>   And since your coming hither have done enough
>   To put him quite besides his patience;
>   You must needs learn, lord, to amend this fault.
>   Though sometimes it show greatness, courage, blood,

---

159. is] *Qq1,2;* was *Qq3–5,F.*   160. Exceedingly] *Qq1,2;* Exceeding *Qq3–5,F.*
161–3.] *As Qq;* In . . . Concealements: / Valiant . . . affable, / And . . . India. /
Shall . . . Cousin, / *F.*   166. come 'cross] *Qq* (come crosse)*;* doe crosse *F.*
173. besides] *Qq1,3–5,F;* beside *Q2.*

---

the belly]", and Davenport, *New Trick to cheat the Devil,* I. ii (Bullen, *Old Plays,* New ser., iii. 208), "Rather then feast where they shall domineere . . . Ile feede on Cheese, and Onions". Windmills were noisy and often unsteady; cf. Jonson, *Silent W.,* v. iii. 61–3 (H. & S., v. 258)—"My very house turnes round with the tumult! I dwell in a windmill!" "Have us out of thy windmil here", a guest in a noisy tavern protests (Brome [Shepherd, vol. II], *Covent Garden Weeded* [p. 35]).

157. *cates*] delicacies.

158. *summer house*] "Beauregard: m. A Summer-house, or Graunge; a house for pleasure and recreation" (Cotgrave). It was a luxury; Dekker and Webster's *West-ward Hoe,* I. i. 188–90 (Bowers, ii. 324) has "Your prodigality, your diceing . . . your building a Summer house hath vndone vs".

160–1. *profited . . . concealments*] proficient in secret arts.

171. *are . . . blame*] are blamable for too much self-will. "The dat. infin. *to blame* is much used as the predicate after *be*. In the 16–17th c. the *to* was misunderstood as *too,* and *blame* taken as adj." (*OED,* "Blame, *vb.* 6"). Cf. *Lr.,* I. ii. 45 (F text)—"The Contents [of Edgar's supposed letter] . . . Are too blame". *2H4,* II. iv. 395, reads in Q "I feele me much too blame", where F has "to blame".

175. *Though . . . blood*] "blood" = "mettle, spirit". Elyot, *Governour,* III. xv, has a similar observation—"In height and greatnesse of courage is moste soneste ingendred obstinacie. . . Undoughtedly this is an horrible and perylouse vice, and very familiar with them whiche be of moste noble courage". For contemporary comment on

—And that's the dearest grace it renders you—   176
Yet oftentimes it doth present harsh rage,
Defect of manners, want of government,
Pride, haughtiness, opinion, and disdain,
The least of which haunting a nobleman   180
Loseth men's hearts and leaves behind a stain
Upon the beauty of all parts besides,
Beguiling them of commendation.

Hot. Well, I am school'd—good manners be your speed!
Here come our wives, and let us take our leave.   185

[Re-]enter GLENDOWER *with the ladies.*

Mort. This is the deadly spite that angers me,
My wife can speak no English, I no Welsh.
Glend. My daughter weeps, she'll not part with you,
She'll be a soldier too, she'll to the wars.
Mort. Good father, tell her that she and my aunt Percy   190
Shall follow in your conduct speedily.

*Glendower speaks to her in Welsh, and she
answers him in the same.*

180. nobleman] *QqF* (*Qq1–4* noble man).   184.] *As Qq;* Well . . . school'd: /
Good- . . . speede; / *F.*   185. come our] *Qq1,2;* come your *Qq3–5,F.*   S.D.
Re-enter] *QqF* (*Enter*), *Capell.*   188. she'll] *QqF;* she will *T. Johnson, Pope.*

valour and discretion see v. iv. 119,
note.

176. *dearest*] noblest; see iv. iv. 31,
note.

184. *good . . . speed*] Sardonic; "let us
hope good manners will win you the
day".

185. *and*] "And" could connect an
affirmation and a command; cf. v. iv.
33—"I will assay thee, and defend
thyself" (Qq: changed in F to "so");
and *Ado,* i. ii. 20–1—"I will send for
him; and question him yourself"; also
R2, v. iii. 144—"Your mother well
hath pray'd, and prove you true."
Chaucer has the same usage in *Tr. &
Cris.,* i. 693.

188. *she'll*] Pope and most edd.
change QqF's "sheele" to "she will".
The protraction, however, may be
Glendower's Welsh inflection (see

notes on ll. 112, 205, 259), even
though in l. 189 the word is mono-
syllabic, as "difference" has three syllables in l. 212 and two in l. 213, or
"cowards" one and two syllables in
"Cowards father cowards, and base
things sire base" (*Cym.,* iv. ii. 25).

190. *my aunt Percy*] More Mortimer
confusion; cf. notes on i. iii. 79, 83–4,
144, and Appendix VIII. As Glendower's son-in-law the speaker was
Lady Percy's brother, not nephew (cf.
ii. iii. 82); as heir to the throne he was
her nephew, not brother, and not
Glendower's son-in-law.

191. S.D. Glendower . . . same]
Dramatists often introduced Welsh
songs or speeches (Max Förster, *Die
Kymr. Einlagen bei Sh.,* 1924, 356);
Glendower and Lady Percy were
doubtless played by Welsh actors.

Glend. She is desperate here, a peevish, self-willed har-
　　lotry, one that no persuasion can do good upon.

　　　　　　　　　　　　The lady speaks in Welsh.

Mort. I understand thy looks, that pretty Welsh
　　Which thou pourest down from these swelling heavens
　　I am too perfect in, and but for shame　　　　　196
　　In such a parley should I answer thee.

　　　　　　　　　　The lady [speaks] again in Welsh.

　　I understand thy kisses, and thou mine,
　　And that's a feeling disputation,
　　But I will never be a truant, love,　　　　　　200
　　Till I have learnt thy language, for thy tongue
　　Makes Welsh as sweet as ditties highly penn'd,
　　Sung by a fair queen in a summer's bow'r
　　With ravishing division to her lute.

Glend. Nay, if you melt, then will she run mad.　　205

　　　　　　　　　　　The lady speaks again in Welsh.

Mort. O, I am ignorance itself in this!

Glend. She bids you on the wanton rushes lay you down,
　　And rest your gentle head upon her lap,
　　And she will sing the song that pleaseth you,

192–3.] *As Cambr. (prose);* She . . . here, / A . . . vpon. *Qq (first phrase verse, rest prose);* Shee . . . heere: / A . . . Harlotry, / One . . . vpon. *F (verse).*　195. pourest] *Qq* (powrest); powr'st *F.*　197. S.D. *speaks*] *Malone; not in QqF.*　198. I] *Theobald; Mor.* I *QqF.*　202. sweet] *Qq1–4,F;* sweets *Q5.*　205. you] *Qq1–3;* thou *Qq4,5,F.*　207.] *As Qq;* She bids you, / On . . . downe, *F.*　209. song] *Qq1–3,5,F;* sung *Q4.*

192–3. *harlotry*] Here, as often (e.g. ii. iv. 390), an unsexual term of indignity; cf. *Rom.*, IV. ii. 14—"a peevish self-will'd harlotry it is".

194–5. *that . . . heavens*] that language of yours (your tears) streaming from your brimming eyes.

199. *feeling disputation*] contest, contention, in the speechless exchange of feelings.

202. *highly penn'd*] As in *Ado*, v. ii. 6–7, where Benedick proposes a sonnet "in so high a style . . . that no man living shall come over it".

204. *division*] "A brilliant passage, of short notes, which is founded essentially on a much simpler passage of

longer notes" (Naylor, *Sh. and Music*, 28).

205. *Nay*] For the protraction cf. notes on ll. 112 and 188. Hemingway (New Var.) cites Coleridge (*Lectures and Notes of 1818*, sec. iii)—"This 'nay' so to be dwelt on in speaking, as to be equivalent to a dissyllable . . . is characteristic of the solemn [Ed.: or the Welsh?] Glendower".

207. *wanton*] Either lush, luxuriant, as in *MND*, II. i. 99—"the wanton green"; or luxurious, comfortable, as in *2H4*, I. i. 147–9, where Northumberland's "sickly quoif" is "a guard too wanton for the head / Which princes . . . aim to hit."

And on your eyelids crown the god of sleep,   210
Charming your blood with pleasing heaviness,
Making such difference 'twixt wake and sleep
As is the difference betwixt day and night,
The hour before the heavenly-harness'd team
Begins his golden progress in the east.   215

Mort. With all my heart I'll sit and hear her sing,
By that time will our book I think be drawn.

Glend. Do so, and those musicians that shall play to you
Hang in the air a thousand leagues from hence,
And straight they shall be here: sit, and attend.   220

Hot. Come, Kate, thou art perfect in lying down:
Come, quick, quick, that I may lay my head in thy lap.

Lady P. Go, ye giddy goose.   *The music plays.*

Hot. Now I perceive the devil understands Welsh,
And 'tis no marvel he is so humorous,   225
By'r lady, he is a good musician.

Lady P. Then should you be nothing but musical,
For you are altogether govern'd by humours.
Lie still, ye thief, and hear the lady sing in Welsh.

Hot. I had rather hear Lady my brach howl in Irish.   230

212. 'twixt] *Qq1–3;* betwixt *Qq4,5,F.*   218.] *As Qq;* Doe so: / And ... you, / *F.*
219. hence] *Qq1–3;* thence *Qq4,5,F.*   221–2.] *As QqF (verse); prose, Pope, most edd.*   224–6.] *As QqF (verse); prose, Pope, some edd.*   225. marvel he is] *QqF;* marvel, he is *Theobald;* marvel, he's *Capell.*   226. he is] *Qq;* hee's *F.*   227–9.] *As QqF (verse); prose, Pope, most edd.*   227. should] *Qq1–3;* would *Qq4,5,F.*   230. hear Lady my] *Q1* (heare lady my), *Qq2–3* (heare, lady, my), *Q4* (heare Lady, my), *Q5* (heare *Lady,* my), *F* (heare (Lady) my).

210. *crown ... sleep*] i.e. give him "sovereign dominion" (Malone).

217. *book*] deed, here of partition.

218. *Do ... you*] One line in Qq; divided at "so" in F and many edd. The problem is quite trivial, but Qq maintain Glendower's flow and enable "to you" to be a delicate extrametrical cadence.

221–2.] As also in ll. 227–9 I keep QqF's lineation, though the rhythms (as often in this scene) wander in the no-man's land between prose and verse, and most edd. enlist them for the former.

225. *'tis ... humorous*] Qq's comma after "humorous" allows the syntax to

work both backward ("No wonder he's so capricious—he's a Welsh linguist") and, as Lady Percy takes it, forward ("No wonder he's so capricious—he's a musician").

230. *Lady my brach ... Irish*] A. Fleming, *Of English Dogs,* 1576, says "We Englishmen call bitches, belonging to the hunting kind of dogs, by the term [viz. Brache]" (Arber, *Engl. Garner,* iii. 237). "Irish" may refer to the supposed uncouthness of Erse or the supposed similarity of its sounds to canine ululation. In *AYL,* v. ii. 121, Rosalind compares the lovers' protestations to "the howling of Irish wolves".

Lady P. Wouldst thou have thy head broken?
Hot. No.
Lady P. Then be still.
Hot. Neither, 'tis a woman's fault.
Lady P. Now God help thee!   235
Hot. To the Welsh lady's bed.
Lady P. What's that?
Hot. Peace, she sings.   *Here the lady sings a Welsh song.*
        Come, Kate, I'll have your song too.
Lady P. Not mine, in good sooth.   240
Hot. Not yours, in good sooth! Heart, you swear like a
        comfit-maker's wife—"Not you, in good sooth!",
        and "As true as I live!", and "As God shall mend
        me!", and "As sure as day!"—
        And givest such sarcenet surety for thy oaths   245
        As if thou never walk'st further than Finsbury.
        Swear me, Kate, like a lady as thou art,
        A good mouth-filling oath, and leave "In sooth",
        And such protest of pepper-gingerbread,

231. thou have] *Qq1,2;* haue *Qq3–5,F.*   239. Come] *Rowe; Hot.* Come *QqF.*
Kate] *Qq1,2; not in Qq3–5,F.*   241–4.] *As Qq (prose);* Not . . . sooth? / You . . .
Wife: / Not . . . liue; / And . . . day: / *F (verse).*   241. Heart, you] *Qq;* You *F.*

233. *still*] Stillness is not, according
to popular wit, among woman's
faults. Either Hotspur is ironical or,
aware of his own masculine restless-
ness, he says, "It would be a fault of
effeminacy in me to lie still and lack
spirit".

241–4. *you swear . . . day*] Cf. R.
Brathwaite, *Strappado for the Divell* (ed.
Ebsworth, 1878, 40)—"A ciuill matron, lisping with forsooth, / As one
that had not heart to sweare an oath".
"Comfit-maker"=confectioner. "Puritans condemned swearing, and
many citizens were Puritans" (Wilson,
N.C.S.); see Fal. on the "rascally yea-
forsooth knave" (*2H4,* I. ii. 40). These
protestations belong to the "city-
words" which, in Brome's *Covent Garden Weeded* (Shepherd, vol. II), III. i
(p. 40), "gaine you credit, and bring
you into good and civil estimation".
Gentlefolk scorned them and writers

made fun of them; cf. Lyly, *Pappe with
a Hatchet* (Bond, iii. 340)—"Martin
will not sweare, but with indeede, in
sooth, & in truth hee'le cog the die of
deceit"; and Jonson, *Poetaster,* IV. i.
33–4 (H. & S., iv. 263)—"your citie
mannerly word (forsooth) vse it not
too often".

245. *sarcenet*] thin silk, light and insubstantial. Cf. Jonson, *Alchemist,* II.
ii. 89–90 (H. & S., v. 320)—"taffata-
sarsnet, soft, and light / As cob-
webs".

246. *Finsbury*] Finsbury Fields,
north of Moorfields, were a favourite
resort of citizens.

247. *a lady*] i.e. an aristocrat; cf.
Elyot, *Governour,* I. xxvi—"they wyll
say he that swereth depe, swereth like
a lorde".

249. *pepper-gingerbread*] R.I.'s *English Huswife,* 1615, 73, gives "a pennyworth of pepper" as an ingredient of

> To velvet-guards, and Sunday citizens.   250
> Come, sing.

Lady P. I will not sing.

Hot. 'Tis the next way to turn tailor, or be redbreast
> teacher. And the indentures be drawn I'll away
> within these two hours; and so come in when ye   255
> will.   *Exit.*

Glend. Come, come, Lord Mortimer, you are as slow
> As hot Lord Percy is on fire to go:
> By this our book is drawn—we'll but seal,
> And then to horse immediately.

Mort.   With all my heart.   260
>   *Exeunt.*

SCENE II.—[*London. The Palace.*]

Enter the KING, PRINCE OF WALES, *and others.*

King. Lords, give us leave; the Prince of Wales and I
> Must have some private conference: but be near at hand,
> For we shall presently have need of you.   *Exeunt Lords.*

257. as slow] *Qq1–4,F; slow Q5.*   258. hot]*F; Hot. Qq1–3; Hot, Q4; Hot | Q5.*

Scene II

SCENE II.] *F (Scæna Secunda.); not in Qq.   Location.] Capell (subst.).   S.D.
others] Qq1–3,F; other Qq4,5.   1–2.] As Qq; Lords . . . leaue: | The . . . I, | Must
. . . conference: | But . . . hand, |F.*

"coarse Ginger-bread". Pepper-gingerbread oaths, doubtless, like crumb-
ly confections, make a fleeting tang in
the mouth.

250. *velvet-guards . . . Sunday citizens*]
citizens in their Sunday finery;
"guards" = trimmings. Cf. Dekker,
Seuen Deadly Sinnes (Grosart, ii. 24)—
"O veluet garded Theeues! O yea-
and-by-nay [sic] Cheaters! O Ciuill, ô
Graue and Right Worshipful Couzen-
ers!" Fynes Moryson's *Itinerary*, 1617,
pt III, iv. 179, says "At publike meetings the Aldermen of London weare
Scarlet gownes, and their wives a close
gowne of skarlet laid with gards of

black velvet", i.e. black velvet facings.

253–4. *'Tis . . . teacher*] "All right,
don't sing! Singing's the quickest way
to turn into a tailor or song-bird
teacher." Tailors sang at work, like
weavers (cf. II. iv. 130); robins were
esteemed for their song. Nicholas Cox,
in *The Gentleman's Recreation (A short
Account of Singing-Birds),* 1686, pt iii.
167, says: "It is the opinion of some,
that this little King of Birds [the
Robin-Redbreast] for sweetness of
Note comes not much short of the
Nightingale".

259. *we'll*] Cf. notes on ll. 112, 188,
205.

KING HENRY THE FOURTH 101

I know not whether God will have it so
For some displeasing service I have done,   5
That in his secret doom out of my blood
He'll breed revengement and a scourge for me;
But thou dost in thy passages of life
Make me believe that thou art only mark'd
For the hot vengeance and the rod of heaven,   10
To punish my mistreadings. Tell me else
Could such inordinate and low desires,
Such poor, such bare, such lewd, such mean attempts,
Such barren pleasures, rude society,
As thou art match'd withal, and grafted to,   15
Accompany the greatness of thy blood,
And hold their level with thy princely heart?
Prince. So please your Majesty, I would I could
Quit all offences with as clear excuse
As well as I am doubtless I can purge   20
Myself of many I am charg'd withal:
Yet such extenuation let me beg
As, in reproof of many tales devis'd,
Which oft the ear of greatness needs must hear,
By smiling pickthanks, and base newsmongers,   25
I may for some things true, wherein my youth
Hath faulty wander'd and irregular,
Find pardon on my true submission.

4. God] *Qq;* Heauen *F.*   8. thy] *Q1,F;* the *Qq2–5.*   15. to] *Qq;* too *F.*

4–11. *I know . . . mistreadings*] In *R2,*
v. iii. 1–3, Bolingbroke already looks
on Hal's dissoluteness as ominous—
"Can no man tell me of my unworthy
son? . . . If any plague hang over us, 'tis
he". His merely covert sense of guilt
here is psychologically interesting.

8. *passages*] courses.

9–11. *mark'd . . . mistreadings*] Logi-
cally the sense is "To punish my sins
Heaven's vengeance will fall on you"
or alternatively "To punish my sins
Heaven has sent you to afflict me".
But Shakespeare's flexible syntax
allows both senses, in a general formula
"Heaven is punishing me through
you".

12. *inordinate*] unworthy of your
rank.

13. *bare . . . lewd . . . attempts*]
wretched . . . base . . . exploits. For
"bare" cf. I. iii. 107.

17. *hold . . . level*] put themselves on a
level.

22–8. *Yet . . . submission*] "Let me beg
so much extenuation that upon con-
futation of many false charges I may be
pardoned some that are true" (Johnson).

23. *reproof*] disproof.

25. *pickthanks*] A clear echo of Hol.,
when "pickthanks had sowne diuision"
between father and son; cf. App. III,
p. 179.

King. God pardon thee! Yet let me wonder, **Harry**,
    At thy affections, which do hold a wing   30
    Quite from the flight of all thy ancestors.
    Thy place in Council thou hast rudely lost,
    Which by thy younger brother is supply'd,
    And art almost an alien to the hearts
    Of all the court and princes of my blood: 35
    The hope and expectation of thy time
    Is ruin'd, and the soul of every man
    Prophetically do forethink thy fall.
    Had I so lavish of my presence been,
    So common-hackney'd in the eyes of men,   40
    So stale and cheap to vulgar company,
    Opinion, that did help me to the crown,
    Had still kept loyal to possession,
    And left me in reputeless banishment,
    A fellow of no mark nor likelihood.   45
    By being seldom seen, I could not stir
    But like a comet I was wonder'd at,
    That men would tell their children, "This is he!"
    Others would say, "Where, which is Bolingbroke?"
    And then I stole all courtesy from heaven,   50
    And dress'd myself in such humility
    That I did pluck allegiance from men's hearts,

29.] *As Qq;* Heauen ... thee: / Yet ... *Harry,* / *F.*

30. *affections*] propensities.

32–3. *Thy place ... supply'd*] Shakespeare saves Hal's reputation by omitting (save for the vague "rudely") reference to the famous quarrel with the Lord Chief Justice as related in Elyot's *Governour* (II. vi), Hall (with the addition of the physical assault), Hol., Stow, and *F.V.* The story is probably apocryphal but was an article of popular faith.

38. *do*] The plural follows the plurality implied in "every man".

39.] See App. VI.

40. *common-hackney'd*] A word retaining the concrete force of its original sense, of a workaday horse.

43. *possession*] Both abstract and concrete (= "possessor"); cf. I. iii. 86, note.

50. *I stole ... heaven*] I assumed a courteous demeanour as of Heaven itself. Henry is describing that "courtship to the common people" which Richard accounts politically significant in *R2*, I. iv. 23–36. On ll. 50–2 Spurgeon remarks "One of [Shakespeare's] outstanding characteristics is the way in which by introducing verbs of movement [e.g. 'stole', 'dress'd', 'pluck'] about things which are motionless, or rather which are abstractions and cannot have physical movement, he gives life to the whole phrase" (Spurgeon, 51).

Loud shouts and salutations from their mouths,
Even in the presence of the crowned King.
Thus did I keep my person fresh and new,   55
My presence, like a robe pontifical,
Ne'er seen but wonder'd at, and so my state,
Seldom, but sumptuous, show'd like a feast,
And wan by rareness such solemnity.
The skipping King, he ambled up and down,   60
With shallow jesters, and rash bavin wits,
Soon kindled and soon burnt, carded his state,
Mingled his royalty with cap'ring fools,

---

54. the presence] *Qq1,3–5,F; presence Q2.*   55. did I] *Qq1–4; I did Q5,F.*
58. Seldom, but] *Qq; Seldome but F.*   show'd] *Q1; shewed Qq2–5,F.*   59.
wan] *Qq; wonne F.*   61. bavin] *QqF; braine Dering MS.*   63. cap'ring] *Q1*
(capring); carping *Qq2–5,F.*

55–7. *my person . . . wonder'd at*]
Tilley, M20, quotes the proverb "A
maid oft seen, a gown oft worn / Are
disesteemed and held in scorn".

56. *pontifical*] of bishop or archbishop.

58. *Seldom*] Adjectival, as still in
Scots (e.g. "the seldom time"), and
in sonnet lii. 4—"seldom pleasure".
This sonnet, on the enhanced value of
unhackneyed pleasures, may be echoed here as it is at I. ii. 202.

59. *wan*] Frequent form of preter-
ite.

60 ff. *The skipping King . . .*] There is
nothing like this behaviour in *R2*, but
there is in *Woodstock* (Mal. Soc., 1929,
ll. 1204 ff.), when Richard and his
companions "ride through London
only to be gaz'd at", fantastically
dressed. Hol. does not record this incident but he does comment "He kept
the greatest port, and maintained the
most plentiful house, that euer any
king in England did either before his
time or since. For there resorted dailie
to his court aboue ten thousand persons that had meat and drinke there
allowed them" (ii. 868); Shakespeare
echoes this in *R2*, IV. i. 281–3. Remarking on Shakespeare's mature
style, Madeleine Doran observes

"Notice the rapid succession of images,
the quick suggestion rather than elab-
oration in such compact and elliptical
lines as 'To laugh at gibing boys' and
'Enfeoff'd himself to popularity', the
fusion of one image with another; the
skipping and capering with the quick
burning of faggots ('rash bavin') and
with the adulteration suggested by
carding; the enfeoffment with the idea
of surfeit (itself boldly linked with
eyes); it in turn with the common
sight of the cuckoo in June, and with
the drowsiness of men in constant sun-
shine, and this latter image shifting
ground with 'cloudy men'" ('Imagery
in *R2* and in *H4*', *MLR*, xxxvii, 1942,
115).

61. *rash bavin*] "rash" = briefly in-
flammable; "bavin" = kindling,
faggot. Tilley, B107, illustrates the
proverb "The Bavin burns bright but
it is but a blaze".

62. *carded his state*] degraded his dignity by indiscriminate mingling. "To
card" = mix together and (often)
adulterate. Greene's *Quippe for an Vpstart Courtier* (Grosart, xi. 275) denounces a dishonest tapster with "You
. . . carde your beere (if you see your
guests begin to be drunke) halfe smal
& halfe strong".

Had his great name profaned with their scorns,
And gave his countenance against his name   65
To laugh at gibing boys, and stand the push
Of every beardless vain comparative,
Grew a companion to the common streets,
Enfeoff'd himself to popularity,
That, being daily swallow'd by men's eyes,   70
They surfeited with honey, and began
To loathe the taste of sweetness, whereof a little
More than a little is by much too much.
So, when he had occasion to be seen,
He was but as the cuckoo is in June,   75
Heard, not regarded; seen, but with such eyes
As, sick and blunted with community,
Afford no extraordinary gaze,
Such as is bent on sun-like majesty
When it shines seldom in admiring eyes,   80
But rather drows'd and hung their eyelids down,
Slept in his face, and render'd such aspect
As cloudy men use to their adversaries,
Being with his presence glutted, gorg'd, and full.
And in that very line, Harry, standest thou,   85
For thou hast lost thy princely privilege
With vile participation. Not an eye

---

70. swallow'd] *Pope;* swallowed *QqF.*   71–2. began / To loathe the] *As
T. Johnson, Pope;* began to loath / The *QqF (subst.).*   83. to] *Qq1,2;* to doe to
Qq3–5,F.

65. *against his name*] Both (*a*) contrary to his kingly title, and (*b*) to the
detriment of his authority.
66. *stand the push*] submit to the
impudence.
67. *comparative*] dealer in insults (cf.
i. ii. 78). The word could also mean
"rival, compeer" (cf. Beau. & Fl.,
*Four Plays in One, Triumph of Love
(Works,* x. 324)—"*Gerard* ever was /
His full comparative"), and both
senses may well be present.
69. *Enfeoff'd*] Surrendered himself—
a legal term meaning surrender of pro-
perty to complete possession.
71–3. *They . . . too much*] Noble cites

Prov., xxv. 16—"If thou findest honie,
eate so muche as is sufficient for thee:
lest thou be ouer full, and parbreake it
out agayne".
77. *community*] commonness, familiarity (that breeds contempt).
79. *sun-like*] Symbolic of royalty; cf.
Chettle, *England's Mourning Garment*
(ed. Ingleby, 103)—"Such maiestie
had her presence . . . that guiltie mor-
talitie durst not beholde her but with
sun dazeled eyes".
83. *cloudy*] (*a*) sullen; (*b*) hostile to
"sun-like majesty".
85. *line*] category; cf. i. iii. 166–7,
note.

But is a-weary of thy common sight,
Save mine, which hath desir'd to see thee more,
Which now doth that I would not have it do,   90
Make blind itself with foolish tenderness.
Prince. I shall hereafter, my thrice gracious lord,
Be more myself.
King.   For all the world
As thou art to this hour was Richard then
When I from France set foot at Ravenspurgh,   95
And even as I was then is Percy now.
Now by my sceptre, and my soul to boot,
He hath more worthy interest to the state
Than thou the shadow of succession.
For of no right, nor colour like to right,   100
He doth fill fields with harness in the realm,
Turns head against the lion's armed jaws,
And being no more in debt to years than thou
Leads ancient lords and reverend bishops on
To bloody battles, and to bruising arms.   105
What never-dying honour hath he got
Against renowned Douglas! whose high deeds,
Whose hot incursions and great name in arms,
Holds from all soldiers chief majority
And military title capital   110
Through all the kingdoms that acknowledge Christ.
Thrice hath this Hotspur, Mars in swathling clothes,

---

89. desir'd] *F;* desired *Qq.*   99. thou the] *Q1;* thou, the *Qq2–5,F.*   107. renowned] *Qq4,5,F;* renowmed *Qq1–3.*   109. soldiers] *Qq1,2,4,5,F* (*subst.*); souldier: *Q3.*   110. capital] *Qq2,3;* capitall. *Qq1,5,F;* capitall, *Q4.*   111. Christ.] *Qq1–3;* Christ, *Qq4,5,F.*   112. this] *Qq1–4;* the *Q5,F.*   Hotspur, Mars] *Qq1–4* (Hotspur Mars), *Q5* (*Hotspur Mars*), *F* (*Hotspur Mars,*), *Warburton.* swathling] *Qq1–3;* swathing *Qq4,5,F.*

---

91. *Make . . . tenderness*] This touch, as Wilson (N.C.S.) notes, probably comes from Hol. ("shedding teares", iii. 54); or the original of *F.V.* (vi. 114, 120, S.D.s "*He weepes*"), though this reconciliation scene is quite different from theirs.

98–9. *He . . . succession*] i.e. He has a claim based upon worth, while you have merely insubstantial hereditary custom to depend on. "Succession" as

an inherited right is a shadow unless confirmed by merit, as Richard II had found when faced with Bolingbroke.

100. *colour*] semblance.

101. *harness*] i.e. armed men.

103. *no more in debt*] Born in 1364, Hotspur was in fact twenty-three years Hal's senior.

109. *majority*] pre-eminence.

112. *Thrice*] The main engagements Hol. records are Otterburn (19 Aug.

This infant warrior, in his enterprises
Discomfited great Douglas, ta'en him once,
Enlarged him, and made a friend of him,   115
To fill the mouth of deep defiance up,
And shake the peace and safety of our throne.
And what say you to this? Percy, Northumberland,
The Archbishop's Grace of York, Douglas, Mortimer,
Capitulate against us and are up.   120
But wherefore do I tell these news to thee?
Why, Harry, do I tell thee of my foes,
Which art my nearest and dearest enemy?
Thou that art like enough, through vassal fear,
Base inclination, and the start of spleen,   125
To fight against me under Percy's pay,
To dog his heels, and curtsy at his frowns,
To show how much thou art degenerate.
Prince. Do not think so, you shall not find it so;

---

115. Enlarged] *Qq2–5,F*; Enlargd *Q1*.   123. nearest] *Qq1–4*; neer'st *Q5,F*.

1388; ii. 797), Nesbit (22 June 1402; iii. 20), and Holmedon (14 Sept. 1402; ibid.). The first, however, though the then Douglas was slain, was an English defeat, and Hotspur was captured.

114. *ta'en him once*] That Douglas was taken at Holmedon is clear in Hol.'s *Historie of Scotland* (v. 406) though ambiguous in that of England (iii. 21), where, though in fact a prisoner, he might appear to be named not as such but merely as the captured "Mordake"'s father; cf. App. III, p. 169.

116. *To fill . . . up*] Perhaps "to swell the chorus of defiance"; or "cram defiance's appetite full". Cf. Barnabe Barnes, *Divils Charter* (ed. McKerrow, 1904, ll. 2745–6)—"Thus doth one hideous act succeed an other, / Vntill the mouth of mischeife be made vp".

120. *Capitulate*] Draw up articles of agreement.

123. *dearest*] Both (*a*) "most cherished", and (*b*) "direst", with the sense of "affecting very intimately"; cf. "my

dearest foe" (*Ham.*, i. ii. 182). This gives simultaneously the bond of affection and distrust between father and son. Most edd. follow Q5's "near'st", but there is no need to eliminate the metrical unevenness.

125. *start of spleen*] fit of ill-temper.

126. *To fight . . . pay*] Since Hotspur died when Hal was 16 this suspicion is antedated, but the germ of it was a proposed usurpation in 1412. Without going into detail Hol. says (iii. 53) that informers' tales "brought no small suspicion into the king's head, least his sonne would presume to vsurpe the crowne". In 1411–12, according to *An Engl. Chron. . . . of Richard II, Henry IV, Henry V, and Henry VI* (ed. J. S. Davies, Camden Soc., 1856, 37), "it was acorded betuene the Prince, king Harries son, and Harri [Beaufort] bisshoppe of Wynchestre, and many othir lordis of this lond, that certayn of thaym sholde speke to the king, and entrete him to resigne the croune to the said Prince Harri . . . but he wolde in no wise".

And God forgive them that so much have sway'd   130
Your Majesty's good thoughts away from me!
I will redeem all this on Percy's head,
And in the closing of some glorious day
Be bold to tell you that I am your son,
When I will wear a garment all of blood,   135
And stain my favours in a bloody mask,
Which, wash'd away, shall scour my shame with it;
And that shall be the day, whene'er it lights,
That this same child of honour and renown,
This gallant Hotspur, this all-praised knight,   140
And your unthought-of Harry chance to meet.
For every honour sitting on his helm,
Would they were multitudes, and on my head
My shames redoubled! For the time will come
That I shall make this northern youth exchange   145
His glorious deeds for my indignities.
Percy is but my factor, good my lord,
To engross up glorious deeds on my behalf,
And I will call him to so strict account
That he shall render every glory up,   150
Yea, even the slightest worship of his time,
Or I will tear the reckoning from his heart.
This in the name of God I promise here,
The which if He be pleas'd I shall perform,
I do beseech your Majesty may salve   155
The long-grown wounds of my intemperance:

130. God] *Qq*; Heauen *F.*   142. sitting] *Qq1,2*; fitting *Qq3–5,F.*   148. up] *Qq1,2,F*; my *Qq3–5.*   153. God] *Qq*; Heauen *F.*   154. He . . . perform] *Qq*; I performe, and doe suruiue *F.*   pleas'd I] *Qq1,5 (subst.)*; pleas'd, I *Qq2–4 (subst.).*   perform,] *F*; performe *Qq4,5*; performe: *Qq1–3.*   156. intemperance] *Qq*; intemperature *F.*

136. *favours*] features. The sense of "insignia" (the scarf or glove witnessing a mistress's favour; cf. v. iv. 95) is implied too, leading on from "garment", but the uppermost idea is of the blood-masked face to be washed clean, a sign of regeneration.

147. *factor*] agent.

148. *engross up*] amass in gross.

150. *render . . . up*] "The idea is that one who subdues a champion succeeds

to all the honours he has won. Percy, at the moment of death, subscribes to this doctrine [v. iv. 77–9]" (Kittredge).

151. *worship . . . time*] honour of his life.

154. *if He . . . perform*] Having substituted "Heauen" for "God" (l. 153), F avoids a hiatus of sense by amending this phrase (see collation).

156. *intemperance*] F's "intempera-

If not, the end of life cancels all bands,
And I will die a hundred thousand deaths
Ere break the smallest parcel of this vow.
King. A hundred thousand rebels die in this—   160
Thou shalt have charge and sovereign trust herein.

Enter BLUNT.

How now, good Blunt? Thy looks are full of speed.
Blunt. So hath the business that I come to speak of.
Lord Mortimer of Scotland hath sent word
That Douglas and the English rebels met   165
The eleventh of this month at Shrewsbury.
A mighty and a fearful head they are,
If promises be kept on every hand,
As ever offer'd foul play in a state.
King. The Earl of Westmoreland set forth today,   170
With him my son, Lord John of Lancaster,
For this advertisement is five days old.
On Wednesday next, Harry, you shall set forward,
On Thursday we ourselves will march.
Our meeting is Bridgnorth, and, Harry, you   175
Shall march through Gloucestershire, by which
account,

158. thousand] *Qq1–3,5,F;* thousands *Q4.*   161. S.D.] *F; Qq (after l. 162).*
173. you shall] *Qq1,2;* thou shalt *Qq3–5,F.*   174–5. march. / Our meeting is]
F; march. Our meeting / Is *Qq.*   175–6. you / Shall march through] *T.*
Johnson, Capell; you shall march / Through *QqF.*

ture", as Wilson (N.C.S.) points out,
means both "licentiousness" and "dis-
tempered condition of the body"
(*OED*). It is in fact the better word,
but I do not accept its authority;
cf. Intro., pp. lxxiv–lxxv.

157. *bands*] bonds. The sentiment is
proverbial: "Death pays all debts"
(Tilley, D148).

159. *parcel*] portion, as in the phrase
"part and parcel".

163. *So hath the business*] " 'So also
the business . . . *hath* speed', i.e. requires immediate attention and des-
patch" (Malone).

164. *Lord . . . Scotland*] Shakespeare
assumed that the Scottish Earls of

March were Mortimers like the English. See App. III, p. 173, for reference
to "the Scot, the earle of March" (i.e.
George Dunbar, Earl of the "March",
or borderland, of Scotland).

172. *advertisement*] information.

174–9.] As Wilson suggests (N.C.S.),
these lines may indicate imperfect
revision in the repetition of the
Bridgnorth meeting (ll. 175, 178),
"march" (ll. 174, 176), and "business"
(ll. 177, 179).

176. *Gloucestershire*] The regular
London – Bridgnorth – Shrewsbury
road was through Daventry, Coventry, and Birmingham. A second main
route, through High Wycombe, More-

Our business valued, some twelve days hence
Our general forces at Bridgnorth shall meet.
Our hands are full of business, let's away,
Advantage feeds him fat while men delay.   *Exeunt.* 180

SCENE III.—[*Eastcheap. The Boar's Head Tavern.*]

Enter FALSTAFF *and* BARDOLPH.

Fal. Bardolph, am I not fallen away vilely since this last
action? Do I not bate? Do I not dwindle? Why, my
skin hangs about me like an old lady's loose gown.
I am withered like an old apple-john. Well, I'll repent, and that suddenly, while I am in some liking;   5
I shall be out of heart shortly, and then I shall have
no strength to repent. And I have not forgotten what

Scene III

SCENE III.] F (*Scena Tertia.*); *not in Qq.*   Location.] Theobald (*subst.*).   S.D.
Bardolph] F; Bardol Qq (*subst.*).   1. Bardolph] F (*Bardolph*); Bardoll Qq
(*subst.*).

ton-in-the-Marsh (traversing northern
Gloucestershire), and Worcester, was
rather longer and Hal is given a day's
start. But Shakespeare apparently
forgets the King's order, for in IV.
ii Hal meets Fal. on the other route
near Coventry (J. V. Crofts, 'Fal.'s
March to Bridgnorth', *TLS*, 8 Jan.
1931).

177. *Our business valued*] Absolute
clause; = What we have to do being
weighed up.

Scene III

1–2. *last action*] i.e. the Gad's Hill
exploit, including the near-arrest at
the end of II. iv. "Fal. speaks of it as a
military encounter" (Kittredge).

2. *bate*] lose weight.

3. *loose gown*] A shapeless garment
for elderly ladies. R. Brathwaite,
Strappado for the Divell (ed. Ebsworth,
1878, 40–1), describes "A ciuill
matron . . . / In Graue attire . . . / Her

outward rayment in a loose-gowne
made".

4. *apple-john*] A kind of apple associated with St John's (Midsummer)
Day, 24 June; it keeps well but the skin
shrivels. Cf. *2H4*, II. iv. 4–9—"The
prince once set a dish of apple-johns
before him, and told him there were
five more Sir Johns; and, putting off
his hat, said, 'I will now take my leave
of these six dry, round, old withered
knights' ". See p. 203.

5. *suddenly*] at once, immediately.

am in some liking] A quibble: (*a*) feel
like it; (*b*) still have some flesh on me.
"Grasselet . . . Fattish, fattie, somewhat fat, in pretie good liking" (Cotgrave).

6. *out of heart*] A parallel quibble to
"in some liking": (*a*) disinclined; (*b*)
in poor condition—still in this sense
applied to unproductive land.

7. *strength*] A third parallel quibble:
strength (*a*) of purpose; (*b*) of body.

the inside of a church is made of, I am a peppercorn,
a brewer's horse: the inside of a church! Company,
villainous company, hath been the spoil of me.   10

Bard. Sir John, you are so fretful you cannot live long.

Fal. Why, there is it: come, sing me a bawdy song, make
me merry. I was as virtuously given as a gentleman
need to be; virtuous enough; swore little; diced not
above seven times—a week; went to a bawdy-house   15
not above once in a quarter—of an hour; paid money
that I borrowed—three or four times; lived well, and
in good compass; and now I live out of all order, out
of all compass.

Bard. Why, you are so fat, Sir John, that you must needs   20
be out of all compass, out of all reasonable compass,
Sir John.

Fal. Do thou amend thy face, and I'll amend my life:
thou art our admiral, thou bearest the lantern in the
poop, but 'tis in the nose of thee: thou art the Knight   25
of the Burning Lamp.

---

15. times—] *Staunton;* times *QqF.*   16. quarter—] *Hanmer;* quarter *QqF.*
17. borrowed—] *Hanmer;* borrowed *Qq;* borrowed, *F.*   19. all compass]
Qq1–4; compasse *Q5,F.*   23. my] *Qq;* thy *F.*

8. *peppercorn*] An improbably dimi-
nutive comparison, like the shotten
herring, bunch of radish, or rabbit
sucker (II. iv. 127, 183, 431).

9. *brewer's horse*] An animal notori-
ously decrepit: cf. Dekker, *If This be
not a good Play* (Shepherd, iii. 307)—"as
noble-men vse their great horses, when
they are past seruice: sell 'em to
brewers and make 'em drey-horses'';
and *History of the Triall of Cheualry*, 1605
(Bullen, *Old Plays,* iii. 303)—"S'hart,
I have been stumbling up and downe
all this night like a Brewers horse that
has ne're a good eye in his head''.

11. *fretful . . . long*] "*Fretful (a)* given
to worry; (*b*) wearing away'' (Wilson,
N.C.S.). Noble quotes *Ecclus.,* xxx.
23–4—"As for sorowe & heauinesse,
dryue it farre from thee, for heauinesse
hath slayne many a man, and bringeth
no profit . . . carefulnesse and sorowe
bring age before the time''.

12. *there is it*] that's it.

18. *in good compass*] within bounds,
an orderly life. Fal. tosses Bardolph an
unmissable pun.

24. *admiral*] flagship.

24–5. *lantern in the poop*] As Mr J. C.
Maxwell points out to me, this association between illumination and Bardolph recurs to Fal. in *2H4,* I. ii. 51–4,
when he speaks of light shining
through a lantern and then suddenly
asks "Where's Bardolph?" Dekker,
Wonderfull Yeare, 1603 (Grosart, i.
138–9), has the same idea—"The
Hamburgers offered I know not how
many Dollars, for his companie in an
East-Indian voyage, to haue stoode a
nightes in the Poope of their Admi-
rall, onely to saue the charges of
candles''.

25–6. *Knight . . . Lamp*] "Parodying
Amadis, Knight of the Burning Sword,
as does *The Knight of the Burning Pestle*''

Bard. Why, Sir John, my face does you no harm.

Fal. No, I'll be sworn, I make as good use of it as many a
    man doth of a death's-head, or a *memento mori.* I
    never see thy face but I think upon hell-fire, and   30
    Dives that lived in purple: for there he is in his robes,
    burning, burning. If thou wert any way given to
    virtue, I would swear by thy face: my oath should be
    "By this fire, that's God's angel!" But thou art alto-
    gether given over; and wert indeed, but for the light   35
    in thy face, the son of utter darkness. When thou
    ran'st up Gad's Hill in the night to catch my horse, if
    I did not think thou hadst been an *ignis fatuus,* or a
    ball of wildfire, there's no purchase in money. O,
    thou art a perpetual triumph, an everlasting bonfire-   40
    light! Thou hast saved me a thousand marks in
    links and torches, walking with thee in the night be-

---

34. that's God's angel] *Qq3–5; that Gods Angell Qq1,2; not in F.*   36. son]
Qq1–4 (sonne Qq1–3; son Q4); Sunne Q5,F.   38. thou] *Qq1,2; that thou
Qq3–5,F.*

(G. C. Moore Smith, cited by Wilson, N.C.S.).

29. *death's-head*] ring with a skull as a memento mori; cf. Beau. & Fl., *Chances,* I. vi (*Works,* iv. 183)—"they keep deaths heads in rings, / To cry *Memento*"; and Brome (Shepherd, vol. iii), *Northern Lasse,* II. v (p. 36)—"She broke me a Tooth once with a Deaths Head-Ring on her finger, it had like to ha' cost me my life! 'thas been a true *memento* to me ever since".

29–31. *I never...purple*] Fal. refers to the Dives-and-Lazarus parable again at IV. ii. 25–6, and the association between Bardolph, hell-fire, and Dives the "glutton" recurs, Mr J. C. Maxwell reminds me, at *2H4,* I. ii. 35–9. Even on his death-bed Fal. jests on the resemblance between Bardolph's nose and the flames of hell (*H5,* II. iii. 42–4).

34. *By . . . angel*] F omits as profane. Proverbial, deriving doubtless from *Exodus,* iii. 2—"And the angell of the Lorde appeared vnto hym in a flambe of fire"; or *Ps.,* civ. 4—"He maketh his angels spirites: and his

ministers a flaming fire" (similarly *Hebr.,* i. 7; echoed in *Oth.,* v. ii. 8). Kittredge cites *Misogonus,* c. 1570, III. i. 240—"By this fier that bournez thats gods aungell I sweare a great oth" (Bond, *Early Plays from the Italian,* 1911, 231).

36. *son . . . darkness*] More Scripture, combining the "children . . . of darkness" (cf. II. iv. 170, note), and the "utter [i.e. outer] darknesse" of *Matt.,* viii. 12, xxii. 13, and xxv. 30.

38. ignis fatuus] will o' the wisp.

39. *ball of wildfire*] A flaming ball of gunpowder, for entertainment or naval warfare; also, globular lightning. These senses are what the phrase primarily conveys, though Wilson (N.C.S.) suggests a further quibble on erysipelas (called also "St. Anthony's fire" or "the rose"), a "local inflammatory cutaneous disease... in which the skin assumes a deep red colour" (*OED,* "Wildfire. 4").

40. *triumph*] illumination for a festival.

42. *links*] flares.

> twixt tavern and tavern: but the sack that thou hast
> drunk me would have bought me lights as good
> cheap at the dearest chandler's in Europe. I have   45
> maintained that salamander of yours with fire any
> time this two and thirty years, God reward me for it!

Bard. 'Sblood, I would my face were in your belly!

Fal. God-a-mercy! so should I be sure to be heartburnt.

Enter Hostess.

> How now, dame Partlet the hen, have you enquired   50
> yet who picked my pocket?

Host. Why, Sir John, what do you think, Sir John, do you
> think I keep thieves in my house? I have searched, I
> have enquired, so has my husband, man by man,
> boy by boy, servant by servant—the tithe of a hair   55
> was never lost in my house before.

Fal. Ye lie, hostess: Bardolph was shaved and lost many
> a hair, and I'll be sworn my pocket was picked: go to,
> you are a woman, go.

Host. Who, I? No, I defy thee: God's light, I was never   60
> called so in mine own house before.

Fal. Go to, I know you well enough.

Host. No, Sir John, you do not know me, Sir John, I know

---

45. at] *Qq1–4;* as *Q5,F.*   47. God] *Qq;* Heauen *F.*   48. 'Sblood] *Qq; not
in F.*   49. God-a-mercy] *Qq; not in F.*   49. S.D.] *F; Enter host.* | *Qq1,2
(opposite line 50), Qq3–5 (after line 51).*   54. has] *Qq1,2;* haz *Qq3–5,F.*   55.
tithe] *Theobald;* tight *QqF;* right *Dering MS;* weight *Vaughan.*   57. Bardolph]
F (Bardolph); Bardoll *Qq (subst.).*   60. No, I] *Qq1–4;* I *Q5,F.*   God's light]
Qq; not in F.

44–5. *good cheap*] cheaply.

46. *salamander*] A species of lizard
supposedly able to live in fire alone,
says Pliny (*Nat. Hist.*, x. lxxxvi), it is so
cold-blooded as to be unaffected.

48. *I would . . . belly*] Cf. Tilley,
B299—"I wish it were in your belly
for me"; a proverbial retort to dispose
of anything irritating.

49. *be heartburnt*] have indigestion.

50. *dame Partlet*] A traditional name
for a hen (cf. Chaucer, *Nonne Pr. T.*)
and so for a fussy or scolding woman;
Fal. refers to her clucking agitation.

In *Wint.*, II. iii. 75, Leontes calls the
sharp-tongued Paulina "dame Partlet".

55. *tithe*] QqF's "tight", Hemingway (New Var.) suggests, may be
"a typical Quickly-Malapropism".
"Tith" occurs as a variant of "tight"
several times (e.g. in Beau. & Fl.; cf.
Skeat & Mayhew, *Glossar of Tudor . . .
Words*). But the reverse variant does
not seem to occur, and in any case the
ear would make little of it on the stage.
Sisson suggests that "tithe" may in the
copy have been misspelt "tithte".

you, Sir John, you owe me money, Sir John, and now
you pick a quarrel to beguile me of it. I bought you   65
a dozen of shirts to your back.

Fal. Dowlas, filthy dowlas. I have given them away to
bakers' wives; they have made bolters of them.

Host. Now as I am a true woman, holland of eight shillings an ell! You owe money here besides, Sir John,   70
for your diet, and by-drinkings, and money lent you,
four and twenty pound.

Fal. He had his part of it, let him pay.

Host. He? Alas, he is poor, he hath nothing.

Fal. How? Poor? Look upon his face. What call you   75
rich? Let them coin his nose, let them coin his cheeks,
I'll not pay a denier. What, will you make a younker

68. they] *Qq;* and they *F.*   69. as] *Qq1–4,F;* at *Q5.*   69–70. eight shillings]
Qq (viii s.), *F.*   72. four and twenty] *Qq* (xxiiii.), *F.*   pound] *Qq;* pounds *F.*

65–6. *I bought . . . shirts*] Other hos-
tesses seem to have been similarly vic-
timized; in Dekker & Webster,
North-ward Hoe, IV. iii. 80–2 (Bowers,
ii. 459), a bawd says "I . . . lend
Gentlemen holland shirts, and they
sweat 'em out at tennis; and no restitution, and no restitution".

67. *Dowlas*] coarse linen named
from Doulas in Brittany. According to
Strype, *Eccl. Mem.* (Bk II, "Repository
of Divers Letters", QQ), the justices of
Cornwall priced it in 1550 at nine-
pence a yard.

68. *bolters*] cloths for sifting meal.

69. *holland*] fine lawn. Brome (Shepherd, vol. ii), *New Academy,* III. i
(p. 47), contrasts two modes of life—
"from the hurden smock . . . and hem-
pen sheets, to weare and sleepe in
Holland". Provoked by Fal.'s dis-
paragement (l. 67), the Hostess goes to
the other extreme; the price was from
one shilling a yard for cheap quality
(an ell = a yard and a quarter) to four
for fine, though the finest might be
considerably more (Linthicum, 98).

71. *by-drinkings*] drinks between
meals.

76. *rich*] The joke is on Bardolph's
rubicund ("rich") face. Bailey gives

"Rich-*Face,* a red Face"; and Lodge,
A Looking Glasse (Mal. Soc., 1932,
ll. 1712–13), has "you and I haue bene
tossing many a good cup of Ale, your
nose is growne verie rich". His nose,
Bardolph says in *H5,* II. iii. 46, is "all
the riches" he got in Fal.'s service.

77. *denier*] "a small copper coyne
valued at the tenth part of an English
pennie" (Cotgrave).

younker] prodigal, and greenhorn.
For the latter sense, of youthful gulli-
bility, see *3H6,* II. i. 24—"Trimm'd
like a younker prancing to his love";
and Beau. & Fl., *Elder Brother,* III. v
(*Works,* ii. 31)—"I fear he'll make an
Ass of me, a younger". The "prodigal"
sense links up, Dr T. W. Craik informs
me, with interlude incidents when the
prodigal not only loses his money by
gaming but has his pockets picked at
his inn, probably by strumpets; e.g. R.
Simpson, *School of Sh.,* ii, *The Comedy of
the Prodigal Son.* Jan Steen and other
Dutch painters depict such incidents,
which may have had traditional currency. In *Mer. V.* the "scarfed bark"
puts forth "like a younker or a prodigal", only to return "Lean, rent,
and beggar'd by the strumpet wind"
(II. vi. 14–19).

of me? Shall I not take mine ease in mine inn but I
shall have my pocket picked? I have lost a seal-ring
of my grandfather's worth forty mark.   80

Host. O Jesu, I have heard the Prince tell him, I know not
how oft, that that ring was copper.

Fal. How? the Prince is a Jack, a sneak-up. 'Sblood, and
he were here I would cudgel him like a dog if he
would say so.   85

Enter the PRINCE *marching,* [*with* PETO,] *and Falstaff meets him,
playing upon his truncheon like a fife.*

How now, lad? Is the wind in that door, i'faith, must
we all march?

Bard. Yea, two and two, Newgate fashion.

Host. My lord, I pray you hear me.

Prince. What say'st thou, Mistress Quickly? How doth   90
thy husband? I love him well, he is an honest man.

Host. Good my lord, hear me.

Fal. Prithee let her alone, and list to me.

Prince. What say'st thou, Jack?

Fal. The other night I fell asleep here, behind the arras,   95

81. O Jesu] *Qq; not in* F.   83. sneak-up] *Qq1,2* (sneakup); sneak-cup *Qq3–5,* F.
'Sblood] *Qq; not in* F.   and] *Qq; and if* F.   84. I would] *Qq1–4,5 corr.,* F;
would *Q5 uncorr.*   85. S.D. *with Peto*] *Theobald* (*subst.*); *not in QqF.*   *upon*]
Qq1,2; on | *Qq3–5,* F.   86. How] *Dyce; Falst.* How *QqF.*   i'faith] *Qq; not
in* F.   90. doth] *Qq1,4;* doeth *Qq2,3;* dow *Q5;* does *F.*

78. *take . . . inn*] A popular tag:
Tilley, E42.

79. *seal-ring*] Often sentimentally
valued as an heirloom: cf. Overbury,
Characters, An Elder Brother—"His pedi-
gree and his fathers seale-ring, are the
stilts of his crazed disposition"; and
C. Cotton, *The Scoffer Scoft* (1734 ed.,
p. 160)—"a Man would think that
he had lost / The half of his Estate almost, / At least his Grandfathers Seal-
Ring, / Or some most dear-beloved
Thing".

83. *Jack*] knave.

sneak-up] See collation. Though the
second "e" of Q1 can be misread "c"
(so indeed can the first, and others
elsewhere with a blocked loop) the

word is certainly "sneakup" and the
meaning "a cowardly, creeping, insi-
dious rascal" (Johnson).

85. S.D. *with Peto*] QqF omit.
Several edd. follow Johnson in thinking Poins more suitable than Peto in
l. 196 (cf. also II. iv. 497, note) and substitute him there and here. But change
is unnecessary.

truncheon] Fal. deftly transforms
the flourished "cudgel" of l. 84 into a
musical instrument.

86. *door*] quarter (*OED*, "Door.
6†c"). Fal.'s phrase was a popular tag;
Tilley, W419.

88. *Newgate fashion*] "As prisoners
are conveyed to Newgate, fastened
two and two together" (Johnson).

and had my pocket picked: this house is turned
bawdy-house, they pick pockets.

Prince. What didst thou lose, Jack?

Fal. Wilt thou believe me, Hal, three or four bonds of
forty pound apiece, and a seal-ring of my grand-   100
father's.

Prince. A trifle, some eightpenny matter.

Host. So I told him, my lord, and I said I heard your
Grace say so: and, my lord, he speaks most vilely of
you, like a foul-mouthed man as he is, and said he   105
would cudgel you.

Prince. What! he did not?

Host. There's neither faith, truth, nor womanhood in
me else.

Fal. There's no more faith in thee than in a stewed   110
prune, nor no more truth in thee than in a drawn
fox—and for womanhood, Maid Marian may be
the deputy's wife of the ward to thee. Go, you thing,
go!

110. in a] *Q1; a Qq2–5,F.*   113. thing] *Qq; nothing F.*

102. *eightpenny*] trifling.

110–11. *There's . . . stewed prune*] i.e.
"You're as faithless as if you made your
living out of a brothel." Stewed prunes
were often associated with brothel-
keeping; Steevens cites Lodge, *Wit's
Misery*, 1596—"you shall know her [a
bawd's] dwelling by a dish of stewed
prunes in the window". W. Clowes,
Treatise on Lues Venerea, 1596, recom-
mends them as a preventative of disease. In *2H4*, II. iv. 154–7, Doll scarifies
Pistol for "tearing a poor whore's ruff
in a bawdy-house" and says "he lives
upon mouldy stewed prunes and dried
cakes". So "a stewed prune" or "dish
of stewed prunes" became a term for
a bawd; cf. Dekker, *2 Honest Whore*,
IV. iii. 36 (Bowers, ii. 197)—"two
dishes of stew'd prunes, a Bawde and
a Pander".

111–12. *drawn fox*] hunted fox,
drawn from cover; less appropriately
explained as a disembowelled fox,
dead fox dragged to leave a false trail,
and a drawn sword.

112. *Maid Marian*] i.e. "Maid
Marian would be a model of respect-
ability compared with you". This was
a May-game and morris-dance character, often played by a man, attacked
by Puritans for impropriety, and a by-
word for grotesque attire and impudence. Kittredge cites *Misogonus*, II. iv.
75–6 (Bond, *Early Plays from the Italian*,
1911, 206)—"This a smurkynge
wenche indeede, this a fare Mayde
Marion, She is none of thes coy
dames". Thomas Heywood, *Iron Age*
(Shepherd, iii. 302), has "Should I
venter / To damme my selfe for paint-
ing, fanne my face / With a dyde
Ostritch plume, plaster my wrinkles /
With some old Ladies Trowell I might
passe / Perhaps for some maide-
marrian". Kemp's reference to a
country wench he danced with is,
however, a friendly one—"my merry
Maydemarian" (*Nine Daies Wonder*,
Camden Soc., 1840, 10).

113. *deputy's . . . ward*] The deputy of
the ward was its most responsible citi-

Host. Say, what thing, what thing?   115

Fal. What thing? Why, a thing to thank God on.

Host. I am no thing to thank God on, I would thou
    shouldst know it, I am an honest man's wife, and
    setting thy knighthood aside, thou art a knave to
    call me so.   120

Fal. Setting thy womanhood aside, thou art a beast to
    say otherwise.

Host. Say, what beast, thou knave, thou?

Fal. What beast? Why, an otter.

Prince. An otter, Sir John? Why an otter?   125

Fal. Why? She's neither fish nor flesh, a man knows not
    where to have her.

Host. Thou art an unjust man in saying so, thou or any
    man knows where to have me, thou knave, thou.

Prince. Thou say'st true, hostess, and he slanders thee   130
    most grossly.

Host. So he doth you, my lord, and said this other day
    you ought him a thousand pound.

Prince. Sirrah, do I owe you a thousand pound?

Fal. A thousand pound, Hal? A million, thy love is   135
    worth a million, thou owest me thy love.

Host. Nay, my lord, he called you Jack, and said he
    would cudgel you.

Fal. Did I, Bardolph?

Bard. Indeed, Sir John, you said so.   140

Fal. Yea, if he said my ring was copper.

Prince. I say 'tis copper, darest thou be as good as thy
    word now?

Fal. Why, Hal, thou knowest as thou art but man I dare,

116, 117. God] *Qq*; heauen *F*.   117. no thing] *Q5,F*; nothing *Qq1–4*.   128.
art an] *Qq*; art *F*.   139. Bardolph] *F (Bardolph)*; Bardol *Qq (subst.)*.   144.
man] *Qq1,2*; a man *Qq3–5,F*.

zen; his wife would naturally be irre-
proachable.

116. *thing ... on*] "i.e. She is as God
made her" (Wilson, N.C.S.).

126. *She's ... flesh*] = She's an incomprehensible creature. Proverbial;
Tilley, F319. The question whether
the otter be beast or fish, says Izaak
Walton, "hath been debated among

many great clerks: and they seem to
differ about it: yet most agree that his
tail is fish" (*Compleat Angler*, I. ii).

127. *where ... her*] how to take her.

129. *where ... me*] "how to get the
better of me" is what the Hostess
means, but she blunders on an equivoque.

133. *ought*] owed; archaic use.

but as thou art prince, I fear thee as I fear the roar-   145
ing of the lion's whelp.

Prince. And why not as the lion?

Fal. The King himself is to be feared as the lion: dost
thou think I'll fear thee as I fear thy father? Nay,
and I do, I pray God my girdle break.   150

Prince. O, if it should, how would thy guts fall about thy
knees! But sirrah, there's no room for faith, truth,
nor honesty in this bosom of thine; it is all filled up
with guts and midriff. Charge an honest woman
with picking thy pocket? Why, thou whoreson   155
impudent embossed rascal, if there were anything
in thy pocket but tavern reckonings, memorandums
of bawdy-houses, and one poor pennyworth of
sugar-candy to make thee long-winded, if thy
pocket were enriched with any other injuries but   160
these, I am a villain: and yet you will stand to it,
you will not pocket up wrong! Art thou not ashamed?

Fal. Dost thou hear, Hal? Thou knowest in the state of
innocency Adam fell, and what should poor Jack   165
Falstaff do in the days of villainy? Thou seest I have
more flesh than another man, and therefore more

---

145. prince] *Qq*; a Prince *F*.   150. and] *Qq*; if *F*.   I pray God] *Qq*; let *F*.

148. *The King . . . lion*] A standard
symbol of kingship; with an echo of
Prov., xix. 12—"The kynges displeasure is lyke the roaryng of a
Lion"; and ibid., xx. 2—"The feare of
the king is as the roaring of a Lion".

150. *pray . . . break*] "Ungirt un-
blessed" was proverbial: Tilley, U10.
Browne, discussing it in *Pseudodoxia
Epidemica*, v. xxii. 13, says that the
girdle signifies "Truth, Resolution,
and Readiness unto action, which are
parts and vertues required in the service of God". Fal.'s version was frequent too; e.g. S. Rowlands, *Well met
Gossip; or 'Tis merrie when Gossips meet*,
1602—"If I make one pray God my
girdle break" (1656 ed., sig. C3);
and W. Rowley, *Match at Midnight*,
I. i (Hazlitt's *Dodsley*, XIII. 10)—

"Would my girdle may break if I do".

156. *embossed rascal*] Probable quibbles on both words. "Embossed" is (a)
swollen (cf. *Lr.*, II. iv. 227—"embossed
carbuncle"); (b) slavering like a hunted deer; Madden (54) quotes *The
Noble Arte of Venerie*, 1575—"When he
[the hart] is foamy at the mouth, we
say that he is embost". "Rascal" is
(a) rogue; (b) "the young, lean, or
inferior deer" (*OED*, "Rascal. †4.")
—and so splendidly sarcastic in this
context.

159. *long-winded*] Fighting cocks
were given sugar to prolong their
breath (Wright).

160. *injuries*] things whose loss you
complain of as injuries.

167–8. *more flesh . . . frailty*] "Flesh
is frail" is proverbial, deriving from

frailty. You confess then, you picked my pocket?

Prince. It appears so by the story.

Fal. Hostess, I forgive thee, go make ready breakfast, 170
love thy husband, look to thy servants, cherish thy
guests, thou shalt find me tractable to any honest
reason, thou seest I am pacified still, nay prithee be
gone. (*Exit Hostess.*) Now, Hal, to the news at court:
for the robbery, lad, how is that answered?   175

Prince. O my sweet beef, I must still be good angel to
thee—the money is paid back again.

Fal. O, I do not like that paying back, 'tis a double
labour.

Prince. I am good friends with my father and may do 180
anything.

Fal. Rob me the exchequer the first thing thou dost, and
do it with unwashed hands too.

Bard. Do, my lord.

Prince. I have procured thee, Jack, a charge of foot. 185

Fal. I would it had been of horse. Where shall I find one
that can steal well? O for a fine thief of the age of
two and twenty or thereabouts: I am heinously un-
provided. Well, God be thanked for these rebels,
they offend none but the virtuous; I laud them, I 190
praise them.

Prince. Bardolph!

Bard. My lord?

170–4. Hostess . . . gone.] *As Qq (prose)*; Hostesse . . . thee / Go . . . Husband, /
Looke . . . Guests: / Thou . . . reason: / Thou . . . still. / Nay . . . gone. / *F (verse)*.
171. cherish] *Qq*; and cherish *F*.   172. guests] *Q1* (ghesse), *Qq2–4* (ghests),
Q5 (Ghestes), *F* (Guests).   173. prithee] *Qq1–4*; I prethee *Q5*,F.   174–5.
court: for] *Theobald*; court for *QqF*.   176–7.] *As Qq (prose)*; O . . . Beefe / I . . .
thee. / The . . . againe. / *F (verse)*.   176. beef] *Qq1–4* (beoffe), *Q5* (beeffe), *F*
(Beefe).   187. of the age of] *Qq*; of *F*.   188. two and twenty] *Qq* (xxii.), *F*.
thereabouts] *Qq1–3*; ther about *Qq4,5*; thereabout *F*.   192. Bardolph] *F*
(*Bardolph*); Bardoll *Qq*.

Matt., xxvi. 41, and *Mark*, xiv. 38—
"The fleshe is weake": cf. Tilley, F363.

173. *pacified still*] always easily pacified.

176. *beef*] ox; a suitably meaty
image.

183. *with . . . hands*] without a
moment's delay—don't pause for any

scruples of propriety. A proverbial
tag; Tilley, H125.

185. *a charge of foot*] Cf. II. iv. 538–9,
note.

189–90. *God . . . virtuous*] As Wilson
observes (*Fortunes*, 84), Fal.'s attitude
to war is blatantly, and indeed blas-
phemously, predatory.

Prince. Go bear this letter to Lord John of Lancaster,
  To my brother John, this to my Lord of Westmoreland.
                                  [Exit Bardolph.]
  Go, Peto, to horse, to horse, for thou and I   196
  Have thirty miles to ride yet ere dinner-time. *[Exit Peto.]*
  Jack, meet me tomorrow in the Temple hall
  At two o'clock in the afternoon:
  There shalt thou know thy charge, and there receive 200
  Money and order for their furniture.
  The land is burning, Percy stands on high,
  And either we or they must lower lie.   *[Exit.]*
Fal. Rare words! Brave world! Hostess, my breakfast, come!
  O, I could wish this tavern were my drum.   *Exit.* 205

194–201.] *As QqF (verse); prose, T. Johnson 2, Pope, some edd.* 195. S.D.] *Dyce; not in QqF.* 196. Peto] *QqF;* Poins *Dering MS, var. 1773, conj. Johnson.* to horse, to horse] *Qq1,2;* to horse *Qq3–5,F.* 197. to ride yet] *Qq1–4,F;* yet to ride *Q5.* 197. S.D.] *Cambr.; Exit Pointz. | Dyce; not in QqF.* 199. o'] *Qq2–5,F* (a), *Theobald;* of *Q1.* 203. we or they] *Qq1–3;* they or we *Qq4,5,F.* 203. S.D.] *Dyce; not in QqF.* 204.] *As Qq;* Rare . . . world. / Hostesse . . . come: / *F.* 205. S.D.] *Capell; Exeunt. | Qq2–5; Exeunt omnes. | F; not in Q1.*

194–9.] Edd. have tried to smooth these lines, here given as in QqF, or have printed them as prose. However printed, on the stage they will sound like exhilarated urgency.

196. *Peto*] Since at IV. ii. 9 Peto is not with Hal but with Fal., Johnson suggested Poins here, and some edd. follow; cf. II. iv. 497 and III. iii. 85, notes. But the two occasions are quite different, and no change is needed.

201. *furniture*] equipment.

205. *O . . . drum*] I wish this tavern were always my rallying-point. To Wilson's suggestion (N.C.S.) of a quibble on "tavern" and "taborn" or "tabern" (= tabor, a small drum), there is the objection that "taborn" or "tabern" was "chiefly north. Eng. and Scots" (*OED*, "taborn"). The normal English "tabor" provides no quibble.

ACT IV

SCENE I.—[*Shrewsbury. The Rebel Camp.*]

Enter HOTSPUR, WORCESTER, *and* DOUGLAS.

Hot. Well said, my noble Scot! If speaking truth
In this fine age were not thought flattery,
Such attribution should the Douglas have
As not a soldier of this season's stamp
Should go so general current through the world.   5
By God, I cannot flatter, I do defy
The tongues of soothers, but a braver place
In my heart's love hath no man than yourself:
Nay, task me to my word, approve me, lord.
Doug. Thou art the king of honour: 10
No man so potent breathes upon the ground
But I will beard him.
Hot.   Do so, and 'tis well.

Enter a Messenger with letters.

What letters hast thou there?—I can but thank you.

ACT IV

Scene i

ACT IV SCENE I.] *F* (*Actus Quartus. Scœna Prima.*); *not in Qq.*   *Location.*] *Capell*
(*subst.*).   S.D.] *Qq2–5,F* (*Enter Harrie Hotspurre ... Dowglas.* / *F*); *not in Q1.*
1. *Hot.*] *Qq2–5,F; Per.* / *Q1* (*so to line 90*).   2. thought] *Qq1–4,5 corr., F;*
though *Q5 uncorr.*   6. God] *Qq;* heauen *F.*   I do] *Q1;* I *Qq2–5,F.*   12.
S.D.] *Malone; Enter one with letters.* / *Qq* (*after* beard him)*; Enter a Messenger.* / *F*
(*after* beard him).   12–13.] *As Capell;* But ... him. / Do ... there? / I ... you.
Qq1,2,F; But ... him. / Do ... you. / *Qq3–5* (*first phrase verse, the rest prose*).
13. hast thou] *Qq;* hast *F.*

3. *attribution*] praise, recognition of
qualities.
6. *defy*] distrust.
7. *soothers*] flatterers.
a ... place] a more splendid place as
being a brave man.

9. *task ... approve me*] put my word,
and me, to the proof.
13. *I ... you*] Wilson (N.C.S.) points
out the "characteristically delayed
reply" also at II. iii. 91 and II. iv.
106.

Mess. These letters come from your father.

Hot. Letters from him? Why comes he not himself?   15

Mess. He cannot come, my lord, he is grievous sick.

Hot. 'Zounds, how has he the leisure to be sick
         In such a justling time? Who leads his power?
         Under whose government come they along?

Mess. His letters bear his mind, not I, my lord.   20

Wor. I prithee tell me, doth he keep his bed?

Mess. He did, my lord, four days ere I set forth,
         And at the time of my departure thence
         He was much fear'd by his physicians.

Wor. I would the state of time had first been whole   25
         Ere he by sickness had been visited:
         His health was never better worth than now.

Hot. Sick now? Droop now? This sickness doth infect
         The very life-blood of our enterprise;
         'Tis catching hither, even to our camp.   30
         He writes me here that inward sickness [   ],
         And that his friends by deputation could not
         So soon be drawn, nor did he think it meet
         To lay so dangerous and dear a trust

15–16.] *As Qq*; Letters . . . him? / Why . . . himselfe? / He . . . Lord, / He . . . sicke. / *F.*   17. 'Zounds, how] *Qq*; How? *F.*   has] *Qq1,2*; haz *Qq3–5,F.* sick] *Qq*; sicke now, *F.*   20. letters] *Qq1–4,5 corr.,F*; litters *Q5 uncorr.*   bear] *Q7*; beares *QqF.*   I, my lord] *Capell*; I my mind *Qq1,2*; I his mind *Qq3–5,F* (*subst.*)   24. physicians] *Qq1–3* (Phisitions [*subst.*]); Phisition *Qq4,5*; Physician *F.*   31. sickness [   ],] *This edn*; sicknesse, *QqF*; sickness— *Rowe.*   32–3. deputation could not / So] *As Capell*; deputation / Could not so *QqF.*

16. *sick*] In Hol. this sickness occurs early in the rebellion (cf. App. III, p. 171); Shakespeare conjoins it with Shrewsbury to precipitate the rebels' peril and throw Hotspur's impatient valour into relief against Northumberland's evasion.

19. *government*] command.

20. *bear . . . lord*] The line suffers in Q1 from the compositor's confusion, and QqF's "beares" is probably part of this, though a plural subject and singular verb are not unknown: Miss G. D. Willcock cites *Oth.,* II. i. 83 (F)— "The Riches of the Ship is come on Shore", and *Tp.,* III. iii. 2—"My old bones akes" ('Sh. and Elizabethan

English', *Sh. Survey* 7, 1954). Q1's further reading "not I my mind" is most improbably brusque (though Sisson supports it), and Capell rightly emended.

24. *fear'd*] sc. "for"; *R3,* I. i. 137, has "His physicians fear him mightily".

31.] QqF end the line at "sicknesse," and, since there is no evident reason why Hotspur should break off tantalizingly, a phrase (Capell suggested "holds him") may have been lost. But he may be giving Northumberland's gist as Kent does Cordelia's, *Lr.,* II. ii. 175–7.

32. *deputation*] means of a deputy.

On any soul remov'd but on his own.   35
Yet doth he give us bold advertisement
That with our small conjunction we should on,
To see how fortune is dispos'd to us;
For, as he writes, there is no quailing now,
Because the King is certainly possess'd   40
Of all our purposes. What say you to it?
Wor. Your father's sickness is a maim to us.
Hot. A perilous gash, a very limb lopp'd off—
And yet, in faith, it is not! His present want
Seems more than we shall find it. Were it good   45
To set the exact wealth of all our states
All at one cast? to set so rich a main
On the nice hazard of one doubtful hour?
It were not good, for therein should we read
The very bottom and the soul of hope,   50
The very list, the very utmost bound
Of all our fortunes.
Doug. Faith, and so we should, where now remains
A sweet reversion—we may boldly spend
Upon the hope of what is to come in.   55
A comfort of retirement lives in this.
Hot. A rendezvous, a home to fly unto,
If that the devil and mischance look big

45–6. it. Were it good / To] *Qq;* it. / Were it good, to *F.*   48. hour?] *Qq1,2;*
houre, *Qq3–5,F.*   53–5.] *As Collier 3, conj. Walker;* Faith . . . should, / Where
. . . reuersion, / We . . . in, / *Qq;* Faith . . . should, / Where . . . reuersion. / We
. . . hope / Of . . . in: / *F.*   55. is] *F;* tis *Qq (subst.).*

35. *remov'd but*] less nearly concerned
than.

42. *maim*] "Maim" in law signified
"where . . . any member is hurt, or
taken away, whereby the partie so
hurt, is made . . . the lesse able to
defend himselfe" (Minsheu: "Mahim,
or Maime").

47–8. *main . . . hazard*] As Wilson
(N.C.S.) points out, an elaborate
quibble. "Main" = (*a*) army; (*b*)
stake at "hazard": "hazard" = (*a*)
chance; (*b*) game at dice.

49–52. *therein . . . fortunes*] "if we did
so we should be scanning the very
bases of our hopes, the limits and ex-

tremities of our fortunes." The style is
bold but needs no emendation: cf.
Intro., p. lxi.

50, 51. *soul . . . list*] Probably subconscious quibbles: "soul" as sole:
and "list" as (*a*) schedule; (*b*) extreme
edge (lit. the selvedge of cloth).

54. *reversion*] inheritance in pros-
pect.

56. *comfort of retirement*] protection to
fall back upon.

58. *look big*] look threateningly. A
popular tag; cf. Thomas Heywood,
Wise-Woman of Hogsdon, IV. iv (Shepherd, v. 337)—"Ile goe, although the
Devill and mischance looke bigge".

Upon the maidenhead of our affairs.

Wor. But yet I would your father had been here: 60
  The quality and hair of our attempt
  Brooks no division; it will be thought,
  By some that know not why he is away,
  That wisdom, loyalty, and mere dislike
  Of our proceedings kept the Earl from hence; 65
  And think how such an apprehension
  May turn the tide of fearful faction,
  And breed a kind of question in our cause:
  For well you know we of the off'ring side
  Must keep aloof from strict arbitrement, 70
  And stop all sight-holes, every loop from whence
  The eye of reason may pry in upon us:
  This absence of your father's draws a curtain
  That shows the ignorant a kind of fear
  Before not dreamt of.

Hot.   You strain too far. 75
  I rather of his absence make this use:
  It lends a lustre and more great opinion,
  A larger dare to our great enterprise,
  Than if the Earl were here; for men must think
  If we without his help can make a head 80
  To push against a kingdom, with his help
  We shall o'erturn it topsy-turvy down.
  Yet all goes well, yet all our joints are whole.

---

61. hair] *Qq1–3* (haire); heaire *Q4*; heire *Q5,F*.   73. father's] *Qq1–4* (fathers);
Father *Q5,F*.   78. our] *Qq1,2*; your *Qq3–5,F*.   81. a] *Qq1–4*; the *Q5,F*.
82. shall o'erturn] *Q1* (shal oreturne), *Q2* (shall or'eturne), *F* (shall o're-turne);
shall or turne *Q3*; shall, or turne *Qq4,5*.

61. *hair*] sort, kind, nature. Cf.
Dekker & Webster, *West-ward Hoe*, II.
iii. 34 (Bowers, ii. 346)—"Am not I
(gentlemen) a Ferret of the right
haire?"; and North's *Plutarch, Sertorius* (Tudor Trans., iv. 108–9)—"a
young hynde, and of a straunge heare,
for she was all milke white". Cf.
OED, "Hair. 6".

64. *mere*] pure, downright.

66. *apprehension*] The sense of "conception" "tends to pass into the

modern sense 'anticipation with
dread'" (Onions).

67. *fearful*] timorous.

69. *the off'ring side*] the side taking the
offensive.

70. *strict arbitrement*] critical and impartial adjudication.

71. *loop*] sc. "-hole".

77. *opinion*] prestige.

80. *make a head*] Both "raise a force"
and "make a hostile advance"; cf.
I. iii. 278, note, and III. i. 60.

Doug. As heart can think: there is not such a word
     Spoke of in Scotland as this term of fear.   85

Enter SIR RICHARD VERNON.

Hot. My cousin Vernon! Welcome, by my soul!
Ver. Pray God my news be worth a welcome, lord.
     The Earl of Westmoreland seven thousand strong
     Is marching hitherwards, with him Prince John.
Hot. No harm, what more?
Ver.   And further, I have learn'd,   90
     The King himself in person is set forth,
     Or hitherwards intended speedily,
     With strong and mighty preparation.
Hot. He shall be welcome too: where is his son,
     The nimble-footed madcap Prince of Wales,   95
     And his comrades that daft the world aside
     And bid it pass?
Ver.   All furnish'd, all in arms;
     All plum'd like estridges that with the wind

84–5.] *As Qq (subst.);* As . . . thinke: / There . . . Scotland, / At . . . feare. / F.
85. as] *Qq1–4;* at *Q5,F.*   term] *Qq1–4* (tearme); deame *Q5;* Dreame *F.*
S.D. *Richard] Qq1–4 (Ri:), Q5 (Rih.), F.*   89. with him] *Q1;* with *Qq2–5,F.*
91. is] *Qq1,2;* hath *Qq3–5,F.*   94.] *As Qq;* He . . . too. / Where . . . Sonne, / F.
98. with] *QqF;* wing *Rowe;* vie *Cowl & Morgan.*

95. *nimble-footed*] "In strength and nimblenesse of bodie from his youth few to him comparable" (Hol., iii. 133). Stow's *Annales,* 1592, 547, repeats almost verbatim the following passage from *The First Engl. Life of Henry V* (ed. Kingsford, 17), and William Harrison's *Description of England* (Hol., i. 380) gives its gist also—"He was passing swift in runninge, in so much that he with two other of his Lords by force of runninge, without any manner of hounds or grayhounds, or without bowe or other engine, would take a wilde bucke or doe at large in a parke".

96. *daft*] toss(ed) aside. This, like "bid" (l. 96), may be the present tense (daff; cf. *Oth.,* IV. ii. 176, "dofftst" [Q], "dafts" [F], for daffest), or past (daff'd). Its ambivalence makes the transition

from the present "is" (l. 94) to Vernon's past tenses.

97. *bid it pass*] "Let the world pass" ("wag", "wind", or "slide") was a popular tag; Tilley, W879.

97–110. *All . . . horsemanship*] This famous passage is exceptionally vivid in its imagery, its symbolism of royalty (eagles, gold, sun, heavenly messengers), rich display (plumes, golden coats, spring and summer splendour, gallant arms), and vital energy (beating wings, eagles, spirited warriors, youthful goats, young bulls, horses and their riders): cf. I. i. 60, 63, note.

98–9. *All plum'd . . . bath'd*] "All plumed like ostriches that bated [beat their wings] in the wind, like newly-bathed eagles". A much-disputed passage, argument arising over (*a*) estridges; (*b*) with; (*c*) bated (Q bait-

Bated, like eagles having lately bath'd,
Glittering in golden coats like images,   100
As full of spirit as the month of May,
And gorgeous as the sun at midsummer;
Wanton as youthful goats, wild as young bulls.
I saw young Harry with his beaver on,
His cushes on his thighs, gallantly arm'd,   105
Rise from the ground like feather'd Mercury,
And vaulted with such ease into his seat
As if an angel dropp'd down from the clouds   *anti - medusa*
To turn and wind a fiery Pegasus,

99. Bated] *Qq1–4* (Baited), *Q5,F* (Bayted), *Heath, Var. 1778;* Baiting *Hanmer;* Bating *Capell.*   eagles having] *Qq1–4;* Eagles, hauing *Q5,F.*   106. feather'd] *Rowe;* feathered *QqF.*   108. dropp'd] *Qq2–5,F* (dropt); drop *Q1.*

ed). (*a*) "estridge" can mean either goshawk or ostrich, and Douce (*Illust. of Sh.*, 1807, i. 435) puts up a strong case for the former, citing *Ant.*, III. xi. 196 ("The dove will peck the estridge"), where the sense is certainly goshawk (cf. *3H6*, I. iv. 41, "So doves do peck the falcon's piercing talons"). Goshawks can spiritedly ruffle their feathers and have an attacking valour which, with "eagles" (l. 99), would well suit the knights (cf. "Valure Estridge-like" at the end of App. VII). Yet the preference here is for "ostrich", on the score of a strikingly relevant Nashe passage which probably suggested "eagles" (l. 99) and "Pegasus" (l. 109) also (cf. App. VII), and of "plum'd", a word which brings to mind not primarily the goshawk but the ostrich; cf. Dekker, *Old Fortunatus*, II. ii. 233–4 (Bowers, i. 147)—"From beggerie / I plum'd thee like an Estridge". The "goshawk" ambiguity may, however, have carried Shakespeare's mind on to the "eagles". (*b*) "with" sometimes is emended (Rowe's "wing" is the best alternative), but change is unnecessary. (*c*) "bated" ("baited") could mean either "fluttered the wings" (a falconry term; Fr. *battre*), or "refreshed". The latter sense, however, refers rather to refreshment by food

and rest at an inn than to the stimulating shock of cold water (*OED*, "Bait, *v.*¹ 7"), and the idea is rather of eagles beating their wings after bathing. For source passages see App. VII; for a further illustration see p. 203.

100. *coats . . . images*] Probably gilded effigies (e.g. of warriors) rather than images of saints, which were abolished in 1538 (M. St Clare Byrne, 'Like Images', *TLS*, 1 June 1946, 259). "Coats" = both coats of mail, and heraldic coats of arms.

104. *beaver*] helmet; strictly, face-guard.

105. *cushes*] thigh-armour. This spelling (in QqF) of "cuisses" represents the pronunciation.

107–10. *vaulted . . . horsemanship*] The climax of the horsemanship references; cf. I. i. 60, 63, note. Vaulting fully-armed needed uncommon strength and skill; in *H5*, v. ii. 141–2, Henry speaks of himself as "vaulting into my saddle with my armour on my back". "In wrestling, leaping, and running no man well able to compare with him" (Hol., iii. 133).

109. *turn and wind*] Madden (286) refers to Blundevill, *Foure Chiefest Offices of Horsemanship*, 1565; the fourth stage of the courser's manage is "To turne, readilie, on both hands with single turne and double turne".

medusa

   And witch the world with noble horsemanship.   110
Hot. No more, no more! Worse than the sun in March,
   This praise doth nourish agues. Let them come!
   They come like sacrifices in their trim,
   And to the fire-ey'd maid of smoky war
   All hot and bleeding will we offer them: 115
   The mailed Mars shall on his altar sit
   Up to the ears in blood. I am on fire
   To hear this rich reprisal is so nigh,
   And yet not ours! Come, let me taste my horse,
   Who is to bear me like a thunderbolt   120
   Against the bosom of the Prince of Wales.
   Harry to Harry shall, hot horse to horse,
   Meet and ne'er part till one drop down a corse.
   O that Glendower were come!
Ver.   There is more news:
   I learn'd in Worcester as I rode along   125
   He cannot draw his power this fourteen days.
Doug. That's the worst tidings that I hear of yet.
Wor. Ay, by my faith, that bears a frosty sound.

111.] *As Qq*; No more, no more, / Worse ... March: / *F.*   116. altar] *Qq4,5,F;*
altars *Qq1–3.*   119. taste] *Qq1,2*; take *Qq3–5,F.*   122. Harry shall, hot] *Q1*
(Harry shal hot), *Johnson*; Harry, shall hot *Q2*; Harry, shall hot *Qq3–5,F (subst.).*
123. corse.] *Q1* (coarse,), *Qq2–5* (coarse:), *T. Johnson, Rowe 3* (coarse.); Coarse?
F.   126. cannot] *Q5 corr., F;* can *Qq1–4, Q5 uncorr.*   127. yet] *Q5,F;* it
Qq1–4.

Blundevill, he observes, devotes 29 pages to the mysteries of single turns, whole turns, and double turns. "Wind" = wheel about.

111–12. *Worse ... agues*] "The March sun breeds agues" (Overbury, *Characters, A Canting Rogue*). It was thought strong enough to agitate but not strong enough to dispel the body's evil humours; Donne, *Biathanatos*, preface (1648 ed., 22), says "It may have as much vigour ... as the Sunne in March; it may stirre and dissolve humors, though not expell them". Ray, *Proverbs*, remarks that "an Ague is nothing else but a strong fermentation of the blood ... easily excited at this time [spring] by the return of

the Sun"; cf. Tilley, S975. "Nourish agues" = give the shudders.

113. *sacrifices ... trim*] beasts decked out for sacrifice.

114. *the fire-ey'd ... war*] Bellona. The Senecan violence of this speech is another touch of Hotspur's valiant rant.

118. *reprisal*] prize, booty.

126. *He ... days*] Having heightened the drama of Northumberland's defection (l. 16, note), Shakespeare here increases the heroic isolation of Hotspur by following Daniel rather than Hol.; the latter makes the Welsh to be present while the former (*C. W.*, iii. 99) says that the King's rapid advance prevented them from joining with Hotspur.

Hot. What may the King's whole battle reach unto?
Ver. To thirty thousand.
Hot.   Forty let it be: 130
     My father and Glendower being both away,
     The powers of us may serve so great a day.
     Come, let us take a muster speedily—
     Doomsday is near; die all, die merrily.
Doug. Talk not of dying, I am out of fear   135
     Of death or death's hand for this one half year.   *Exeunt.*

SCENE II.—[*A public road near Coventry.*]

Enter FALSTAFF *and* BARDOLPH.

Fal. Bardolph, get thee before to Coventry; fill me a
     bottle of sack. Our soldiers shall march through;
     we'll to Sutton Co'fil' tonight.
Bard. Will you give me money, captain?
Fal. Lay out, lay out.   5
Bard. This bottle makes an angel.

134. merrily] *Q1* (merely), *Qq2–5,F*.   136. S.D.] *Qq; Exeunt Omnes.* / *F*.

Scene II

SCENE II.] *F (Scæna Secunda.); not in QqF.   Location.] Theobald.   S.D. and
Bardolph] F; Bardoll / Q1; and Bardoll / Qq2–5.   1. Bardolph] F (Bardolph);
Bardol Qq (subst.).   3. Sutton Co'fil'] Cambr.; Sutton cop-/hill Qq1,3,4;
Sutton cophill Q2; Sutton-cop-/hill Q5; Sutton-cop-hill F.*

129. *battle*] forces (in battle array).
130. *thirty . . . Forty*] Wright points out that Wyntown's *Cronykil of Scotland* gives 30,000; but Shakespeare's figures are probably chosen merely to show a marked superiority over the 14,000 which Hol. gives for Hotspur's forces. Neither Hol. nor Daniel estimates the King's numbers; Hall says that above 40,000 were engaged on both sides. The *Battle of Otterburn* (stanza 35) relates how when "the Perssy and the Dowglas mette" the former was faced by "forty thowsande . . . and fowre" Scots (*Engl. and Scot. Popular Ballads,* ed. Child).

Scene II

3. *Co fil'*] Sutton Coldfield in Warwickshire is 20 miles beyond Coventry, so Fal. is marching with unexpected vigour, though why he is making thither, miles off the Coventry–Shrewsbury road, remains a mystery.
5. *Lay out*] "Pay out of your own pocket" (Kittredge), rather than "take it out of expenses" Wilson (N.C.S.). Were it the latter, the drain on public funds would be vastly more than "an angel".
6. *makes*] brings the outlay up to. *angel*] coin with the archangel

Fal. And if it do, take it for thy labour—and if it make
twenty, take them all, I'll answer the coinage. Bid
my lieutenant Peto meet me at town's end.

Bard. I will, captain: farewell.   *Exit.*   10

Fal. If I be not ashamed of my soldiers, I am a soused
gurnet; I have misused the King's press damnably.
I have got in exchange of a hundred and fifty soldiers
three hundred and odd pounds. I press me none but
good householders, yeomen's sons, inquire me out   15
contracted bachelors, such as had been asked twice
on the banns, such a commodity of warm slaves as
had as lief hear the devil as a drum, such as fear the

---

9. at] *Qq1–4; a Q5;* at the *F.*   11. be not] *Qq1,2,F;* be *Qq3–5.*   13. a hundred
and fifty] *Qq* (150.), *F.*   14. three hundred] *Qq* (300.), *F.*

Michael stamped on it; generally
reckoned as 6s. 8d.

8. *answer*] "be answerable for.
Alluding to the illegality of private
minting" (Wilson, N.C.S.).

9. *Peto*] Cf. III. iii. 196, note.

11–12. *soused gurnet*] pickled gurnet,
a small fish esteemed as a delicacy,
with large head and tapering body.
The effectiveness of the phrase involves (*a*) its incongruity with Fal.;
(*b*) its currency as a term of contempt;
e.g. Dekker, *1 Honest Whore*, II. i. 201
(Bowers, ii. 49)—"Puncke, you sowcde
gurnet?"; (*c*) Fal.'s promptness to
think of food, especially of such as promotes thirst, like the anchovies at II. iv.
531.

12. *misused . . . press*] Examples
abound of the misuse of the royal commission for impressment. Steevens
quotes *The Voyage to Cadiz*, 1597
(Hakluyt Soc., i. 607)—"a certaine
Lieutenant was degraded and cashier-
ed, &c., for the taking of money by the
way of corruption of certaine prest
souldiers in the countrey, and for
placing of others in their roomes, more
unfit for service and of less sufficiency
and abilitie". Elizabethan military
texts are usually respectful about
generals but sardonic about captains;

Barnabe Riche, himself a captain, says
"wee neuer number his [the captain's]
yeeres, we neither consider his know-
ledg, we little regard his worthines, we
lesse esteeme his experience, we scarce
examine his honestye" (*Path-way to
Military practise*, 1587, sig. C2).
"[Fal.'s] behaviour is so accurately
opposed to that recommended for captains that it might serve as a model in
reverse. . . His comic appeal as captain
is due to the accuracy with which he
violates all the carefully formulated
requirements for this responsible
office" (Jorgensen). G. B. Harrison
describes some corruptions of the
1590s and points out that since England was engaged in a considerable
war they were matters of sinister
importance (*Sh. at Work*, 1933, 129–
30, 313).

14–15. *press . . . householders*] Steevens
quotes Barnabe Riche, *Souldier's Wishe
to Briton's Welfare*, 1604, 62—"we
should take up honest householders,
men that are of wealth and abilitie to
live at home, such as your captaines
might chop and change, and make
merchandise of". "Good" = substantial.

17. *warm*] "*Warm,* well lined or flush
in the Pocket" (Bailey).

report of a caliver worse than a struck fowl or a hurt
wild duck. I pressed me none but such toasts-and-   20
butter, with hearts in their bellies no bigger than
pins' heads, and they have bought out their services;
and now my whole charge consists of ancients, cor-
porals, lieutenants, gentlemen of companies—slaves
as ragged as Lazarus in the painted cloth, where the   25
glutton's dogs licked his sores: and such as indeed
were never soldiers, but discarded unjust serving-
men, younger sons to younger brothers, revolted
tapsters, and ostlers trade-fallen, the cankers of a

---

19. fowl] *Qq1–3* (foule); foole *Qq4,5,F*; sorel *conj. Johnson.*   26. sores:]
Qq2–5,F (*subst.*); sores, *Q1.*   29. tapsters, and ostlers] *Qq2,3* (tapsters,
and Ostlers); tapsters, and Ostlers, *Q1*; tapsters & Ostlers *Q4*; Tapsters and
Ostlers *Q5*; Tapsters and Ostlers, *F.*

---

19. *caliver*] light musket. Wright
cites contemporary spellings of "calee-
uer" and "calieuers" to show the long
second syllable.

struck fowl] Since this seems merely
to anticipate "hurt wild duck",
emendations have been proposed, the
best being Johnson's "sorel" (= young
buck). "Strike" as a hunting term was
particularly used of deer; cf. *OED*,
"Strike, *v.* 33.b. To kill or wound
(deer) with an arrow or spear". Or
"fowl" may = woodcock (Schmidt).

20–1. *toasts-and-butter*] milksops,
pampered citizens. Fynes Moryson's
Itinerary, 1617, pt III, i. 53, says
"Londiners, and all within the sound
of Bow-Bell, are in reproch called
Cocknies, and eaters of buttered
tostes".

23. *ancients*] i.e. ensigns, standard-
bearers.

24. *gentlemen of companies*] These
were imprecisely ranked somewhere
between privates and officers. To
Pistol's question "Art thou officer, /
Or art thou base, common, and popular?" Henry judiciously replies "I am
a gentleman of a company" (*H5*, IV. i.
37–9). Sir J. Turner, *Pallas Armata*,
1683, 218, 220–1, says that they were
not officers but were more honourable

than sergeants—"I encounter'd once
with a Country man of my own. . .
I enquir'd then if he had attain'd to
any degree better than a Serjeants
place? he told me, yes; for . . . he was
the oldest Gentleman of a Company".

25–6. *Lazarus . . . sores*] For Fal. and
this parable, cf. III. iii. 29–31, note.
Cloth painted with pictures was a
cheap substitute for tapestry; when the
hostess complains (*2H4*, II. i. 157) that
she is "fain to pawn . . . the tapestry",
Fal. replies ". . . for thy walls . . . the
story of the Prodigal, or the German
hunting, in water-work, is worth a
thousand of these . . . fly-bitten
tapestries".

26. *sores:*] Q1 has only a comma, but
Fal. divides his men into (*a*) old
soldiers who, though ragged, had seen
service; and (*b*) such as never were
soldiers, whose impressment represents the depths of corruption.

28. *revolted*] runaway.

29–30. *cankers . . . peace*] Steevens and
Wilson (N.C.S.) cite Nashe parallels,
Pierce Penilesse (McKerrow, i. 213, 211)
—"all the cankerwormes that breede
on the rust of peace", and "There is a
certain waste of the people for whome
there is no vse, but warre: and these
men must haue some employment still

calm world and a long peace, ten times more dis-   30
honourable-ragged than an old fazed ancient; and
such have I to fill up the rooms of them as have
bought out their services, that you would think that
I had a hundred and fifty tattered prodigals lately
come from swine-keeping, from eating draff and   35
husks. A mad fellow met me on the way, and told me
I had unloaded all the gibbets and pressed the dead
bodies. No eye hath seen such scarecrows. I'll not
march through Coventry with them, that's flat: nay,
and the villains march wide betwixt the legs as if they   40
had gyves on, for indeed I had the most of them out
of prison. There's not a shirt and a half in all my
company, and the half shirt is two napkins tacked together and thrown over the shoulders like a herald's
coat without sleeves; and the shirt to say the truth   45
stolen from my host at Saint Albans, or the red-nose
innkeeper of Daventry. But that's all one, they'll
find linen enough on every hedge.

30. a long] *Qq1–4;* long *Q5,F.*   31. fazed] *Qq1–4* (fazd *or* fazde); faczde *Q5;* fac'd *F.*   32. as] *Qq;* that *F.*   34. tattered] *QqFf1,2* (tottered [*subst.*]), *F3* (tatter'd).   46. at] *Qq1–4;* of *Q5,F.*

to cut them off". Elizabethan references to the supposed unhealthiness
of a long peace abound; cf. *Ham.,*
IV. iv. 27–8—"the imposthume of
much wealth and peace, / That inward breaks"; and Daniel, *C.W.,* i. 83
—"For now this Peace with *France*
had shut in here / The overgrowing
Humours Wars do spend".

31. *old fazed ancient*] a tattered old
flag: "faze", "feaze" = fray, unravel
(*OED,* "Feaze, *v.*"). F's "old-fac'd"
may mean the same thing but is ambiguous. Fal. presumably means that
his men are more ragged in a dis-
honourable way than an ensign is in an
honourable one.

34–6. *prodigals . . . husks*] "The most
frequently mentioned Parable . . . in
the plays" (Noble, 277). Shakespeare
recollects the Geneva Bible's "huskes"
(*Luke,* xv. 16) rather than the Bishops'
or Great Bible's "coddes".

35. *draff*] pig-swill.

41–2. *out of prison*] "The Privy
Council emptied the London prisons in 1596 to furnish recruits for
the Cadiz expedition" (Wilson,
N.C.S.).

42. *not*] Rowe emended to "but"
and many edd. follow. But this free
hand with arithmetic is thoroughly
Falstaffian. For an exact parallel see
v. iii. 37–8.

46–7. *Saint Albans . . . Daventry*] Both
on the main road from London to
Coventry. Q6's "Daintry" ("Dauin-
try" *Qq1–5,*F) indicates the pronunciation.

47–8. *they'll . . . hedge*] A frequent
recourse for snappers-up of uncon-
sidered trifles, like Autolycus ("My
traffic is sheets"—*Wint.,* IV. ii. 23).
John Awdeley's *Fraternitye of Vaca-
bondes,* 1575, mentions the "Prygman"
whose "propertye is to steale cloathes

Enter the PRINCE *and the* LORD OF WESTMORELAND.

Prince. How now, blown Jack? How now, quilt?

Fal. What, Hal! How now, mad wag? What a devil dost   50
thou in Warwickshire? My good Lord of Westmoreland, I cry you mercy, I thought your honour had
already been at Shrewsbury.

West. Faith, Sir John, 'tis more than time that I were
there, and you too, but my powers are there already;   55
the King I can tell you looks for us all, we must away
all night.

Fal. Tut, never fear me, I am as vigilant as a cat to steal
cream.

Prince. I think, to steal cream indeed, for thy theft hath   60
already made thee butter; but tell me, Jack, whose
fellows are these that come after?

Fal. Mine, Hal, mine.

Prince. I did never see such pitiful rascals.

Fal. Tut, tut, good enough to toss, food for powder, food   65
for powder, they'll fill a pit as well as better; tush,
man, mortal men, mortal men.

West. Ay, but, Sir John, methinks they are exceeding
poor and bare, too beggarly.

Fal. Faith, for their poverty I know not where they had   70
that; and for their bareness I am sure they never
learned that of me.

48. S.D. *and the*] *Qq2–5,F; not in Q1.*   56. can tell] *Qq1–4, Q5 corr., F;* can *Q5
uncorr.*   57. all night] *Qq;* all to Night *F.*   58. fear me] *Qq1–4,F;* feare tell
me *Q5.*   66. better] *Qq1,3–5,F;* a better *Q2.*

of the hedge" (EETS, Extra ser., ix. 3);
and Harman's *Caveat for Commen Cur-
setors*, 1567, calls for vigilance so that
"our lynnen clothes shall and maye
lye safelye one our hedges vntouched"
(ibid., 21).

49. *blown . . . quilt*] "blown" = (a)
swollen; (b) short-winded. "Jack" is
also a quibble, a "jack" being a soldier's quilted or wadded jacket.

50–3. *What . . . Shrewsbury*] Fal. gets
his innuendos in first.

60–1. *I think . . . butter*] It must be
cream indeed, for whatever you steal
runs to fat.

65. *good . . . powder*] Remarking on
"the terrible anonymity of Fal.'s
'food for powder'" (like "cannon-
fodder" in the 1914–18 war), Jorgensen cites Thomas Digges, *Foure Paradoxes*, 1604, 47, on the indifference of
captains and men to each other—"The
Captaine neither knowes his Souldiers,
nor the Souldiers their Captaine before the Seruice, nor euer meane to
meete againe when the warres are
ended". Fal.'s nonchalance reflects the
Elizabethan captains' readiness to lose
their men so that they could retain the
pay; cf. v. iii. 36, note.

Prince. No, I'll be sworn, unless you call three fingers in
        the ribs bare. But sirrah, make haste; Percy is
        already in the field.   *Exit.*   75
Fal. What, is the King encamped?
West. He is, Sir John, I fear we shall stay too long.   [*Exit.*]
Fal. Well,
        To the latter end of a fray, and the beginning of a feast
        Fits a dull fighter and a keen guest.   *Exit.*   80

SCENE III.—[*Shrewsbury. The Rebel Camp.*]

Enter HOTSPUR, WORCESTER, DOUGLAS, VERNON.

Hot. We'll fight with him tonight.
Wor.   It may not be.
Doug. You give him then advantage.
Ver.   Not a whit.
Hot. Why say you so, looks he not for supply?
Ver. So do we.
Hot.   His is certain, ours is doubtful.
Wor. Good cousin, be advis'd, stir not tonight.   5
Ver. Do not, my lord.
Doug.   You do not counsel well.
        You speak it out of fear and cold heart.
Ver. Do me no slander, Douglas; by my life,
        And I dare well maintain it with my life,
        If well-respected honour bid me on,   10
        I hold as little counsel with weak fear

73. in] *Qq1,2*; on *Qq3–5,F.*   75. S.D.] *Qq; not in F.*   77. S.D.] *Capell; not in
QqF.*   78–80.] *As verse, Pope; prose, QqF.*   80. S.D.] *Capell; Exeunt. | QqF.*

Scene III

SCENE III.] *F* (*Scœna Tertia.*); *not in Qq.   Location.*] *Malone* (*subst.*).   S.D.
Douglas,] *Q1* (*Doug:*); *Douglas, and | Qq2–5,F.*

73. *fingers*] The finger is a measure of
¾ inch; *OED* ("Finger, *sb.*5") cites
Eden, *Arte of Navig.*, 1561, I. xviii. 19—
"Foure graines of barlye make a
fynger; foure fyngers a hande; foure
handes a foote".

79–80. *To . . . guest*] A proverbial
sentiment; Tilley, C547.

Scene III

3. *supply*] reinforcements.
10. *well-respected*] well-considered—

　　　As you, my lord, or any Scot that this day lives;
　　　Let it be seen tomorrow in the battle
　　　Which of us fears.
Doug.　　　　　　　　Yea, or tonight.
Ver.　　　　　　　　　　　　Content.
Hot. Tonight, say I.　　　　　　　　　　　　　　15
Ver. Come, come, it may not be. I wonder much,
　　　Being men of such great leading as you are,
　　　That you foresee not what impediments
　　　Drag back our expedition: certain horse
　　　Of my cousin Vernon's are not yet come up,　　　20
　　　Your uncle Worcester's horse came but today,
　　　And now their pride and mettle is asleep,
　　　Their courage with hard labour tame and dull,
　　　That not a horse is half the half himself.
Hot. So are the horses of the enemy　　　　　　　25
　　　In general journey-bated and brought low.
　　　The better part of ours are full of rest.
Wor. The number of the King exceedeth ours:
　　　For God's sake, cousin, stay till all come in.

　　　　　　　　　　The trumpet sounds a parley.

Enter SIR WALTER BLUNT.

13. Let it] *Qq1,5,F*; Let *Qq2–4.*　　13–14. Let ... battle / Which ... fears.] *As F*;
Let . . . battle which . . . feares. / *Qq.*　　14. Doug.] *Qq1,2,5,F*; *not in Qq3,4.*
16–17.] *As T. Johnson, Pope;* Come . . . be. / I . . . are, / *QqF* (*subst.*).　　21. horse]
Q5,F; horses *Qq1–4.*　　24. the half] *Steevens;* the halfe of *QqF*; half of *Pope.*
28. ours] *Q6,F;* our *Qq1–5.*

"i.e. as understood by wise campaigners, not mere fire-eaters" (Wilson, N.C.S.).

　17. *of such . . . leading*] so experienced in generalship.

　19. *Drag . . . expedition*] Prevent our moving fast.

　19, 21. *horse*] Cf. II. i. 3, note.

　24. *That . . . himself*] For metre Pope dropped "the" and Steevens, more effectively, "of" (see collation). "Half the half of himself", Dr Harold Brooks comments to me, sounds un-Shakespearean in rhythm, even granted the play's occasional roughness.

　26. *journey-bated*] dejected, weakened, by travel.

　28. *ours*] *Qq1–5*'s "our" may be right. Jespersen, *Mod. Engl. Grammar*, ii. 16, 27, says "The form without *s* was used as late as 1550"; but *OED* ("Our. † 2 . . . = OURS") cites a later usage, in Daniel, *C.W.*, 1601, VI. lxi— "We rule who liue: the dead are none of our" (rhyming with "pow'r").

　29 S.D. Sir Walter Blunt] Hol. says "the abbat of Shrewesburie, and one of the clearks of the priuie seale were sent from the king vnto the Persies" (iii. 25), but Shakespeare heightens Blunt's role.

Blunt. I come with gracious offers from the King,   30
    If you vouchsafe me hearing and respect.
Hot. Welcome, Sir Walter Blunt: and would to God
    You were of our determination!
    Some of us love you well, and even those some
    Envy your great deservings and good name,   35
    Because you are not of our quality,
    But stand against us like an enemy.
Blunt. And God defend but still I should stand so,
    So long as out of limit and true rule
    You stand against anointed majesty.   40
    But to my charge. The King hath sent to know
    The nature of your griefs, and whereupon
    You conjure from the breast of civil peace
    Such bold hostility, teaching his duteous land
    Audacious cruelty. If that the King   45
    Have any way your good deserts forgot,
    Which he confesseth to be manifold,
    He bids you name your griefs, and with all speed
    You shall have your desires with interest
    And pardon absolute for yourself, and these   50
    Herein misled by your suggestion.
Hot. The King is kind, and well we know the King
    Knows at what time to promise, when to pay:
    My father, and my uncle, and myself

32-3.] *As Qq;* Welcome . . . *Blunt.* / And . . . determination. / *F.*   38. God] *Qq;*
Heauen *F.*   41.] *As Qq;* But . . . Charge. / The . . . know / *F.*   52.] *As Qq;*
The . . . kinde: / And . . . King / *F.*   54. and my] *Qq1,2;* my *Qq3-5,F.*

35. *Envy*] Begrudge.
36. *quality*] company, party. It signified a profession (especially the
actor's), and so a fellowship; cf. *Tp.*,
I. ii. 193—"Ariel and all his quality".
38. *defend*] forbid.
39. *limit*] bounds of allegiance.
51. *suggestion*] instigation, temptation—a word of sinister implication;
cf. *2H4,* IV. iv. 45—"venom of suggestion"; *Mac.*, I. iii. 134—"Why do I
yield to that suggestion . . .?"; and
Lr., II. i. 75—"Thy suggestion, plot,
and damned practice".
54. *My father . . .*] "At his comming

vnto Doncaster, the earle of Northumberland, and his sonne sir Henrie
Persie . . . with the erle of Westmerland, came vnto him, where he sware
vnto those Lords, that he would
demand no more, but the lands that
were to him descended by inheritance
from his father and in right of his wife"
(Hol., ii. 853). For the Percys' accusation of "manifest periurie" see App.
III, p. 174. Actually Hall's *Chronicle*
more clearly makes the Percys the first
supporters on his landing. But it does
not follow that Hall was a source, for
Shakespeare undoubtedly derives from

Did give him that same royalty he wears,   55
And when he was not six and twenty strong,
Sick in the world's regard, wretched and low,
A poor unminded outlaw sneaking home,
My father gave him welcome to the shore:
And when he heard him swear and vow to God   60
He came but to be Duke of Lancaster,
To sue his livery, and beg his peace
With tears of innocency, and terms of zeal,
My father, in kind heart and pity mov'd,
Swore him assistance, and perform'd it too.   65
Now when the lords and barons of the realm
Perceiv'd Northumberland did lean to him,
The more and less came in with cap and knee,
Met him in boroughs, cities, villages,
Attended him on bridges, stood in lanes,   70
Laid gifts before him, proffer'd him their oaths,
Gave him their heirs as pages, follow'd him

61. but to be] *Qq1-3,5 corr.,F;* but to the *Qq4,5 uncorr.*   70. Attended] *Qq1-3,F;*
Attend *Qq4,5.*   72. heirs as pages,] *F4* (Heires, as Pages,); heires, as Pages
QqFf1-3 (subst.).   follow'd] *Capell;* followed *QqF.*

Hol. in some details (e.g. in naming
Beaumont among the supporters—*R2,*
II. ii. 54), and in any case the Percys,
whether or not present at Ravenspurgh, are clearly the greatest of
Bolingbroke's allies (cf. Northumberland's initiative in *R2,* II. i. 278 ff.).

56. *six and twenty*] A number not
apparent in the sources. Hol. says that
Bolingbroke "landed . . . at . . . Rauen-
spur . . . and with him not past threescore persons" (ii. 853).

62. *sue his livery*] sue for the delivery
of his lands which, by law, on the
death of his father, John of Gaunt,
reverted to the King.

beg his peace] i.e. from Richard II.
Cf. *OED,* "Peace. *sb.* I.I.C. . . . peace-
ful recognition of the authority or
claims, and acceptance of the protection, of a king or lord".

68. *with cap and knee*] An accepted
phrase; cf. Sidney, *Lady of the May*
(*Wks,* ed. Feuillerat, 1922, ii. 334)—

"With cap and knee be it spoken, is it
your pleasure neighbour *Rixus* to be
a wild foole?"; and Dekker, *Sun's
Darling* (Shepherd, iv. 299)—*"Follie.*
I am sure the Times were never more
beggerly and proud . . . knaves over-
brave wise men, while wise men stand
with cap and knee to fooles".

70. *lanes*] The sense "rows, files"
(*OED,* "Lane. 2*b.* A passage between
two lines of persons; a way to pass
through a crowd") is apter than that
of "country paths"; Bolingbroke's
triumph is a matter rather for high-
roads.

72. *Gave him . . . him*] QqF have the
comma after "heirs", not "pages".
But (*a*) the young heirs rather than the
fathers would be the pages; (*b*) pages
normally preceded their masters, as in
Three Lords and Three Ladies of London
(Hazlitt's *Dodsley,* vi. 472–3)—*"Pomp.*
But, Fealty, canst thou declare to me /
The cause why all their pages follow

Even at the heels in golden multitudes.
He presently, as greatness knows itself,
Steps me a little higher than his vow   75
Made to my father while his blood was poor
Upon the naked shore at Ravenspurgh;
And now forsooth takes on him to reform
Some certain edicts and some strait decrees
That lie too heavy on the commonwealth;   80
Cries out upon abuses, seems to weep
Over his country's wrongs; and by this face,
This seeming brow of justice, did he win
The hearts of all that he did angle for;
Proceeded further—cut me off the heads   85
Of all the favourites that the absent King
In deputation left behind him here,
When he was personal in the Irish war.
Blunt. Tut, I came not to hear this.
Hot.   Then to the point.
In short time after he depos'd the King,   90
Soon after that depriv'd him of his life,
And in the neck of that task'd the whole state;
To make that worse, suffer'd his kinsman March
(Who is, if every owner were well plac'd,
Indeed his King) to be engag'd in Wales,   95
There without ransom to lie forfeited;
Disgrac'd me in my happy victories,
Sought to entrap me by intelligence,

80. lie] *Qq1–4,5 uncorr.;* lay *Q5 corr., F.*   82. country's] *Rowe;* Countries *Q5 corr., F;* Countrey *Q1;* Countrie *Qq2,3;* Country *Qq4,5 uncorr.*   94. were well] *Qq1–4;* were *Q5,F.*

them, / When ours in show do ever go before? / *Fealty.* In war they follow, and the Spaniard is / Warring in mind".

73. *golden*] (a) resplendent; (b) auspicious. Cf. Pistol's "golden times" and "golden joys" (*2H4,* v. iii. 98, 101).

78–80. *reform . . . commonwealth*] "He vndertooke to cause the paiment of taxes and tallages to be laid downe, & to bring the king to good gouernment" (Hol., ii. 853).

87. *In deputation*] As deputies; cf. iv. i. 32, note.

88. *personal*] personally engaged.

92. *in the neck of*] immediately after.
task'd] Almost identical with "taxed", though technically a particular levy of a "fifteenth" authorized to the king by Magna Carta.

95. *engag'd*] held as hostage; cf. v. ii. 43.

98. *intelligence*] secret information. For the rebels' complaint of "slan-

Rated mine uncle from the Council-board,
In rage dismiss'd my father from the court,   100
Broke oath on oath, committed wrong on wrong,
And in conclusion drove us to seek out
This head of safety, and withal to pry
Into his title, the which we find
Too indirect for long continuance.   105
Blunt. Shall I return this answer to the King?
Hot. Not so, Sir Walter. We'll withdraw awhile.
Go to the King, and let there be impawn'd
Some surety for a safe return again,
And in the morning early shall mine uncle   110
Bring him our purposes—and so, farewell.
Blunt. I would you would accept of grace and love.
Hot. And may be so we shall.
Blunt.   Pray God you do.   *Exeunt.*

SCENE IV.—[*York. The Archbishop's Palace.*]

Enter the ARCHBISHOP OF YORK *and* SIR MICHAEL.

Arch. Hie, good Sir Michael, bear this sealed brief
With winged haste to the lord marshal,

99. mine] *Qq1–4;* my *Q5,F.*   104. title] *QqF;* title too *Pope.*   107.] *As Qq;*
Not . . . *Walter.* / Wee'le . . . a while: / *F.*   110. mine] *Qq1,2;* my *Qq3–5,F.*
111. purposes] *Qq1–3;* porpose *Q4;* purpose *Q5,F.*   113. And] *Qq;* And't *F.*
God] *Qq;* Heauen *F.*   113. S.D.] *F; not in Qq.*

Scene IV
SCENE IV.] *F (Scena Quarta.); not in Qq.*   Location.] *Theobald (subst.).*   S.D.
the] *F; not in Qq.*   and] *Qq2–5,F; not in Q1.*

derous reports" see App. III, p. 172.
  99. *Rated mine uncle*] Cf. I. iii. 14–20.
  100. *In rage . . . court*] Cf. I. iii. 120–2.
  103. *head of safety*] self-defensive army.
  105. *indirect*] (a) not in the direct line; (b) morally crooked.
  113. *And . . . shall*] This unexpectedly moderate reply corresponds to Hol.;
  App. III, p. 174.

Scene IV
  1. *Sir Michael*] Unknown to history. "Sir" was a courtesy title for priests (like Sir Hugh Evans in *Wiv.*), but, Evans (*Supp.*) suggests, Sir Michael might equally well be a knight, in view of his military interests. The name was very variously spelt, and Q1's *Mighell,* Wilson (N.C.S.) notes, occurs twice in Nashe (McKerrow, iii. 88, ll. 17, 26).
    brief] letter.
  2. *marshal*] He was Thomas Mow-

This to my cousin Scroop, and all the rest
To whom they are directed. If you knew
How much they do import you would make haste.   5
Sir M. My good lord,
     I guess their tenor.
Arch.   Like enough you do.
Tomorrow, good Sir Michael, is a day
Wherein the fortune of ten thousand men
Must bide the touch; for, sir, at Shrewsbury,   10
As I am truly given to understand,
The King with mighty and quick-raised power
Meets with Lord Harry: and I fear, Sir Michael,
What with the sickness of Northumberland,
Whose power was in the first proportion,   15
And what with Owen Glendower's absence thence,
Who with them was a rated sinew too,
And comes not in, o'er-rul'd by prophecies,
I fear the power of Percy is too weak
To wage an instant trial with the King.   20
Sir M. Why, my good lord, you need not fear,
     There is Douglas, and Lord Mortimer.
Arch. No, Mortimer is not there.

4–5.] *As Qq*; To . . . directed. / If . . . import, / You . . . haste. / *F.*   6–7.] *As Var. 1773*; My . . . tenor. / Like . . . do. / *QqF (subst.).*   16. what with] *Qq1,2,F;* what *Qq3–5.*   17. a rated sinew] *Qq1–3;* rated sinew *Q4;* rated firmely *Q5,F.* 18. o'er-rul'd] *QqF* (ouerrulde *or* ouer-rul'd), *T. Johnson 2, Pope.*

---

bray, Duke of Norfolk, an insurgent leader in *2H4.* "Marshal" sometimes is trisyllabic (Fr. maréschal); cf. *Lr.,* IV. iii. 9—"The Marshal of France, Monsieur la Far".

     3. *my cousin Scroop*] If this fleeting reference is to be elucidated, the identification is probably with (*a*) below. Various Scropes in the plays fall foul of the Bolingbroke line, viz. (*a*) Sir Stephen, who tells Richard II of Wiltshire's execution (*R2*, III. ii. 142); (*b*) William, Earl of Wiltshire, younger brother of Sir Stephen, executed by Bolingbroke at Bristol; (*c*) the Archbishop, Richard, who resents "his brother's death at Bristow" (*1H4,* I. iii.

265)—really a distant cousin of Wiltshire (though Hol. calls him a brother, iii. 23); (*d*) Sir Henry, son of Sir Stephen above, the treacherous Scrope of *H5,* II. ii.

     10. *bide the touch*] be put to the test, as gold is tried by the touchstone.

     15. *proportion*] magnitude, i.e. a larger proportion than any other.

     17. *rated sinew*] valued source of strength.

     18. *o'er-rul'd by prophecies*] Hol. says that the Welsh were at Shrewsbury, Daniel that they were absent. The "prophecies" are a Shakespearean invention in keeping with Glendower's character.

Sir M. But there is Mordake, Vernon, Lord Harry Percy,
    And there is my Lord of Worcester, and a head   25
    Of gallant warriors, noble gentlemen.
Arch. And so there is: but yet the King hath drawn
    The special head of all the land together:
    The Prince of Wales, Lord John of Lancaster,
    The noble Westmoreland, and warlike Blunt,   30
    And many mo corrivals and dear men
    Of estimation and command in arms.
Sir M. Doubt not, my lord, they shall be well oppos'd.
Arch. I hope no less, yet needful 'tis to fear;
    And to prevent the worst, Sir Michael, speed.   35
    For if Lord Percy thrive not, ere the King
    Dismiss his power he means to visit us,
    For he hath heard of our confederacy,
    And 'tis but wisdom to make strong against him:
    Therefore make haste—I must go write again   40
    To other friends; and so, farewell, Sir Michael.   *Exeunt.*

25–6.] *As Qq;* And . . . Worcester, / And . . . Warriors, / Noble Gentlemen. / *F.*
33. they] *Qq1–3;* he *Qq4,5,F.*   36. not,] *Qq2,3,F;* not *Qq1,4,5.*   38. our]
Qq1–3,5,F; out *Q4.*

31. *mo*] more. "Mo" generally =
more in number, while "more" =
more in quantity; cf. North's *Plutarch,
Fabius Maximus* (Tudor Trans., II. 60)
—"the one chaunced to have moe
prisoners than the other . . . Hannibal
had . . . of Romaine prisoners, two
hundred and fortie moe, then Fabius
had".

    corrivals] partners, associates; cf.

"Without corrival" at I. iii. 205.
    dear] noble, honourable; as in *Troil.*,
v. iii. 27–8—"the dear man / Holds
honour far more precious-dear than
life".

    38. *our confederacy*] our combining
against him. The chief, and very real,
interest of this otherwise unremarkable
scene is in its foreshadowing of further
trouble after Shrewsbury.

ACT V

SCENE I.—[*Shrewsbury. The King's Camp.*]

Enter the KING, PRINCE OF WALES, LORD JOHN OF LANCASTER,
SIR WALTER BLUNT, FALSTAFF.

King. How bloodily the sun begins to peer
    Above yon bulky hill! The day looks pale
    At his distemp'rature.
Prince.   The southern wind
    Doth play the trumpet to his purposes,
    And by his hollow whistling in the leaves   5
    Foretells a tempest and a blust'ring day.
King. Then with the losers let it sympathise,
    For nothing can seem foul to those that win.

                                The trumpet sounds.

Enter WORCESTER [*and* VERNON.]

ACT V

Scene 1

ACT V SCENE I.] F (*Actus Quintus. Scena Prima.*); *not in Qq.*   *Location.*] *Capell*
(*subst.*).   S.D. *Lancaster, Sir*] *Hanmer*; Lancaster, Earle of Westmerland, Sir | QqF.
Blunt,] *Q1*; Blunt, and | *Qq2–5,F.*   2. bulky] *Q1*; busky *Qq2–5,F.*   5. by his]
Qq1,2,F; by the *Q3*; by *Qq4,5.*   8. S.D. *and Vernon*] *Theobald* (*and Sir Richard*
Vernon), *Capell*; *not in QqF.*

2. *bulky*] All previous edd. have
followed Qq2–5,F's "busky". But Q1
certainly (though faintly) reads
"bulky", and though "busky" would
connect poetically with the "whistling
in the leaves" (l. 5) "bulky" has its
own atmospheric quality. Elizabethan
maps (e.g. Christopher Saxton's, of
Shropshire, 1577) show a hump-like
mound for "Wrekin hill" for which
"bulky" would be a most suitable epithet, and if Shakespeare examined
such a map the word might leap to his
mind. Shaaber (*MLN*, 1939, lix. 276–
8) argues that Shakespeare uses "bulk"

often enough (cf. l. 62, below), sometimes for "a thing of great size looming
up before the speaker", and that as a
neologism (*OED*'s earliest citation is in
1672) "bulky" would have "none of
those prosaic connotations which it has
for us". Nashe refers to a "gorbellied
Volume" as "bigger bulkt than a
Dutch Hoy" (*Haue with You*; McKerrow, iii. 35); and for "bulk" as the
swelling of a ship's hull Cotgrave
gives "vaisseau d'un navire. *The bulke,*
bellie, or *bodie of a ship*". The idea is of
swelling magnitude.

   3. *distemp'rature*] Cf. III. i. 31, note.

How now, my Lord of Worcester! 'Tis not well
That you and I should meet upon such terms   10
As now we meet. You have deceiv'd our trust,
And made us doff our easy robes of peace
To crush our old limbs in ungentle steel:
This is not well, my lord, this is not well.
What say you to it? Will you again unknit   15
This churlish knot of all-abhorred war,
And move in that obedient orb again
Where you did give a fair and natural light,
And be no more an exhal'd meteor,
A prodigy of fear, and a portent   20
Of broached mischief to the unborn times?
Wor. Hear me, my liege:
For mine own part I could be well content
To entertain the lag end of my life
With quiet hours. For I protest   25
I have not sought the day of this dislike.
King. You have not sought it? How comes it, then?
Fal. Rebellion lay in his way, and he found it.
Prince. Peace, chewet, peace!
Wor. It pleas'd your Majesty to turn your looks   30
Of favour from myself, and all our house,
And yet I must remember you, my lord,
We were the first and dearest of your friends;
For you my staff of office did I break

---

9. How] *Var. 1778; King.* Now *QqF.*   25. I] *Qq;* I do *F.*

13. *our old limbs*] Henry was about 36, but the whole conception here is of an elderly and careworn ruler.

17. *obedient orb*] proper sphere of obedience. In the Ptolemaic cosmology the stars revolve in fixed orbs. The analogy between celestial and social order is an Elizabethan axiom.

19. *exhal'd*] (*a*) drawn up of vapours (cf. I. i. 11, note); (*b*) dragged from the orderly course proper to celestial bodies.

25. *I protest*] It is tempting to read F's "I do protest", but the metre is

often irregular; cf. l. 27. If a word has dropped out, there is no certainty that F's is the right correction.

29. *chewet*] A quibble; (*a*) chough, jackdaw (= chatterer); (*b*) minced-meat pie (*OED*, "A dish . . . of meat or fish, chopped fine").

33. *We . . . friends*] For the Percys' early support, cf. IV. iii. 54, note.

34–5. *For you . . . time*] "Sir Thomas Persie, earle of Worcester . . . brake his white staffe, which is the representing signe and token of his office, and without delaie went to duke Henrie" (Hol., ii. 855). Shakespeare follows this in

In Richard's time, and posted day and night   35
To meet you on the way, and kiss your hand,
When yet you were in place and in account
Nothing so strong and fortunate as I.
It was myself, my brother, and his son,
That brought you home, and boldly did outdare   40
The dangers of the time. You swore to us,
And you did swear that oath at Doncaster,
That you did nothing purpose 'gainst the state,
Nor claim no further than your new-fall'n right,
The seat of Gaunt, dukedom of Lancaster.   45
To this we swore our aid: but in short space
It rain'd down fortune show'ring on your head,
And such a flood of greatness fell on you,
What with our help, what with the absent King,
What with the injuries of a wanton time,   50
The seeming sufferances that you had borne,
And the contrarious winds that held the King
So long in his unlucky Irish wars
That all in England did repute him dead:
And from this swarm of fair advantages   55
You took occasion to be quickly woo'd
To gripe the general sway into your hand,
Forgot your oath to us at Doncaster,
And being fed by us, you us'd us so
As that ungentle gull the cuckoo's bird   60
Useth the sparrow—did oppress our nest,
Grew by our feeding to so great a bulk
That even our love durst not come near your sight
For fear of swallowing; but with nimble wing

40. outdare] *Q1,F;* outdate *Qq2-5.*   41. dangers] *Qq1-4;* danger *Q5,F.*
43. purpose] *Qq1-4;* of purpose *Q5,F.*   46. swore] *Qq1-4;* sweare *Q5;* sware
F.   50. of a] *Qq1-4;* of *Q5,F.*   53. his] *Qq1-4;* the *Q5,F.*   56. woo'd] *F;*
wooed *Qq.*

R2—"the Earl of Worcester / Hath
broke his staff" (II. ii. 58–9), and "He
hath forsook the court, / Broken his
staff of office" (II. iii. 26–7).

41. *You swore to us*] Cf. IV. iii. 54 ff.,
note.

44. *new-fall'n*] i.e. newly fallen due
to you.

60. *gull . . . bird*] nestling. *OED,*
"gull. *sb.*[2] Now dial. . . . An unfledged
bird . . ." (quoting this passage),
and also "bird *orig.* . . . a young
bird . . . a nestling. The only sense
in *OE;* found in literature down
to 1600". Cf. *3H6,* II. i. 91—"that
princely eagle's bird".

We were enforc'd for safety sake to fly   65
Out of your sight, and raise this present head,
Whereby we stand opposed by such means
As you yourself have forg'd against yourself,
By unkind usage, dangerous countenance,
And violation of all faith and troth   70
Sworn to us in your younger enterprise.

King. These things indeed you have articulate,
     Proclaim'd at market crosses, read in churches,
     To face the garment of rebellion
     With some fine colour that may please the eye   75
     Of fickle changelings and poor discontents,
     Which gape and rub the elbow at the news
     Of hurlyburly innovation;
     And never yet did insurrection want
     Such water-colours to impaint his cause,   80
     Nor moody beggars starving for a time
     Of pellmell havoc and confusion.

Prince. In both your armies there is many a soul
     Shall pay full dearly for this encounter
     If once they join in trial. Tell your nephew,   85
     The Prince of Wales doth join with all the world
     In praise of Henry Percy: by my hopes,
     This present enterprise set off his head,

---

71. in your] *Qq;* in *F.*   72. articulate] *Qq;* articulated *F.*   73. Proclaim'd]
Q1,F; Proclaimed *Qq2–5.*   83. your] *Qq;* our *F.*

69. *dangerous countenance*] threatening
demeanour.

74. *face*] trim with ornament.

75. *colour*] A quibble on the literal
and metaphorical (= a specious excuse) senses. "Colour is when men
make a way for themselves to have a
construction made of their faults or
wants, as proceeding from a better
cause" (Bacon, *Adv. of Learning*, xxiii.
32; *Works*, ed. Spedding & Ellis, iii.
464).

77. *rub the elbow*] hug themselves
(with pleasure), arms crossed and
hands on elbows. Joy supposedly made
the elbows itch; cf. Nashe, *Unfortunate
Traveller* (McKerrow, ii. 321)—"My

hart hopt and danst, my elbowes itcht
. . . I wist not . . . what I did for joy";
and *LLL.*, v. ii. 109–10—"One rubb'd
his elbow thus, and fleer'd, and swore /
A better speech was never spoke
before".

78. *innovation*] disturbance of the
accepted order, commotion. In *Sir
Thomas More*, II. iv. 114–15, More calls
on the rioters to "perceaue howe horrible a shape / Your ynnouation
beres". See p. 203.

80. *water-colours*] "colours" (cf. l. 75,
note) hastily applied and not lasting.

81. *moody*] sullen, angry.

88. *set off his head*] not being counted
against him.

I do not think a braver gentleman,
More active-valiant or more valiant-young,   90
More daring or more bold, is now alive
To grace this latter age with noble deeds.
For my part, I may speak it to my shame,
I have a truant been to chivalry,
And so I hear he doth account me too;   95
Yet this before my father's majesty—
I am content that he shall take the odds
Of his great name and estimation,
And will, to save the blood on either side,
Try fortune with him in a single fight.   100
King. And, Prince of Wales, so dare we venture thee,
Albeit, considerations infinite
Do make against it: no, good Worcester, no,
We love our people well, even those we love
That are misled upon your cousin's part,   105
And will they take the offer of our grace,
Both he, and they, and you, yea, every man
Shall be my friend again, and I'll be his:
So tell your cousin, and bring me word
What he will do. But if he will not yield,   110
Rebuke and dread correction wait on us,
And they shall do their office. So, be gone;
We will not now be troubled with reply:
We offer fair, take it advisedly.

Exit Worcester[, with Vernon].

Prince. It will not be accepted, on my life;   115
The Douglas and the Hotspur both together
Are confident against the world in arms.
King. Hence, therefore, every leader to his charge;
For on their answer will we set on them,

---

90. active-valiant] *Theobald;* actiue, valiant *Qq1,2,F;* actiue, more valiant *Qq3–5.*   valiant-young] *Theobald;* valiant yong *QqF* (*subst.*).   100. in a] *Q1,F;* in *Qq2–5.*   114. S.D. *with Vernon*] *Theobald; not in QqF.*

---

90. *active- . . . -young*] In Sidney's *Astrophel and Stella*, sonnet lxxv, Edward IV is "young-wise, wise-valiant". Shakespeare may be echoing this.

100. *single fight*] There is no chronicle-precedent for this challenge.
102. *Albeit*] Yet on the other hand.
105. *cousin's*] The frequent extended use of the word; here = nephew's.

And God befriend us as our cause is just!   120

Exeunt all but the Prince and Falstaff.

Fal. Hal, if thou see me down in the battle and bestride
me, so; 'tis a point of friendship.

Prince. Nothing but a Colossus can do thee that friendship. Say thy prayers, and farewell.

Fal. I would 'twere bed-time, Hal, and all well.   125

Prince. Why, thou owest God a death.   [*Exit.*]

Fal. 'Tis not due yet, I would be loath to pay him before
his day—what need I be so forward with him that
calls not on me? Well, 'tis no matter, honour pricks
me on. Yea, but how if honour prick me off when I   130
come on, how then? Can honour set to a leg? No.
Or an arm? No. Or take away the grief of a wound?
No. Honour hath no skill in surgery then? No.
What is honour? A word. What is in that word

[margin handwritten notes]

120. S.D. *all but the*] *Cambr.; manent | Qq; Manet | F.   and*] *F; not in Qq.*
121–4.] *As Pope (prose)*; Hal...battel / And...friendship. / Nothing...friend-
ship, / Say...farewell. / *QqF, subst. (verse)*.   125. 'twere] *Q1*; it were *Qq2–5,F.*
126. God] *Qq; heauen F.*   126. S.D.] *Hanmer; not in QqF.*   130. Yea, but]
Qq; But F.   131. then? Can] *Qq2,3,F*; then can *Qq1,4,5.*   134–5. in...that
honour?] *Qq1,3*; in that word? honor: what is that honour? *Q2;* that word
honor? what is that honor? *Q4;* that word Honour? *Q5,F.*

126. *thou owest...death*] Proverbial:
Tilley, G237. For the "debt-death"
quibble cf. I. iii. 183–4, note, and
Feeble's "We owe God a death"
(*2H4*, III. ii. 254).

127–8. *to pay...day*] Tilley, T290,
illustrates the proverb, "He does not
desire to die before his time".

129 ff. *Well...*] For a probable
source, see Intro., p. xxxviii. The sentiment may echo Palingenius' *Zodiacus
Vitae*, read in Elizabethan schools;
"Fama quid est, si nil delectat fama
sepultos? / Quid lapis, aut stipes, lau-
dum praeconia curant? / Si non lae-
taris vivens, laetabere nunquam" (ed.
1574, 52), translated by Barnabe
Googe as "Thou nothing art, for what
is fame, / yf it doe nought delight? /
The corps in graue, what doth yᵉ
stone / or stocke reioice in prayes? / If
here thou has not them, thou shalt /
haue neuer happy dayes": cf. T. W.

Baldwin, *Wm. Sh.'s Small Latine &
Lesse Greeke*, 1944, i. 678.

129, 130. *pricks, prick*] spur(s),
quibbling on "pricks" as "marks
down for death"; cf. *Cæs.*, IV. i. 1—
"These many then shall die; their
names are prick'd". G. B. Harrison
('Sh.'s Topical Significances', in *Sh.
Criticism 1919–1935*, ed. Ridler) points
out an echo of this in a letter of Tobie
Matthew to Dudley Carleton on 20
Sept. 1598—"Sir Fras. Vere is coming
towards the Low Countries, and Sir
Alex. Ratcliffe and Sir Robt. Drury
with him. Honour pricks them on, and
the world thinks that honour will
quickly prick them off again" (*Calender
of State Papers, Domestic Series, Elizabeth, 1598–1601*, 97). For other Fal.
jokes cf. Intro., p. xii.

131. *set to a leg*] set a broken leg, or,
perhaps, re-join one lopped off.

132. *grief*] pain, as in I. iii. 50.

honour? What is that honour? Air. A trim reckon-   135
ing! Who hath it? He that died a-Wednesday.
Doth he feel it? No. Doth he hear it? No. 'Tis in-
sensible, then? Yea, to the dead. But will it not live
with the living? No. Why? Detraction will not suffer it. Therefore I'll none of it. Honour is a mere   140
scutcheon—and so ends my catechism.   *Exit.*

SCENE II.—[*Shrewsbury. The Rebel Camp.*]

Enter WORCESTER *and* SIR RICHARD VERNON.

Wor. O no, my nephew must not know, Sir Richard,
    The liberal and kind offer of the King.
Ver. 'Twere best he did.
Wor.   Then are we all undone.
    It is not possible, it cannot be,
    The King should keep his word in loving us;   5
    He will suspect us still, and find a time
    To punish this offence in other faults:
    Supposition all our lives shall be stuck full of eyes,

137. 'Tis] *Qq;* Is it *F.*   138. will it] *Qq2–5,F;* wil *Q1.*

Scene II

SCENE II.] *F (Scena Secunda.); not in Qq.   Location.]* Malone (*subst.*).   S.D.
and] *Qq2–5,F; not in Q1.*   2. and kind] *Q1;* kinde *Qq2–5,F.*   3. are we] *Qq;*
we are *F.*   undone] *Q5,F;* vnder one *Qq1–4.*   5. should] *Qq1–3;* would
Qq4,5,F.   7. other] *Qq1–4;* others *Q5,F.*

141. *scutcheon*] funeral hatchment.
Scutcheons were the lowest form of
heraldic ensign, allotted for funerals.
They were of metal, silk, buckram, or
paper, and were hung in churches.

Scene II

1–2. *O no . . . King*] For Worcester's
misrepresentation see App. III, p. 174.
To Hol.'s account Shakespeare adds a
plausible reason (l. 3 ff.).

8. *Supposition*] Rowe and most edd.
emend to "Suspicion". But nothing is
gained; either word suits the sense,

and the metre is not improved since
"supp'sition" is no longer than "suspicion". Allegorical figures of rumour
and ill report were common; e.g.
Spenser's Envy (*F.Q.*, I. iv. 31) is
"ypainted full of eyes", and Dekker's
King's Entertainment, 1604 (Bowers, ii.
276), introduces Fame as "A Woman
in a Watchet Roabe, thickly set with
open Eyes, and Tongues". The image
may be traced to Virgil's Fama—"cui,
quot sunt corpore plumae / tot vigiles
oculi subter (mirabile dictu), / tot
linguae, totidem ora sonant, tot

For treason is but trusted like the fox,
Who, never so tame, so cherish'd and lock'd up,   10
Will have a wild trick of his ancestors.
Look how we can, or sad or merrily,
Interpretation will misquote our looks,
And we shall feed like oxen at a stall,
The better cherish'd still the nearer death.   15
My nephew's trespass may be well forgot,
It hath the excuse of youth and heat of blood,
And an adopted name of privilege—
A hare-brain'd Hotspur, govern'd by a spleen:
All his offences live upon my head   20
And on his father's. We did train him on,
And, his corruption being ta'en from us,
We as the spring of all shall pay for all:
Therefore, good cousin, let not Harry know
In any case the offer of the King.   25

Ver. Deliver what you will; I'll say 'tis so.
Here comes your cousin.

Enter HOTSPUR [*and* DOUGLAS].

Hot.   My uncle is return'd;
Deliver up my Lord of Westmoreland.
Uncle, what news?
Wor. The King will bid you battle presently.   30
Doug. Defy him by the Lord of Westmoreland.

10. never so] *Qq;* ne're so *F.*   12. we] *Qq1–3;* he *Qq4,5,F.*   merrily] *Q1* (merely), *Qq2,4* (merily), *Qq3,5,F.*   22. being] *Qq1–3,F;* beene *Q4;* benig *Q5.* 26–7.] *As F;* Deliuer . . . coosen. / My . . . returnd, / *Qq.*   27. your] *Qq1–4,F;* you *Q5.*   27. S.D. *Enter Hotspur*] *F; Enter Percy* / *Q1 (opposite l. 25); Enter Hotspur* / *Qq2–5 (opposite l. 25). and Douglas*] *Rowe; not in QqF.*   29. news] *Qq;* newe— *F.*

subrigit aures" (*Aen.*, IV. 181–3).
    11. *trick*] trait; cf. Beau. & Fl., *Maid in the Mill*, III. i (*Works*, vii. 36)—
"In you a wildness is a noble trick".
    18. *an adopted . . . privilege*] a nickname which privileges him to be rash.
    19. *govern'd...spleen*] Cf. II.iii.79, note.
    20. *live*] = "are active"; nearly synonymous with "lie" (cf. I. ii. 185, collation), but with extra vitality; cf. *2H4*,

I. iii. 12, "Our supplies live largely in the hope".
    22. *ta'en*] caught, as an infection.
    28. *Deliver . . . Westmoreland*] This is the first mention of Westmoreland's being the "surety" of IV. iii. 109 but we need not, with Wilson (N.C.S.), suspect revision. The intention was doubtless in Shakespeare's mind; the detail of the name was overlooked.

Hot. Lord Douglas, go you and tell him so.
Doug. Marry, and shall, and very willingly.   *Exit.*
Wor. There is no seeming mercy in the King.
Hot. Did you beg any? God forbid!   35
Wor. I told him gently of our grievances,
    Of his oath-breaking; which he mended thus,
    By now forswearing that he is forsworn:
    He calls us rebels, traitors, and will scourge
    With haughty arms this hateful name in us.   40

                [*Re-*]*enter* DOUGLAS.

Doug. Arm, gentlemen, to arms! for I have thrown
    A brave defiance in King Henry's teeth,
    And Westmoreland that was engag'd did bear it,
    Which cannot choose but bring him quickly on.
Wor. The Prince of Wales stepp'd forth before the King,   45
    And, nephew, challeng'd you to single fight.
Hot. O, would the quarrel lay upon our heads,
    And that no man might draw short breath today
    But I and Harry Monmouth! Tell me, tell me,
    How show'd his tasking? Seem'd it in contempt?   50
Ver. No, by my soul, I never in my life
    Did hear a challenge urg'd more modestly,
    Unless a brother should a brother dare
    To gentle exercise and proof of arms.
    He gave you all the duties of a man,   55
    Trimm'd up your praises with a princely tongue,
    Spoke your deservings like a chronicle,
    Making you ever better than his praise
    By still dispraising praise valu'd with you,

33. S.D.] *QqF* (*Exit Dou.* [*subst.*]), *Capell.*   40. S.D. *Re-enter*] *QqF* (*Enter*), *Capell.*   50. show'd] *Qq3–5,F;* shewed *Qq1,2.*   tasking] *Q1;* talking *Qq2–5,F.*   59. valu'd] *F* (valew'd); valued *Qq.*

32. *Douglas*] Sometimes trisyllabic.
34. *seeming*] semblance of.
38. *forswearing*] denying with a false oath.
43. *engag'd*] held as hostage.
50. *tasking*] challenging.
55. *all . . . man*] all that is due from one man to another; cf. *Ham.,* I. ii. 88 —"To give these mourning duties [= dues of mourning] to your father".
56. *Trimm'd up*] "To Trimme up a Thing, to make it seeme fairer" (Minsheu).
59. *dispraising . . . you*] disparaging

And, which became him like a prince indeed,   60
He made a blushing cital of himself,
And chid his truant youth with such a grace
As if he master'd there a double spirit
Of teaching and of learning instantly.
There did he pause: but let me tell the world—   65
If he outlive the envy of this day,
England did never owe so sweet a hope
So much misconstru'd in his wantonness.

Hot. Cousin, I think thou art enamoured
On his follies: never did I hear   70
Of any prince so wild a liberty.
But be he as he will, yet once ere night
I will embrace him with a soldier's arm,
That he shall shrink under my courtesy.
Arm, arm with speed! And fellows, soldiers, friends, 75
Better consider what you have to do
Than I that have not well the gift of tongue
Can lift your blood up with persuasion.

Enter a Messenger.

Mess. My lord, here are letters for you.
Hot. I cannot read them now.   80
O gentlemen, the time of life is short!

---

68. misconstru'd] *Capell*; misconstrued *QqF* (*subst.*).   70. On] *QqF;* Upon *Pope.*   71. a liberty] *Qq1–4* (a libertie)*;* at libertie *Q5,F* (*subst.*)*;* a libertine *Capell.*   75. fellows] *Qq1–4;* fellow's *Q5,F.*   77. Than] *Qq1,2* (Then)*;* That *Qq3–5,F.*

praise since it could not come up to your merits. This is, as Johnson notes, an extravagant version of what Hal said (v. i. 86–92), but no duplicity on Vernon's part is intended. Shakespeare makes the most of his occasions and gives the high generous spirit of the Prince's tribute.

61. *made . . . himself*] Either (*a*) spoke modestly of himself, or (*b*) called himself blushingly to account.

64. *instantly*] simultaneously.

66. *envy*] ill-will.

67. *owe*] own.

71. *liberty*] reckless freedom, as in the phrase "taking liberties with". "Never did I hear so wild a liberty reported of any prince" (Grant White). Capell's "libertine" is plausible (Shakespeare may have written libertie) but unnecessary.

76–8. *Better . . . persuasion*] Though the impetuous Hotspur telescopes two constructions his sense is clear: (*a*) You can better consider . . . than I can persuade you; (*b*) Consider . . . for I cannot lift your blood up with persuasion.

> To spend that shortness basely were too long
> If life did ride upon a dial's point,
> Still ending at the arrival of an hour.
> And if we live, we live to tread on kings,   85
> If die, brave death when princes die with us!
> Now, for our consciences, the arms are fair
> When the intent of bearing them is just.

Enter another Messenger.

Mess. My lord, prepare, the King comes on apace.
Hot. I thank him that he cuts me from my tale,   90
For I profess not talking: only this—
Let each man do his best; and here draw I
A sword whose temper I intend to stain
With the best blood that I can meet withal
In the adventure of this perilous day.   95
Now, Esperance! Percy! and set on,
Sound all the lofty instruments of war,
And by that music let us all embrace,
For, heaven to earth, some of us never shall
A second time do such a courtesy.   100
Here they embrace, the trumpets sound, [exeunt.]

87. are] *Qq1–4;* is *Q5,F.*   88. of] *Qq1–4;* for *Q5,F.*   88. S.D. *Messenger*] *F;
not in Qq.*   91. talking:] *F;* talking *Q1;* talking, *Qq2–5.*   92–3.] *As Pope;*
Let . . . sword, / Whose . . . staine / *QqF.*   92. draw I] *Qq;* I draw *F.*   93.
whose] *Qq;* Whose worthy *F.*   100. S.D. *Here*] *Qq; not in F.   exeunt.*] *Rowe;
not in QqF.*

82–4. *To spend . . . hour*] If life were a
mere hour long, it would be too long if
spent basely.
     96. *Esperance! Percy!*] Cf. II. iii. 72,

note, and App. III, p. 175. The final
"e" in "Esperance" is sounded.
     99. *heaven to earth*] the odds are as
heaven is to earth.

[SCENE III.—*Shrewsbury. The Field of Battle.*]

The KING *enters with his power. Alarum to the battle. Then enter*
DOUGLAS, *and* SIR WALTER BLUNT [*disguised as the King*].

Blunt. What is thy name that in the battle thus
     Thou crossest me? What honour dost thou seek
     Upon my head?
Doug.   Know then my name is Douglas,
     And I do haunt thee in the battle thus
     Because some tell me that thou art a king.   5
Blunt. They tell thee true.
Doug. The Lord of Stafford dear today hath bought
     Thy likeness, for instead of thee, King Harry,
     This sword hath ended him: so shall it thee
     Unless thou yield thee as my prisoner.   10
Blunt. I was not born a yielder, thou proud Scot,
     And thou shalt find a king that will revenge
     Lord Stafford's death.   *They fight. Douglas kills Blunt.*

Then enter HOTSPUR.

Hot. O Douglas, hadst thou fought at Holmedon thus

Scene III

SCENE III.] *Capell; not in QqF.*   *Location.*] *This edn; Plain near Shrewsbury. | Var.*
1778.   S.D. *disguised as the King*] *Wilson (N.C.S.); not in QqF.*   1–3.] *As*
Hanmer; What . . . me, / What . . . head? / Know . . . Douglas, / *QqF (subst.).*
1. the] *T. Johnson, Hanmer; not in QqF.*   10. my] *Qq1–4;* a *Q5,F.*   11. a
yielder, thou proud] *Qq1–4 (Q1* a yeelder thou proud*);* to yeeld, thou proud *Q5;*
to yeeld, thou haughty *F.*   Scot] *Qq1–4,F; Sot Q5.*   13. Lord] *Qq;* Lords *F.*
13. S.D.] *Qq (subst.); Fight, Blunt is slaine, then enters Hotspur. | F.*

S.D.] QqF envisage no break here
other than that of the departure of
Hotspur's army and the entry of the
King's; this S.D. is continuous with
that at the end of v. ii, and the action
continues too. The break, first made by
Capell, is retained for convenience of
scene- and line-reference, but should
be ignored from every other point of
view. The locality is purely general.

    1. *the*] QqF omit, but in l. 4 Douglas
uses it in echoing Blunt's words.

    7–8. *The Lord . . . likeness*] Hol. does
not say that Stafford was one of the

decoys, but he does say in one paragraph that Blunt and Stafford were
killed while defending the King's standard (iii. 26), and in the next that
Douglas struck the King down and
killed Blunt and three others "apparelled in the kings sute", so Stafford
might well appear to be dressed like
the King. There were in fact two
Blunts (cf. *2H4,* I. i. 16–17—"both
the Blunts / Kill'd by the hand of
Douglas"), but Hol. at this point is
not clear, though Daniel is (*C.W.,* iii.
112).

I never had triumph'd upon a Scot.   15
Doug. All's done, all's won: here breathless lies the King.
Hot. Where?
Doug. Here.
Hot. This, Douglas? No, I know this face full well,
 A gallant knight he was, his name was Blunt,   20
 Semblably furnish'd like the King himself.
Doug. A fool go with thy soul, whither it goes!
 A borrow'd title hast thou bought too dear.
 Why didst thou tell me that thou wert a king?
Hot. The King hath many marching in his coats.   25
Doug. Now, by my sword, I will kill all his coats;
 I'll murder all his wardrobe, piece by piece,
 Until I meet the King.
Hot.   Up and away!
 Our soldiers stand full fairly for the day.   *Exeunt.*

Alarum. Enter FALSTAFF *solus.*

Fal. Though I could scape shot-free at London, I fear   30
the shot here, here's no scoring but upon the
pate. Soft! who are you? Sir Walter Blunt—there's
honour for you! Here's no vanity! I am as hot as
molten lead, and as heavy too: God keep lead out of
me, I need no more weight than mine own bowels.   35

---

15. triumph'd upon] *Qq1,2;* triumpht ouer *Qq3–5;* triumphed o're *F.*   16.
won: here] *Qq2,3;* won here, *Q1;* won, here *Qq4,5,F.*   22. A fool go] *Capell;*
Ah foole, goe *Qq;* Ah foole: go *F.*   23. borrow'd] *Rowe;* borrowed *QqF.*
29. S.D. Exeunt.] *F; not in Qq.   Enter*] *Qq; and enter | F.*   34. God] *Qq;*
heauen *F.*

22. *A fool go with*] = "May the stig-
ma 'A fool' stick to"; Capell's emendation. The formula was quasi-prover-
bial; cf. Thomas Heywood, *Rape of
Lucrece* (Shepherd, v. 229)—"Get thee
to thy Tent and a coward goe with
thee"; and Whetstone, *Promos and
Cassandra*, 1578, II. iv. 15—"Goe and a
knaue with thee".

25. *coats*] the "sleeveless surcoat
with heraldic bearings" (Wright).

29. *stand ... day*] are in a fair way for
victory.

30. *shot-free*] A quibble: (a) un-
wounded; (b) without paying the
"shot", or reckoning. In Dekker,
Satiro-Mastix, v. ii. 329 (Bowers, i.
383), Sir Vaughan makes Horace (Ben
Jonson) "sweare ... [never] at Table
to fling Epigrams, Embleames, or
Play-speeches about you (lyke Hayle-
stones) to keepe you out of the terrible
daunger of the Shot".

31. *scoring*] Another quibble: (a)
notching; (b) charging the reckoning.

33. *no vanity*] Ironical; "if this isn't
futility, what is?"

I have led my ragamuffins where they are peppered;
there's not three of my hundred and fifty left alive,
and they are for the town's end, to beg during life.
But who comes here?

Enter the PRINCE.

Prince. What, stands thou idle here? Lend me thy sword: 40
Many a nobleman lies stark and stiff
Under the hoofs of vaunting enemies,   *mix of verse &*
whose deaths are yet unrevenged. I prithee lend me   *prose*
thy sword.

Fal. O Hal, I prithee give me leave to breathe awhile—   45
Turk Gregory never did such deeds in arms as I have

36. ragamuffins] *Capell;* rag of Muffins *QqF.*   37. hundred and fifty] *QqF* (150.),
Dering MS, Rowe.   38. they are] *Qq;* they *F.*   40. stands] *Q1;* standst
Qq2–5,F (*subst.*).   41. nobleman] *F;* noble man *Qq.*   lies] *Qq;* likes *F.*
43. are yet] *Qq;* are *F.*   I prithee] *Qq;* Prethy *F.*

36. *I have led . . . peppered*] Shakespeare would surely have been surprised to find "led" interpreted, as it sometimes is, as proof of Fal.'s valour. Thomas Digges, *Foure Paradoxes,* 1604, 51, describes captains "leading their men euen to the place of Butcherie, and then to take their leaue (vnder pretence to fetch supplies)", and Thomas Powell, *Tom of all Trades,* 1631 (ed. Furnivall, 170), says that "the land Captaine vseth but to offer his men to the face of the enemy, and than retreateth". Fal.'s motive is indicated in Sir John Smythe's *Certain Discourses Militarie,* 1590 (sig. 3)—"The new discipline of some of our men of warre in the Lowe Countries, hath been, to send, and employe their soldiers into manie daungerous . . . exploits and seruices . . . hauing sure regard to theire owne safeties; as though they desired and hoped to haue more gaine and profite by the dead paies of their soldiers slaine".

37. *not*] Capell conjectured "but"; but cf. IV. ii. 42, note.

40. *stands*] Verbs ending in dentals often had this second-person-singular form; cf. Jespersen, *Mod. Engl. Gram-*

mar, vi. 2.4, 2.5₁: e.g. "chide thee who confounds . . ." (sonnet viii. 7), "thou . . . Reuisits thus . . ." (*Ham.,* F, I. iv. 53), "Thou hotly lusts" (*Lr.,* F, IV. vi. 167), "Thou refts me of my Lands" (*Cym.,* F, III. iii. 103); and cf. l. 51.

43–55.] This, a mixture of prosy verse and versy prose, is given as in Q1.

46. *Turk Gregory*] "TURK, any cruel hard-hearted Man" (Bailey). For Gregory two candidates are proposed: (*a*) Hildebrand, who, as Gregory VII, succeeded Pope Alexander in 1035, and whom Protestant writers cited as a by-word for violence; e.g. *Martin Marprelate, the Epistle,* 1588 (ed. Arber, 22) —"But looke to it brother Canterburie certainly without your repentance I feare me you shalbe Hildebrand in deed", with the marginal gloss "A fyrebrand in deede". Foxe tells how, infuriated with Pope Alexander, "he was stroken in suche a fury, that scharsly he could kepe his hãds of him, while mas was don[.] After the mas being finished, by force of souldiers and strength of men, he had him into a chamber, there all to bepomild Pope Alexander with his fistes" (*Actes & Monuments,* 1563, 14); (*b*) "Gregory

  done this day; I have paid Percy, I have made him
  sure.

Prince. He is indeed, and living to kill thee:
  I prithee lend me thy sword.   50

Fal. Nay, before God, Hal, if Percy be alive thou gets not
  my sword, but take my pistol if thou wilt.

Prince. Give it me: what, is it in the case?

Fal. Ay, Hal, 'tis hot, 'tis hot; there's that will sack a city.
    The Prince draws it out, and finds it to be a bottle of sack.

Prince. What, is it a time to jest and dally now?   55
        He throws the bottle at him. Exit.

Fal. Well, if Percy be alive, I'll pierce him. If he do come
  in my way, so: if he do not, if I come in his willingly,
  let him make a carbonado of me. I like not such
  grinning honour as Sir Walter hath. Give me life,
  which if I can save, so: if not, honour comes unlooked 60
  for, and there's an end.   *Exit.*

---

51. before God] *Qq; not in F.* gets] *Q1;* getst *Qq2–5,F.* 54. 'tis hot, 'tis hot]
Qq1–4; tis hot *Q5,F.* 54. S.D.] *Qq (The . . . finds it a . . . sack. | Q5); The
Prince drawes out a Bottle of Sacke. | F.* 55. S.D.] *Qq; Exit. Throwes it at him. |
F.* 56. Well, if] *Qq1–4;* If *Q5,F.* 61. S.D.] *F; not in Qq.*

XIII (1572–85), ınveterate foe of England, who blessed if he did not insti-
gate the Massacre of St. Bartholomew,
and promised plenary indulgence to
anyone who would murder Elizabeth"
(Wilson, N.C.S.). In 1579 "he was
figuring with Nero and the Grand
Turk as one of 'The Three Tyrants of
the World' in coloured prints sold on
the streets of London" (ibid.). The
conjunction here with the Turk is
striking.

 47. *paid*] killed.

 51. *gets*] Cf. l. 40, note.

 53–4. *what . . . hot*] "It should have
been primed for instant use, and not in

the holster. Fal. pretends he has put it
up to cool after much firing" (Wilson,
N.C.S.).

 56. *pierce*] Pronounced "perse".
Nashe makes the Devil address Pierce
Penilesse as "Persie" (McKerrow, i.
219, 226). Capgrave, *Chron. of Engl.*
(*Book of the Illustrious Henries*, ed. F. C.
Hingeston, 1858, 119, fn), has "Herri
Percy, aftir the propirte of his name,
percid, or presed, in so fer that he was
ded".

 58. *make . . . me*] i.e. "slash me all
over and grill me", a carbonado being
"meat scored across and broiled"
(Onions).

SCENE IV.—[*The Same.*]

Alarum. Excursions. Enter the KING, *the* PRINCE, LORD JOHN OF
LANCASTER, EARL OF WESTMORELAND.

King. I prithee, Harry, withdraw thyself, thou bleed'st
    too much.
    Lord John of Lancaster, go you with him.
Lan. Not I, my lord, unless I did bleed too.
Prince. I beseech your Majesty, make up,
    Lest your retirement do amaze your friends.   5
King. I will do so. My Lord of Westmoreland,
    Lead him to his tent.
West. Come, my lord, I'll lead you to your tent.
Prince. Lead me, my lord? I do not need your help,
    And God forbid a shallow scratch should drive   10
    The Prince of Wales from such a field as this,
    Where stain'd nobility lies trodden on,
    And rebels' arms triumph in massacres!
Lan. We breathe too long: come, cousin Westmoreland,
    Our duty this way lies: for God's sake, come.   15
        [*Exeunt Lancaster and Westmoreland.*]
Prince. By God, thou hast deceiv'd me, Lancaster,
    I did not think thee lord of such a spirit:
    Before, I lov'd thee as a brother, John,
    But now I do respect thee as my soul.
King. I saw him hold Lord Percy at the point   20
    With lustier maintenance than I did look for

Scene IV

SCENE IV.] *Capell; Scena Tertia.* / F; *not in Qq.*   Location.] *This edn; Another part
of the Field.* / *Var. 1778.*   S.D. *Earl*] Q1; *and Earle* / Qq2–5,F.   1–2.] *As* Q1;
I prithee, / Harry, . . . much. / Lord . . . him. / *Steevens; prose,* Qq2–5,F.   1.
bleed'st] *Capell;* bleedest QqF.   5. Lest your] Qq; Least you F.   6–7.] *As
Capell;* I . . . so: / My . . . Tent. / F; I . . . so. My . . . tent. / Qq (*one line*).
10. God] Qq; heauen F.   15. God's] Qq; heauens F.   15. S.D.] *Capell
(subst.); not in* QqF.   16. God] Qq; heauen F.

1.] Almost all edd. since Steevens
divide this line after "prithee", but
this impairs its velocity.
    4. *make up*] go to the front.
    5. *amaze*] dismay; cf. Drayton,
Ballad of Agincourt—"Though they

to one be ten / Be not amazed".
    12. *stain'd*] Both literal ("bemired")
and figurative ("disgraced"); cf. *Ant.*,
III. iv. 26–7—"I'll raise the preparation of a war / Shall stain your brother".

Of such an ungrown warrior.
Prince.   O, this boy
   Lends mettle to us all!   *Exit.*

Enter DOUGLAS.

Doug. Another king! They grow like Hydra's heads:
   I am the Douglas, fatal to all those   25
   That wear those colours on them. What art thou
   That counterfeit'st the person of a king?
King. The King himself, who, Douglas, grieves at heart
   So many of his shadows thou hast met,
   And not the very King. I have two boys   30
   Seek Percy and thyself about the field,
   But seeing thou fall'st on me so luckily
   I will assay thee, and defend thyself.
Doug. I fear thou art another counterfeit,
   And yet, in faith, thou bearest thee like a king;   35
   But mine I am sure thou art, whoe'er thou be,
   And thus I win thee.   *They fight, the King being in danger.*

[*Re-*]*enter* PRINCE OF WALES.

Prince. Hold up thy head, vile Scot, or thou art like
   Never to hold it up again! The spirits
   Of valiant Shirley, Stafford, Blunt are in my arms.   40
   It is the Prince of Wales that threatens thee,
   Who never promiseth but he means to pay.
                              They fight: Douglas flieth.

22–3.] *As Pope;* Of . . . warrior. / O . . . all. / *QqF.*   23. S.D. *Enter Douglas*] *F;
not in Qq.*   33. thee, and] *Qq2–5;* thee and *Q1;* thee: so *F.*   35. bearest]
Qq1–5; bear'st *F.*   37. S.D. *Re-enter*] *QqF* (*enter*), *Dyce.   Prince of Wales*] *Qq;
Prince* / *F.*   38. thy] *Qq;* they *F.*

24. *Hydra's heads*] The Hydra grew
two heads for each one cut off. Shakespeare echoes Daniel; cf. I. i. 5–18,
note.

33. *and*] "And" could connect an
affirmation and a command; cf. III. i.
185, and note.

38–40. *Hold up . . . arms*] Hol.
describes the King's falling before
Douglas, his rising again, and the

slaying of Hotspur in a general mêlée
(App. III, pp. 175–6). Daniel credits
the Prince with the King's rescue
(*C.W.*, iii. 111) and with encountering
Hotspur (*C.W.*, iii. 97). Shakespeare
follows Daniel in this, and also in l. 40
echoes his praise of "Heroycall Cour-
ageous *Blunt*" (*C.W.*, iii. 111), "Magnanimous *Stafford*" and "valiant *Shor-
ley*" (*C.W.*, iii. 113).

Cheerly, my lord, how fares your grace?
Sir Nicholas Gawsey hath for succour sent,
And so hath Clifton—I'll to Clifton straight.   45
King. Stay and breathe a while:
Thou hast redeem'd thy lost opinion,
And show'd thou mak'st some tender of my life,
In this fair rescue thou hast brought to me.
Prince. O God, they did me too much injury   50
That ever said I hearken'd for your death.
If it were so, I might have let alone
The insulting hand of Douglas over you,
Which would have been as speedy in your end
As all the poisonous potions in the world,   55
And sav'd the treacherous labour of your son.
King. Make up to Clifton, I'll to Sir Nicholas Gawsey.   *Exit.*

Enter HOTSPUR.

Hot. If I mistake not, thou art Harry Monmouth.
Prince. Thou speak'st as if I would deny my name.
Hot. My name is Harry Percy.
Prince.   Why then I see   60
A very valiant rebel of the name.
I am the Prince of Wales, and think not, Percy,
To share with me in glory any more:
Two stars keep not their motion in one sphere,
Nor can one England brook a double reign   65
Of Harry Percy and the Prince of Wales.
Hot. Nor shall it, Harry, for the hour is come
To end the one of us, and would to God
Thy name in arms were now as great as mine!

47. redeem'd] *Q5,F*; redeemed *Qq1-4*.   50. God] *Qq*; heauen *F*.   51.
hearken'd] *Q1,F* (harkned [*subst.*]); harkened *Qq2-5*.   for] *Qq1-3*; to
Qq4,5,F.   57. Sir] *Qq* (S.), *F*.   57. S.D.] *Qq1-3* (*Exit Ki:*), *Q4* (*Exit K.*),
Q5,F.   60-1.] *As Rowe 3*; My . . . Percy. / Why . . . name; *QqF* (*subst.*).
61. the] *Qq1,2*; that *Qq3-5,F*.   67. Nor] *F*; Now *Qq*.   68. God] *Qq*;
heauen *F*.

47. *opinion*] reputation.
48. *mak'st some tender of*] hast some
regard for.
53. *insulting*] exultantly triumphing.
64. *Two . . . sphere*] One star, one

sphere, was the Ptolemaic principle;
cf. v. i. 17, note. Proverbial; Tilley,
S992.
67. *Nor*] F. Qq's "Now" is clearly
wrong.

Prince. I'll make it greater ere I part from thee,   70
    And all the budding honours on thy crest
    I'll crop to make a garland for my head.
Hot. I can no longer brook thy vanities.   *They fight.*

Enter FALSTAFF.

Fal. Well said, Hal! To it, Hal! Nay, you shall find no
    boy's play here, I can tell you.   75

[*Re-*]*enter* DOUGLAS; *he fighteth with Falstaff, who falls down as if he were dead.* [*Exit Douglas.*] *The Prince mortally wounds Hotspur.*

Hot. O Harry, thou hast robb'd me of my youth!
    I better brook the loss of brittle life
    Than those proud titles thou hast won of me;
    They wound my thoughts worse than thy sword my
        flesh:
    But thoughts, the slaves of life, and life, time's fool,   80
    And time, that takes survey of all the world,
    Must have a stop. O, I could prophesy,
    But that the earthy and cold hand of death
    Lies on my tongue: no, Percy, thou art dust,
    And food for—   [*Dies.*]   85

---

71. the] *Qq1–4,F;* thy *Q5.*   73. S.D.] *Qq;* Fight. | *F.*   75. S.D. Re-enter] *QqF* (Enter), *Dyce.*   fighteth] *Qq1–4;* fights *Q5,F.*   who] *F;* he | *Qq.*   Exit Douglas.] *Capell;* not in *QqF.*   mortally . . . Hotspur] *This edn;* killeth Percy | *QqF* (*subst.*); wounds Hotspur | *Hanmer.*   77. brook] *Qq1–4,F;* broke *Q5.*   79. thy] *Qq1–4;* the *Q5,F.*   80. thoughts, the slaves] *Q1;* thought's the slaue *Qq2–5,F.*   83. earthy] *Q1;* earth *Qq2–5,F.*   and] *Qq;* and the *F.*   85. for—] *F;* for. *Qq1,2;* for *Qq3–5.*   85. S.D.] *Rowe;* not in *QqF.*

---

74. *Well said*] = "Well done". Often used even when nothing has been said; e.g. "*Tit.* Now, masters, draw. [*They shoot.*] O, well said, Lucius" (*Tit.*, IV. iii. 63).

75. *boy's play*] Proverbial phrase: "It is no child's play" (Tilley, C324).

80–2. *But . . . stop*] Q1. Qq2–5,F (reading "thought's the slaue") produce successive moralizing clauses, instead of Q1's successive subjects all governing "must have a stop". Q1 is

accepted since (*a*) Hotspur has already mentioned "thoughts" in the plural (l. 79), and (*b*), dying, he recognizes the simultaneous stoppage at death of thoughts, life, and cognizance of time alike.

82. *prophesy*] Cf. Tilley, M514— "Dying Men speak true [prophesy]"; an allusion to the belief that a dying man can foretell the future like Gaunt in *R2*, II. i. 31 ff.—"Methinks I am a prophet new inspir'd, / And thus expiring do foretell of him . . ."

Prince. For worms, brave Percy. Fare thee well, great heart!
    Ill-weav'd ambition, how much art thou shrunk!
    When that this body did contain a spirit,
    A kingdom for it was too small a bound;
    But now two paces of the vilest earth   90
    Is room enough. This earth that bears thee dead
    Bears not alive so stout a gentleman.
    If thou wert sensible of courtesy
    I should not make so dear a show of zeal;
    But let my favours hide thy mangled face,   95
    And even in thy behalf I'll thank myself
    For doing these fair rites of tenderness.
    Adieu, and take thy praise with thee to heaven!
    Thy ignominy sleep with thee in the grave,
    But not remember'd in thy epitaph!   100
                        He spieth Falstaff on the ground.
    What, old acquaintance, could not all this flesh

86. Fare thee well] *Qq;* Farewell *F.*   91. thee dead] *Q7;* the dead *Qq1–6,F.*
94. dear] *Q1;* great *Qq2–5,F.*   97. rites] *Qq2–5,F;* rights *Q1.*   99. ignominy]
Qq1–3; ignomy *Qq4,5,F.*   100. S.D.]*Qq; not in F.*

87. *Ill-weav'd . . . shrunk*] Loosely and
badly woven cloth shrinks. "Not
meant of ambition in general but only
of such as Hotspur's, which, the Prince
thinks, was ill-conceived" (Kittredge).
    88–91. *When that . . . enough*] Many
"sources" have been proposed for this
idea; e.g. Ovid, *Amores*, III. ix. 33, 40;
Juvenal, *Satires*, x. 147–8; Lyly,
Letters writ by Euphues (Bond, i. 314)—
"*Philip* falling in the dust, and seeing
the figure of his shape perfect in shewe:
Good God sayd he, we desire y° whole
earth and see how little serveth";
similarly Lyly, *Campaspe*, v. iv. 49–53
(Bond, ii. 355), and *Midas*, III. i. 12–14
(Bond, iii. 130). But multiple parallels
prove only that it is a commonplace.
Shakespeare had treated it before (*R2*,
III. iii. 153—"My large kingdom for
a little grave"), and was to treat it
again (*Cæs.*, III. i. 148 ff.—"O mighty
Caesar! dost thou lie so low? . . .").
    92. *stout*] valiant.
    94. *dear*] heartfelt.

95. *favours*] These could be scarves
or gloves, signs of a lady's favour. But
the days when Hal "would unto the
stews, / And from the common'st creature pluck a glove, / And wear it as a
favour" (*R2*, v. iii. 16–18) are over,
and the wooing of Katherine of
France is far ahead. Here they are
either "a torse of silk of his own
colours, white and blue, which he unbound from his helm for the purpose"
(C. W. Scott-Giles, *Sh.'s Heraldry*,
1950, 91), or the plumes of his helmet
(H. Hartman, 'Prince Hal's "Shewe
of Zeale" ', *PMLA*, 1931, vol. 46, 720).
    101–9. *What . . . lie*] "The tone,
which may be compared with Hamlet's when confronted with Yorick's
skull, is that of a prince speaking of his
dead jester, not of friend taking leave
of familiar friend: and what there is of
affection is mainly retrospective. . .
The epitaph on Hotspur contains not
a word of triumph; its theme is the
greatness of the slain man's spirit, the

Keep in a little life? Poor Jack, farewell!
I could have better spar'd a better man:
O, I should have a heavy miss of thee
If I were much in love with vanity: 105
Death hath not struck so fat a deer today,
Though many dearer, in this bloody fray.
Embowell'd will I see thee by and by,
Till then in blood by noble Percy lie.   *Exit.*

FALSTAFF *riseth up.*

Fal. Embowelled? If thou embowel me today, I'll give   110
you leave to powder me and eat me too tomorrow.
'Sblood, 'twas time to counterfeit, or that hot ter-
magant Scot had paid me, scot and lot too. Counterfeit? I lie, I am no counterfeit: to die is to be a
counterfeit, for he is but the counterfeit of a man,   115
who hath not the life of a man: but to counterfeit
dying, when a man thereby liveth, is to be no
counterfeit, but the true and perfect image of life
indeed. The better part of valour is discretion, in

106. fat] *Q1,F;* faire *Qq2-5.*   109. S.D. *Exit.*] *Qq1-3,F; not in Qq4,5.*
112. 'Sblood] *Qq; not in F.*   114. I lie, I] *Qq1-4;* I *Q5,F.*

tragedy of his fall, and what may be
done to reverence him in death. With
such solemn thoughts does Shakespeare's hero turn to Fal. Is it surprising that he should be out of love with
vanity at a moment like this? The
point is of interest technically, since
the moment balances and adumbrates
a still more solemn moment at the end
of Part II, in which he also encounters
Fal. and has by then come to be even
less in love with what he represents"
(Wilson, *Fortunes,* 67-8).

104. *heavy*] A quibble.

107. *dearer*] Another quibble; (*a*)
"more beloved", (*b*) "nobler"; cf.
IV. iv. 31, note.

108. *Embowell'd*] i.e. disembowelled
for embalming, though with an equivoque on the "assay" or ceremony of
disembowelling the deer (Madden,
65); cf. l. 161, note.

109. *in blood*] Another equivoque: as
a hunting term it = "in full vigour";
cf. *LLL.,* IV. ii. 3-4—"The deer was, as
you know, *sanguis,* in blood". In this
sense it is literally, and comically, true
of the sham corpse.

111. *powder*] pickle in salt.

113. *paid . . . lot*] Quibbles on "paid"
(cf. v. iii. 47) and "scot", "scot and
lot" being parish rates, and "to pay
scot and lot" being to pay in full: cf.
I. iii. 213, note, and Tilley, S159.

119. *The better . . . discretion*] Proverbial; Tilley, D354. Vincentio Saviolo
(*his Practise,* 1595, sig. Bb) says that
"The wisdom and discretion of a man,
is as great a vertue as his magnanimitie
and courage, which are so much the
greater vertues, by how much they
are accompanied with wisedome: for
without them a man is not to be
accounted valiant, but rather furious".

the which better part I have saved my life. 'Zounds,   120
I am afraid of this gunpowder Percy, though he be
dead; how if he should counterfeit too and rise? By
my faith, I am afraid he would prove the better
counterfeit; therefore I'll make him sure, yea, and
I'll swear I killed him. Why may not he rise as well   125
as I? <u>Nothing</u> confutes me but eyes, and nobody
sees me: therefore, sirrah [*stabbing him*], with a new
wound in your thigh, come you along with me.

                    He takes up Hotspur on his back.

[*Re-*]*enter* PRINCE *and* [LORD] JOHN OF LANCASTER.

Prince. Come, brother John, full bravely hast thou flesh'd
        Thy maiden sword.
Lan.   But soft, whom have we here?   130
        Did you not tell me this fat man was dead?
Prince. I did, I saw him dead,
        Breathless and bleeding on the ground. Art thou alive?
        Or is it fantasy that plays upon our eyesight?
        I prithee speak, we will not trust our eyes   135
        Without our ears: thou art not what thou seem'st.
Fal. No, that's certain, I am not a double-man: but if I
        be not Jack Falstaff, then am I a Jack: there is
        Percy [*throwing the body down*]! If your father will do
        me any honour, so: if not, let him kill the next   140
        Percy himself. I look to be either earl or duke, I can
        assure you.
Prince. Why, Percy I kill'd myself, and saw thee dead.

---

120. 'Zounds] *Qq; not in F.*   122–3. By my faith] *Qq; not in F.*   127. S.D.]
Malone; not in QqF.   128. with me] *Qq;* me *F.*   128. S.D. He takes up] *Qq;*
Takes | *F.*   Re-enter] *QqF (Enter), Capell.*   and Lord John] *Hanmer; Iohn | Q1;*
and Iohn | *Qq2–5,F.*   129–30. Come . . . sword] *As Qq; prose, F.*   130.
whom] *Qq1–4;* who *Q5,F.*   139. S.D.] *Var. 1773; not in QqF.*

"Fal.'s cynical misinterpretation of a
wise maxim is now generally accepted
as its true meaning" (Wilson, N.C.S.).
Both Fal. and Hotspur err at opposite
extremes of true "discretion".

126. *Nothing . . . eyes*] Oddly put, but
the sense is clear—"Only an eye-wit-
ness could prove me a liar".

129–30. *full . . . sword*] Brooks &
Heilman point out how this praise sets
off the ignominy of Fal.'s bogus flesh-
ing of *his* "maiden sword".

137. *double-man*] *OED,* "double.
*sb.*2c. The apparition of a living person: wraith, fetch"; with a quibble on
the extra body he is carrying.

Fal. Didst thou? Lord, Lord, how this world is given to
lying! I grant you I was down, and out of breath,   145
and so was he, but we rose both at an instant, and
fought a long hour by Shrewsbury clock. If I may be
believed, so: if not, let them that should reward
valour bear the sin upon their own heads. I'll take
it upon my death, I gave him this wound in the   150
thigh; if the man were alive, and would deny it,
'zounds, I would make him eat a piece of my sword.

Lan. This is the strangest tale that ever I heard.

Prince. This is the strangest fellow, brother John.
Come, bring your luggage nobly on your back.   155
[*Aside to Falstaff*] For my part, if a lie may do thee grace,
I'll gild it with the happiest terms I have.

A retreat is sounded.

The trumpet sounds retreat, the day is ours.
Come, brother, let us to the highest of the field,
To see what friends are living, who are dead.   160

Exeunt [Prince of Wales and Lancaster].

Fal. I'll follow, as they say, for reward. He that rewards
me, God reward him! If I do grow great, I'll grow
less, for I'll purge, and leave sack, and live cleanly
as a nobleman should do.   *Exit[, bearing off the body].*

144. this] *Qq1–4*; the *Q5,F.*   149–50. take it upon] *Qq*; take't on *F.*   152.
'zounds] *Qq*; not in *F.*   153. ever] *Qq*; e're *F.*   156. S.D.] *Wilson (N.C.S.)*;
not in *QqF.*   158. The] *F*; Prin. The *Qq.*   trumpet sounds] *Qq1–3*; trumpets
sound *Qq4,5,F.*   ours] *Qq2–5,F*; our *Q1.*   159. let us] *Qq1–3*; lets *Qq4,5,F.*
160. S.D.] *Cambr.*; Exeunt. | *QqF.*   162. God] *Qq*; heauen *F.*   great] *Qq*;
great again *F.*   164. nobleman] *Qq4,5,F*; noble man *Qq1–3.*   164. S.D.]
Capell; Exit. *QqF.*

149–50. *I'll . . . death*] An oath of
peculiar solemnity. Perkin Warbeck
on the day of his execution, writes
Bacon, "did again openly read his
confession, and take it upon his death
to be true" (*Hist. of Hy VII: Works*, ed.
Spedding & Ellis, vi. 203).

156. S.D.] I follow Wilson (N.C.S.)
in treating this as a matter between
Hal and Fal. only.

a lie] i.e. "of yours".

158. *ours*] Cf. collation, and IV. iii.
28, note.

161. *I'll . . . reward*] "In hunting, the

hounds 'follow' and are given 'reward', i.e. portions assigned to them
at the 'breaking up of the deer' (v.
Turbervile, *Booke of Hunting*, 1575,
130–5). Fal. claims to have brought
the great quarry down; apparently
his 'reward' is a 'pension' (*2H4*, I.
ii. 280—'My pension shall seem
the more reasonable')" (Wilson,
N.C.S.).

163. *purge*] repent; cf. *Iacke Drums
Entertainment* (R. Simpson, *School of
Sh.*, ii. 160)—"Old wretch, amend thy
thoughts, purge, purge, repent!"

SCENE V.—[*The Same.*]

The trumpets sound. Enter the KING, PRINCE OF WALES, LORD
JOHN OF LANCASTER, EARL OF WESTMORELAND, *with*
WORCESTER *and* VERNON *prisoners.*

King. Thus ever did rebellion find rebuke.
      Ill-spirited Worcester, did not we send grace,
      Pardon, and terms of love to all of you?
      And wouldst thou turn our offers contrary?
      Misuse the tenor of thy kinsman's trust?   5
      Three knights upon our party slain today,
      A noble earl and many a creature else,
      Had been alive this hour,
      If like a Christian thou hadst truly borne
      Betwixt our armies true intelligence.   10
Wor. What I have done my safety urg'd me to;
      And I embrace this fortune patiently,
      Since not to be avoided it falls on me.
King. Bear Worcester to the death, and Vernon too:
      Other offenders we will pause upon.   15
                 Exeunt Worcester and Vernon[, *guarded*].
      How goes the field?
Prince. The noble Scot, Lord Douglas, when he saw
      The fortune of the day quite turn'd from him,
      The noble Percy slain, and all his men
      Upon the foot of fear, fled with the rest,   20
      And falling from a hill, he was so bruis'd
      That the pursuers took him. At my tent
      The Douglas is; and I beseech your Grace
      I may dispose of him.
King.   With all my heart.

Scene v

SCENE V.] *Capell; Scæna Quarta. | F; not in Qq.*   *Location.*] *This edn; Another Part.|
Capell.*   2. not we] *Qq;* we not *F.*   14. the] *Qq; not in F.*   15. S.D.]
Theobald; Exit Worcester and Vernon. | F; not in Qq.

1. *rebuke*] "violent check" (Wilson,
N.C.S.).
6–7. *Three . . . earl*] This varies oddly
from Hol., who, besides the Earl of
Stafford, names ten knights, adding

that they were all dubbed on the morning of the battle.
20. *Upon . . . fear*] In panic flight. For
the metaphor cf. *Mac.*, II. iii. 132—
"Upon the foot of motion".

Prince. Then, brother John of Lancaster, to you   25
    This honourable bounty shall belong;
    Go to the Douglas and deliver him
    Up to his pleasure, ransomless and free:
    His valours shown upon our crests today
    Have taught us how to cherish such high deeds,   30
    Even in the bosom of our adversaries.

Lan. I thank your Grace for this high courtesy,
    Which I shall give away immediately.

King. Then this remains, that we divide our power:
    You, son John, and my cousin Westmoreland,   35
    Towards York shall bend you with your dearest speed
    To meet Northumberland and the prelate Scroop,
    Who, as we hear, are busily in arms:
    Myself and you, son Harry, will towards Wales,
    To fight with Glendower and the Earl of March.   40
    Rebellion in this land shall lose his sway,
    Meeting the check of such another day,
    And since this business so fair is done,
    Let us not leave till all our own be won.   *Exeunt.*

25–6.] *As Pope;* Then ... Lancaster, / To ... belong, / *QqF.*   29–30. valours
... Have] *Qq1–3;* valour ... Hath *Qq4,5,F.*   32–3.] *Qq1–4; not in Q5,F.*
36. bend you] *Qq4,5,F;* bend, you *Qq1–3.*   41. sway] *Qq1–4;* way *Q5,F.*

34–44. *Then ... won*] "If we are to
consider this 'first part' as an entire
play, King Harry's closing speech
offends sadly against Aristotle, in a
point wherein Aristotle's authority, if
sound in itself, has a jurisdiction
general, and not limited by the usages
of the Greek stage. It is a conclusion in
which nothing is concluded" (Hartley
Coleridge, *Essays*, 1851, ii. 156, cited

by Hemingway, New Var., 337). The
speech, together with IV. iv, undoubtedly involves a further phase in the
action and so a Part II, however effectively Shrewsbury may conclude
Part I. The relationship of the parts is
most ably studied in Harold Jenkins,
Structural Problem in Sh.'s H4, 1956.
    36. *dearest*] most earnest, zealous.
    43. *business*] Trisyllabic.

APPENDIX I

THE TITLE IN Qq2–5, F1

The Qq2–5 title-pages read as follows:

Q2. THE | HISTORY OF | HENRIE THE | FOVRTH; | With the battell at Shrewsburie, | *betweene the King and Lord* Henry | Percy, *surnamed* Henry Hot-|spur of the North. | *VVith the humorous conceits of Sir* | Iohn Falstalffe. | Newly corrected by *W. Shake-speare.* | [Device] | AT LONDON, | Printed by *S.S.* for *Andrew VVise,* dwelling | in Paules Churchyard, at the signe of | the Angell. 1599.

Q3. THE | HISTORY OF | Henrie the fourth, | VVith the battell at Shrewsburie, | *betweene the King, and Lord* | Henry Percy, surnamed Henry Hot-|*spur of the North.* | With the humorous conceits of Sir | Iohn Falstalffe. | Newly corrected by W. *Shake-speare.* | (Ornament] | LONDON | Printed by Valentine Simmes, for *Mathew Law,* and | are to be solde at his shop in Paules Church-yard, | at the signe of the Fox. | 1604.

Q4. THE | HISTORY OF | Henry the fourth, | VVith the battell at Shrewseburie, | *betweene the King, and Lord* | Henry Percy, surnamed Henry | *Hotspur of the North.* | *With the humorous conceites of Sir* | Iohn Falstalffe. | *Newly corrected by W. Shake-speare.* | [ornament] | LONDON, | Printed for *Mathew Law,* and are to be sold at | his shop in Paules Church-yard, neere vnto S. | *Augustines* gate, at the signe of | the Foxe. 1608.

Q5. THE | HISTORY OF | Henrie the fourth, | With the Battell at Shrewseburie, betweene | the King, and Lord Henrie Percy, sur-|named *Henrie Hotspur* of the North. | VVith the humorous conceites of Sir | *Iohn Falstaffe.* | Newly corrected by *W. Shake-speare.* | [White's device] | LONDON, | Printed by *W.W. for Mathew Law,* and are to be sold | at his shop in Paules Church-yard, neere vnto S. | *Augustines* Gate, at the signe of the Foxe. | 1613.

Q6 was printed in 1622 by T. P. for Mathew Law; Q7 in 1632 by John Norton for William Sheares, and Q8 in 1639 by John Norton for Hugh Perry.

The title in the First Folio is, "The First Part of Henry the Fourth, | with the Life and Death of HENRY | Sirnamed HOTSPVRRE".

166 the first part of

Appendix II

THE DATE OF
THE MERRY WIVES OF WINDSOR

The Merry Wives has generally been thought to be of later date
than Henry V (1599), and Sir E. K. Chambers's comment that in it
Nym would hardly be called "corporal" unless he had already
been seen on a battle-field is cogent. Yet the text is confused and
revised, not only in the bad Q of 1602 but in the better F text, and
post-Henry V traces, like post-Hamlet ones (cf. Chambers, W. Sh., i.
429–30), may have crept in. What is more important is that The
Merry Wives (perhaps based on a source-play of about 1592–3)
seems to have been written for a conferment of Garter Knighthoods,
and that the conferment of April–May 1597 seems the likely occasion. The case for this, in Dr Leslie Hotson's Shakespeare versus
Shallow (1931), has gained much acceptance—an acceptance not
extending, however, to Hotson's other suggestion, that Shakespeare's Robert Shallow, justice of the peace in Gloucestershire, is
drawn from William Gardiner, justice of the peace in Southwark.

In 1865 W. B. Rye translated a German travel journal of 1592
kept by the secretary of Frederick, Count of Mömpelgart, heir to
the Duke of Württemberg. Mömpelgart visited England in 1592,
had trouble with post-horses, was promised Knighthood of the
Garter by Elizabeth, and returned to Germany expecting his election to that Order. The Queen kept "our Cousin Mumpellgart"
waiting until in 1597 she capitulated. His election then took place
though without his being informed until too late—the insignia
were not sent until James I's reign.

To these rather absurd events it has long been recognized that
The Merry Wives alludes. In iv. iii Bardolph tells the Host of the
Garter Inn that there are Germans desiring horses of him, and that
their Duke will appear at Court on the morrow. In iv. v the
"Germans" are said to have absconded with the horses, and in
the 1602 Q Sir Hugh Evans mentions "three sorts of cosen garmombles, is cosen [i.e. have cheated] all the Host of Maidenhead and Readings". "Garmomble" is an actual word meaning
"confusion" (literally "bruise") but "Cousin Mumpellgart" must
surely be the target. The Folio makes the joke less private and less
funny—"cosen garmombles" becomes "Cozen-Iermans". Finally,
Dr Caius addresses the Host (iv. v. 88–91):

it is tell-a-me, dat you make grand preparation for a Duke de
Iamanie: by my trot: der is no Duke that the Court is know, to come.

One has, then, a Garter-celebration play (as Anne's speech at v. v. 61–79 makes clear), with Mömpelgart jokes about horse-trickery and the Duke's arrival or non-arrival at Windsor. The likeliest occasion for such jests would be the ceremony of 1597, when the Duke was elected but not informed, so that reports of a hasty belated arrival would greatly amuse the assembled Knights. A second of the new Knights in that year was Lord Hunsdon, the new Lord Chamberlain, who appeared with extreme splendour at the Windsor installation in May.[1] His prospective election would, of course, be known some time before the election ceremony on 23 April, St George's Day. As patron of Shakespeare's company, he might be expected to entertain the assembly with a play, and if the play were new (or, as *The Merry Wives* seems, an old one re-worked) it would need to be rushed through, the more so if the Queen, who did not go to Windsor, were to see it at Greenwich Palace beforehand. This may be the basis of the tradition recorded by Dennis.

Appendix III

SOURCE MATERIAL

1. *Raphael Holinshed: "The Chronicles of England, Scotlande, and Ire-lande" (2nd edition, 1587)*. The references are to the 6-volume reprint of 1807–8.

OWEN GLENDOWER

"This Owen Glendouer was sonne to an esquier of Wales, named Griffith Vichan; he dwelled in the parish of Conwaie, within the county of Merioneth, in North Wales...

"He was first set to studie the lawes of the realme, and became an vtter barrester, or an apprentise of the law (as they terme him) and serued king Richard at Flint castell, when he was taken by Henrie duke of Lancaster, though other haue written that he serued this king Henrie the fourth, before he came to atteine the crowne, in roome of an esquier." (iii. 17)

KING HENRY'S UNQUIET REIGN

After relating an abortive attempt on the King's life Holinshed continues thus:

"Howbeit he was not so soone deliuered from feare; for he might well haue his liĩe in suspicion, & prouide for the preseruation of the

1. L. Hotson, *Sh. versus Shallow*, 117–19.

same; sith perils of death crept into his secret chamber, and laie lurking in the bed of downe where his bodie was to be reposed and to take rest. Oh what a suspected state therefore is that of a king holding his regiment with the hatred of his people, the hart grudgings of his courtiers, and the peremptorie practises of both togither? Could he confidentlie compose or setle himselfe to sleepe for feare of strangling? Durst he boldly eat and drinke without dreade of poisoning? Might he aduenture to shew himselfe in great meetings or solemne assemblies without mistrust of mischeefe against his person intended? What pleasure or what felicitie could he take in his princelie pompe, which he knew by manifest and fearfull experience to be enuied and maligned to the verie death? The state of such a king is noted by the poet in Dionysius, as in a mirror, concerning whome it is said,

> Districtus ensis cui super impia　　　*Hor. lib. ca. 3*
> Ceruice pendet, non Siculae dapes　　*Ode 1.*
> Dulcem elaborabunt saporem
> Non auium cytharæq. cantus."　　　　(iii. 18–19)

THE PERCYS' REBELLION

"Owen Glendouer, according to his accustomed manner, robbing and spoiling within the English borders, caused all the forces of the shire of Hereford to assemble togither against them, vnder the conduct of Edmund Mortimer earle of March. But coming to trie the matter by battell, whether by treason or otherwise, so it fortuned, that the English power was discomfited, the earle taken prisoner, and aboue a thousand of his people slaine in the place. The shamefull villanie vsed by the Welshwomen towards the dead carcasses, was such, as honest eares would be ashamed to heare, and continent toongs to speake thereof. The dead bodies might not be buried, without great summes of monie giuen for libertie to conueie them awaie.

"The king was not hastie to purchase the deliuerance of the earle March, bicause his title to the crowne was well inough knowen, and therefore suffered him to remaine in miserable prison, wishing both the said earle, and all other of his linage out of this life, with God and his saincts in heauen, so they had beene out of the waie, for then all had beene well inough as he thought... About mid of August, the king to chastise the presumptuous attempts of the Welshmen, went with a great power of men into Wales, to pursue the capteine of the Welsh rebell Owen Glendouer, but in effect he lost his labor; for Owen conueied himselfe out of the waie, into his knowen lurking places, and (as was thought) through art magike, he caused such foule weather of winds, tempest, raine, snow, and haile to be raised, for the annoiance of the kings armie, that the like had not beene heard of; in such sort, that the king was constreined to return home, hauing caused his people yet to spoile and burne first a great part of the countrie. . . The Scots vnder the leding of Patrike Hepborne, of the Hales the yoonger, entring into England, were ouerthrowen at Nesbit, in the marches, as in the Scotish chronicle ye may find more at large. This battell was fought the two and twentith of Iune, in this yeare of our Lord 1402.

"Archembald earle Dowglas sore displeased in his mind for this ouerthrow, procured a commission to inuade England, and that to his cost, as ye may likewise read in the Scotish histories. For at a place called Homildon, they were so fiercelie assailed by the Englishmen, vnder the leading of the lord Persie, surnamed Henrie Hotspur, and George earle of March, that with violence of the English shot they were quite vanquished and put to flight, on the Rood daie in haruest, with a great slaughter made by the Englishmen. We know that the Scotish writers note this battell to haue chanced in the yeare 1403. But we following Tho. Walsingham in this place, and other English writers, for the accompt of times, haue thought good to place it in this yeare 1402, as in the same writers we find it. There were slaine of men of estimation, sir Iohn Swinton, sir Adam Gordon, sir Iohn Leuiston, sir Alexander Ramsie of Dalehousie, and three and twentie knights, besides ten thousand of the commons: and of prisoners among other were these, Mordacke earle of Fife, son to the gouernour Archembald earle Dowglas, which in the fight lost one of his eies, Thomas erle of Murrey, Robert earle of Angus, and (as some writers haue) the earles of Atholl & Menteith, with fiue hundred other of meaner degrees.

". . . Edmund Mortimer earle of March, prisoner with Owen Glendouer, whether for irkesomnesse of cruell captiuitie, or feare of death, or for what other cause, it is vncerteine, agreed to take part with Owen, against the king of England, and tooke to wife the daughter of the said Owen.

"Strange wonders happened (as men reported) at the natiuitie of this man, for the same night he was borne, all his fathers horsses in the stable were found to stand in bloud vp to the bellies. . .

"Henrie earle of Northumberland, with his brother Thomas earle of Worcester, and his sonne the lord Henrie Persie, surnamed Hotspur, which were to king Henrie in the beginning of his reigne, both faithfull freends, and earnest aiders, began now to enuie his wealth and felicitie; and especiallie they were greeued, bicause the king demanded of the earle and his sonne such Scotish prisoners as were taken at Homeldon and Nesbit: for of all the captiues which were taken in the conflicts foughten in those two places, there was deliuered to the kings possession onelie Mordake earle of Fife, the duke of Albanies sonne, though the king did diuers and sundrie times require deliuerance of the residue, and that with great threatnings: wherewith the Persies being sore offended, for that they claimed them as their owne proper prisoners, and their peculiar preies, by the counsell of the lord Thomas Persie earle of Worcester, whose studie was euer (as some write) to procure malice, and set things in a broile, came to the king vnto Windsore (vpon a purpose to prooue him) and there required of him, that either by ransome or otherwise, he would cause to be deliuered out of prison Edmund Mortimer earle of March, their cousine germane, whome (as they reported) Owen Glendouer kept in filthie prison, shakled with irons, onelie for that he tooke his part, and was to him faithfull and true.

"The king began not a little to muse at this request, and not without cause: for in deed it touched him somewhat neere, sith this Edmund was sonne to Roger earle of March, sonne to the ladie Philip, daughter of Lionell duke of Clarence, the third sonne of king Edward the third; which Edmund at king Richards going into Ireland, was proclaimed heire apparant to the crowne and realme, whose aunt called Elianor, the lord Henrie Persie had married; and therefore king Henrie could not well heare, that anie man should be earnest about the aduancement of that linage. The king when he had studied on the matter, made answer, that the earle of March was not taken prisoner for his cause, nor in his seruice, but willinglie suffered himselfe to be taken, bicause he would not withstand the attempts of Owen Glendouer, and his complices, and therefore he would neither ransome him, nor releeue him.

"The Persies with this answer and fraudulent excuse were not a little fumed, insomuch that Henrie Hotspur said openlie: Behold, the heire of the relme is robbed of his right, and yet the robber with his owne will not redeeme him. So in this furie the Persies departed, minding nothing more than to depose king Henrie from the high type of his roialtie, and to place in his seat their cousine Edmund earle of March, whom they did not onlie deliuer out of captiuitie, but also (to the high displeasure of king Henrie) entered in league with the foresaid Owen Glendouer. Heerewith, they by their deputies in the house of the archdeacon of Bangor, diuided the realme amongst them, causing a tripartite indenture to be made and sealed with their seales, by the couenants whereof, all England from Seuerne and Trent, south and eastward, was assigned to the earle of March: all Wales, & the lands beyond Seuerne westward, were appointed to Owen Glendouer: and all the remnant from Trent northward, to the lord Persie.

"This was doone (as some haue said) through a foolish credit giuen to a vaine prophesie, as though king Henrie was the mold-warpe, curssed of Gods owne mouth, and they three were the dragon, the lion, and the woolfe, which should diuide this realme betweene them. Such is the deuiation (saith Hall) and not diuination of those blind and fantasticall dreames of the Welsh pro-phesiers. King Henrie not knowing of this new confederacie, and nothing lesse minding than that which after happened, gathered a great armie to go againe into Wales, whereof the earle of Northum-berland and his sonne were aduertised by the earle of Worcester, and with all diligence raised all the power they could make, and sent to the Scots which before were taken prisoners at Homeldon, for aid of men, promising to the earle of Dowglas the towne of Ber-wike, and a part of Northumberland, and to other Scotish lords, great lordships and seigniories, if they obteined the upper hand. The Scots in hope of gaine, and desirous to be reuenged of their old greefes, came to the earle with a great companie well appointed.

"The Persies to make their part seeme good, deuised certeine articles, by the aduise of Richard Scroope, archbishop of Yorke, brother to the lord Scroope, whome king Henrie had caused to be beheaded at Bristow. These articles being shewed to diuerse noble-men, and other states of the realme, mooued them to fauour their purpose, in so much that manie of them did not onelie promise to the Persies aid and succour by words, but also by their writings and seales confirmed the same. Howbeit when the matter came to triall, the most part of the confederates abandoned them, and at the daie of the conflict left them alone. Thus after that the conspirators had discouered themselues, the lord Henrie Persie desirous to proceed in the enterprise, vpon trust to be assisted by Owen Glendouer, the earle of March, & other, assembled an armie of men of armes and archers foorth of Cheshire and Wales. Incontinentlie his vncle Thomas Persie earle of Worcester, that had the gouernement of the prince of Wales, who as then laie at London in secret manner, con-ueied himselfe out of the princes house, and comming to Stafford (where he met his nephue) they increased their power by all waies and meanes they could deuise. The earle of Northumberland him-selfe was not with them, but being sicke, had promised vpon his amendement to repair vnto them (as some write) with all con-uenient speed.

"These noble men, to make their conspiracie to seeme excus-

able, besides the articles aboue mentioned, sent letters abroad,
wherein was conteined, that their gathering of an armie tended to
none other end, but onlie for the safegard of their owne persons, and
to put some better gouernment in the commonwealth. For whereas
taxes and tallages were dailie leuied, vnder pretense to be imploied
in defense of the realme, the same were vainlie wasted, and vnpro-
fitablie consumed: and where through the slanderous reports of
their enimies, the king had taken a greeuous displeasure with them,
they durst not appeare personallie in the kings presence, vntill the
prelats and barons of the realme had obteined of the king licence
for them to come and purge themselues before him, by lawfull triall
of their peeres, whose iudgement (as they pretended) they would in
no wise refuse. Manie that saw and heard these letters, did com-
mend their diligence, and highlie praised their assured fidelitie and
trustinesse towards the commonwealth.

"But the king vnderstanding their cloaked drift, deuised (by
what meanes he might) to quiet and appease the commons, and
deface their contriued forgeries; and therefore he wrote an answer
to their libels, that he maruelled much, sith the earle of Northumberland, and the lord Henrie Persie his sonne, had receiued the
most part of the summes of monie granted to him by the cleargie
and communaltie, for defense of the marches, as he could euidentlie
prooue, what should mooue them to complaine and raise such
manifest slanders. And whereas he vnderstood, that the earles of
Northumberland and Worcester, and the lord Persie had by their
letters signified to their freends abroad, that by reason of the slanderous reports of their enimies, they durst not appeare in his
presence, without the mediation of the prelats and nobles of the
realme, so as they required pledges, whereby they might safelie
come afore him, to declare and alledge what they had to saie in
proofe of their innocencie, he protested by letters sent foorth vnder
his seale, that they might safelie come and go, without all danger,
or anie manner of indamagement to be offered to their persons.

"But this could not satisfie those men, but that resolued to go
forwards with their enterprise, they marched towards Shrewesburie, vpon hope to be aided (as men thought) by Owen Glendouer, and his Welshmen, publishing abroad throughout the
countries on each side, that king Richard was aliue, whome if they
wished to see, they willed them to repaire in armour vnto the
castell of Chester, where (without all doubt) he was at that present,
and redie to come forward. This tale being raised, though it were
most vntrue, yet it bred variable motions in mens minds, causing
them to wauer, so as they knew not to which part they should

sticke; and verelie, diuers were well affected towards king Richard, speciallie such as had tasted of his princelie bountifulnes, of which there was no small number. And to speake a truth, no maruell it was, if manie enuied the prosperous state of king Henrie, sith it was euident inough to the world, that he had with wrong vsurped the crowne, and not onelie violentlie deposed king Richard, but also cruellie procured his death; for the which vndoubtedlie, both he and his posteritie tasted such troubles, as put them still in danger of their states, till their direct succeeding line was quite rooted out by the contrarie faction, as in Henrie the sixt and Edward the fourth it may appeare.

"But now to return where we left. King Henrie aduertised of the proceedings of the Persies, foorthwith gathered about him such power as he might make, and being earnestlie called vpon by the Scot, the earle of March, to make hast and giue battell to his enimies, before their power by delaieng of time should still too much increase, he passed forward with such speed, that he was in sight of his enimies, lieng in campe neere to Shrewesburie, before they were in doubt of anie such thing, for the Persies thought that he would have staied at Burton vpon Trent, till his councell had come thither to him to giue their aduise what he were best to doo. But herein the enimie was deceiued of his expectation, sith the king had great regard of expedition and making speed for the safetie of his owne person, wherevnto the earle of March incited him, considering that in delaie is danger, & losse in lingering, as the poet in the like case saith:

> Tolle moras, nocuit semper differre paratis,
> Dum trepidant nullo firmatæ robore partes.

"By reason of the kings sudden côming in this sort, they staied from assaulting the towne of Shrewesburie, which enterprise they were readie at that instant to haue taken in hand, and foorthwith the lord Persie (as a capteine of high courage) began to exhort the capteines and souldiers to prepare themselues to battell, sith the matter was growen to that point, that by no meanes it could be auoided, so that (said he) this daie shall either bring vs all to aduancement & honor, or else if it shall chance vs to be ouercome, shall deliuer vs from the kings spitefull malice and cruell disdaine: for plaieng the men (as we ought to doo) better it is to die in battell for the commonwealths cause, than through cowardlike feare to prolong life, which after shall be taken from vs, by sentence of the enimie.

"Herevpon, the whole armie being in number about fourteene

thousand chosen men, promised to stand with him so long as life lasted. There were with the Persies as chiefteines of this armie, the earle of Dowglas a Scotish man, the baron of Kinderton, sir Hugh Browne, and sir Richard Vernon knights, with diuerse other stout and right valiant capteins. Now when the two armies were in-camped, the one against the other, the earle of Worcester and the lord Persie with their complices sent the articles (whereof I spake before) by Thomas Caiton, and Thomas Saluain esquiers to king Henrie, vnder their hands and seales, which articles in effect charged him with manifest periurie, in that (contrarie to his oth receiued vpon the euangelists at Doncaster, when he first entred the realme after his exile) he had taken vpon him the crowne and roiall dignitie, imprisoned king Richard, caused him to resigne his title, and finallie to be murthered. Diuerse other matters they laid to his charge, as leuieng of taxes and tallages, contrarie to his promise, infringing of lawes & customes of the realme, and suffering the earle of March to remaine in prison, without trauelling to haue him deliuered. All which things they as procurors & protectors of the common-wealth, tooke vpon them to prooue against him, as they protested vnto the whole world.

"King Henrie after he had read their articles, with the defiance which they annexed to the same, answered the esquiers, that he was readie with dint of sword and fierce battell to prooue their quarrell false, and nothing else than a forged matter, not doubting, but that God would aid and assist him in his righteous cause, against the disloiall and false forsworne traitors. The next daie in the morning earlie, being the euen of Marie Magdalene, they set their battels in order on both sides, and now whilest the warriors looked when the token of battell should be giuen, the abbat of Shrewesburie, and one of the clearks of the priuie seale, were sent from the king vnto the Persies, to offer them pardon, if they would come to any reasonable agreement. By their persuasions, the lord Henrie Persie began to giue eare vnto the kings offers, & so sent with them his vncle the earle of Worcester, to declare vnto the king the causes of those troubles, and to require some effectuall reformation in the same.

"It was reported for a truth, that now when the king had con-descended vnto all that was resonable at his hands to be required, and seemed to humble himselfe more than was meet for his estate, the earle of Worcester (vpon his returne to his nephue) made rela-tion cleane contrarie to that the king had said, in such sort that he set his nephues hart more in displeasure towards the king, than euer it was before, driuing him by that meanes to fight whether he would or not: then suddenlie blew the trumpets, the kings part crieng S. George vpon them, the aduersaries cried *Esperance Persie*, and so the two armies furiouslie ioined. The archers on both sides shot for the best game, laieng on such load with arrowes, that manie died, and were driuen downe that neuer rose againe.

"The Scots (as some write) which had the fore ward on the Persies side, intending to be reuenged of their old displeasures doone to them by the English nation, set so fiercelie on the kings fore ward, led by the earle of Stafford, that they made the same draw backe, and had almost broken their aduersaries arraie. The Welshmen also which before had laine lurking in the woods, mounteines, and marishes, hearing of this battell toward, came to the aid of the Persies, and refreshed the wearied people with new succours. The king perceiuing that his men were thus put to distresse, what with the violent impression of the Scots, and the tempestuous stormes of arrowes, that his aduersaries discharged freely against him and his people, it was no need to will him to stirre: for suddenlie with his fresh battell, he approched and relieued his men; so that the battell began more fierce than before. Here the lord Henrie Persie, and the earle Dowglas, a right stout and hardie capteine, not regarding the shot of the kings battell, nor the close order of the ranks, pressing forward togither bent their whole forces towards the kings person, comming vpon him with speares and swords so fiercelie, that the earle of March the Scot, perceiuing their purpose, withdrew the king from that side of the field (as some write) for his great benefit and safegard (as it appeared) for they gaue such a violent onset vpon them that stood about the kings standard, that slaieng his standard-bearer sir Walter Blunt, and ouerthrowing the standard, they made slaughter of all those that stood about it, as the earle of Stafford, that daie made by the king constable of the realme, and diuerse other.

"The prince that daie holpe his father like a lustie yoong gentleman: for although he was hurt in the face with an arrow, so that diuerse noble men that were about him, would haue conueied him foorth of the field, yet he would not suffer them so to doo, least his departure from amongst his men might happilie haue striken some feare into their harts: and so without regard of his hurt, he continued with his men, & neuer ceassed, either to fight where the battell was most hot, or to incourage his men where it seemed most need. This battell lasted three long houres, with indifferent fortune on both parts, till at length, the king crieng saint George victorie, brake the arraie of his enimies, and aduentured so farre, that (as some write) the earle Dowglas strake him downe, & at that instant

slue Sir Walter Blunt, and three other, apparelled in the kings sute
and clothing, saieng: I maruell to see so many kings thus suddenlie
arise one in the necke of an other. The king in deed was raised, &
did that daie manie a noble feat of armes, for as it is written, he slue
that daie with his owne hands six and thirtie persons of his enimies.
The other on his part incouraged by his doings, fought valiantlie,
and slue the lord Persie, called sir Henrie Hotspurre. To conclude,
the kings enimies were vanquished, and put to flight, in which
flight, the earle of Dowglas, for hast, falling from the crag of an hie
mounteine, brake one of his cullions, and was taken, and for his
valiantnesse, of the king frankelie and freelie deliuered.

"There was also taken the earle of Worcester, the procuror and
setter foorth of all this mischeefe, sir Richard Vernon, and the
baron of Kinderton, with diuerse other. There were slaine vpon the
kings part, beside the earle of Stafford, to the number of ten
knights, sir Hugh Shorlie, sir Iohn Clifton, sir Iohn Cokaine, sir
Nicholas Gausell, sir Walter Blunt, sir Iohn Caluerleie, Sir Iohn
Massie of Podington, sir Hugh Mortimer, and sir Robert Gausell,
all the which receiued the same morning the order of knighthood:
sir Thomas Wendesleie was wounded to death, and so passed out of
this life shortlie after. There died in all vpon the kings side sixteene
hundred, and foure thousand were greeuouslie wounded. On the
contrarie side were slaine, besides the lord Persie, the most part of
the knights and esquiers of the countie of Chester, to the number of
two hundred, besides yeomen and footmen, in all there died of those
that fought on the Persies side, about fiue thousand. This battell
was fought on Marie Magdalene euen, being saturdaie. Vpon the
mondaie folowing, the earle of Worcester, the baron of Kinderton,
and sir Richard Vernon knights, were condemned and beheaded.
The earles head was sent to London, there to be set on the bridge.

"The earle of Northumberland was now marching forward with
great power, which he had got thither, either to aid his sonne and
brother (as was thought) or at the least towards the king, to procure
a peace: but the earle of Westmerland, and sir Robert Waterton
knight, had got an armie on foot, and meant to meet him. The earle
of Northumberland, taking neither of them to be his freend, turned
suddenlie back, and withdrew himselfe into Warkewoorth castell.
The king hauing set a staie in things about Shrewesburie, went
straight to Yorke, from whence he wrote to the earle of Northumberland, willing him to dismisse his companies that he had with
him, and to come vnto him in peaceable wise. The earle vpon
receipt of the kings letters came vnto him the morow after saint
Laurence daie, hauing but a few of his seruants to attend him, and

so excused himselfe, that the king (bicause the earle had Berwike in
his possession, and further, had his castels of Alnewike, Warkewoorth, and other, fortified with Scots) dissembled the matter,
gaue him faire words, and suffered him (as saith Hall) to depart
home, although by other it should seeme, that he was committed
for a time to safe custodie.

"The king returning foorth of Yorkshire, determined to go into
Northwales, to chastise the presumptuous dooings of the vnrulie
Welshmen, who (after his comming from Shrewesburie, and the
marches there) had doone much harme to the English subiects."
(iii. 20–7)

THE INTERVIEW BETWEEN PRINCE HENRY AND THE KING

"Whilest these things were a dooing in France, the lord Henrie
prince of Wales, eldest sonne to king Henrie, got knowledge that
certeine of his fathers seruants were busie to giue informations
against him, whereby discord might arise betwixt him and his
father: for they put into the kings head, not onelie what euill rule
(according to the course of youth) the prince kept to the offense of
manie: but also what great resort of people came to his house, so
that the court was nothing furnished with such a traine as dailie
followed the prince. These tales brought no small suspicion into the
kings head, least his sonne would presume to vsurpe the crowne, he
being yet aliue, through which suspicious gelousie, it was perceiued
that he fauoured not his sonne, as in times past he had doone.

"The Prince sore offended with such persons, as by slanderous
reports, sought not onelie to spot his good name abrode in the
realme, but to sowe discord also betwixt him and his father, wrote
his letters into euerie part of the realme, to reproue all such slanderous deuises of those that sought his discredit. And to cleare himselfe the better, that the world might vnderstand what wrong he
had to be slandered in such wise: about the feast of Peter and Paule,
to wit, the nine and twentith daie of Iune, he came to the court with
such a number of noble men and other his freends that wished him
well, as the like traine had beene sildome seene repairing to the
court at any one time in those daies. He was apparelled in a gowne
of blew satten, full of small oilet holes, at euerie hole the needle
hanging by a silke thred with which it was sewed. About his arme
he ware an hounds collar set full of SS of gold, and the tirets likewise
being of the same metall.

"The court was then at Westminster, where he being entred into
the hall, not one of his companie durst once aduance himselfe
further than the fire in the same hall, notwithstanding they were

earnestlie requested by the lords to come higher: but they regarding what they had in commandement of the prince, would not presume to doo in any thing contrarie there vnto. He himselfe onelie
accompanied with those of the kings house, was streight admitted
to the presence of the king his father, who being at that time
greeuouslie diseased, yet caused himselfe in his chaire to be borne
into his priuie chamber, where in the presence of three or foure persons, in whome he had most confidence, he commanded the prince
to shew what he had to saie concerning the cause of his comming.

"The prince kneeling downe before his father said: Most re-
doubted and souereigne lord and father, I am at this time come to
your presence as your liege man, and as your naturall sonne, in all
things to be at your commandement. And where I vnderstand you
haue in suspicion my demeanour against your grace, you know
verie well, that if I knew any man within this realme, of whome you
should stand in feare, my duetie were to punish that person, thereby to remooue that greefe from your heart. Then how much more
ought I to suffer death, to ease your grace of that greefe which you
haue of me, being your naturall sonne and liege man: and to that
end I haue this daie made my selfe readie by confession and
receiuing of the sacrament. And therefore I beseech you most re-
doubted lord and deare father, for the honour of God, to ease your
heart of all such suspicion as you haue of me, and to dispatch me
heere before your knees, with this same dagger, [and withall he
deliuered vnto the king his dagger, in all humble reuerence; adding
further, that his life was not so deare to him, that he wished to liue
one daie with his displeasure] and therefore in thus ridding me out
of life, and your selfe from all suspicion, here in presence of these
lords, and before God at the daie of the generall iudgement, I
faithfullie protest clearlie to forgiue you.

"The king mooued herewith, cast from him the dagger, and
imbracing the prince kissed him, and with shedding teares confessed, that in deed he had him partlie in suspicion, though now (as
he perceiued) not with iust cause, and therefore from thencefoorth
no misreport should cause him to haue him in mistrust, and this he
promised of his honour. So by his great wisedome was the wrong-
full suspicion which his father had conceiued against him remoou-
ed, and he restored to his fauour. And further, where he could not
but greeuouslie complaine of them that had slandered him so
greatlie, to the defacing not onelie of his honor, but also putting
him in danger of his life, he humblie besought the king that they
might answer their vniust accusation; and in case they were found
to haue forged such matters vpon a malicious purpose, that then

they might suffer some punishment for their faults, though not to
the full of that they had deserued. The king seeming to grant his
resonable desire, yet told him that he must tarrie a parlement, that
such offendors might be punished by iudgement of their peeres:
and so for that time he was dismissed, with great loue and signes of
fatherlie affection.

"Thus were the father and the sonne reconciled, betwixt whom
the said pickthanks had sowne diuision, insomuch that the sonne
vpon a vehement conceit of vnkindnesse sproong in the father, was
in the waie to be worne out of fauour. Which was the more likelie to
come to passe, by their informations that priuilie charged him with
riot and other vnciuill demeanor vnseemelie for a prince. Indeed
he was youthfullie giuen, growne to audacitie, and had chosen him
companions agreeable to his age; with whome he spent the time in
such recreations, exercises, and delights as he fansied. But yet (it
should seeme by the report of some writers) that his behauiour was
not offensiue or at least tending to the damage of anie bodie; sith he
had a care to auoid dooing of wrong, and to tedder his affections
within the tract of vertue, whereby he opened vnto himselfe a redie
passage of good liking among the prudent sort, and was beloued of
such as could discerne his disposition, which was in no degree so
excessiue, as that he deserued in such vehement maner to be suspected. In whose dispraise I find little, but to his praise verie much,
parcell whereof I will deliuer by the waie as a metyard whereby the
residue may be measured. The late poet that versified the warres of
the valorous Englishmen, speaking of the issue of Henrie the fourth
saith of this prince (among other things) as followeth:

> —procero qui natu maximus hæres
> Corpore, progressus cum pubertatis ad annos
> Esset, res gessit multas iuueniliter audax,
> Asciscens comites quos par sibi iunxerat ætas,
> Nil tamen iniuste commisit, nil tamen vnquam
> Extra virtutis normam, sapientibus æque
> Ac aliis charus." (iii. 53–5)

2. *Samuel Daniel:* "*The First Fowre Bookes of the Ciuile Wars Between
the Two Houses of Lancaster and Yorke*" (*1595*)

Book III

86   And yet new *Hydraes* lo, new heades appeare
        T'afflict that peace reputed then so sure,
        And gaue him much to do, and much to feare,

And long and daungerous tumults did procure,
And those euen of his chiefest followers were
Of whom he might presume him most secure,
Who whether not so grac'd or so preferd
As they expected, these new factions stird.

87   The *Percyes* were the men, men of great might,
Strong in alliance, and in courage strong
That thus conspire, vnder pretence to right
The crooked courses they had suffered long:
Whether their conscience vrgd them or despight,
Or that they saw the part they tooke was wrong,
Or that ambition hereto did them call,
Or others enuide grace, or rather all.

88   What cause soeuer were, strong was their plot,
Their parties great, meanes good, th'occasion fit:
Their practice close, their faith suspected not,
Their states far off and they of wary wit:
Who with large promises draw in the Scot
To ayde their cause, he likes, and yeeldes to it,
Not for the loue of them or for their good,
But glad hereby of meanes to shed our bloud.

89   Then ioyne they with the *Welsh*, who fitly traind
And all in armes vnder a mightie head
Owen   Great *Glendowr*, who long warr'd, and much attaind,
Glendor. Sharp conflicts made, and many vanquished:
With whom was *Edmond Earle* of *March* retaind
Being first his prisoner, now confedered,
A man the king much fear'd, and well he might
Least he should looke whether his Crown stood right.

90   For *Richard*, for the quiet of the state,
Before he tooke those *Irish* warres in hand
About succession doth deliberate,
Rich. 2nd And finding how the certaine right did stand,
With full consent this man did ordinate
The heyre apparent in the crowne and land:
Then iudge if this the king might nerely touch,
Although his might were smal, his right being much.

91 With these the *Percyes* them confederate
And as three heades they league in one intent,
And instituting a Triumuirate
Do part the land in triple gouerment:
Deuiding thus among themselues the state,
The *Percyes* should rule all the *North* from *Trent*
And *Glendowr Wales*: the *Earle* of *March* should bee
Lord of the *South* from *Trent*; and thus they gree.

92 Then those two helpes which still such actors find
Pretence of common good, the kings disgrace
Doth fit their course, and draw the vulgar mind
To further them and aide them in this case;
The king they accusd for cruell, and vnkind
That did the state, and crowne, and all deface;
A periurde man that held all faith in skorne,
Whose trusted othes had others made forsworne.

93 Besides the odious detestable act
Of that late murdered king they aggrauate,
Making it his that so had will'd the fact
That he the doers did remunerate:
And then such taxes daily doth exact
That were against the orders of the state,
And with all these or worse they him assaild
Who late of others with the like preuaild.

94 Thus doth contentious proud mortality
Afflict each other and itselfe torment:
And thus o thou mind-tortring misery
Restles ambition, borne in discontent,
Turn'st and retossest with iniquity
The vnconstant courses frailty did inuent:
And fowlst faire order and defilst the earth
Fostring vp warre, father of bloud and dearth.

95 Great seemd the cause, and greatly to, did ad
The peoples loue thereto these crimes rehearst,
That manie gathered to the troupes they had
And many more do flocke from costs disperst:
But when the king had heard these newes so bad,

Th'vnlookt for dangerous toyle more nearly perst;
For bēt t'wards *Wales* t'appease those tumults there,
H'is for'st diuert his course, and them forbeare.

96   Not to giue time vnto th'increasing rage
And gathering fury, forth he hastes with speed,
Lest more delay or giuing longer age
To th'euill growne, it might the cure exceed:
All his best men at armes, and leaders sage
All he prepard he could, and all did need;
For to a mighty worke thou goest ô king,
To such a field that power to power shall bring.

97   There shall young *Hotespur* with a fury lead   *The Son*
Meete with thy forward sonne as fierce as he: *to the*
There warlike *Worster* long experienced   *Earle of*
In forraine armes, shall come t'incounter thee: *Northū-*
There *Dowglas* to thy *Stafford* shall make head: *berland.*
There *Vernon* for thy valiant *Blunt* shalbe:
There shalt thou find a doubtfull bloudy day,
Though sicknesse keepe *Northumberland* away.

98   Who yet reseru'd, though after quit for this,
Another tempest on thy head to raise,
As if still wrong reuenging *Nemesis*
Did meane t'afflict all thy continuall dayes:
And yet this field he happely might misse
For thy great good, and therefore well he staies:
What might his force haue done being ioynd thereto
When that already gaue so much to do?

99   The swift approch and vnexpected speed
The king had made vpon this new-raisd force
In th'vnconfirmed troupes much feare did breed,
Vntimely hindring their intended course;
The ioyning with the *Welsh* they had decreed
Was hereby stopt, which made their part the worse,
Northumberland with forces from the *North*
Expected to be there, was not set forth.

100   And yet vndaunted *Hotspur* seeing the king
So nere approch'd, leauing the worke in hand

With forward speed his forces marshalling,
Sets forth his farther comming to withstand:
And with a cheerfull voice incouraging
By his great spirit his well imboldened band,
Bringes a strong host of firme resolued might,
And plac'd his troupes before the king in sight.

101   This day (saith he) ô faithfull valiaunt frendes,
What euer it doth giue, shall glorie giue:
This day with honor frees our state, or endes
Our misery with fame, that still shall liue,
And do but thinke how well this day he spendes
That spendes his bloud his countrey to relieue:
Our holie cause, our freedome, and our right,
Sufficient are to moue good mindes to fight.

102   Besides th'assured hope of victory
That wee may euen promise on our side
Against this weake-constrained companie
Whom force & feare, not will, and loue doth guide
Against a prince whose foule impiety
The heauens do hate, the earth cannot abide,
Our number being no lesse, our courage more,
What need we doubt if we but worke therefore.

103   This said, and thus resolu'd euen bent to charge
Vpon the king, who well their order viewd
And carefull noted all the forme at large
Of their proceeding, and their multitude:
And deeming better if he could discharge
The day with safetie, and some peace conclude,
Great proffers sendes of pardon, and of grace
If they would yeeld, and quietnes imbrace.

104   But this refusd, the king with wrath incensd
Rage against fury doth with speed prepare:
And ô saith he, though I could haue dispensd
With this daies bloud, which I haue sought to spare
That greater glory might haue recompensd
The forward worth of these that so much dare,
That we might honor had by th'ouerthrown
That th'wounds we make, might not haue bin our own.

105
    Yet since that other mens iniquity
Calles on the sword of wrath against my will,
And that themselues exact this cruelty,
And I constrained am this bloud to spill:
Then on my maisters, on couragiously
True-harted subiects against traitors ill,
And spare them not who seeke to spoile vs all,
Whose fowle confused end soone see you shall.

106
    Straight moues with equall motion equall rage
The like incensed armies vnto bloud,
One to defend, another side to wage
Foule ciuill war, both vowes their quarrell good:
Ah too much heate to bloud doth nowe inrage
Both who the deed prouokes and who withstood,
That valor here is vice, here manhood sin,
The forward'st hands doth ô least honor win.

107
    But now begin these fury-mouing soundes
The notes of wrath that musicke brought from hell,
The ratling drums which trumpets voice côfounds,
The cryes, th'incouragements, the shouting shrell;
That all about the beaten ayre reboundes,
Thundring confused, murmurs horrible,
To rob all sence except the sence to fight,
Well hands may worke, the mind hath lost his sight.

108
    O war! begot in pride and luxury,
The child of wrath and of dissention,
Horrible good; mischiefe necessarie,
The fowle reformer of confusion,
Vniust-iust scourge of our iniquitie,
Cruell recurer of corruption:
O that these sin-sicke states in need should stand
To be let bloud with such a boystrous hand!

109
    And ô how well thou hadst been spar'd this day
Had not wrong counsail'd *Percy* bene peruers,
Whose yong vndanger'd hand now rash makes way
Vpon the sharpest fronts of the most fierce:
Where now an equall fury thrusts to stay
And rebeat-backe that force and his disperse,

Then these assaile, then those chace backe againe,
Till staid with new-made hils of bodies slaine.

110

There lo that new-appearing glorious starre
Wonder of Armes, the terror of the field

*The Prince
of Wales.*

Young *Henrie*, laboring where the stoutest are,
And euen the stoutest forces backe to yeild,
There is that hand boldned to bloud and warre
That must the sword in woundrous actions weild:
But better hadst thou learnd with others bloud
A lesse expence to vs, to thee more good.

111

Hadst thou not there lent present speedy ayd
To thy indaungerde father nerely tyrde,
Whom fierce incountring *Dowglas* ouerlaid,
That day had there his troublous life expirde:

*Which was
sir Walter
Blunt.*

Heroycall Couragious *Blunt* araid
In habite like as was the king attirde
And deemd for him, excusd that fate with his,
For he had what his Lord did hardly misse.

112

For thought a king he would not now disgrace
The person then supposd, but princelike shewes
Glorious effects of worth that fit his place,

*Another
Blunt which
was the
kings Stand-
ard bearer.*

And fighting dyes, and dying ouerthrowes:
Another of that forward name and race
In that hotte worke his valiant life bestowes,
Who bare the standard of the king that day,
Whose colours ouerthrowne did much dismaie.

113

And deare it cost, and ô much bloud is shed
To purchase thee this loosing victory
O trauayld king: yet hast thou conquered
A doubtfull day, a mightie enemy:
But ô what woundes, what famous worth lyes dead!
That makes the winner looke with sorrowing eye,

*Sir Hugh
Shorly.*

Magnanimous *Stafford* lost that much had wrought,
And valiant *Shorly* who great glory gote.

114

Such wracke of others bloud thou didst behold
O furious *Hotspur*, ere thou lost thine owne!
Which now once lost that heate in thine waxt cold,

And soone became thy Armie ouerthrowne;
And ô that this great spirit, this courage bold,
Had in some good cause bene rightly showne!
So had not we thus violently then
Haue termd that rage, which valor should haue ben.

3. *Anon.*: "*The Famous Victories of Henry the fifth: Containing the Honourable Battell of Agin-court*" (*1598*)—passages utilized for the first part of *Henry IV*.[1]

THE HIGHWAY ROBBERY.

[*Sc. I.*] *Enter the yoong Prince*, Ned, *and* Tom.

Henry the fifth.

    Come away Ned and Tom.

Both. Here my Lord.

Henr. 5. Come away my Lads:

    Tell me sirs, how much gold haue you got?   [4]

Ned. Faith my Lord, I haue got fiue hundred pound.

Hen. 5. But tell me Tom, how much hast thou got?

Tom. Faith my Lord, some foure hundred pound.

Hen. 5. Foure hundred pounds, brauely spoken Lads.   [8]

    But tell me sirs, thinke you not that it was a villainous

    part of me to rob my fathers Receiuers?

Ned. Why no my Lord, it was but a tricke of youth.

Hen. 5. Faith Ned, thou sayest true.   [12]

    But tell me sirs, whereabouts are we?

Tom. My Lord, we are now about a mile off London.

Hen. 5. But sirs, I maruell that Sir Iohn Old-Castle

    Comes not away: Sounds see where he comes.   [16]

Enters Iockey.

How now Iockey, what newes with thee?

Iockey. Faith my Lord, such newes as passeth,

    For the Towne of Detfort is risen,

    With hue and crie after your man,   [20]

    Which parted from vs the last night,

    And has set vpon, and hath robd a poore Carrier.

Hen. 5. Sownes, the vilaine that was wont to spie

    Out our booties.   [24]

   1. The original (1598) is in black letter. Scene- and line-divisions here are from the Praetorius-Daniel facsimile, 1887.

Iock. I my Lord, euen the very same.

Hen. 5. Now base minded rascal to rob a poore carrier,
Wel it skils not, ile saue the base vilaines life:
I, I may: but tel me Iockey, wherabout be the
Receiuers? [28]

Ioc. Faith my Lord, they are hard by,
But the best is, we are a horse backe and they be a foote,
So we may escape them.

Hen. 5. Wel, I the vilaines come, let me alone with [32]
them.

But tel me Iockey, how much gots thou from the
knaues?

For I am sure I got something, for one of the
vilaines

So belamd me about the shoulders, [36]
As I shal feele it this moneth.

Iock. Faith my Lord, I haue got a hundred pound.

Hen. 5. A hundred pound, now brauely spoken Iockey:
But come sirs, laie al your money before me, [40]
Now by heauen here is a braue shewe:
But as I am true Gentleman, I will haue the halfe
Of this spent to night, but sirs take vp your bags,
Here comes the Receiuers, let me alone. [44]

Enters two Receiuers.

One. Alas good fellow, what shal we do?
I dare neuer go home to the Court, for I shall be hangd.
But looke, here is the yong Prince, what shal we doo?

Hen. 5. How now you vilaines, what are you? [48]

One Recei. Speake you to him.

Other. No I pray, speake you to him.

Hen. 5. Why how now you rascals, why speak you not?

One. Forsooth we be. Pray speake you to him. [52]

Hen. 5. Sowns, vilains speak, or ile cut off your heads.

Other. Forsooth he can tel the tale better then I.

One Forsooth we be your fathers Receiuers.

Hen. 5. Are you my fathers Receiuers? [56]
Then I hope ye haue brought me some money.

One. Money, Alas sir we be robd.

Hen. 5. Robd, how many were there of them?

One. Marry sir, there were foure of them: [60]
And one of them had sir Iohn Old-Castles bay Hobbie,
And your blacke Nag.

Hen. 5. Gogs wounds how like you this Iockey?
    Blood you vilaines: my father robd of his money
        abroad, [64]
    And we robd in our stables.
    But tell me, how many were of them?
One recei. If it please you, there were foure of them,
    And there was one about the bignesse of you: [68]
    But I am sure I so belambd him about the shoulders,
    That he wil feele it this month.
Hen. 5. Gogs wounds you lamd them faierly,
    So that they haue carried away your money. [72]
    But come sirs, what shall we do with the vilaines?
Both recei. I beseech your grace, be good to vs.
Ned. I pray you my Lord forgiue them this once.
    Well stand vp and get you gone, [76]
    And looke that you speake not a word of it,
    For if there be, sownes ile hang you and all your kin.
                          Exit Purseuant.
Hen. 5 Now sirs, how like you this?
    Was not this brauely done? [80]
    For now the vilaines dare not speake a word of it,
    I haue so feared them with words.
    Now whither shall we goe?
All. Why my Lord, you know our old hostes [84]
    At Feuersham.
Hen. 5. Our hostes at Feuersham, blood what shal we do there?
    We haue a thousand pound about vs,
    And we shall go to a pettie Ale-house. [88]
    No, no: you know the olde Tauerne in Eastcheape,
    There is good wine: besides, there is a pretie wench
    That can talke well, for I delight as much in their toongs,
    As any part about them. [92]
All. We are readie to waite vpon your grace.
Hen. 5. Gogs wounds wait, we will go altogither,
    We are all fellowes, I tell you sirs, and the King
    My father were dead, we would be all Kings, [96]
    Therefore come away.
Ned. Gogs wounds, brauely spoken Harry.   [*Exeunt.*]

[*Sc. II.*] *Enter Iohn Cobler, Robin Pewterer, Lawrence Costermonger.*

*　　　*　　　*

Law. Neighbor, what newes heare you of ye young Prince? [12]

Iohn. Marry neighbor, I heare say, he is a toward yoong Prince,
    For if he met any by the hie way,
    He will not let to talke with him,
    I dare not call him theefe, but sure he is one of these taking
      fellowes.   [16]

Law. Indeed neighbour I heare say he is as liuely
    A young Prince as euer was.

Iohn. I, and I heare say, if he vse it long,
    His father will cut him off from the Crowne: [20]
    But neighbour say nothing of that.

*　　　*　　　*

Iohn. How now, who's there?   [64]

Enter the Theefe.

Theefe. Here is a good fellow, I praye you which is the
    Way to the old Tauerne in Eastcheape?

Der. Whoope hollo, now Gads Hill, knowest thou me?

Theef. I know thee for an Asse.   [68]

Der. And I know thee for a taking fellow,
    Vpon Gads hill in Kent:
    A bots light vpon ye.

Theef. The whorson villaine would be knockt.   [72]

Der. Maisters, vilaine, and ye be men stand to him,
    And take his weapon from him, let him not passe you.

Iohn. My friend, what make you abroad now?
    It is too late to walke now.   [76]

Theef. It is not too late for true men to walke.

Law. We know thee not to be a true man.

PRINCE HENRY COMMITTED TO PRISON.

[*Sc. III.*] *Enter Henry the Fourth.*

*　　　*　　　*

Hen. 4. Ah Harry, Harry, now thrice accursed Harry,
    That hath gotten a sonne, which with greefe   [44]
    Will end his fathers dayes.
    Oh my sonne, a Prince thou art, I a Prince indeed,
    And to deserue imprisonment.

PRINCE HENRY STRIKES THE LORD CHIEF JUSTICE.

[*Sc. IV.*] *Enter Lord chiefe Iustice, Clarke of the Office, Iayler, Iohn Cobler,*
Dericke, and the Theefe.

*   *   *

Clearke. Is not thy name Cutbert Cutter?

Theefe. What the Diuell need you ask, and know it so well.

Cleark. Why then Cutbert Cutter, I indite thee by the [20] name of
      Cutbert Cutter, for robbing a poore carrier the 20 day of May
      last past, in the fourteen yeare of the raigne of our soueraigne
      Lord King Henry the fourth, for setting vpon a poore Carrier
      vpon Gads hill in Kent, and hauing [24] beaten and wounded
      the said Carrier, and taken his goods from him.

Der. Oh maisters stay there, nay lets neuer belie the man, for he
      hath not beaten and wounded me also, but hee [28] hath
      beaten and wounded my packe, and hath taken the great rase
      of Ginger, that bouncing Besse with the iolly buttocks should
      haue had, that greeues me most.

Iudge. Well, what sayest thou, art thou guiltie, or not   [32]
      guiltie?

Theefe. Not guiltie, my Lord.

Iudge. By whom wilt thou be tride?

Theefe. By my Lord the young Prince, or by my selfe   [36]
      whether you will.

            Enter the young Prince, with Ned and Tom.

Hen. 5. Come away my lads, Gogs wounds ye villain, what
      make you heere? I must goe about my businesse my
      selfe, and you must stand loytering here.   [40]

Theefe. Why my Lord, they haue bound me, and will not let
      me goe.

Hen. 5. Haue they bound thee villain, why how now my
      Lord?   [44]

Iudge. I am glad to see your grace in good health.

Hen. 5. Why my Lord, this is my man,
      Tis maruell you knew him not long before this,
      I tell you he is a man of his hands.   [48]

Theefe. I Gogs wounds that I am, try me who dare.

Iudge. Your Grace shal finde small credit by acknowledging
      him to be your man.

Hen. 5. Why my Lord, what hath he done?   [52]

Iud. And it please your Maiestie, he hath robbed a poore
      Carrier.

Der. Heare you sir, marry it was one Dericke,
Goodman Hoblings man of Kent.

Hen. 5. What wast you butten-breech? [56]
Of my word my Lord, he did it but in iest.

Der. Heare you sir, is it your mans qualitie to rob folks in iest?
In faith, he shall be hangd in earnest.

Hen. 5. Well my Lord, what do you meane to do with my [60]
man?

Iudg. And please your grace, the law must passe on him,
According to iustice, then he must be executed.

Der. Heare you sir, I pray you, is it your mans quality to rob [64]
folkes in iest? In faith he shall be hangd in iest.

Hen. 5. Well my Lord, what meane you to do with my man?

Iudg. And please your grace the law must passe on him, [68]
According to iustice, then he must be executed.

Hen. 5. Why then belike you meane to hang my man?

Iudge. I am sorrie that it falles out so.

Hen. 5. Why my Lord, I pray ye who am I? [72]

Iudge. And please your Grace, you are my Lord the yong
Prince, our King that shall be after the decease of our
soueraigne Lord, King Henry the fourth, whom God
graunt long to raigne. [76]

Hen. 5. You say true my Lord:
And you will hang my man.

Iudge. And like your grace, I must needs do iustice.

Hen. 5. Tell me my Lord, shall I haue my man? [80]

Iudge. I cannot my Lord.

Hen. 5. But will you not let him go?

Iud. I am sorie that his case is so ill.

Hen. 5. Tush, case me no casings, shal I haue my man? [84]

Iudge. I cannot, nor I may not my Lord.

Hen. 5. Nay, and I shal not say, & then I am answered?

Iudge. No.

Hen. 5. No: then I will haue him. [88]
He giueth him a boxe on the eare.

Ned. Gogs wounds my Lord, shall I cut off his head?

Hen. 5. No, I charge you draw not your swords,
But get you hence, prouide a noyse of Musitians,
Away, be gone. *Exeunt the Theefe.* [92]

Iudge. Well my Lord, I am content to take it at your hands.

Hen. 5. Nay and you be not, you shall haue more.

Iudge. Why I pray you my Lord, who am I? [96]

Hen. 5. You, who knowes not you?

Why man, you are Lord chiefe Iustice of England.

Iudge. Your Grace hath said truth, therfore in striking me in this
    place, you greatly abuse me, and not me onely, [100] but also
    your father: whose liuely person here in this place I doo repre-
    sent. And therefore to teach you what prerogatiues meane, I
    commit you to the Fleete, vntill wee haue spoken with your
    father.   [104]

Hen. 5. Why then belike you meane to send me to the Fleete?

Iudge. I indeed, and therefore carry him away.

                               Exeunt Hen. 5. with the Officers.

Iudge. Iayler, carry the prisoner to Newgate againe, vntil   [108]
    the next Sises.

Iay. At your commandement my Lord, it shalbe done.

THE TAVERN PLAY-ACTING.

[Sc. V.] Enter Dericke and Iohn Cobler.

Der. Sownds maisters, heres adoo,
    When Princes must go to prison:
    Why Iohn, didst euer see the like?

Iohn. O Dericke, trust me, I neuer saw the like.   [4]

Der. Why Iohn thou maist see what princes be in choller,
    A Iudge a boxe on the eare, Ile tel thee Iohn, O Iohn,
    I would not haue done it for twentie shillings.

Iohn. No nor I, there had bene no way but one with vs,   [8]
    We should haue bene hangde.

Der. Faith Iohn, Ile tel thee what, thou shalt be my Lord chiefe
      Iustice, and thou shalt sit in the chaire,
    And ile be the yong Prince, and hit thee a box on the
      eare,   [12]
    And then thou shalt say, to teach you what prerogatiues
    Meane, I commit you to the Fleete.

Iohn. Come on, Ile be your Iudge,
    But thou shalt not hit me hard.   [16]

Der. No, no.

Iohn. What hath he done?

Det. Marry he hath robd Dericke.

Iohn. Why then I cannot let him go.   [20]

Der. I must needs haue my man.

Iohn. You shall not haue him.

Der. Shall I not haue my man, say no and you dare:
    How say you, shall I not haue my man?   [24]

Iohn. No marry shall you not.

Der. Shall I not Iohn?

Iohn. No Dericke.

Der. Why then take you that till more come,
    Sownes, shall I not haue him?   [28]

Iohn. Well I am content to take this at your hand,
    But I pray you, who am I?

Der. Who art thou, Sownds, doost not know thy self?

Iohn. No.   [32]

Der. Now away simple fellow,
    Why man, thou art Iohn the Cobler.

Iohn. No, I am my Lord chiefe Iustice of England. [36]

Der. Oh Iohn, Masse thou saist true, thou art indeed.

Iohn. Why then to teach you what prerogatiues mean I commit
    you to the Fleete.

Der. Wel I wil go, but yfaith you gray beard knaue, Ile [40]
    course you.   *Exit. And straight enters again.*
    Oh Iohn, Come, come out of thy chair, why what a clown
    weart thou, to let me hit thee a box on the eare, and now thou
    seest they will not take me to the Fleete, I thinke that [44]
    thou art one of these Worenday Clownes.

PROSPECTS OF MISRULE.

[*Sc.* VI.] *Enter the yoong Prince, with Ned and Tom.*

Hen. 5. Come away sirs, Gogs wounds Ned,
    Didst thou not see what a boxe on the eare
    I tooke my Lord chiefe Iustice?

Tom. By gogs blood it did me good to see it,
    It made his teeth iarre in his head.   [4]

                    Enter sir Iohn Old-Castle.

Hen. 5. How now sir Iohn Old-Castle,
    What newes with you?

Ioh. Old. I am glad to see your grace at libertie,   [8]
    I was come I, to visit you in prison.

Hen. 5. To visit me, didst thou not know that I am a Princes son,
    why tis inough for me to looke into a prison, though I come not
    in my selfe, but heres such adoo now a [12] days, heres prison-
    ing, heres hanging, whipping, and the diuel and all: but I tel
    you sirs, when I am King, we will haue no such things, but my
    lads, if the old king my father were dead, we would be all
    kings.   [16]

Ioh. Old. Hee is a good olde man, God take him to his mercy the
    sooner.

Hen. 5. But Ned, so soone as I am King, the first thing I wil do, shal
be to put my Lord chiefe Iustice out of office. [20] And thou
shalt be my Lord chiefe Iustice of England.

Ned. Shall I be Lord chiefe Iustice?
By gogs wounds, ile be the brauest Lord chiefe Iustice
That euer was in England.   [24]

Hen. 5. Then Ned, Ile turne all these prisons into fence Schooles,
and I will endue thee with them, with landes to maintaine
them withall: then I wil haue a bout with my Lord chiefe
Iustice, thou shalt hang none but picke purses [28] and horse
stealers, and such base minded villaines, but that fellow that
will stand by the high way side couragiously with his sword
and buckler and take a purse, that fellow giue him commen-
dations, beside that, send him to me and [32] I wil giue him an
anuall pension out of my Exchequer, to maintaine him all the
dayes of his life.

Ioh. Nobly spoken Harry, we shall neuer haue a mery world til
the old king be dead.   [36]

THE KING AND PRINCE RECONCILED.

*   *   *

[*Sc. VI.*] *Enters the Prince with a dagger in his hand.*

Hen. 4. Come my sonne, come on a God's name,   [108]
I know wherefore thy comming is,
Oh my sonne, my sonne, what cause hath euer bene,
That thou shouldst forsake me, and follow this vilde and
Reprobate company, which abuseth youth so mani-
   festly: [112]
Oh my sonne, thou knowest that these thy doings
Wil end thy fathers dayes.   *He weepes.*
I so, so, my sonne, thou fearest not to approach the presence of
thy sick father, in that disguised sort, I tel thee my sonne, [116]
that there is neuer a needle in thy cloke, but it is a prick to my
heart, & neuer an ilat-hole, but it is a hole to my soule: and
wherefore thou bringest that dagger in thy hande I know not,
but by coniecture.   *He weepes.* [120]

Hen. 5. My cōscience accuseth me, most soueraign Lord, and
welbeloued father, to answere first to the last point, That is,
whereas you coniecture that this hand and this dagger shall be
armde against your life: no, know my be[124]loued father,
far be the thoughts of your sonne, sonne said I, an vnworthie

sonne for so good a father: but farre be the thoughts of any
such pretended mischiefe: and I most humbly render it to
your Maiesties hand, and liue my Lord and [128] soueraigne
for euer: and with your dagger arme show like vengeance
vpon the bodie of that your sonne, I was about say and dare
not, ah woe is me therefore, that your wilde slaue, tis not the
Crowne that I come for, sweete father, [132] because I am
vnworthie, and those vilde & reprobate company I abandon,
& vtterly abolish their company for euer. . . . Pardō me,
sweet father, pardon me: good my Lord of Exeter speak for
me: pardon me, pardō good father, not a word: ah he wil not
speak one word: A Harry, now thrice vnhap[140]pie Harry.
But what shal I do? I wil go take me into some solitarie place,
and there lament my sinfull life, and when I haue done, I wil
laie me downe and die.   *Exit.*

Hen. 4. Call him againe, call my sonne againe.   [144]
Hen. 5. And doth my father call me again? now Harry,
    Happie be the time that thy father calleth thee againe.
Hen. 4. Stand vp my son, and do not think thy father,
    But at the request of thee my sonne I wil pardon thee, [148]
    And God blesse thee, and make thee his seruant.
Hen. 5. Thanks good my Lord, & no doubt but this day,
    Euen this day, I am borne new againe.
Hen. 4. Come my son and Lords, take me by the hands.   [152]
                                            Exeunt omnes.

Appendix IV

DOUBTFUL SOURCES

The claims sometimes made that the following works were possible direct sources for *1 Henry IV* seem ill-founded; they are therefore discussed here rather than in the Introduction.

1. *Edward Hall*: "*Chronicle of the Vnion of the Two Noble and Illustre
    Famelies of Lancastre and Yorke*" (*1542, 1548, 1550*). The page
    references are to the 1809 reprint.

Hall's direct contribution to the *Henry IV*s seems to amount to
nothing: I, like Hemingway, "have found no passage in *1 Henry IV*
which is taken directly from Hall" (Hemingway, New Var., 364).
Indirectly, since Holinshed incorporated much from Hall, and
Hall's reading of history meant much to the Elizabethans, the con-

tribution was great. His theme of the "Union" of Lancaster and York set the pattern for interpreting the reigns from Richard II to Henry VII; the title-page of Stow's *Annales* (1592), for instance, shows Edward III's family tree divided, the Lancastrians branching up the left side of the page, the Yorkists up the right, uniting across the top in the marriage of Henry of Richmond and Elizabeth of York, and bearing joint fruit in Henry VIII and his successors. This is the spirit of Daniel's *Ciuile Wars*, too, and of Shakespeare's double tetralogy which begins, as Hall had begun, with the Mowbray–Bolingbroke quarrel leading to Richard II's fall.

Hall doubtless suggested the starting-point for this whole sequence of plays. At first glance it might seem also that he suggested starting-points for both parts of *Henry IV*; the first paragraphs of his sections "The Thirde Yere" and "The Sixt Yere" outline the material for each part. Dover Wilson believes that Shakespeare noticed the reference (not in Holinshed) to "that mawmet Merlin" in "The Thirde Yere". Yet Phaer's story of Glendower in *A Myrroure for Magistrates* could give him the Merlin reference (cf. Intro., p. xxxvii), and had he read nine lines more in Hall he would have found what the writer of *1 Henry VI* had known (whether Shakespeare or another), namely, that the Earl of March, who was heir to the throne, was "euer kept in the courte vnder suche a keeper that he could nether doo or attempte any thyng againste the kyng" (Hall, 28). In "The Sixt Yere" the account of the Archbishop's rising differs widely from Shakespeare's, which closely follows Holinshed and could find its cue in Holinshed's glosses, "A new cōspiracie against King Henrie by the earle of Northumberland & others" . . . "The archbishop of yorke one of the chief conspirators" (Hol. iii. 36). Hall omits the Welsh villainies (cf. I. i. 43–6), and the fact that Holmedon was fought on Holy Rood Day (I. i. 52); he is not misleading as to Mordake's parentage (I. i. 71–2, note); he associates no portents or magic with "Owen Glendor" (III. i. 11 ff.); he separates Glendower's victory over Mortimer by a considerable space from Hotspur's over Douglas (I. i. 38, 67); he makes no reference to Henry's distrust of Hal or, consequently, to any reconciliation; he does not show the King offering terms through Worcester on the eve of Shrewsbury (v. i. 106 ff.) or, consequently, that Machiavellian concealing them (v. ii. 1); he attributes to a vague "they" at Stafford the battle-oration which Holinshed, Daniel, and Shakespeare give to Hotspur at Shrewsbury (v. ii. 81 ff.); and he strikingly makes Lord Stafford the only nobleman who "kept his promise & ioined with the Percies to his destructiō" (Hall, 29), whereas in Holinshed, Daniel, and Shakespeare (v. iii.

7) he loses his life for the King. Of Henry's other supporters at
Shrewsbury, whereas Holinshed gives Shakespeare the names
of Blunt, "Shorlie" (Shirley), "Gausell" (Gawsey), and Clifton,
Hall names only the first. Finally, Hall makes the death of Glendower—"in maner desperate of all comfort by reason of the king's
late victory" (Hall, 31)—follow quickly on Shrewsbury, as a result
of an expedition led by the Prince. Shaaber surmises that in thus
placing Glendower's death earlier than Holinshed (who puts it in
Henry's tenth year; Hol., iii. 48) Hall may have made Shakespeare
mention it less than half-way through Part 2 (2H4, III. i. 103). Yet
surely the conclusion is the opposite; had Shakespeare attended to
Hall here he would have made Glendower's fall an accompani-
ment of Shrewsbury. The conclusion is inevitable; Shakespeare
could hardly have differentiated himself more from Hall if he had
deliberately tried.

2. Holinshed: "The Historie of Scotland"[1]

The English-Scottish wars, with the valour of Hotspur and the
Earls of Douglas, occur again in the *Historie of Scotland*. The only
details that might suggest Shakespeare's indebtedness are the reference (not paralleled in the *Chronicles of England*) to "Mordake" as
the *eldest* son (cf. I. i. 71–2 and note), and the allusion to Douglas's
capture at Holmedon on which the Scottish history is clearer than
the English (cf. III. ii. 114 and note). The former point may well,
however, derive from Stow (cf. Intro., p. xxxii). Otherwise Shakespeare keeps decidedly to the English version, not least in the error
over "Mordake"'s parentage (cf. I. i. 71–2 and note) and at
Shrewsbury, where the Scottish history says plainly "The king got
the victorie, and slue the lord Persie" (v. 406). Once in the Scottish
version (never in the English, but repeatedly in the play—e.g. I. iii.
257, II. iii. 26, IV. i. 3, v. i. 116, v. iv. 25, v. v. 23, 27) Douglas is
called, in characteristic Scottish manner, "the Dowglasse" (v.
405); but this may derive from ballad-usage (cf. p. xxxviii). All in
all, the signs of indebtedness are not strong enough to be convincing.

3. Sir John Hayward: "The Life and Raigne of King Henry IV" (1599)[2]

Since Hayward averred that his *Henry IV* was started in 1598 and
contemplated (though he consulted no-one) a dozen years before
that, it has been suggested that Shakespeare may have seen it in
MS (Hemingway, New Var., 372–3), or alternatively that Hay-

1. The references are to the 1807–8 reprint.
2. The references are to the 1642 reprint.

ward borrowed from Shakespeare. Unless Hayward erred in his dates, the former possibility is ruled out; even if he did so err, the similarities are shared with Holinshed and no indebtedness on Shakespeare's part need be assumed. These similarities are:

(a) that Hayward (7) describes Henry's bearing as "courteous and familiar respectively towards all men, whereby he procured great reputation and regard, especially with those of the meaner sort" (cf. *R2*, v. ii. 7 ff., *1H4*, III. ii. 50 ff.). But Holinshed mentions his "cheerful and right courteous countenance regarding the people" (ii. 867), his popularity on landing (ii. 855, 858), and his being "gentle" in later years (iii. 58).

(b) that Shakespeare is confused about the oath Bolingbroke swore on landing from exile; in *1 Henry IV*, IV. iii. 59–77, we learn that Northumberland heard the oath sworn "upon the naked shore" at Ravenspurgh, whereas in v. i. 41–2 the oath is sworn at Doncaster. Since Hayward says (69–70) that "presently after his arrival" Henry swore the oath to "Lord Henrie Percie . . . and many other personages of honour", it has been suggested that Shakespeare was combining Hayward's version with Holinshed's (cf. Hemingway, New Var., 373, citing Cowl, *Sources*). But Shakespeare's ambiguity can all derive from Holinshed, who says (*i*) that the Lincolnshire lords greeted Henry at Ravenspurgh, the Percys only at Doncaster, where he swore the oath (ii. 853, iii. 25); but also (*ii*) that he swore the oath "at his entring into the lande, vpon his returne from exile" (iii. 58; cf. IV. iii. 54 ff., v. i. 33, notes); and, moreover, (*iii*) that the Percys were "in the beginning of his reigne both faithfull friends, and earnest aiders" (iii. 22).

4. *Another Hotspur Play?*

As possible evidence for an earlier (Shakespearean?) version of the Hotspur story, Professor Morgan[1] adduces some lines in John Day's hand on the back of a letter from Samuel Rowley to Henslowe, to which Greg queryingly assigns the date 4 June 1601.[2] They seem to be spoken by Prince Hal to Prince John on the field of Shrewsbury:

> brother, they were too nebers of our state
> yet both infected wth a strong disease
> & mortal sicknes proud ambytion
> wch being ranck & villanously neare
> had they not been prevented might have proved
> fatall & dangerouse then synce [proud] *scornfull* death

1. A. E. Morgan, *Some Problems of Sh.'s "Henry the Fourth"*, 1924, 41–2.
2. *Henslowe Papers*, ed. W. W. Greg, 1907, 57–8.

> hath like a skillfull artist cured that feare
> wch might have proved so hurtefull to o^r selves
> lets [bear them hence] *vs Commit* in sad and mournfull sound
> there worthes to fame there bodyes to the ground
> for the [brave] *dead* percy bore a gallant mynd
> Jngland has my prayers left behind.

Morgan thinks them "not incompatible with Shakespeare's earlier manner"—i.e. that of his supposed first *1 Henry IV*. But since in the original the italicized words have replaced those in brackets one wonders why, if the lines were Shakespeare's, Day should have copied not only the corrections but the original words too. Day was surely himself drafting the lines, for some purpose unknown; they are unShakespearean in their flat expository manner, and the reference to "too neighbours" must be to a Shrewsbury different from Shakespeare's, where only Hotspur is seen slain on the field.

In 1592 Greene, Nashe, and Harvey were bandying about some phrases which have been thought to echo an early *Henry IV*— "hypocriticall hot-spurres", "lad of the Castle", and "buckram giants" (cf. J. M. Purcell and H. W. Crundell, *NQ*, June–July 1935). But these seem merely casual blooms in the floral display of Elizabethan pamphlet exuberance, quite unrelated to Shakespeare.

APPENDIX V

II. iv. 382—"KING CAMBYSES' VEIN"
(contributed by J. C. Maxwell)

In his note on *1 Henry IV*, II. iv. 382, Professor Dover Wilson writes: "I suspect that quotations from Preston figured in the old *Henry IV*, and that Shakespeare rewrote them to burlesque the more up-to-date style of Kyd or Greene. By 1596–8 Preston and fourteeners were *vieux jeu*". This explanation has the disadvantage of supposing that Shakespeare went out of his way to leave traces of the "old play" in a passage which must have been thoroughly rewritten. I think the truth is simpler. Whatever the previous stage history of *Henry IV*, here we have Shakespeare about 1597 referring to "King Cambyses' vein" as a well-known style. It is true that the lines actually spoken are, as Dover Wilson says, more in the style of Kyd or Greene, but Shakespeare's methods become clearer in the light of his other reminiscences of *Cambises*. M. P. Tilley long ago pointed out (*MLN*, xxiv, 1909, 244–7) that there is an affinity be-

tween all the passages in which Shakespeare uses the word "perpend" and the opening lines of *Cambises* where it also occurs (l. 5).
In none of these passages is there any attempt to recall the four-
teener: on the contrary almost all the Shakespeare characters who
use the word are as well able to bombast out a blank verse as the
best, and one of them does so even in a prose setting—"therefore
perpend, my princess, and give ear" (*Twelfth Night*, v. i. 310–11).
The whole process is perfectly natural. *Cambises* was a stock joke,
and evidently remained so till the turn of the century, and the substance of certain passages, and a few words, were vaguely remembered, as Dover Wilson's own notes indicate. But Shakespeare
could achieve a double purpose by using this well-worn butt, while
at the same time he parodied the style not of *Cambises* but of its
more recent analogues. It was a much more telling hit at Kyd
and Greene than an acknowledged parody would have been—the
impression created is that they are really as absurd as everyone
admits *Cambises* to be. There may have been an old *Henry IV*, and it
may have contained quotations from *Cambises*, but there is nothing
in this passage of Shakespeare that needs any such hypothesis to
explain it.

Appendix VI

iii. ii. 39 ff.—

"HAD I SO LAVISH OF MY PRESENCE BEEN . . ."

Dr Harold Brooks adduces parallel ideas in Hoccleve which,
though not directly connected with Shakespeare, suggest a traditional warning against kingly familiarity:

> Bet is the peples eres thriste and yerne
> Hir Kyng or princes wordes for to here,
> Than that his tongue goo so faste and yerne
> That mennes eres dul of his mateere;
> For dullynge hem, dulleth the herte in fere
> Of hem that yeven to him audience;
> In mochil speche wantith nat offence.
>
> (*Works*, iii: EETS, Extra ser., lxxii, 1897,
> st. 347, ll. 2423 ff.)

A gloss refers to the pseudo-Aristotelian *Secreta Secretorum*—
"Melius est quod aures hominum sint sitibundi ad Regis eloquia,
quam suis affatibus sacientur, quia saturatis auribus anima etiam
saturatur". This is translated in *Three Prose Versions of the Secreta*

Secretorum (EETS, Extra ser., lxxiv, 1898, 12–13): "It is a precious and an honurabille thing to a Kyng for to kepe sylence and speke but litille but if it be nede, for it were better that the eeris of the peple were brennynge in desire to here the speche of her Kyng then the pepille wofulle and wery in the listenyng of hir Kyng, and the hert is envenymyd of his presence and his sight. And also a King oweth not to shewe him ouer oftene to his peple, ne ouer oft haunte the company of his sugetis, and specially of chorlis and ruralle folke, for bi ouyr moche homelynes he shalle be the lasse honourid". The clash between this tradition and the behaviour of Richard II and Hal is highly dramatic.

Appendix VII

iv. i. 98–9—"ALL PLUM'D LIKE ESTRIDGES..."

Shakespeare probably telescoped the first two and perhaps all three possible sources below:

(*i*) Nashe, *Unfortunate Traveller* (McKerrow, ii. 272; suggested by G. R. Coffman, *MLN*, 1927, 318).

The trappings of his horse were pounced and bolstered out with rough plumed siluer plush, in full proportion and shape of an Estrich. On the breast of the horse were the fore-parts of this greedie bird aduanced... His wings, which he neuer vseth but running, beeing spread full saile, made his lustie stead as proud vnder him as he had bin some other *Pegasus*, & so quiueringly and tenderly were these his broade winges bounde to either side of him, that as he paced vp and downe the tilt-yard in his maiesty ere the knights were entered, they seemed wantonly to fan in his face and make a flickering sound, such as Eagles doe, swiftly pursuing their praie in the ayre.

The continuation tells how a knight, moved by his mistress's eyes,

perswaded himselfe he should outstrip all other in running to the goale of glorie.

(*ii*) Spenser, *Faerie Queene*, i. xi. 33–4. The Red Cross Knight, rising from the Well of Life,

> upstarted brave
> Out of the well, wherein he drenched lay:
> As Eagle, fresh out of the ocean wave,
> Where he had left his plumes all hoary gray,

And deckt himself with feathers youthly gay,
Like Eyas hauke up mounts unto the skies,
His newly-budded pineons to assay,
And marvailes at himself still as he flies:
So new this new-borne knight to battell new did rise.

(*iii*) George Chapman, *De Guiana Carmen Epicum* (prefixed to Lawrence Keymis, *Relation of the Second Voyage* [of Ralegh] *to Guiana*, 1596; suggested by Kathleen Lea and Ethel Seaton, *RES*, 1945, xxi. 319). Its last paragraph describes Ralegh, blessed by the Queen, going forth to his fleet attended by nobles, and the phrases "his bating Colores", "a wind as forward as their spirits", and "Valure Estridge-like" occur within eleven lines.

Appendix VIII

THE MORTIMERS

Daniel's *Civile Wars* conflated the last two Edmunds shown below into a single "Mortimer" combining the circumstances of both. Shakespeare follows Daniel, and his "Mortimer" is not only Earl of March and heir-designate but also son-in-law and fellow-rebel of Glendower. Shakespeare did not notice, or did not care, that one and the same person cannot call Hotspur's wife "aunt Percy" (III. i. 190) and be called by her "my brother Mortimer" (II. iii. 82).

Edmund Mortimer, = Philippa, daughter of
Earl of March,   Lionel, Duke of
d. 1381   Clarence

Elizabeth (1371–?1444), "Kate" in the play, wife of Hotspur	Roger (1374–98), Earl of March, and heir-designate to succeed Richard II (not in the play)	Sir Edmund (1376–1409), never Earl of March or heir to the throne; son-in-law and fellow-rebel of Glendower
	Edmund (1391–1425), Earl of March, and heir-designate to the crown after his father's death in 1398	

ADDITIONAL NOTES TO TEXT AND COMMENTARY

p. 109, iii. 4: *apple-John*] The usual explanation that it is so called because gathered about St John's Day cannot be right, that date being altogether too early. Mr I. I. Jeffries of Cullompton, once a professional fruit-grower, writes to me, "I know of no apple in this country which is mature, or anything like it, by this date. If the name has anything to do with St John's Day it would perhaps be more likely that the apple *kept* to around that date. It was famed for its long keeping properties (vide H. V. Taylor, *The Apples of England*, 3rd edn, 1946, pp. 20–21)".

p. 125, iv. i. 98–9: *estridges*] A relevant example is cited in W. Green, *Sh.'s 'Merry Wives of Windsor'*, 1962, p. 43, from Bodl. Ashm. MS. 1112, fol. 16v—"Next after him came riding the Lord Mountjoy, with all his men in blew Coates, every one a plume of purple estridge feathers in their Hattes".

p. 143, v. i. 78: *innovation*] Remarking on the turmoil which followed on Bolingbroke's overthrow of Richard, Daniel writes (C.W., ii. 4): "And thus these mighty actors sonnes of change, / These partizans of factions, often tride / That in the smoake of innovations strange / Build huge vncertaine plots of vnsure pride. . ."